READINGS IN THE WESTERN HUMANITIES

VOLUME I

Edited by

JULIE WILDHABER

KATHLEEN ENGELBERG

C. LANSING HAYS

Mayfield Publishing Company
Mountain View, California
London • Toronto

Library of Congress Cataloging-in-Publication Data

Readings in the Western humanities / edited by Julie Wildhaber,
  Kathleen Engelberg, C. Lansing Hays.
      p.   cm.
    ISBN 1-55934-198-X (v. 1). — ISBN 1-55934-199-8 (v. 2)
    1. College readers. 2. Humanities—Problems, exercises, etc.
  3. Readers—Humanities. I. Wildhaber, Julie. II. Engelberg,
  Kathleen.   III. Hays, C. Lansing.
  PE1122.G625   1992
  082—dc20   92-13134
                                                     CIP

Manufactured in the United States of America

10 9 8 7 6 5 4 3 2 1

Mayfield Publishing Company
1240 Villa Street
Mountain View, California 94041

Sponsoring editor, C. Lansing Hays; managing editor,
April Wells-Hayes; production editor, Lynn Rabin Bauer;
text designer, Wendy Calmenson; manufacturing manager,
Martha Branch. The text was set in 9/11 Palatino by ExecuStaff
and printed on 50# White by Malloy Lithographing.

Preface

This collection of literary and philosophical writings is designed to accompany Roy Matthews and DeWitt Platt's *The Western Humanities*, a textbook that surveys the artistic, cultural, and intellectual heritage of Western civilization from prehistory to the present. Volume I covers ancient Mesopotamia through the Renaissance; Volume II covers the Renaissance through the twentieth century.

Our principal goal in assembling this volume has been to bring the student into contact with as many diverse and representative voices as possible. Compiling an anthology is a quixotic process; the giants of Western thought stand before us, and we, armed with computers and liberal educations, cannot force them into a modest volume without compromises. Thus, we had to make choices.

Our first choice was to include certain voices and not others. The range of Western literature and philosophy is vast, and to keep these books within manageable length we had to exclude many worthwhile writers. Our second choice was to include particular selections and excerpts. Again, our desire for diversity and broad representation compelled us to reproduce relatively brief samples of many writers' work. We hope these samples will entice students into reading more of each of these writers.

The third choice we made was to devote each page to the selections themselves rather than to introductions, notes, annotations, or biographical material. This choice allows the instructor the freedom and flexibility to provide his or her own commentary and interpretations. The student will find in these pages only the unadorned, original works.

We have been aided in selecting these writings by a number of experienced humanities faculties from around the country. We wish to thank them for their generous and thoughtful advice. Special thanks must go to Roy Matthews and DeWitt Platt for their counsel and for their superb work on *The Western Humanities*, which inspired the demand for this anthology.

Contents

Chapter

1

Prehistory and Near Eastern Civilizations

from *Inanna:* *Queen of Heaven and Earth*

From the Great Above to the Great Below

From the Great Above she opened her ear to the Great
  Below.
From the Great Above the goddess opened her ear to the
  Great Below.
From the Great Above Inanna opened her ear to the
  Great Below.

My Lady abandoned heaven and earth to descend to the
  underworld.
Inanna abandoned heaven and earth to descend to the
  underworld.
She abandoned her office of holy priestess to descend to
  the underworld.

In Uruk she abandoned her temple to descend to the
  underworld.
In Badtibira she abandoned her temple to descend to the
  underworld.
In Zabalam she abandoned her temple to descend to the
  underworld.
In Adab she abandoned her temple to descend to the
  underworld.

In Nippur she abandoned her temple to descend to the
  underworld.
In Kish she abandoned her temple to descend to the
  underworld.
In Akkad she abandoned her temple to descend to the
  underworld.

She gathered together the seven *me*.
She took them into her hands.
With the *me* in her possession, she prepared herself:

She placed the *shugurra*, the crown of the steppe, on
  her head.
She arranged the dark locks of hair across her forehead.
She tied the small lapis beads around her neck,
Let the double strand of beads fall to her breast,
And wrapped the royal robe around her body.
She daubed her eyes with ointment called "Let him
  come, Let him come,"
Bound the breastplate called "Come, man, come!"
  around her chest,

1

Slipped the gold ring over her wrist,
And took the lapis measuring rod and line in her hand.

Inanna set out for the underworld.
Ninshubur, her faithful servant, went with her.
Inanna spoke to her, saying:
> "Ninshubur, my constant support,
> My *sukkal* who gives me wise advice,
> My warrior who fights by my side,
> I am descending to the *kur*, to the underworld.
> If I do not return,
> Set up a lament for me by the ruins.
> Beat the drum for me in the assembly places.
> Circle the houses of the gods.
> Tear at your eyes, at your mouth, at your thighs.
> Dress yourself in a single garment like a beggar.
> Go to Nippur, to the temple of Enlil.
>
> When you enter his holy shrine, cry out:
> 'O Father Enlil, do not let your daughter
> Be put to death in the underworld.
> Do not let your bright silver
> Be covered with the dust of the underworld.
> Do not let your precious lapis
> Be broken into stone for the stoneworker.
> Do not let your fragrant boxwood
> Be cut into wood for the woodworker.
> Do not let the holy priestess of heaven
> Be put to death in the underworld.'
>
> If Enlil will not help you,
> Go to Ur, to the temple of Nanna.
> Weep before Father Nanna.
> If Nanna will not help you,
> Go to Eridu, to the temple of Enki.
> Weep before Father Enki.
> Father Enki, the God of Wisdom, knows the food
>   of life,
> He knows the water of life;
> He knows the secrets.
> Surely he will not let me die."

Inanna continued on her way to the underworld.
Then she stopped and said:
> "Go now, Ninshubur—
> Do not forget the words I have commanded you."

When Inanna arrived at the outer gates of the
    underworld,
She knocked loudly.

She cried out in a fierce voice:
> "Open the door, gatekeeper!
> Open the door, Neti!
> I alone would enter!"

Neti, the chief gatekeeper of the *kur*, asked:
> "Who are you?"

She answered:
> "I am Inanna, Queen of Heaven,
> On my way to the East."

Neti said:
> "If you are truly Inanna, Queen of Heaven,
> On your way to the East,
> Why has your heart led you on the road
> From which no traveler returns?"

Inanna answered:
> "Because . . . of my older sister, Ereshkigal,
> Her husband, Gugalanna, the Bull of Heaven,
>   has died.
> I have come to witness the funeral rites.
> Let the beer of his funeral rites be poured into
>   the cup.
> Let it be done."

Neti spoke:
> "Stay here, Inanna, I will speak to my queen.
> I will give her your message."

Neti, the chief gatekeeper of the *kur*,
Entered the palace of Ereshkigal, the Queen of the
    Underworld, and said:
> "My queen, a maid
> As tall as heaven,
> As wide as the earth,
> As strong as the foundations of the city wall,
> Waits outside the palace gates.
>
> She has gathered together the seven *me*.
> She has taken them into her hands.
> With the *me* in her possession, she has
>   prepared herself:
>
> On her head she wears the *shugurra*, the crown
>   of the steppe.
> Across her forehead her dark locks of hair are
>   carefully arranged.
> Around her neck she wears the small lapis beads.
> At her breast she wears the double strand of beads.
> Her body is wrapped with the royal robe.
> Her eyes are daubed with the ointment called, 'Let
>   him come, let him come.'
> Around her chest she wears the breastplate called
>   'Come, man, come!'
> On her wrist she wears the gold ring.
> In her hand she carries the lapis measuring
>   rod and line."

When Ereshkigal heard this,
She slapped her thigh and bit her lip.
She took the matter into her heart and dwelt on it.
Then she spoke:
> "Come, Neti, my chief gatekeeper of the *kur*,
> Heed my words:

Bolt the seven gates of the underworld.
Then, one by one, open each gate a crack.
Let Inanna enter.
As she enters, remove her royal garments.
Let the holy priestess of heaven enter
      bowed low." . . .

Naked and bowed low, Inanna entered the throne room.
Ereshkigal rose from her throne.
Inanna started toward the throne.
The Annuna, the judges of the underworld, surrounded
      her.
They passed judgment against her.

Then Ereshkigal fastened on Inanna the eye of death.
She spoke against her the word of wrath.
She uttered against her the cry of guilt.

She struck her.

Inanna was turned into a corpse,
A piece of rotting meat,
And was hung from a hook on the wall.

When, after three days and three nights, Inanna had not
      returned,
Ninshubur set up a lament for her by the ruins.
She beat the drum for her in the assembly places.
She circled the houses of the gods.
She tore at her eyes; she tore at her mouth; she tore at
      her thighs.
She dressed herself in a single garment like a beggar.
Alone, she set out for Nippur and the temple of Enlil. . . .

Father Enki said:
      "What has happened?
      What has my daughter done?
      Inanna! Queen of All the Lands! Holy Priestess
            of Heaven!
      What has happened?
      I am troubled. I am grieved."

From under his fingernail Father Enki brought forth dirt.
He fashioned the dirt into a *kurgarra*, a creature neither
      male nor female.
From under the fingernail of his other hand he brought
      forth dirt.
He fashioned the dirt into a *galatur*, a creature neither
      male nor female.
He gave the food of life to the *kurgarra*.
He gave the water of life to the *galatur*.
Enki spoke to the *kurgarra* and *galatur*, saying:
      "Go to the underworld,
      Enter the door like flies.
      Ereshkigal, the Queen of the Underworld,
            is moaning
      With the cries of a woman about to give birth.
      No linen is spread over her body.

Her breasts are uncovered.
Her hair swirls about her head like leeks.
When she cries, 'Oh! Oh! My inside!'
Cry also, 'Oh! Oh! Your inside!'
When she cries, 'Oh! Oh! My outside!'
Cry also, 'Oh! Oh! Your outside!'
The queen will be pleased.
She will offer you a gift.
Ask her only for the corpse that hangs from the
      hook on the wall.
One of you will sprinkle the food of life on it.
The other will sprinkle the water of life.
Inanna will arise."

The *kurgarra* and the *galatur* heeded Enki's words.
They set out for the underworld.
Like flies, they slipped through the cracks of the gates.
They entered the throne room of the Queen of the
      Underworld.
No linen was spread over her body.
Her breasts were uncovered.
Her hair swirled around her head like leeks.

Ereshkigal was moaning:
      "Oh! Oh! My inside!"

They moaned:
      "Oh! Oh! Your inside!"

She moaned:
      "Ohhhh! Oh! My outside!"

They moaned:
      "Ohhhh! Oh! Your outside!"

She groaned:
      "Oh! Oh! My belly!"

They groaned:
      "Oh! Oh! Your belly!"

She groaned:
      "Oh! Ohhhh! My back!!"

They groaned:
      "Oh! Ohhhh! Your back!!"

She sighed:
      "Ah! Ah! My heart!"

They sighed:
      "Ah! Ah! Your heart!"

She sighed:
      "Ah! Ahhhh! My liver!"

They sighed:
      "Ah! Ahhhh! Your liver!"

Ereshkigal stopped.
She looked at them.
She asked:
"Who are you,
Moaning—groaning—sighing with me?
If you are gods, I will bless you.
If you are mortals, I will give you a gift.
I will give you the water-gift, the river
in its fullness."

The *kurgarra* and *galatur* answered:
"We do not wish it."

Ereshkigal said:
"I will give you the grain-gift, the fields in harvest."

The *kurgarra* and *galatur* said:
"We do not wish it."

Ereshkigal said:
"Speak then! What do you wish?"

They answered:
"We wish only the corpse that hangs from the
hook on the wall."

Ereshkigal said:
"The corpse belongs to Inanna."

They said:
"Whether it belongs to our queen,
Whether it belongs to our king,
That is what we wish."

The corpse was given to them.

The *kurgarra* sprinkled the food of life on the corpse.
The *galatur* sprinkled the water of life on the corpse.
Inanna arose. . . .

from *The Epic of Gilgamesh*

Ishtar and Gilgamesh, and the Death of Enkidu

Gilgamesh washed out his long locks and cleaned his weapons; he flung back his hair from his shoulders; he threw off his stained clothes and changed them for new. He put on his royal robes and made them fast. When Gilgamesh had put on the crown, glorious Ishtar lifted her eyes, seeing the beauty of Gilgamesh. She said, 'Come to me Gilgamesh, and be my bridegroom; grant me seed of your body, let me be your bride and you shall be my husband. I will harness for you a chariot of lapis lazuli and of gold, with wheels of gold and horns of copper; and you shall have mighty demons of the storm for draft-mules. When you enter our house in the fragrance of cedar-wood, threshold and throne will kiss your feet. Kings, rulers, and princes will bow down before you; they shall bring you tribute from the mountains and the plain. Your ewes shall drop twins and your goats triplets; your pack-ass shall outrun mules; your oxen shall have no rivals, and your chariot horses shall be famous far-off for their swiftness.'

Gilgamesh opened his mouth and answered glorious Ishtar, 'If I take you in marriage, what gifts can I give in return? What ointments and clothing for your body? I would gladly give you bread and all sorts of food fit for a god. I would give you wine to drink fit for a queen. I would pour out barley to stuff your granary; but as for making you my wife—that I will not. How would it go with me? Your lovers have found you like a brazier which smoulders in the cold, a backdoor which keeps out neither squall of wind nor storm, a castle which crushes the garrison, pitch that blackens the bearer, a water-skin that chafes the carrier, a stone which falls from the parapet, a battering-ram turned back from the enemy, a sandal that trips the wearer. Which of your lovers did you ever love for ever? What shepherd of yours has pleased you for all time? Listen to me while I tell the tale of your lovers. There was Tammuz, the lover of your youth, for him you decreed wailing, year after year. You loved the many-coloured roller, but still you struck and broke his wing; now in the grove he sits and cries, "kappi, kappi, my wing, my wing." You have loved the lion tremendous in strength: seven pits you dug for him, and seven. You have loved the stallion magnificent in battle, and for him you decreed whip and spur and a thong, to gallop seven leagues by force and to muddy the water before he drinks; and for his mother Silili lamentations. You have loved the shepherd of the flock; he made meal-cake for you day after day, he killed kids for your sake. You struck and turned him into a wolf; now his own herd-boys chase him away, his own hounds worry his flanks. And did you not love Ishullanu, the gardener of your father's palm-grove? He brought you baskets filled with dates without end; every day he loaded your table. Then you turned your eyes on him and said, "Dearest Ishullanu, come here to me, let us enjoy your manhood, come forward and take me, I am yours." Ishullanu answered, "What are you asking from me? My mother has baked and I have eaten; why should I come to such as you for food that is tainted and rotten? For when was a screen of rushes sufficient protection from frosts?" But when you had heard his answer you struck him. He was changed to a blind mole deep in the earth, one whose desire is always beyond his reach. And if you and I should be lovers, should not I be served in the same fashion as all these others whom you loved once?'

When Ishtar heard this she fell into a bitter rage, she went up to high heaven. Her tears poured down in front of her father Anu, and Antum her mother. She said, 'My father, Gilgamesh has heaped insults on me, he has told over all my abominable behaviour, my foul and hideous acts.' Anu opened his mouth and said, 'Are you a father of gods? Did not you quarrel with Gilgamesh the king, so now he has related your abominable behaviour, your foul and hideous acts.'

Ishtar opened her mouth and said again, 'My father, give me the Bull of Heaven to destroy Gilgamesh. Fill Gilgamesh, I say, with arrogance to his destruction; but if you refuse to give me the Bull of Heaven I will break in the doors of hell and smash the bolts; there will be confusion of people, those above with those from the lower depths. I shall bring up the dead to eat food like the living; and the hosts of dead will outnumber the living.' Anu said to great Ishtar, 'If I do what you desire there will be seven years of drought throughout Uruk when corn will be seedless husks. Have you saved grain enough for the people and grass for the cattle?' Ishtar replied. 'I have saved grain for the people, grass for the cattle; for seven years of seedless husks there is grain and there is grass enough.'

When Anu heard what Ishtar had said he gave her the Bull of Heaven to lead by the halter down to Uruk. When they reached the gates of Uruk the Bull went to the river; with his first snort cracks opened in the earth and a hundred young men fell down to death. With his second snort cracks opened and two hundred fell down to death. With his third snort cracks opened, Enkidu doubled over but instantly recovered, he dodged aside and leapt on the Bull and seized it by the horns. The Bull of Heaven foamed in his face, it brushed him with the thick of its tail. Enkidu cried to Gilgamesh, 'My friend, we boasted that we would leave enduring names behind us. Now thrust in your sword between the nape and the horns.' So Gilgamesh followed the Bull, he seized the thick of its tail, he thrust the sword between the nape and the horns and slew the Bull. When they had killed the Bull of Heaven they cut out its heart and gave it to Shamash, and the brothers rested.

But Ishtar rose up and mounted the great wall of Uruk; she sprang on to the tower and uttered a curse: 'Woe to Gilgamesh, for he has scorned me in killing the Bull of Heaven.' When Enkidu heard these words he tore out the Bull's right thigh and tossed it in her face saying, 'If I could lay my hands on you, it is this I should do to you, and lash the entrails to your side.' Then Ishtar called together her people, the dancing and singing girls, the prostitutes of the temple, the courtesans. Over the thigh of the Bull of Heaven she set up lamentation.

But Gilgamesh called the smiths and the armourers, all of them together. They admired the immensity of the horns. They were plated with lapis lazuli two fingers thick. They were thirty pounds each in weight, and their capacity in oil was six measures, which he gave to his guardian god, Lugulbanda. But he carried the horns into the palace and hung them on the wall. Then they washed their hands in Euphrates, they embraced each other and went away. They drove through the streets of Uruk where the heroes were gathered to see them, and Gilgamesh called to the singing girls, 'Who is most glorious of the heroes, who is most eminent among men?' 'Gilgamesh is the most glorious of heroes, Gilgamesh is most eminent among men.' And now there was feasting, and celebrations and joy in the palace, till the heroes lay down saying, 'Now we will rest for the night.'

When the daylight came Enkidu got up and cried to Gilgamesh, 'Oh my brother, such a dream I had last night. Anu, Enlil, Ea and heavenly Shamash took counsel together, and Anu said to Enlil, "Because they have killed the Bull of Heaven, and because they have killed Humbaba who guarded the Cedar Mountain one of the two must die." Then glorious Shamash answered the hero Enlil, "It was by your command they killed the Bull of Heaven, and killed Humbaba, and must Enkidu die although innocent?" Enlil flung round in rage at glorious Shamash, "You dare to say this, you who went about with them every day like one of themselves!" '

So Enkidu lay stretched out before Gilgamesh; his tears ran down in streams and he said to Gilgamesh, 'O my brother, so dear as you are to me, brother, yet they will take me from you.' Again he said, 'I must sit down on the threshold of the dead and never again will I see my dear brother with my eyes.'

While Enkidu lay alone in his sickness he cursed the gate as though it was living flesh, 'You there, wood of the gate, dull and insensible, witless, I searched for you over twenty leagues until I saw the towering cedar. There is no wood like you in our land. Seventy-two cubits high and twenty-four wide, the pivot and the ferrule and the jambs are perfect. A master craftsman from Nippur has made you; but O, if I had known the conclusion! If I had known that this was all the good that would come of it, I would have raised the axe and split you into little pieces and set up here a gate of wattle instead. Ah, if only some future king had brought you here, or some god had fashioned you. Let him obliterate my name and write his own, and the curse fall on him instead of on Enkidu.'

With the first brightening of dawn Enkidu raised his head and wept before the Sun God, in the brilliance of the sunlight his tears streamed down. 'Sun God, I beseech you, about that vile Trapper, that Trapper of nothing because of whom I was to catch less than my comrade; let him catch least; make his game scarce, make him feeble, taking the smaller of every share, let his quarry escape from his nets.'

When he had cursed the Trapper to his heart's content he turned on the harlot. He was roused to curse her also. 'As for you, woman, with a great curse I curse you! I will promise you a destiny to all eternity. My curse shall come on you soon and sudden. You shall be without a roof for your commerce, for you shall not keep house with other girls in the tavern, but do your business in places fouled by the vomit of the drunkard. Your hire will be potter's earth, your thievings will be flung into the hovel, you will sit at the crossroads in the dust of the potter's quarter, you will make your bed on the dunghill at night, and by day take your stand in the wall's shadow. Brambles and thorns will tear your feet, the drunk and the dry will strike your cheek and your mouth will ache. Let you be stripped of your purple dyes, for I too once in the wilderness with my wife had all the treasure I wished.'

When Shamash heard the words of Enkidu he called to him from heaven: 'Enkidu, why are you cursing the woman, the mistress who taught you to eat bread fit for gods and drink wine of kings? She who put upon you a magnificent garment, did she not give you glorious Gilgamesh for your companion, and has not Gilgamesh, your own brother, made you rest on a royal bed and recline on a couch at his left hand? He has made the princes of the earth kiss your feet, and now all the people of Uruk lament and wail over you. When you are dead he will let his hair grow long for your sake, he will wear a lion's pelt and wander through the desert.'

When Enkidu heard glorious Shamash his angry heart grew quiet, he called back the curse and said, 'Woman, I promise you another destiny. The mouth which cursed you shall bless you! Kings, princes and nobles shall adore you. On your account a man though twelve miles off will clap his hand to his thigh and his hair will twitch. For you he will undo his belt and open his treasure and you shall have your desire; lapis lazuli, gold and carnelian from the heap in the treasury. A ring for your hand and a robe shall be yours. The priest will lead you into the presence of the gods. On your account a wife, a mother of seven, was forsaken.'

As Enkidu slept alone in his sickness, in bitterness of spirit he poured out his heart to his friend. 'It was I who cut down the cedar, I who levelled the forest, I who slew Humbaba and now see what has become of me. Listen, my friend, this is the dream I dreamed last night. The heavens roared, and earth rumbled back an answer; between them stood I before an awful being, the somber-faced man-bird; he had directed on me his purpose. His was a vampire face, his foot was a lion's foot, his hand was an eagle's talon. He fell on me and his claws were in my hair, he held me fast and I smothered; then he transformed me so that my arms became wings covered with feathers. He turned his stare towards me, and he led me away to the palace of Irkalla, the Queen of Darkness, to the house from which none who enters ever returns, down the road from which there is no coming back.

'There is the house whose people sit in darkness; dust is their food and clay their meat. They are clothed like birds with wings for covering, they see no light, they sit in darkness. I entered the house of dust and I saw the kings of the earth, their crowns put away for ever; rulers and princes, all those who once wore kingly crowns and ruled the world in the days of old. They who had stood in the place of the gods like Anu and Enlil, stood now like servants to fetch baked meats in the house of dust, to carry cooked meat and cold water from the water-skin. In the house of dust which I entered were high priests and acolytes, priests of the incantation and of ecstasy; there were servers of the temple, and there was Etana, that King of Kish whom the eagle carried to heaven in the days of old. I saw also Samuqan, god of cattle, and there was Ereshkigal the Queen of the Underworld; and Belit-Sheri squatted in front of her, she who is recorder of the gods and keeps the book of death. She held a tablet from which she read. She raised her head, she saw me and spoke: "Who has brought this one here?" Then I awoke like a man drained of blood who wanders alone in a waste of rushes; like one whom the bailiff has seized and his heart pounds with terror.'

Gilgamesh had peeled off his clothes, he listened to his words and wept quick tears, Gilgamesh listened and his tears flowed. He opened his mouth and spoke to Enkidu: 'Who is there in strong-walled Uruk who has wisdom like this? Strange things have been spoken, why does your heart speak strangely? The dream was marvellous but the terror was great; we must treasure the dream whatever the terror; for the dream has shown that misery comes at last to the healthy man, the end of life is sorrow.' And Gilgamesh lamented, 'Now I will pray to the great gods, for my friend had an ominous dream.'

This day on which Enkidu dreamed came to an end and he lay stricken with sickness. One whole day he lay on his bed and his suffering increased. He said to Gilgamesh, the friend on whose account he had left the wilderness, 'Once I ran for you, for the water of life, and I now have nothing.' A second day he lay on his bed and Gilgamesh watched over him but the sickness increased. A third day he lay on his bed, he called out to Gilgamesh, rousing him up. Now he was weak and his eyes were blind with weeping. Ten days he lay and his suffering increased, eleven and twelve days he lay on his bed of pain. Then he called to Gilgamesh, 'My friend, the great goddess cursed me and I must die in shame. I shall not die like a man fallen in battle; I feared to fall, but happy is the man who falls in the battle, for I must die in shame.' And Gilgamesh wept over Enkidu. . . .

He touched his heart but it did not beat, nor did he lift his eyes again. When Gilgamesh touched his heart it did not beat. So Gilgamesh laid a veil, as one veils the bride, over his friend. He began to rage like a lion, like a lioness robbed of her whelps. This way and that he paced round the bed, he tore out his hair and strewed it around. He dragged off his splendid robes and flung them down as though they were abominations.

In the first light of dawn Gilgamesh cried out, 'I made you rest on a royal bed, you reclined on a couch at my left hand, the princes of the earth kissed your feet. I will cause all the people of Uruk to weep over you and raise the dirge of the dead. The joyful people will stoop with sorrow; and when you have gone to the earth I will let my hair grow long for your sake, I will wander through the wilderness in the skin of a lion.' The next day also, in the first light, Gilgamesh lamented; seven days and seven nights he wept for Enkidu, until the worm fastened on him. Only then he gave him up to the earth, for the Anunnaki, the judges, had seized him.

Then Gilgamesh issued a proclamation through the land, he summoned them all, the coppersmiths, the goldsmiths, the stone-workers, and commanded them, 'Make a statue of my friend.' The statue was fashioned with a great weight of lapis lazuli for the breast and of gold for the body. A table of hard-wood was set out, and on it a bowl of carnelian filled with honey, and a bowl of lapis lazuli filled with butter. These he exposed and offered to the Sun; and weeping he went away.

The Story of the Flood

'You know the city Shurrupak, it stands on the banks of Euphrates? That city grew old and the gods that were in it were old. There was Anu, lord of the firmament, their father, and warrior Enlil their counsellor, Ninurta the helper, and Ennugi watcher over canals; and with them also was Ea. In those days the world teemed, the people multiplied, the world bellowed like a wild bull, and the great god was aroused by the clamour. Enlil heard the clamour and he said to the gods in council, "The uproar of mankind is intolerable and sleep is no longer possible by reason of the babel." So the gods agreed to exterminate mankind. Enlil did this, but Ea because of his oath warned me in a dream. He whispered their words to my house of reeds, "Reed-house, reed-house! Wall, O wall, hearken reed-house, wall reflect; O man of Shurrupak, son of Ubara-Tutu; tear down your house and build a boat, abandon possessions and look for life, despise worldly goods and save your soul alive. Tear down your house, I say, and build a boat. These are the measurements of the barque as you shall build her: let her beam equal her length, let her deck be roofed like the vault that covers the abyss; then take up into the boat the seed of all living creatures."

'When I had understood I said to my lord, "Behold, what you have commanded I will honour and perform, but how shall I answer the people, the city, the elders?" Then Ea opened his mouth and said to me, his servant, "Tell them this: I have learnt that Enlil is wrathful against me, I dare no longer walk in his land nor live in his city; I will go down to the Gulf to dwell with Ea my lord. But on you he will rain down abundance, rare fish and shy wild-fowl, a rich harvest-tide. In the evening the rider of the storm will bring you wheat in torrents."

'In the first light of dawn all my household gathered round me, the children brought pitch and the men whatever was necessary. On the fifth day I laid the keel and the ribs, then I made fast the planking. The ground-space was one acre, each side of the deck measured one hundred and twenty cubits, making a square. I built six decks below, seven in all, I divided them into nine sections with bulkheads between.

I drove in wedges where needed, I saw to the punt-poles, and laid in supplies. The carriers brought oil in baskets, I poured pitch into the furnace and asphalt and oil; more oil was consumed in caulking, and more again the master of the board took into his stores. I slaughtered bullocks for the people and every day I killed sheep. I gave the shipwrights wine to drink as though it were river water, raw wine and red wine and oil and white wine. There was feasting then as there is at the time of the New Year's festival; I myself anointed my head. On the seventh day the boat was complete.

'Then was the launching full of difficulty; there was shifting of ballast above and below till two thirds was submerged. I loaded into her all that I had of gold and of living things, my family, my kin, the beast of the field both wild and tame, and all the craftsmen. I sent them on board, for the time that Shamash had ordained was already fulfilled when he said, "In the evening, when the rider of the storm sends down the destroying rain, enter the boat and batten her down." The time was fulfilled, the evening came, the rider of the storm sent down the rain. I looked out at the weather and it was terrible, so I too boarded the boat and battened her down. All was now complete, the battening and the caulking; so I handed the tiller to Puzur-Amurri the steersman, with the navigation and the care of the whole boat.

'With the first light of dawn a black cloud came from the horizon; it thundered within where Adad, lord of the storm was riding. In front over hill and plain Shullat and Hanish, heralds of the storm, led on. Then the gods of the abyss rose up; Nergal pulled out the dams of the nether waters, Ninurta the war-lord threw down the dykes, and the seven judges of hell, the Annunaki, raised their torches, lighting the land with their livid flame. A stupor of despair went up to heaven when the god of the storm turned daylight to darkness, when he smashed the land like a cup. One whole day the tempest raged, gathering fury as it went, it poured over the people like the tides of battle; a man could not see his brother nor the people be seen from heaven. Even the gods were terrified at the flood, they fled to the highest heaven, the firmament of Anu; they crouched against the walls, cowering like curs. Then Ishtar the sweet-voiced Queen of Heaven cried out like a woman in travail: "Alas the days of old are turned to dust because I commanded evil; why did I command this evil in the council of all the gods? I commanded wars to destroy the people, but are they not my people, for I brought them forth? Now like the spawn of fish they float in the ocean." The great gods of heaven and of hell wept, they covered their mouths.

'For six days and six nights the winds blew, torrent and tempest and flood overwhelmed the world, tempest and flood raged together like warring hosts. When the seventh day dawned the storm from the south subsided, the sea grew calm, the flood was stilled; I looked at the face of the world and there was silence, all mankind was turned to clay. The surface of the sea stretched as flat as a roof-top; I opened a hatch and the light fell on my face. Then I bowed low, I sat down and I wept, the tears streamed down my face, for on every side was the waste of water. I looked for land in vain, but fourteen leagues distant there appeared a mountain, and there the boat grounded; on the mountain of Nisir the boat held fast, she held fast and did not budge. One day she held, and a second day on the mountain of Nisir she held fast and did not budge. A third day, and a fourth day she held fast on the mountain and did not budge; a fifth day and a sixth day she held fast on the mountain. When the seventh day dawned I loosed a dove and let her go. She flew away, but finding no resting-place she returned. Then I loosed a swallow, and she flew away but finding no resting-place she returned. I loosed a raven, she saw that the waters had retreated, she ate, she flew around, she cawed, and she did not come back. Then I threw everything open to the four winds, I made a sacrifice and poured out a libation on the mountain top. Seven and again seven cauldrons I set up on their stands, I heaped up wood and cane and cedar and myrtle. When the gods smelled the sweet savour, they gathered like flies over the sacrifice. Then, at last, Ishtar also came, she lifted her necklace with the jewels of heaven that once Anu had made to please her. "O you gods here present,

by the lapis lazuli round my neck I shall remember these days as I remember the jewels of my throat; these last days I shall not forget. Let all the gods gather round the sacrifice, except Enlil. He shall not approach this offering, for without reflection he brought the flood; he consigned my people to destruction."

'When Enlil had come, when he saw the boat, he was wrath and swelled with anger at the gods, the host of heaven, "Has any of these mortals escaped? Not one was to have survived the destruction." Then the god of the wells and canals Ninurta opened his mouth and said to the warrior Enlil, "Who is there of the gods that can devise without Ea? It is Ea alone who knows all things." Then Ea opened his mouth and spoke to warrior Enlil, "Wisest of gods, hero Enlil, how could you so senselessly bring down the flood?

> *Lay upon the sinner his sin,*
> *Lay upon the transgressor his transgression,*
> *Punish him a little when he breaks loose,*
> *Do not drive him too hard or he perishes;*
> *Would that a lion had ravaged mankind*
> *Rather than the flood,*
> *Would that a wolf had ravaged mankind*
> *Rather than the flood,*
> *Would that famine had wasted the world*
> *Rather than the flood,*
> *Would that pestilence had wasted mankind*
> *Rather than the flood.*

It was not I that revealed the secret of the gods; the wise man learned it in a dream. Now take your counsel what shall be done with him."

'Then Enlil went up into the boat, he took me by the hand and my wife and made us enter the boat and kneel down on either side, he standing between us. He touched our foreheads to bless us saying, "In time past Utnapishtim was a mortal man; henceforth he and his wife shall live in the distance at the mouth of the rivers." Thus it was that the gods took me and placed me here to live in the distance, at the mouth of the rivers.'

---

from the Unas Pyramid Texts

Utterance 217

Sarcophagus Chamber, South Wall
The king joins the sun-god

Re-Atum, this Unas comes to you,
A spirit indestructible
Who lays claim to the place of the four pillars!
Your son comes to you, this Unas comes to you,
May you cross the sky united in the dark,
May you rise in lightland, the place in which you shine!

Seth, Nephthys, go proclaim to Upper Egypt's gods
And their spirits:
"This Unas comes, a spirit indestructible,
If he wishes you to die, you will die,
If he wishes you to live, you will live!"
Re-Atum, this Unas comes to you,

A spirit indestructible
Who lays claim to the place of the four pillars!
Your son comes to you, this Unas comes to you,
May you cross the sky united in the dark,
May you rise in lightland, the place in which you shine!
Osiris, Isis, go proclaim to Lower Egypt's gods
And their spirits:
"This Unas comes, a spirit indestructible,
Like the morning star above Hapy,
Whom the water-spirits worship;
Whom he wishes to live will live,
Whom he wishes to die will die!"

Re-Atum, this Unas comes to you,
A spirit indestructible
Who lays claim to the place of the four pillars!
Your son comes to you, this Unas comes to you,
May you cross the sky united in the dark,
May you rise in lightland, the place in which you shine!
Thoth, go proclaim to the gods of the west
And their spirits:
"This Unas comes, a spirit indestructible,

Decked above the neck as Anubis,
Lord of the western height,
He will count hearts, he will claim hearts,
Whom he wishes to live will live,
Whom he wishes to die will die!"

Re-Atum, this Unas comes to you,
A spirit indestructible
Who lays claim to the place of the four pillars!
Your son comes to you, this Unas comes to you,
May you cross the sky united in the dark,
May you rise in lightland, the place in which you shine!
Horus, go proclaim to the powers of the east
And their spirits:
"This Unas comes, a spirit indestructible,
Whom he wishes to live will live,
Whom he wishes to die will die!"

Re-Atum, your son comes to you,
Unas comes to you,
Raise him to you, hold him in your arms,
He is your son, of your body, forever!

The Dispute of a Man With His Soul

. . . Then I opened my mouth to my soul, that I might answer what it had said: "This is too much for me now, that my soul does not speak with me. My soul goes forth; let it stand and wait for me!

"Behold, my soul disobeys me because I did not hearken to it, and drag myself to death ere I have come to it, to cast myself upon the fire in order to consume myself. Rather, let it be near to me on this day of misfortune, and wait on the other side!

"My soul is foolish to hold back one wretched over life and delay me from death before I have come to it. Rather, make the West pleasant for me! Is it something bad? The period of life is limited in any case: even the trees must fall! Thoth, who contents the gods, he will judge me! Khonsu, the Scribe in Truth, he will defend me! Ra, who guides the Solar Bark, he will hear my words! My distress is heavy, and he bears it for me!"

And this is what my soul said to me: "And are you not a plain man? Yet you are as concerned as if you were a possessor of wealth!"

I said: "If my soul will hearken to me, and its heart agrees with me, it will be happy. I will cause it to reach the West, like one who is in his pyramid, and at whose burial there has stood a survivor. I shall drink from the river whose water is drawn, and look down on the souls that are unsatisfied!"

Then my soul opened its mouth to me, to answer what I had said: "If you are calling burial to mind, that is a distress of the heart; it is a bringing of tears, it is making a man sorrowful. It is haling a man from his house and throwing him upon the hill. Never shall you go up above to behold the sun. They who built in granite and fashioned pyramids—fine things of good work—when the builders have become gods, their offering tables are as empty as those of the wretches who die on the riverbank—part of their bodies held by the water and part by the heat of the sun, and the fish of the bank hold converse with them! Listen, then, to me; lo, it is good to listen to people! Follow the happy day and forget care!

"Take the case of a poor man who plows his field and then loads his harvest on to a boat, and hurries to tow the boat since his feast day approaches. He sees a flood coming on in the night, and keeps vigil when Ra goes down. He comes forth with his wife, but his children perish upon the water, dangerous with crocodiles in the night. At last he sits down, when he can regain his voice, and says: 'I do not weep for that girl; there is no coming forth into the West for her. I am troubled for her children that are broken in the egg, that behold the face of the crocodile-god before they had lived.'"

Then I opened my mouth to my soul, that I might answer what it had said:

"Behold, you make my name reek,
  lo, more than the stench of carrion
  on days in summer, when the sky is hot.

"Behold, you make my name reek
   lo, more than a fisherman
   on the day of the catch, when the sky is hot.

"Behold, you make my name reek
   lo, more than the stench of bird droppings,
   more than the hill of willows with the geese.

"Behold, you make my name reek
   lo, more than the odor of fishermen,
   more than the shores of the swamps when they have
      fished.

"Behold, you make my name reek
   lo, more than the stench of crocodiles,
   more than sitting among crocodiles.

"Behold, you make my name reek
   lo, more than that of a woman
   when lies are told about her to her man.

"Behold, you make my name reek
   lo, more than that of a lusty boy
   against whom it is said, 'He belongs to his hated one!'

"Behold, you make my name reek
   lo, more than a treacherous city,
   more than a traitor who turns his back.

"To whom shall I speak today?
   One's fellows are evil;
   the friends of today do not love.

"To whom shall I speak today?
   Men are rapacious;
   every one seizes his neighbor's goods.

"To whom shall I speak today?
   Gentleness has perished;
   insolence has access to all men.

"To whom shall I speak today?
   The evil have a contented countenance;
   good is rejected in every place.

"To whom shall I speak today?
   He who by his evil deeds should arouse wrath
   moves all men to laughter, though his iniquity is
      grievous.

"To whom shall I speak today?
   Men rob;
   Every man seizes his neighbor's goods.

"To whom shall I speak today?
   The foul man is trusted,
   but one who was a brother to him has become an
      enemy.

"To whom shall I speak today?
   No one remembers yesterday;
   no one now requites good to him who has done it.

"To whom shall I speak today?
   Brothers are evil;
   a man is treated as an enemy for his uprightness.

"To whom shall I speak today?
   Faces are not seen;
   every man's face is downcast toward his brethren.

"To whom shall I speak today?
   Hearts are greedy;
   the man on whom men rely has no heart.

"To whom shall I speak today?
   There are no righteous onces;
   the land is given over to the doers of evil.

"To whom shall I speak today?
   There is lack of a trusty friend;
   one must go to an unknown in order to complain.

"To whom shall I speak today?
   There is none that is peaceable;
   the one with whom one went no longer exists.

"To whom shall I speak today?
   I am laden with misery,
   and lack a trusted friend.

"To whom shall I speak today?
   The evil which treads the earth,
   it has no end.

"Death is in my sight today
   as when a sick man becomes whole,
   as when one goes out after an illness.

"Death is in my sight today
   as the odor of myrrh,
   as when sitting under sail on a breezy day.

"Death is in my sight today
   as the odor of lotus flowers,
   as when sitting on the riverbank getting drunk.

"Death is in my sight today
   as a well-trodden path,
   as when a man returns home to his house from war.

"Death is in my sight today
   as a clearing of the sky,
   as a man discerning what he knew not.

"Death is in my sight today
   as when a man longs to see his home again
   after he has spent many years in captivity.

"Nay, but he who is Yonder
 will be as a living god,
 inflicting punishment for evil upon him who does it.

"Nay, but he who is Yonder
 will stand in the bark of the Sun-god
 and will assign the choicest things therein to the temples.

"Nay, but he who is Yonder
 will be a man of knowledge,
 not hindered from petitioning Ra when he speaks."

This is what my soul said to me: "Set aside lamentation, you who are mine, my brother! Although offered up on the brazier, still you shall cling to life, as you say. Whether I remain here if you reject the West, or whether you reach the West and your body is joined with the earth, I will alight after you go to rest. Then we shall make an abode together!"

The Story of Sinuhe the Egyptian

The Hereditary Prince and Chief, Treasurer of the King, and Unique Courtier, Administrative Dignitary of the districts and estates of the Sovereign in the lands of the Syrians, Actual Acquaintance of the King and beloved of him, the King's Retainer Sinuhe says:

I was a retainer who followed his lord, a servant of the Royal Harem and of the Princess great of praise, the wife of King Sen-Wesret and daughter of King Amen-em-Hat, namely, Neferu, Lady of Reverence.

In the year 30 of his reign, in the third month of the season of Inundation, the god ascended unto his horizon; the King of Upper and Lower Egypt, Amen-em-Hat, was taken up to heaven and united with the sun. The body of the god was united with him who made him. The city of royal residence was silent, all hearts were in grief, and the great Double Gates were sealed. The courtiers sat with heads bent down upon their laps, and the people were in mourning.

Now His Majesty had sent a great army to the land of the Lybians, with his eldest son in command of it, namely, the beautiful god Sen-Wesret. He had been sent to smite the foreign lands, to strike down the dwellers in Lybia. Indeed, even now was he returning, bringing living prisoners from among the Lybians and all kinds of cattle without limit.

The courtiers of the palace sent to the western border, advising the King's son of what had come about in the Palace. The messengers found him on the road, having reached him at the time of evening. Not a moment at all did he delay: The Falcon flew with his attendants, not letting his army know what had happened.

Now those others of the King's sons who were following him in this expedition were sought out, and one of them was called aside. And lo, I happened to be standing near by, and heard his voice as he was speaking. My heart was distraught, my arms flung apart, and trembling seized all my limbs. I sprang bounding away to seek myself a place to hide. I placed myself between two bushes to hide from the passers-by. I certainly had no intention of returning to the Residence, for I expected civil strife to break out, and I did not think I would live after the King's death.

I crossed Lake Maati near Nehet and landed at the island of Senefru. I passed the day at the edge of the fields, and at dawn the next morning I set forth again. I met a man standing on the road. He was frightened of me, and stood in awe. When it was time for supper, I reached the town of Negau. I crossed the river on a barge without a rudder, with the aid of a westerly wind. I passed eastward of the quarry, above the temple of Hathor, Lady of the Red Hill. I gave road to my legs and went northward.

I arrived at the Walls of the Ruler, which were made to repel the Syrians and to defeat the Sand-crossers. I took up a crouching position under a bush, in fear lest the watch of the day standing on the wall would see me. At the time of late evening I journeyed on, and when the sun came forth again I reached Peten, and halted at the island of Kem-Wer. A great attack of thirst overtook me. My throat was hot and dry, and I said, "This is the taste of death."

Then I lifted up my heart and pulled my limbs together, for I heard the sound of the lowing of cattle and I spied some Syrians. A distinguished chieftain among them, who had been in Egypt, recognized me. Then he gave me water and cooked milk for me. I proceeded with him to his tribe, and they treated me well.

Land gave me to land. I went forth to Byblos, and then I turned back to Kedem. There I spent a year and a half. Then Amu-nenshi, a ruler in Palestine, fetched me. He said to me, "You will fare well with me; here you will hear the speech of Egypt." He said this since he knew my character and had heard of my capacities. The Egyptians who were there with him bore witness for me.

He said to me, "For what reason have you come to this place? What is it? Has something happened at the Residence?"

Then I said to him, "King Amen-em-Hat has proceeded to the Horizon. No one knows what can happen because of it." But I added, untruthfully:

"I was returning from an expedition to the land of the Lybians when it was reported to me. My mind became unquiet. My heart was not in my body, and it drew me to the desert roads. I had not been accused of anything, no one had spat in my face, and no wretched remarks had been heard about me. My name had not been heard in the mouth of the herald. I do not know what brought me to this land. It is like the dispensation of some god; or like a dream in which a man of the Delta might see himself in Nubia!"

Then he said to me, "What, then, will the land be without him, that excellent god, the fear of whom pervaded the foreign lands like Sekhmet in a year of pestilence?"

I spoke to him in reply, "Indeed his son has entered into the Palace and has assumed the heritance of his father.

For he is a god; there is none his equal,
  and there is none other who surpasses him.
He is a master of understanding, excellent in plans
    and beneficent of decrees;
  and going and coming are according to his commands.
He it was who subdued the foreign lands while his father
    was within the palace;
  and he reported to him that what he was ordered had
    been done.
Mighty indeed is he, achieving with his strong arm;
  a valiant one, and there is not his equal!
He slakes his wrath by smashing skulls;
  and no one can stand up about him.
He is robust of heart at the moment of attack;
  and does not let sloth rest upon his heart.
Bold of countenance is he when sees the mêlée;
  to attack the barbarian is his joy.
He girds his shield and crushes the foe;
  and does not strike twice in order to kill!
But he is lord of charm and great of sweetness;
  and through love has he conquered!
His city loves him more than itself;
  it rejoices in him more than in its god;
  men and women salute and rejoice with him now that
    he is King!
He conquered while still in the egg,
  and his face was turned to royal deeds since he
    was born.
He makes multiply those who were born with him;
  he is unique, the gift of the god.
He is one who makes wide the boundaries;
  he will seize the southern countries, and the northern
    ones with ease,
  having been created to smite the Syrians and to crush
    the Sand-crossers.
How this land rejoices now that he is come to rule!

Send to him, cause him to know your name as an inquirer far from His Majesty. He will not cease to make happy a land which will be loyal to him!"

Then he said to me, "Well, assuredly then, Egypt is happy, knowing that he flourishes. Behold, you are here, and you shall stay with me. I will treat you well."

He placed me at the head of his children, and he married me to his eldest daughter. He let me choose for myself from his land, from the choicest that he had, on his boundary adjoining another territory. It was a good land, and Yaa was its name. There were figs in it, together with grapes. It had more wine than water; great was its honey and abundant its olives. Every fruit was on its trees. There was barley there, and emmer wheat, and all kinds of cattle without limit.

And much, indeed, accrued to me as a result of the love of me. He appointed me as ruler of a tribe of the choicest of his country. Provisions were assigned for me daily, and wine for each day's needs; cooked meat and roasted fowl besides desert game. They used to snare for me and set aside game for me over and above what my hounds caught. Much wine was made for me, and milk was used in every kind of cooking.

Thus I spent many years. My children became strong men, each man in control of a tribe. The couriers who went north or south to the Palace would tarry because of me, and I made all travelers tarry. I gave water to the thirsty; I put on the road those who had become lost, and I rescued those who were plundered.

When the Bedouin became so bold as to oppose the "Chiefs of the Foreign Lands," I advised them how to proceed. This ruler of the Syrians caused me to spend many years as commander of his army. Every foreign territory against which I went forth, I attacked and it was driven away from its pasturage and its wells. I plundered its cattle, I carried away its inhabitants, and seized their food. I slew people thereof with my strong arm, and by my movements and my excellent devices, I found favor in the ruler's heart, and he loved me. He recognized my valor, and placed me even before his children, since he saw that my arms flourished.

There came a powerful man of the Syrians to taunt me with challenges in my tent. He was a hero without peer, and he had beaten all the Syrians. He said he would fight with me. He expected to despoil me and plunder my cattle, being so counseled by his tribe.

The ruler discussed the matter with me, and I said, "I do not know him, and I certainly am not an associate of his going about in his camp. Is it that I have opened his gate, or thrown down his fence? It is envy, because he sees me carrying out your orders. Assuredly, I am like a bull who has wandered into the herd, and whom the long-horned steer of the herd attacks. Is there any man of humble origin who is loved when he becomes a superior? Well, if he wants to fight, let him speak out what he has in mind. Is a god ignorant of the fact that the nature of whatever he has ordained will eventually be known?"

During the night I strung my bow and practised my shooting. I made my dagger loose and free and polished my weapons. At dawn all Syria came, its tribes stirred up and half its peoples assembled; this fight had been planned.

Then he came toward me as I waited, and I placed myself in position near him. Every heart burned for me, and the women and even the men were murmuring. Every heart was sick for me as they said, "Is there another strong enough to fight him?"

But I escaped his missiles and made his arrows pass me by until none remained, and his shield, his ax, and his armful of spears fell down before me. Then he charged at me. I shot him; my arrow stuck in his neck. He shrieked and fell on his nose. I killed him with his own battle-ax. I gave forth my shout of victory on his back while every Syrian roared. I gave jubilant praise to Montu while his partisans mourned him.

This ruler Amu-nenshi took me in his embrace. Then I carried away my enemy's goods, and I plundered his cattle. What he had planned to do to me, this I did to him. I seized all that was in his tent, and stripped his encampment. Thus I widened my possessions and became numerous in cattle. I became great there. Thus has the god done, in being gracious unto one against whom he had been angered, and whom he had sent astray into another land. Today is his heart appeased.

> *A fugitive has fled in his straitened moment;*
>   *now my good report is in the Palace.*
> *A lingerer lingered because of hunger;*
>   *now I give bread to my neighbor.*
> *A man left his land because of nakedness;*
>   *now I am bright of raiment and of linen.*
> *A man ran for lack of someone to send;*
>   *now I am rich in slaves.*
> *My house is beautiful, and broad is my abode.*
>   *The memory of me is in the Palace.*

O whichever God ordained this flight, show mercy and return me to the Palace! Surely you will grant that I see the place where dwells my heart!

What is more important than that my body be buried in Egypt, the land where I was born? O come to my aid!

That which has occurred is a fortunate event—the god has shown mercy. May he do the like to bring to a good end him whom he has afflicted!

May his heart be sick for him whom he has cast out to live in a foreign land. Is it true that today he is appeased? Then let him hear the prayer of one who is afar! Let him turn his hand toward him who trod the earth, leading him back to the place whence he drew him forth!

May the King of Egypt be gracious unto me, who lives in his grace! May I hail the Lady of the Land, who is in his Palace, and may I hear word of his children! Then might my limbs flourish, since old age has befallen me, and infirmity has overtaken me.

My arms are weak, and my legs have slackened. My heart is weary; I am near to departure, and they will take me away to the City of Eternity!

Might I once more serve the Lady of All! Then will she tell me that it is well with her children! May she spend eternity over me!

Now, it was told to the Majesty of the King of Upper and Lower Egypt, Kheper-Ka-Ra [Senusret I], regarding the circumstances under which I was living. And His Majesty kept sending to me bearers of gifts of the royal bounty, that he might gladden the heart of this his servant like the ruler of any foreign land. And the children of the King, who were in the Palace, let me hear word from them.

[Here Sinuhe inserts the text of the message sent by King Senusret inviting him to return to Egypt:]

Copy of the decree brought to this servant about bringing him back to Egypt:

"The Horus Living-of-Births, the Two Ladies Living-of-Births, the King of Upper and Lower Egypt, Kheper-Ka-Ra, Son of Ra, Senusret, Living forever unto eternity!

"A decree of the King to the Retainer Sinuhe:

"Behold, this decree of the King is brought to you to advise you as follows: You have wandered about foreign lands—you have gone from Kedem to Tenu. Under the counsel of your own heart, land gave you to land! What have you done, that anything should be done against you? You have not blasphemed, that your words should be reproved. Your words have not been evil in the Council of the Nobles, that your utterances should be opposed. This plan of yours carried away your heart. It was not in my heart against you.

"This your 'Heaven,' who is in the Palace, today prospers and flourishes. Her head is covered with the royalty of the land. Her children are in the Residence; you shall heap up precious things of what they will give you, and you shall live by their largesse.

"Do you return to Egypt, that you may see the Residence wherein you grew up. You shall kiss the earth at the Great Double Door, and you shall join the courtiers.

"For today indeed you have begun to grow old, and have lost your virile powers. Be mindful of the day of burial, of passing to a revered state! A night will be assigned for you for oils and wrappings from the hands of Tayit. A funeral cortege will be made for you on the day of interment a mummy case of gold with a headpiece of lapis lazuli, and a heaven canopy above you. You will be placed upon a bier, with oxen drawing you and singers going before you, and the mortuary dances will be performed at the door of your tomb. The lists of the offering-table shall be invoked for you, sacrifices shall be made before your tomb stelae, and your tomb columns shall be built of white limestone amidst the tombs of the royal children.

"You must not die in a foreign land! The Asiatics shall not escort you to burial. You shall not be put in a sheepskin and a mound made over you!

"This is too long to tread the earth. Be mindful of illness, and come back!"

This decree reached me as I was standing in the midst of my tribe. It was recited to me; I placed myself on my belly. I touched the earth and scattered it upon my hair. I went about my camp rejoicing and saying, "How can such things be done to a servant whom his heart led astray to foreign and barbarous lands? Good indeed is the clemency which rescued me from the hand of death! Your Divine Essence will allow me to make my end with my body in the Residence!"

[Sinuhe now gives the text of his reply:]

Copy of the answer to this decree:
"The Servant of the Palace, Sinuhe, says:

"In very good peace! It is known to your Divine Essence, this flight made by your servant in his ignorance, O good God, Lord of the Two Lands, Beloved of Ra, Favored of Montu, Lord of Thebes!

"Amen, Lord of the Thrones of the Two Lands, Sebek, Ra, Horus, Hathor, Atum with his Ennead, Soped, Nefer-Bau, Semseru, the Eastern Horus, the Lady of Yemet—The Serpent-goddess, may she continue to enfold your head—the Council over the Nile waters, Min-Horus amidst the foreign lands, Wereret Lady of Punt, Nut, Ra-Horus the Elder, and all the Gods of Egypt and the Islands of the Sea, may they give life and strength to your nostrils, may they endow you with their bounty, may they give you eternity without bound and everlasting without limit! May the fear of you be repeated in the lowlands and the highlands, when you have subdued all that the sun encircles! This is the prayer of your servant for his Lord, who saves from the West!

"The lord of perception who perceives his people, he perceives in the Majesty of his Palace that which your servant feared to say, and which is a grave thing to repeat. O great God, likeness of Ra, make prudent one who is laboring on his own behalf! Your servant is in the hand of one who takes counsel concerning him, and verily am I placed under his guidance. Your Majesty is Horus the Conqueror; your arms are mighty over all lands.

"Lo, this flight your servant made, I did not plan it; it was not in my heart, I did not devise it. I do not know what separated me from my place. It was like some sort of dream, as when a man of the Delta marshes sees himself in Elephantine, or a man of the northern swamps in Nubia. I did not take fright, no one was pursuing me, I had heard no reviling word. My name had not been heard in the mouth of the herald.

"However, my limbs began to quiver, and my legs began to tremble. My heart led me away. The god who ordained this flight drew me, although I had not been rebellious.

"Any man who knows his land stands in awe, for Ra has set the fear of you throughout the earth, and the dread of you in every foreign land. Whether I am at the Palace or whether I am in this place, it is you, indeed, who clothes this horizon. The sun shines at your pleasure; the water in the rivers, it is drunk at your desire; the air is in the heaven, it is breathed when you so say.

"This your servant will resign the viziership which he has exercised in this place; it was a function they had requested your servant to perform. Your Majesty will act as he pleases; one lives by the breath which you bestow. Ra, Horus, and Hathor love this thy noble nose, which Montu, Lord of Thebes, desires shall live for ever!"

They came for me. I was allowed to spend a day in Yaa for transferring my possessions to my children, my eldest son having charge of my tribe—my tribe and all my property in his hands, my serfs and all my cattle, my stores of fruit and every pleasant tree of mine.

Then this servant went southward. I halted at the Roads of Horus. The commander there who was in charge of the frontier patrol sent a message to the Palace to make it known. Then His Majesty sent a capable overseer of the peasants who belonged to the Palace, followed by ships laden with gifts of the King for the Syrians who had come escorting me to the Roads of Horus. I introduced each of them by his name. Every servant was at his task when I set out and hoisted sail. They kneaded and strained before me, until I reached the vicinity of Yetchet-Tawy.

And when it dawned, very early, they came to call me, ten men coming and ten men going, to conduct me to the Palace. I touched my forehead to the ground beneath the sphinxes. The King's children were standing in the gateway to meet me. The courtiers who had been led into the Great Hall took me on the way to the royal chambers.

I found His Majesty on a great throne in a gilded niche. Then when I was stretched out on my belly, I lost consciousness before him. This god addressed me joyfully, but I was like a man overcome by dusk. My soul departed; my limbs were powerless, my heart, it was not in my body, that I should know life from death.

Then His Majesty said to one of the courtiers, "Raise him, and let him speak to me."

And His Majesty said, "Behold, you have returned! You have trodden foreign lands; you fled away. Now infirmity has seized you, and you have reached old age. It is of no little importance for your body to be buried, that you should not be interred by the Bedouin. Come, do not behave thus, not to speak when your name is pronounced!"

But I still feared punishment, and I answered with the response of one afraid, "What does my Lord say to me? I should answer, but I can do nothing. It is indeed the hand of a god. There is a terror in my belly, like that which brought about that destined flight. Behold me before you; life is yours; may Your Majesty do as he desires!"

Then they had the King's children brought in, and His Majesty said to the Queen, "Behold Sinuhe, come as a Bedouin, as if born a Syrian!"

She uttered a very great cry, and the King's children all shouted together. And they said to His Majesty, "Is it not he, in truth, O King, My Lord?"

And His Majesty said, "It is he, in truth!"

Now they had brought with them their *menit* collars and their rattles and sistra of Hathor, and they presented them before His Majesty, saying:

"Put forth your hands to these beautiful things.
    O enduring King,
    the adornments of the Lady of Heaven!
May the Golden One give life to your nostrils;
    may she join with you, the Lady of the Stars!
May the Crown-goddess of Upper Egypt sail northward
    and the Crown-goddess of Lower Egypt sail southward,
    joined and united by the utterance of Your Majesty!
The Cobra-goddess is set upon your brow,
    and you have removed your subjects from evil.
May Ra, Lord of the Two Lands, be gracious unto you;
    hail to you, as to the Lady of All!
Slacken your bow, make loose your arrow,
    give breath to him who is stifling!
Give us as good festal gift this sheik, son of the North,
    a barbarian born in Egypt!
He made flight through fear of you,
    he left the land through dread of you!
May the face of him who has seen your face not be afraid;
    may the eye which has looked at you not be terrified!"

Then said His Majesty, "Let him not fear, and let him not fall into dread. He shall be a courtier among the nobles, and he shall be placed in the midst of the courtiers. Proceed you to the Morning-chamber, and wait upon him!"

And so I went forth from the royal chambers, the King's children giving me their hands. We proceeded afterward to the Great Double Door. I was placed in the house of a son of the King, which had fine things in it; there was a cooling room in it, and landscape decoration. There were valuables of the Treasury in it, and in every room was clothing of royal linen, and myrrh, and the best oil of the King, and of the courtiers, whom he loves. Every servingman was at his task.

The years were made to pass away from my limbs as I was shaved and my hair was combed. A load of dirt was given back to the desert, and their clothes to the sand farers. I was clothed in fine linen, and anointed with fine oil. I slept upon a bed. I gave back the sand to those who live in it, and tree oil to those who rub themselves with it.

There was given to me a house with grounds, which had belonged to a courtier. Many craftsmen restored it, and all its trees made to flourish anew. Meals from the Palace were brought to me three or four times a day besides what the King's children kept on giving me.

There was built for me a pyramid-tomb of stone, in the midst of the pyramids. The chief pyramid mason took charge of its ground, the chief draftsman designed it, the chief sculptor carved in it, and the chief builders of the necropolis concerned themselves with it. All the equipment which is placed in a tomb, those were supplied therein. Ka-priests were assigned to me. A funerary domain was made for me with fields in it, as is done for a foremost courtier. My statue was overlaid with gold, its kilt with fine gold.

By His Majesty was it caused to be done. There is no commoner for whom the like has been done. I was bestowed the favors of the King until there came the day of mooring.

IT HAS COME FROM ITS BEGINNING TO ITS END, AS WAS FOUND IN THE WRITING.

The Great Hymn to the Aten

Praise of the Living Ra, Horus of the Double Horizon, Rejoicing on the Horizon, in His Name of Shu Who is in the Aten, living forever unto eternity; Aten living and great, he who is in the Jubilee Festival, Lord of all that the Aten encircles, Lord of the Heavens and Lord of the Earth, Lord of the House of Aten in Akhet-Aten. The King of Upper and Lower Egypt, Living in Truth, the Lord of the Two Lands, Nefer-Kheperu-Ra Wa-en-Ra, Son of Ra, Living in Truth, Lord of Diadems, Akh-en-Aten, Great in his Duration, and the Great Wife of the King, his Beloved, the Lady of the Two Lands, Nefer-Neferu-Aten Nefert-Iti, living, healthy, and youthful forever unto eternity. He says:

Beautiful is your shining forth on the horizon,
  O living Aten, beginning of life!
When you arise on the eastern horizon,
  you fill every land with your beauty.
You are bright and great and gleaming,
  and are high above every land.
Your rays envelop the lands,
  as far as all you have created.
You are Ra, and you reach unto their end,
  and subdue them all for your beloved son.
You are afar, yet are your rays upon earth;
  you are before their face, yet one knows not their going!
When you go down in the western horizon,
  the earth is in darkness, as if it were dead.
They sleep in their chamber, their heads enwrapped,
  and no eye sees the other.
Though all their things were taken while under their heads,
  yet would they not perceive it.
Every lion comes forth from his den,
  and all serpents that bite.

Darkness is without and the earth is silent,
  for he who created it rests in his horizon.
When the earth brightens and you rise on the horizon,
  and shine as the Aten in the day,
When you scatter the darkness and offer your beams,
  the Two Lands are in festival,
They are awake and they stand on their feet,
  for you have raised them up.
They wash their bodies, and they take their garments,
  and their hands praise your arising.
    The whole land, it performs its work!

All beasts are content upon their pasture,
  and the trees and herbs are verdant.
The birds fly out of their nests,
  and their wings praise your Divine Essence.
All wild beasts prance upon their feet,
  and all that fly and alight.
    They live when you shine forth for them!

The ships voyage downstream and upstream likewise,
  and every way is open, since you have arisen.
The fish in the river leap up before your face,
  and your rays are in the midst of the Great Green.

You who bring children into being in women,
  and make fluid into mankind,
Who nourishes the son in the womb of his mother,
  who soothes him so that he weeps not,
    O nurse in the womb!
Who gives breath in order to keep alive
  all that he has made;

When he comes forth from the womb on the day of his
   birth,
   you open his mouth in speech, and give all that he
      needs.
The chick in the egg chirps in the shell,
   for you give it breath therein to sustain its life.
You make its completion for it in the egg in order to
      break it;
It comes forth from the egg at its completion,
   and walks on its feet when it comes forth therefrom.

How manifold are the things which you have made,
   and they are hidden from before man!
      O unique god, who has no second to him!
You have created the earth according to your desire,
   while you were alone,
With men, cattle, and wild beasts,
   all that is upon earth and goes upon feet,
      and all that soars above and flies with its wings.

The lands of Syria and Kush,
   and the land of Egypt,
You put every man in his place,
   and supply their needs.
Each one has provision
   and his lifetime is reckoned.
Their tongues are diverse in speech,
   and their form likewise;
Their skins are distinguished,
   for you distinguish the peoples of foreign lands.

You make the Nile in the Other World,
   and bring it whither you wish,
In order to sustain the people,
   even as you have made them.
For you are lord of them all,
   who weary yourself on their behalf,
The lord of every land, who arises for them,
   O Aten of the day, great of majesty!

All strange foreign lands,
   you make that whereon they live.
You have put a Nile in the sky,
   that it may come down for them,
And make waves on the hills like the sea,
   to water their fields in their townships.

How excellently made are your designs, O Lord of
   Eternity!
   the Nile in heaven, you appoint it for foreign peoples,
      and all beasts of the wilderness which walk upon feet;
The Nile upon earth,
   it proceeds from the Other World for the Beloved Land.

Your rays suckle every field,
   and when you shine forth
      they live and flourish for you.
You make the seasons
   to cause to continue all you have created:
The winter to cool them,
   and the warmth that they may taste of you.
You have made the sky afar off to shine therein,
   in order to behold all you have made.
You are alone, shining in your forms as living Aten,
   appearing, shining, withdrawing, returning,
      you make millions of forms of yourself alone!
Cities, townships, fields, road, and river,
   all eyes behold you against them,
      O Aten of the day above the earth!

You are in my heart,
   and there is no one who knows you save your son,
Nefer-Kheperu-Ra Wa-en-Ra,
   whom you made understanding of your designs and
      your might.
The earth came into being by your hand,
   even as you have created them.
When you arise they live,
   and when you set they die.
But you have eternity in your members,
   and all creatures live in you.
The eyes look on your beauty until you set;
   all work is laid aside when you set in the west.
When you rise you make all to flourish for the King,
   you who made the foundations of the earth.
You raise them up for your son,
   he who came forth from your body,
the King of Upper and Lower Egypt, Living in Truth, the Lord
of the Two Lands, Nefer-Kheperu-Ra Wa-en-Ra, Son of Ra,
Living in Truth, Lord of Diadems, Akh-en-Aten, Great in His
Duration, and for the Great Wife of the King, his Beloved,
the Lady of the Two Lands, Nefer-Neferu-Aten Nefert-Iti,
living and youthful forever unto eternity.

from *The New English Bible*

Genesis 1–3

The Creation of the World

In the beginning of creation, when God made heaven and earth, the earth was without form and void, with darkness over the face of the abyss, and a mighty wind that swept over the surface of the waters. God said, 'Let there be light', and there was light; and God saw that the light was good, and he separated light from darkness. He called the light day, and the darkness night. So evening came, and morning came, the first day.

God said, 'Let there be a vault between the waters, to separate water from water.' So God made the vault, and separated the water under the vault from the water above it, and so it was; and God called the vault heaven. Evening came, and morning came, a second day.

God said, 'Let the waters under heaven be gathered into one place, so that dry land may appear'; and so it was. God called the dry land earth, and the gathering of the waters he called seas; and God saw that it was good. Then God said, 'Let the earth produce fresh growth, let there be on the earth plants bearing seed, fruit-trees bearing fruit each with seed according to its kind.' So it was; the earth yielded fresh growth, plants bearing seed according to their kind and trees bearing fruit each with seed according to its kind; and God saw that it was good. Evening came, and morning came, a third day.

God said, 'Let there be lights in the vault of heaven to separate day from night, and let them serve as signs both for festivals and for seasons and years. Let them also shine in the vault of heaven to give light on earth.' So it was; God made the two great lights, the greater to govern the day and the lesser to govern the night; and with them he made the stars. God put these lights in the vault of heaven to give light on earth, to govern day and night, and to separate light from darkness; and God saw that it was good. Evening came, and morning came, a fourth day.

God said, 'Let the waters teem with countless living creatures, and let birds fly above the earth across the vault of heaven.' God then created the great sea-monsters and all living creatures that move and swarm in the waters, according to their kind, and every kind of bird; and God saw that it was good. So he blessed them and said, 'Be fruitful and increase, fill the waters of the seas; and let the birds increase on land.' Evening came, and morning came, a fifth day.

God said, 'Let the earth bring forth living creatures, according to their kind: cattle, reptiles, and wild animals, all according to their kind.' So it was; God made wild animals, cattle, and all reptiles, each according to its kind; and he saw that it was good. Then God said, 'Let us make man in our image and likeness to rule the fish in the sea, the birds of heaven, the cattle, all wild animals on earth, and all reptiles that crawl upon the earth.' So God created man in his own image; in the image of God he created him; male and female he created them. God blessed them and said to them, 'Be fruitful and increase, fill the earth and subdue it, rule over the fish in the sea, the birds of heaven, and every living thing that moves upon the earth.' God also said, 'I give you all plants that bear seed everywhere on earth, and every tree bearing fruit which yields seed: they shall be yours for food. All green plants I give for food to the wild animals, to all the birds of heaven, and to all reptiles on earth, every living creature.' So it was; and God saw all that he had made, and it was very good. Evening came, and morning came, a sixth day.

Thus heaven and earth were completed with all their mighty throng. On the sixth day God completed all the work he had been doing, and on the seventh day he ceased from all his work. God blessed the seventh day and made it holy, because on that day he ceased from all the work he had set himself to do.

This is the story of the making of heaven and earth when they were created.

The Beginnings of History

When the Lord God made earth and heaven, there was neither shrub nor plant growing wild upon the earth, because the Lord God had sent no rain on the earth; nor was there any man to till the ground. A flood used to rise out of the earth and water all the surface of the ground. Then the Lord God formed a man from the dust of the ground and breathed into his nostrils the breath of life. Thus the man became a living creature. Then the Lord God planted a garden in Eden away to the east, and there he put the man whom he had formed. The Lord God made trees spring from the ground, all trees pleasant to look at and good for food; and in the middle of the garden he set the tree of life and the tree of the knowledge of good and evil.

There was a river flowing from Eden to water the garden, and when it left the garden it branched into four streams. The name of the first is Pishon; that is the river which encircles all the land of Havilah, where the gold is. The gold of that land is good; bdellium and cornelians are also to be found there. The name of the second river is Gihon; this is the one which encircles all the land of Cush. The name of the third is Tigris; this is the river which runs east of Asshur. The fourth river is the Euphrates.

The Lord God took the man and put him in the garden of Eden to till it and care for it. He told the man, 'You may eat from every tree in the garden, but not from the tree of the knowledge of good and evil; for on the day that you eat from it, you will certainly die.' Then the Lord God said, 'It is not good for the man to be alone. I will provide a partner for him.' So God formed out of the ground all the wild animals and all the birds of heaven. He brought them to the man to see what he would call them, and whatever the man called each living creature, that was its name. Thus the man gave names to all cattle, to the birds of heaven, and to every wild animal; but for the man himself no partner had yet been found. And so the Lord God put the man into a trance, and while he slept, he took one of his ribs and closed the flesh over the place. The Lord God then built up the rib, which he had taken out of the man, into a woman. He brought her to the man, and the man said:

> 'Now this, at last—
> bone from my bones,
> flesh from my flesh!—
> this shall be called woman,
> for from man was this taken.'

That is why a man leaves his father and mother and is united to his wife, and the two become one flesh. Now they were both naked, the man and his wife, but they had no feeling of shame towards one another.

The serpent was more crafty than any wild creature that the Lord God had made. He said to the woman, 'Is it true that God has forbidden you to eat from any tree in the garden?' The woman answered the serpent, 'We may eat the fruit of any tree in the garden, except for the tree in the middle of the garden; God has forbidden us either to eat or to touch the fruit of that; if we do, we shall die.' The serpent said, 'Of course you will not die. God knows that as soon as you eat it, your eyes will be opened and you will be like gods knowing both good and evil.' When the woman saw that the fruit of the tree was good to eat, and that it was pleasing to the eye and tempting to contemplate, she took some and ate it. She also gave her husband some and he ate it. Then the eyes of both of them were opened and they discovered that they were naked; so they stitched fig-leaves together and made themselves loincloths.

The man and his wife heard the sound of the Lord God walking in the garden at the time of the evening breeze and hid from the Lord God among the trees of the garden. But the Lord God called to the man and said to him, 'Where are you?' He replied, 'I heard the sound as you were walking in the garden, and I was afraid because I was naked, and I hid myself.' God answered, 'Who told you that you were naked? Have you eaten from the tree which I forbade you?'

The man said, 'The woman you gave me for a companion, she gave me fruit from the tree and I ate it.' Then the Lord God said to the woman, 'What is this that you have done?' The woman said, 'The serpent tricked me, and I ate.' Then the Lord God said to the serpent:

> 'Because you have done this you are accursed
> more than all cattle and all wild creatures.
> On your belly you shall crawl, and dust you shall eat
> all the days of your life.
> I will put enmity between you and the woman,
> between your brood and hers.
> They shall strike at your head,
> and you shall strike at their heel.'

To the woman he said:

> 'I will increase your labour and your groaning,
> and in labour you shall bear children.
> You shall be eager for your husband,
> and he shall be your master.'

And to the man he said:

> 'Because you have listened to your wife
> and have eaten from the tree which I forbade you,
> accursed shall be the ground on your account.
> With labour you shall win your food from it
> all the days of your life.
> It will grow thorns and thistles for you,
> none but wild plants for you to eat.
> You shall gain your bread by the sweat of your brow
> until you return to the ground;
> for from it you were taken.
> Dust you are, to dust you shall return.'

The man called his wife Eve because she was the mother of all who live. The Lord God made tunics of skins for Adam and his wife and clothed them. He said, 'The man has become like one of us, knowing good and evil; what if he now reaches out his hand and takes fruit from the tree of life also, eats it and lives for ever?' So the Lord God drove him out of the garden of Eden to till the ground from which he had been taken. He cast him out, and to the east of the garden of Eden he stationed the cherubim and a sword whirling and flashing to guard the way to the tree of life.

Isaiah

42:5–9

Thus speaks the Lord who is God,
  he who created the skies and stretched them out,
  who fashioned the earth and all that grows in it,
who gave breath to its people,
  the breath of life to all who walk upon it:
I, the Lord, have called you with righteous purpose
    and taken you by the hand;
  I have formed you, and appointed you
  to be a light to all peoples,
  a beacon for the nations,
  to open eyes that are blind,
  to bring captives out of prison,
    out of the dungeons where they lie in darkness.
I am the Lord; the Lord is my name;
  I will not give my glory to another god,
    nor my praise to any idol.
  See how the first prophecies have come to pass,
  and now I declare new things;
before they break from the bud I announce them to you.

44:6–8

Thus says the Lord, Israel's King,
  the Lord of Hosts, his ransomer:
I am the first and I am the last,
    and there is no god but me.
  Who is like me? Let him stand up,
  let him declare himself and speak and show me his
    evidence,
  let him announce beforehand things to come,
  let him declare what is yet to happen.

Take heart, do not be afraid.
Did I not foretell this long ago?
I declared it, and you are my witnesses.
Is there any god beside me,
  or any creator, even one that I do not know?

49:22–26

The Lord God says,
Now is the time: I will beckon to the nations
  and hoist a signal to the peoples,
  and they shall bring your sons in their arms
  and carry your daughters on their shoulders;
  kings shall be your foster-fathers
    and their princesses shall be your nurses.
They shall bow to the earth before you
  and lick the dust from your feet;
  and you shall know that I am the Lord
  and that none who look to me will be disappointed.
Can his prey be taken from the strong man,
  or the captive be rescued from the ruthless?
  And the Lord answers,
  The captive shall be taken even from the strong,
    and the prey of the ruthless shall be rescued;
  I will contend with all who contend against you
    and save your children from them.
I will force your oppressors to feed on their own flesh
and make them drunk with their own blood as if with
    fresh wine,
    and all mankind shall know
  that it is I, the Lord, who save you,
    I your ransomer, the Mighty One of Jacob.

Chapter

2

Aegean Civilization:
The Minoans, the Mycenaeans, and the Greeks of the Archaic Age

HOMER

from *The Iliad*

Book XVIII

• • •

He cast on the fire bronze which is weariless, and tin
   with it
and valuable gold, and silver, and thereafter set forth
upon its standard the great anvil, and gripped in one hand
the ponderous hammer, while in the other he grasped
   the pincers.
  First of all he forged a shield that was huge and heavy,
elaborating it about, and threw around it a shining
triple rim that glittered, and the shield strap was cast of
   silver.
There were five folds composing the shield itself, and
   upon it
he elaborated many things in his skill and craftsmanship.
  He made the earth upon it, and the sky, and the sea's
   water,
and the tireless sun, and the moon waxing into her fullness,
and on it all the constellations that festoon the heavens,
the Pleiades and the Hyades and the strength of Orion
and the Bear, whom men give also the name of the Wagon,

who turns about in a fixed place and looks at Orion
and she alone is never plunged in the wash of the
   Ocean.
  On it he wrought in all their beauty two cities of
   mortal
men. And there were marriages in one, and festivals.
They were leading the brides along the city from their
   maiden chambers
under the flaring of torches, and the loud bride song was
   arising.
The young men followed the circles of the dance, and
   among them
the flutes and lyres kept up their clamour as in the
   meantime
the women standing each at the door of her court
   admired them.
The people were assembled in the market place, where a
   quarrel
had arisen, and two men were disputing over the blood
   price

for a man who had been killed. One man promised full
   restitution
in a public statement, but the other refused and would
   accept nothing.
Both then made for an arbitrator, to have a decision;
and people were speaking up on either side, to help
   both men.
But the heralds kept the people in hand, as meanwhile
   the elders
were in session on benches of polished stone in the
   sacred circle
and held in their hands the staves of the heralds who lift
   their voices.
The two men rushed before these, and took turns
   speaking their cases,
and between them lay on the ground two talents of gold,
   to be given
to that judge who in this case spoke the straightest
   opinion.
   But around the other city were lying two forces of
   armed men
shining in their war gear. For one side counsel was
   divided
whether to storm and sack, or share between both sides
   the property
and all the possessions the lovely citadel held hard
   within it.
But the city's people were not giving way, and armed for
   an ambush.
Their beloved wives and their little children stood on the
   rampart
to hold it, and with them the men with age upon them,
   but meanwhile
the others went out. And Ares led them, and Pallas
   Athene.
These were gold, both, and golden raiment upon them,
   and they were
beautiful and huge in their armour, being divinities,
and conspicuous from afar, but the people around them
   were smaller.
These, when they were come to the place that was set
   for their ambush,
in a river, where there was a watering place for all animals,
there they sat down in place shrouding themselves in the
   bright bronze.
But apart from these were sitting two men to watch for
   the rest of them
and waiting until they could see the sheep and the
   shambling cattle,
who appeared presently, and two herdsmen went along
   with them
playing happily on pipes, and took no thought of the
   treachery.
Those others saw them, and made a rush, and quickly
   thereafter
cut off on both sides the herds of cattle and the beautiful
flocks of shining sheep, and killed the shepherds upon them.
But the other army, as soon as they heard the uproar
   arising

from the cattle, as they sat in their councils, suddenly
   mounted
behind their light-foot horses, and went after, and soon
   overtook them.
These stood their ground and fought a battle by the
   banks of the river,
and they were making casts at each other with their
   spears bronze-headed;
and Hate was there with Confusion among them, and
   Death the destructive;
she was holding a live man with a new wound, and
   another
one unhurt, and dragged a dead man by the feet
   through the carnage.
The clothing upon her shoulders showed strong red with
   the men's blood.
All closed together like living men and fought with each
   other
and dragged away from each other the corpses of those
   who had fallen.
   He made upon it a soft field, the pride of the tilled
   land,
wide and triple-ploughed, with many ploughmen upon it
who wheeled their teams at the turn and drove them in
   either direction.
And as these making their turn would reach the end-strip
   of the field,
a man would come up to them at this point and hand
   them a flagon
of honey-sweet wine, and they would turn again to the
   furrows
in their haste to come again to the end-strip of the deep
   field.
The earth darkened behind them and looked like earth
   that has been ploughed
though it was gold. Such was the wonder of the shield's
   forging.
   He made on it the precinct of a king, where the
   labourers
were reaping, with the sharp reaping hooks in their
   hands. Of the cut swathes
some fell along the lines of reaping, one after another,
while the sheaf-binders caught up others and tied them
   with bind-ropes.
There were three sheaf-binders who stood by, and
   behind them
were children picking up the cut swathes, and filled their
   arms with them
and carried and gave them always; and by them the king
   in silence
and holding his staff stood near the line of the reapers,
   happily.
And apart and under a tree the heralds made a feast
   ready
and trimmed a great ox they had slaughtered. Meanwhile
   the women
scattered, for the workmen to eat, abundant white barley.
   He made on it a great vineyard heavy with clusters,
lovely and in gold, but the grapes upon it were darkened

and the vines themselves stood out through poles of
   silver. About them
he made a field-ditch of dark metal, and drove all
   around this
a fence of tin; and there was only one path to the
   vineyard,
and along it ran the grape-bearers for the vineyard's
   stripping.
Young girls and young men, in all their light-hearted
   innocence,
carried the kind, sweet fruit away in their woven baskets,
and in their midst a youth with a singing lyre played
   charmingly
upon it for them, and sang the beautiful song for Linos
in a light voice, and they followed him, and with singing
   and whistling
and light dance-steps of their feet kept time to the music.
   He made upon it a herd of horn-straight oxen. The
   cattle
were wrought of gold and of tin, and thronged in speed
   and with lowing
out of the dung of the farmyard to a pasturing place by a
   sounding
river, and beside the moving field of a reed bed.
The herdsmen were of gold who went along with the
   cattle,
four of them, and nine dogs shifting their feet followed
   them.
But among the foremost of the cattle two formidable lions
had caught hold of a bellowing bull, and he with loud
   lowings
was dragged away, as the dogs and the young men went
   in pursuit of him.
But the two lions, breaking open the hide of the great ox,
gulped the black blood and the inward guts, as
   meanwhile the herdsmen
were in the act of setting and urging the quick dogs on
   them.
But they, before they could get their teeth in, turned
   back from the lions,
but would come and take their stand very close, and
   bayed, and kept clear.
   And the renowned smith of the strong arms made on
   it a meadow
large and in a lovely valley for the glimmering
   sheepflocks,

with dwelling places upon it, and covered shelters, and
   sheepfolds.
   And the renowned smith of the strong arms made
   elaborate on it
a dancing floor, like that which once in the wide spaces
   of Knosos
Daidalos built for Ariadne of the lovely tresses.
And there were young men on it and young girls, sought
   for their beauty
with gifts of oxen, dancing, and holding hands at the
   wrist. These
wore, the maidens long light robes, but the men wore
   tunics
of finespun work and shining softly, touched with olive oil.
And the girls wore fair garlands on their heads, while the
   young men
carried golden knives that hung from sword-belts of silver.
At whiles on their understanding feet they would run very
   lightly,
as when a potter crouching makes trial of his wheel, holding
it close in his hands, to see if it will run smooth. At another
time they would form rows, and run, rows crossing each
   other.
And around the lovely chorus of dancers stood a great
   multitude
happily watching, while among the dancers two acrobats
led the measures of song and dance revolving among them.
   He made on it the great strength of the Ocean River
which ran around the uttermost rim of the shield's strong
   structure.
   Then after he had wrought this shield, which was huge
   and heavy,
he wrought for him a corselet brighter than fire in its shining,
and wrought him a helmet, massive and fitting close to his
   temples,
lovely and intricate work, and laid a gold top-ridge along it,
and out of pliable tin wrought him leg-armour. Thereafter
when the renowned smith of the strong arms had
   finished the armour
he lifted it and laid it before the mother of Achilleus.
And she like a hawk came sweeping down from the
   snows of Olympos
and carried with her the shining armour, the gift of
   Hephaistos. . . .

Book XXII

· · ·

So these two in tears and with much supplication called out
to their dear son, but could not move the spirit in Hektor,
but he awaited Achilleus as he came on, gigantic.
But as a snake waits for a man by his hole, in the mountains,
glutted with evil poisons, and the fell venom has got inside him,
and coiled about the hole he stares malignant, so Hektor
would not give ground but kept unquenched the fury within him
and sloped his shining shield against the jut of the bastion.
Deeply troubled he spoke to his own great-hearted spirit:
'Ah me! If I go now inside the wall and the gateway,
Poulydamas will be first to put a reproach upon me,
since he tried to make me lead the Trojans inside the city
on that accursed night when brilliant Achilleus rose up,
and I would not obey him, but that would have been far better.
Now, since by my own recklessness I have ruined my people,
I feel shame before the Trojans and the Trojan women with trailing
robes, that someone who is less of a man than I will say of me:
"Hektor believed in his own strength and ruined his people."
Thus they will speak; and as for me, it would be much better
at that time, to go against Achilleus, and slay him, and come back,
or else be killed by him in glory in front of the city.
Or if again I set down my shield massive in the middle
and my ponderous helm, and lean my spear up against the rampart
and go out as I am to meet Achilleus the blameless
and promise to give back Helen, and with her all her possessions,
all those things that once in the hollow ships Alexandros
brought back to Troy, and these were the beginning of the quarrel;
to give these to Atreus' sons to take away, and for the Achaians
also to divide up all that is hidden within the city,
and take an oath thereafter for the Trojans in conclave
not to hide anything away, but distribute all of it,
as much as the lovely citadel keeps guarded within it;
yet still, why does the heart within me debate on these things?

I might go up to him, and he take no pity upon me
nor respect my position, but kill me naked so, as if I were
a woman, once I stripped my armour from me. There is no
way any more from a tree or a rock to talk to him gently
whispering like a young man and a young girl, in the way
a young man and a young maiden whisper together.
Better to bring on the fight with him as soon as it may be.
We shall see to which one the Olympian grants the glory.'
    So he pondered, waiting, but Achilleus was closing upon him
in the likeness of the lord of battles, the helm-shining warrior,
and shaking from above his shoulder the dangerous Pelian
ash spear, while the bronze that closed about him was shining
like the flare of blazing fire or the sun in its rising.
And the shivers took hold of Hektor when he saw him, and he could no longer
stand his ground there, but left the gates behind, and fled, frightened,
and Peleus' son went after him in the confidence of his quick feet.
As when a hawk in the mountains who moves lightest of things flying
makes his effortless swoop for a trembling dove, but she slips away
from beneath and flies and he shrill screaming close after her
plunges for her again and again, heart furious to take her;
so Achilleus went straight for him in fury, but Hektor
fled away under the Trojan wall and moved his knees rapidly.
They raced along by the watching point and the windy fig tree
always away from under the wall and along the wagon-way
and came to the two sweet-running well springs. There there are double
springs of water that jet up, the springs of whirling Skamandros.
One of these runs hot water and the steam on all sides
of it rises as if from a fire that was burning inside it.
But the other in the summer-time runs water that is like hail
or chill snow or ice that forms from water. Beside these
in this place, and close to them, are the washing-hollows
of stone, and magnificent, where the wives of the Trojans and their lovely
daughters washed the clothes to shining, in the old days
when there was peace, before the coming of the sons of the Achaians.
They ran beside these, one escaping, the other after him.

It was a great man who fled, but far better he who
    pursued him
rapidly, since here was no festal beast, no ox-hide
they strove for, for these are prizes that are given men
    for their running.
No, they ran for the life of Hektor, breaker of horses.
As when about the turnposts racing single-foot horses
run at full speed, when a great prize is laid up for their
    winning,
a tripod or a woman, in games for a man's funeral,
so these two swept whirling about the city of Priam
in the speed of their feet, while all the gods were
    looking upon them.
First to speak among them was the father of gods and
    mortals:
'Ah me, this is a man beloved whom now my eyes watch
being chased around the wall; my heart is mourning for
    Hektor
who has burned in my honour many thigh pieces of oxen
on the peaks of Ida with all her folds, or again on the
    uttermost
part of the citadel, but now the brilliant Achilleus
drives him in speed of his feet around the city of Priam.
Come then, you immortals, take thought and take
    counsel, whether
to rescue this man or whether to make him, for all his
    valour,
go down under the hands of Achilleus, the son of Peleus.'
    Then in answer the goddess grey-eyed Athene spoke
    to him:
'Father of the shining bolt, dark misted, what is this you
    said?
Do you wish to bring back a man who is mortal, one
    long since
doomed by his destiny, from ill-sounding death and
    release him?
Do it, then; but not all the rest of us gods shall approve
    you.'
    Then Zeus the gatherer of the clouds spoke to her in
    answer:
'Tritogeneia, dear daughter, do not lose heart; for I say this
not in outright anger, and my meaning toward you is
    kindly.
Act as your purpose would have you do, and hold back
    no longer.'
    So he spoke, and stirred on Athene, who was eager
    before this,
and she went in a flash of speed down the pinnacles of
    Olympos.
    But swift Achilleus kept unremittingly after Hektor,
chasing him, as a dog in the mountains who has flushed
    from his covert
a deer's fawn follows him through the folding ways and
    the valleys,
and though the fawn crouched down under a bush and
    be hidden
he keeps running and noses him out until he comes on him;
so Hektor could not lose himself from swift-footed
    Peleion.
If ever he made a dash right on for the gates of Dardanos

to get quickly under the strong-built bastions,
    endeavoring
that they from above with missiles thrown might
    somehow defend him,
each time Achilleus would get in front and force him to
    turn back
into the plain, and himself kept his flying course next
    the city.
As in a dream a man is not able to follow one who runs
from him, nor can the runner escape, nor the other
    pursue him,
so he could not run him down in his speed, nor the
    other get clear.
How then could Hektor have escaped the death spirits,
    had not
Apollo, for this last and uttermost time, stood by him
close, and driven strength into him, and made his knees
    light?
But brilliant Achilleus kept shaking his head at his own
    people
and would not let them throw their bitter projectiles at Hektor
for fear the thrower might win the glory, and himself
    come second.
But when for the fourth time they had come around to
    the well springs
then the Father balanced his golden scales, and in them
he set two fateful portions of death, which lays men
    prostrate,
one for Achilleus, and one for Hektor, breaker of horses,
and balanced it by the middle; and Hektor's death-day
    was heavier
and dragged downward toward death, and Phoibos
    Apollo forsook him.
But the goddess grey-eyed Athene came now to Peleion
and stood close beside him and addressed him in
    winged words: 'Beloved
of Zeus, shining Achilleus, I am hopeful now that you
    and I
will take back great glory to the ships of the Achaians, after
we have killed Hektor, for all his slakeless fury for battle.
Now there is no way for him to get clear away from us,
not though Apollo who strikes from afar should be
    willing to undergo
much, and wallow before our father Zeus of the aegis.
Stand you here then and get your wind again, while I go
to this man and persuade him to stand up to you in combat.'
    So spoke Athene, and he was glad at heart, and
    obeyed her,
and stopped, and stood leaning on his bronze-barbed
    ash spear. Meanwhile
Athene left him there, and caught up with brilliant Hektor,
and likened herself in form and weariless voice to
    Deïphobos.
She came now and stood close to him and addressed
    him in winged words:
'Dear brother, indeed swift-footed Achilleus is using you
    roughly
and chasing you on swift feet around the city of Priam.
Come on, then; let us stand fast against him and beat
    him back from us.'

Then tall Hektor of the shining helm answered her:
  'Deïphobos,
before now you were dearest to me by far of my brothers,
of all those who were sons of Priam and Hekabe, and now
I am minded all the more within my heart to honour you,
you who dared for my sake, when your eyes saw me, to
  come forth
from the fortifications, while the others stand fast inside
  them.'
  Then in turn the goddess grey-eyed Athene answered
  him:
'My brother, it is true our father and the lady our
  mother, taking
my knees in turn, and my companions about me, entreated
that I stay within, such was the terror upon all of them.
But the heart within me was worn away by hard sorrow
  for you.
But now let us go straight on and fight hard, let there be
  no sparing
of our spears, so that we can find out whether Achilleus
will kill us both and carry our bloody war spoils back
to the hollow ships, or will himself go down under your
  spear.'
  So Athene spoke and led him on by beguilement.
Now as the two in their advance were come close
  together,
first of the two to speak was tall helm-glittering Hektor:
'Son of Peleus, I will no longer run from you, as before this
I fled three times around the great city of Priam, and
  dared not
stand to your onfall. But now my spirit in turn has
  driven me
to stand and face you. I must take you now, or I must be
  taken.
Come then, shall we swear before the gods? For these
  are the highest
who shall be witnesses and watch over our agreements.
Brutal as you are I will not defile you, if Zeus grants
to me that I can wear you out, and take the life from you.
But after I have stripped your glorious armour, Achilleus,
I will give your corpse back to the Achaians. Do you do
  likewise.'
  Then looking darkly at him swift-footed Achilleus
  answered:
'Hektor, argue me no agreements. I cannot forgive you.
As there are no trustworthy oaths between men and lions,
nor wolves and lambs have spirit that can be brought to
  agreement
but forever these hold feelings of hate for each other,
so there can be no love between you and me, nor shall
  there be
oaths between us, but one or the other must fall before then
to glut with his blood Ares the god who fights under the
  shield's guard.
Remember every valour of yours, for now the need comes
hardest upon you to be a spearman and a bold warrior.
There shall be no more escape for you, but Pallas Athene
will kill you soon by my spear. You will pay in a lump
  for all those
sorrows of my companions you killed in your spear's fury.'

So he spoke, and balanced the spear far shadowed,
  and threw it;
but glorious Hektor kept his eyes on him, and avoided it,
for he dropped, watchful, to his knee, and the bronze
  spear flew over his shoulder
and stuck in the ground, but Pallas Athene snatched it,
  and gave it
back to Achilleus, unseen by Hektor shepherd of the
  people.
But now Hektor spoke out to the blameless son of Peleus:
'You missed; and it was not, o Achilleus like the immortals,
from Zeus that you knew my destiny; but you thought
  so; or rather
you are someone clever in speech and spoke to swindle me,
to make me afraid of you and forget my valour and war
  strength.
You will not stick your spear in my back as I run away
  from you
but drive it into my chest as I storm straight in against you;
if the god gives you that; and now look out for my
  brazen
spear. I wish it might be taken full length in your body.
And indeed the war would be a lighter thing for the
  Trojans
if you were dead, seeing that you are their greatest
  affliction.'
  So he spoke, and balanced the spear far shadowed,
  and threw it,
and struck the middle of Peleïdes' shield, nor missed it,
but the spear was driven far back from the shield, and
  Hektor was angered
because his swift weapon had been loosed from his hand
  in a vain cast.
He stood discouraged, and had no other ash spear; but
  lifting
his voice he called aloud on Deïphobos of the pale shield,
and asked him for a long spear, but Deïphobos was not
  near him.
And Hektor knew the truth inside his heart, and spoke
  aloud:
'No use. Here at last the gods have summoned me
  deathward.
I thought Deïphobos the hero was here close beside me,
but he is behind the wall and it was Athene cheating me,
and now evil death is close to me, and no longer far away,
and there is no way out. So it must long since have been
  pleasing
to Zeus, and Zeus' son who strikes from afar, this way;
  though before this
they defended me gladly. But now my death is upon me.
Let me at least not die without a struggle, inglorious,
but do some big thing first, that men to come shall know
  of it.'
  So he spoke, and pulling out the sharp sword that was
  slung
at the hollow of his side, huge and heavy, and gathering
himself together, he made his swoop, like a high-flown
  eagle
who launches himself out of the murk of the clouds on
  the flat land

to catch away a tender lamb or a shivering hare; so
Hektor made his swoop, swinging his sharp sword, and
  Achilleus
charged, the heart within him loaded with savage fury.
In front of his chest the beautiful elaborate great shield
covered him, and with the glittering helm with four horns
he nodded; the lovely golden fringes were shaken about it
which Hephaistos had driven close along the horn of the
  helmet.
And as a star moves among stars in the night's darkening,
Hesper, who is the fairest star who stands in the sky, such
was the shining from the pointed spear Achilleus was
  shaking
in his right hand with evil intention toward brilliant
  Hektor.
He was eyeing Hektor's splendid body, to see where it
  might best
give way, but all the rest of the skin was held in the armour,
brazen and splendid, he stripped when he cut down the
  strength of Patroklos;
yet showed where the collar-bones hold the neck from
  the shoulders,
the throat, where death of the soul comes most swiftly;
  in this place
brilliant Achilleus drove the spear as he came on in fury,
and clean through the soft part of the neck the
  spearpoint was driven.
Yet the ash spear heavy with bronze did not sever the
  windpipe,
so that Hektor could still make exchange of words spoken.
But he dropped in the dust, and brilliant Achilleus
  vaunted above him:
'Hektor, surely you thought as you killed Patroklos you
  would be
safe, and since I was far away you thought nothing of me,
o fool, for an avenger was left, far greater than he was,
behind him and away by the hollow ships. And it was I;
and I have broken your strength; on you the dogs and
  the vultures
shall feed and foully rip you; the Achaians will bury
  Patroklos.'
  In his weakness Hektor of the shining helm spoke to him:
'I entreat you, by your life, by your knees, by your parents,
do not let the dogs feed on me by the ships of the
  Achaians,
but take yourself the bronze and gold that are there in
  abundance,
those gifts that my father and the lady my mother will
  give you,
and give my body to be taken home again, so that the
  Trojans
and the wives of the Trojans may give me in death my
  rite of burning.'
  But looking darkly at him swift-footed Achilleus
  answered:
'No more entreating of me, you dog, by knees or parents.
I wish only that my spirit and fury would drive me
to hack your meat away and eat it raw for the things that
you have done to me. So there is no one who can hold
  the dogs off

from your head, not if they bring here and set before me
  ten times
and twenty times the ransom, and promise more in
  addition,
not if Priam son of Dardanos should offer to weigh out
your bulk in gold; not even so shall the lady your mother
who herself bore you lay you on the death-bed and
  mourn you:
no, but the dogs and the birds will have you all for their
  feasting.'
  Then, dying, Hektor of the shining helmet spoke to him:
'I know you well as I look upon you, I know that I could not
persuade you, since indeed in your breast is a heart of
  iron.
Be careful now; for I might be made into the gods' curse
upon you, on that day when Paris and Phoibos Apollo
destroy you in the Skaian gates, for all your valour.'
  He spoke, and as he spoke the end of death closed in
  upon him,
and the soul fluttering free of the limbs went down into
  Death's house
mourning her destiny, leaving youth and manhood
  behind her.
Now though he was a dead man brilliant Achilleus spoke
  to him:
'Die: and I will take my own death at whatever time
Zeus and the rest of the immortals choose to accomplish it.'
  He spoke, and pulled the brazen spear from the body,
  and laid it
on one side, and stripped away from the shoulders the
  bloody
armour. And the other sons of the Achaians came
  running about him,
and gazed upon the stature and on the imposing beauty
of Hektor; and none stood beside him who did not stab
  him;
and thus they would speak one to another, each looking
  at his neighbour:
'See now, Hektor is much softer to handle than he was
when he set the ships ablaze with the burning firebrand.'
  So as they stood beside him they would speak, and
  stab him.
But now, when he had despoiled the body, swift-footed
  brilliant
Achilleus stood among the Achaians and addressed them
  in winged words:
'Friends, who are leaders of the Argives and keep their
  counsel:
since the gods have granted me the killing of this man
who has done us much damage, such as not all the
  others together
have done, come, let us go in armour about the city
to see if we can find out what purpose is in the Trojans,
whether they will abandon their high city, now that this man
has fallen, or are minded to stay, though Hektor lives no
  longer.
Yet still, why does the heart within me debate on these
  things?
There is a dead man who lies by the ships, unwept,
  unburied:

Patroklos: and I will not forget him, never so long as
I remain among the living and my knees have their
    spring beneath me.
And though the dead forget the dead in the house of
    Hades,
even there I shall still remember my beloved companion.
But now, you young men of the Achaians, let us go back,
    singing
a victory song, to our hollow ships; and take this with us.
We have won ourselves enormous fame; we have killed
    the great Hektor
whom the Trojans glorified as if he were a god in their city.'
    He spoke, and now thought of shameful treatment for
    glorious Hektor.

In both of his feet at the back he made holes by the tendons
in the space between ankle and heel, and drew thongs of
    ox-hide through them,
and fastened them to the chariot so as to let the head drag,
and mounted the chariot, and lifted the glorious armour
    inside it,
then whipped the horses to a run, and they winged their
    way unreluctant.
A cloud of dust rose where Hektor was dragged, his
    dark hair was falling
about him, and all that head that was once so handsome
    was tumbled
in the dust; since by this time Zeus had given him over
to his enemies, to be defiled in the land of his fathers. . . .

Book XXIV

. . .

So Hermes spoke, and went away to the height of
    Olympos,
but Priam vaulted down to the ground from behind the
    horses
and left Idaios where he was, for he stayed behind,
    holding
in hand the horses and mules. The old man made
    straight for the dwelling
where Achilleus the beloved of Zeus was sitting. He
    found him
inside, and his companions were sitting apart, as two
    only,
Automedon the hero and Alkimos, scion of Ares,
were busy beside him. He had just now got through
    with his dinner,
with eating and drinking, and the table still stood by.
    Tall Priam
came in unseen by the other men and stood close beside
    him
and caught the knees of Achilleus in his arms, and
    kissed the hands
that were dangerous and manslaughtering and had killed
    so many
of his sons. As when dense disaster closes on one who
    has murdered
a man in his own land, and he comes to the country of
    others,
to a man of substance, and wonder seizes on those who
    behold him,
so Achilleus wondered as he looked on Priam, a godlike
man, and the rest of them wondered also, and looked at
    each other.
But now Priam spoke to him in the words of a suppliant:
'Achilleus like the gods, remember your father, one who

is of years like mine, and on the door-sill of sorrowful
    old age.
And they who dwell nearby encompass him and afflict
    him,
nor is there any to defend him against the wrath, the
    destruction.
Yet surely he, when he hears of you and that you are
    still living,
is gladdened within his heart and all his days he is
    hopeful
that he will see his beloved son come home from the
    Troad.
But for me, my destiny was evil. I have had the noblest
of sons in Troy, but I say not one of them is left to me.
Fifty were my sons, when the sons of the Achaians came
    here.
Nineteen were born to me from the womb of a single mother,
and other women bore the rest in my palace; and of
    these
violent Ares broke the strength in the knees of most
    of them,
but one was left me who guarded my city and people,
    that one
you killed a few days since as he fought in defence of his
    country,
Hektor; for whose sake I come now to the ships of the
    Achaians
to win him back from you, and I bring you gifts beyond
    number.
Honour then the gods, Achilleus, and take pity upon me
remembering your father, yet I am still more pitiful;
I have gone through what no other mortal on earth has
    gone through;
I put my lips to the hands of the man who has killed my
    children.'

So he spoke, and stirred in the other a passion of
    grieving
for his own father. He took the old man's hand and
    pushed him
gently away, and the two remembered, as Priam sat
    huddled
at the feet of Achilleus and wept close for
    manslaughtering Hektor
and Achilleus wept now for his own father, now again
for Patroklos. The sound of their mourning moved in the
    house. Then
when great Achilleus had taken full satisfaction in sorrow
and the passion for it had gone from his mind and body,
    thereafter
he rose from his chair, and took the old man by the
    hand, and set him
on his feet again, in pity for the grey head and the grey
    beard,
and spoke to him and addressed him in winged words:
    'Ah, unlucky,
surely you have had much evil to endure in your spirit.
How could you dare to come alone to the ships of the
    Achaians
and before my eyes, when I am one who have killed in
    such numbers
such brave sons of yours? The heart in you is iron.
    Come, then,
and sit down upon this chair, and you and I will even let
our sorrows lie still in the heart for all our grieving.
    There is not
any advantage to be won from grim lamentation.
Such is the way the gods spun life for unfortunate mortals,
that we live in unhappiness, but the gods themselves
    have no sorrows.
There are two urns that stand on the door-sill of Zeus.
    They are unlike
for the gifts they bestow: an urn of evils, an urn of blessings.
If Zeus who delights in thunder mingles these and
    bestows them
on man, he shifts, and moves now in evil, again in good
    fortune.
But when Zeus bestows from the urn of sorrows, he
    makes a failure
of man, and the evil hunger drives him over the shining
earth, and he wanders respected neither of gods nor
    mortals.
Such were the shining gifts given by the gods to Peleus
from his birth, who outshone all men beside for his riches
and pride of possession, and was lord over the
    Myrmidons. Thereto
the gods bestowed an immortal wife on him, who was
    mortal.
But even on him the god piled evil also. There was not
any generation of strong sons born to him in his great
    house
but a single all-untimely child he had, and I give him
no care as he grows old, since far from the land of my
    fathers
I sit here in Troy, and bring nothing but sorrow to you
    and your children.

And you, old sir, we are told you prospered once; for as
    much
as Lesbos, Makar's hold, confines to the north above it
and Phrygia from the north confines, and enormous
    Hellespont,
of these, old sir, you were lord once in your wealth and
    your children.
But now the Uranian gods brought us, an affliction upon you,
forever there is fighting about your city, and men killed.
But bear up, nor mourn endlessly in your heart, for
    there is not
anything to be gained from grief for your son; you will
    never
bring him back; sooner you must go through yet another
    sorrow.'
    In answer to him again spoke aged Priam the godlike:
'Do not, beloved of Zeus, make me sit on a chair while
    Hektor
lies yet forlorn among the shelters; rather with all speed
give him back, so my eyes may behold him, and accept
    the ransom
we bring you, which is great. You may have joy of it,
    and go back
to the land of your own fathers, since once you have
    permitted me
to go on living myself and continue to look on the sunlight.'
    Then looking darkly at him spoke swift-footed
    Achilleus:
'No longer stir me up, old sir. I myself am minded
to give Hektor back to you. A messenger came to me
    from Zeus,
my mother, she who bore me, the daughter of the sea's
    ancient.
I know you, Priam, in my heart, and it does not escape me
that some god led you to the running ships of the
    Achaians.
For no mortal would dare come to our encampment, not
    even
one strong in youth. He could not get by the pickets, he
    could not
lightly unbar the bolt that secures our gateway. Therefore
you must not further make my spirit move in my sorrows,
for fear, old sir, I might not let you alone in my shelter,
suppliant as you are; and be guilty before the god's
    orders.'
    He spoke, and the old man was frightened and did as
    he told him.
The son of Peleus bounded to the door of the house like
    a lion,
nor went alone, but the two henchmen followed attending,
the hero Automedon and Alkimos, those whom Achilleus
honoured beyond all companions after Patroklos dead.
    These two
now set free from under the yoke the mules and the horses,
and led inside the herald, the old king's crier, and gave
    him
a chair to sit in, then from the smooth-polished mule
    wagon
lifted out the innumerable spoils for the head of Hektor,
but left inside it two great cloaks and a finespun tunic

to shroud the corpse in when they carried him home.
  Then Achilleus
called out to his serving-maids to wash the body and
  anoint it
all over; but take it first aside, since otherwise Priam
might see his son and in the heart's sorrow not hold in
  his anger
at the sight, and the deep heart in Achilleus be shaken
  to anger;
that he might not kill Priam and be guilty before the
  god's orders.
Then when the serving-maids had washed the corpse
  and anointed it
with olive oil, they threw a fair great cloak and a tunic
about him, and Achilleus himself lifted him and laid him
on a litter, and his friends helped him lift it to the
  smooth-polished
mule wagon. He groaned then, and called by name on
  his beloved companion:
'Be not angry with me, Patroklos, if you discover,
though you be in the house of Hades, that I gave back
  great Hektor
to his loved father, for the ransom he gave me was not
  unworthy.
I will give you your share of the spoils, as much as is
  fitting.'
  So spoke great Achilleus and went back into the
  shelter
and sat down on the elaborate couch from which he had
  risen,
against the inward wall, and now spoke his word to
  Priam:
'Your son is given back to you, aged sir, as you asked it.
He lies on a bier. When dawn shows you yourself shall
  see him
as you take him away. Now you and I must remember
  our supper.
For even Niobe, she of the lovely tresses, remembered
to eat, whose twelve children were destroyed in her
  palace,
six daughters, and six sons in the pride of their youth,
  whom Apollo
killed with arrows from his silver bow, being angered
with Niobe, and shaft-showering Artemis killed the
  daughters;
because Niobe likened herself to Leto of the fair colouring
and said Leto had borne only two, she herself had borne
  many;
but the two, though they were only two, destroyed all
  those others.
Nine days long they lay in their blood, nor was there anyone
to bury them, for the son of Kronos made stones out of
the people; but on the tenth day the Uranian gods
  buried them.
But she remembered to eat when she was worn out with
  weeping.
And now somewhere among the rocks, in the lonely
  mountains,
in Sipylos, where they say is the resting place of the
  goddesses

who are nymphs, and dance beside the waters of
  Acheloios,
there, stone still, she broods on the sorrows that the
  gods gave her.
Come then, we also, aged magnificent sir, must
  remember
to eat, and afterwards you may take your beloved son
  back
to Ilion, and mourn for him; and he will be much
  lamented.'
  So spoke fleet Achilleus and sprang to his feet and
  slaughtered
a gleaming sheep, and his friends skinned it and
  butchered it fairly,
and cut up the meat expertly into small pieces, and
  spitted them,
and roasted all carefully and took off the pieces.
Automedon took the bread and set it out on the table
in fair baskets, while Achilleus served the meats. And
  thereon
they put their hands to the good things that lay ready
  before them.
But when they had put aside their desire for eating and
  drinking,
Priam, son of Dardanos, gazed upon Achilleus,
  wondering
at his size and beauty, for he seemed like an outright
  vision
of gods. Achilleus in turn gazed on Dardanian Priam
and wondered, as he saw his brave looks and listened to
  him talking.
But when they had taken their fill of gazing one on the
  other,
first of the two to speak was the aged man, Priam the
  godlike:
'Give me, beloved of Zeus, a place to sleep presently,
  so that
we may even go to bed and take the pleasure of sweet
  sleep.
For my eyes have not closed underneath my lids since
  that time
when my son lost his life beneath your hands, but always
I have been grieving and brooding over my numberless
  sorrows
and wallowed in the muck about my courtyard's enclosure.
Now I have tasted food again and have let the gleaming
wine go down my throat. Before, I had tasted nothing.'
  He spoke, and Achilleus ordered his serving-maids and
  companions
to make a bed in the porch's shelter and to lay upon it
fine underbedding of purple, and spread blankets above it
and fleecy robes to be an over-all covering. The
  maid-servants
went forth from the main house, and in their hands held
  torches,
and set to work, and presently had two beds made.
  Achilleus
of the swift feet now looked at Priam and said, sarcastic:
'Sleep outside, aged sir and good friend, for fear some
  Achaian

might come in here on a matter of counsel, since they
  keep coming
and sitting by me and making plans; as they are
  supposed to.
But if one of these come through the fleeting black night
  should notice you,
he would go straight and tell Agamemnon, shepherd of
  the people,
and there would be delay in the ransoming of the body.
But come, tell me this and count off for me exactly
how many days you intend for the burial of great Hektor.
Tell me, so I myself shall stay still and hold back the
  people.'
  In answer to him again spoke aged Priam the godlike:
'If you are willing that we accomplish a complete funeral
for great Hektor, this, Achilleus, is what you could do
  and give
me pleasure. For you know surely how we are penned in
  our city,

and wood is far to bring in from the hills, and the
  Trojans are frightened
badly. Nine days we would keep him in our palace and
  mourn him,
and bury him on the tenth day, and the people feast by him,
and on the eleventh day we would make the grave-barrow
  for him,
and on the twelfth day fight again; if so we must do.'
  Then in turn swift-footed brilliant Achilleus answered him:
'Then all this, aged Priam, shall be done as you ask it.
I will hold off our attack for as much time as you bid me.'
  So he spoke, and took the aged king by the right hand
at the wrist, so that his heart might have no fear. Then
  these two,
Priam and the herald who were both men of close counsel,
slept in the place outside the house, in the porch's shelter;
but Achilleus slept in the inward corner of the strong-built
  shelter,
and at his side lay Briseis of the fair colouring. . . .

HOMER

from *The Odyssey*

Book XII

• • •

Then, going back on board my ship, I told my
  companions
also to go aboard, and to cast off the stern cables,
and quickly they went aboard the ship and sat to the
  oarlocks,
and sitting well in order dashed the oars in the gray sea;
but fair-haired Circe, the dread goddess who talks with
  mortals,
sent us an excellent companion, a following wind, filling
the sails, to carry from astern the ship with the dark prow.
We ourselves, over all the ship making fast the running gear,
sat there, and let the wind and the steersman hold her
  steady.
Then, sorrowful as I was, I spoke and told my companions:
"Friends, since it is not right for one or two of us only
to know the divinations that Circe, bright among goddesses,
gave me, so I will tell you, and knowing all we may
  either
die, or turn aside from death and escape destruction.
First of all she tells us to keep away from the magical
Sirens and their singing and their flowery meadow, but only
I, she said, was to listen to them, but you must tie me
hard in hurtful bonds, to hold me fast in position
upright against the mast, with the ropes' ends fastened
  around it;

but if I supplicate you and implore you to set me
free, then you must tie me fast with even more lashings."
  'So as I was telling all the details to my companions,
meanwhile the well-made ship was coming rapidly closer
to the Sirens' isle, for the harmless wind was driving her
  onward;
but immediately then the breeze dropped, and a windless
calm fell there, and some divinity stilled the tossing
waters. My companions stood up, and took the sails
  down,
and stowed them away in the hollow hull, and took their
  places
for rowing, and with their planed oarblades whitened
  the water.
Then I, taking a great wheel of wax, with the sharp
  bronze
cut a little piece off, and rubbed it together in my heavy
hands, and soon the wax grew softer, under the powerful
stress of the sun, and the heat and light of Hyperion's
  lordling.
One after another, I stopped the ears of all my
  companions,
and they then bound me hand and foot in the fast ship,
  standing
upright against the mast with the ropes' ends lashed
  around it,

and sitting then to row they dashed their oars in the
gray sea.
But when we were as far from the land as a voice
shouting
carries, lightly plying, the swift ship as it drew nearer
was seen by the Sirens, and they directed their sweet
song toward us:
"Come this way, honored Odysseus, great glory of the
Achaians,
and stay your ship, so that you can listen here to our
singing;
for no one else has ever sailed past this place in his
black ship
until he has listened to the honey-sweet voice that issues
from our lips; then goes on, well pleased, knowing more
than ever
he did; for we know everything that the Argives and
Trojans
did and suffered in wide Troy through the gods' despite.
Over all the generous earth we know everything that
happens."
   'So they sang, in sweet utterance, and the heart within
me
desired to listen, and I signaled my companions to set me
free, nodding with my brows, but they leaned on and
rowed hard,
and Perimedes and Eurylochos, rising up, straightway
fastened me with even more lashings and squeezed me
tighter.
But when they had rowed on past the Sirens, and we
could no longer
hear their voices and lost the sound of their singing,
presently
my eager companions took away from their ears the
beeswax
with which I had stopped them. Then they set me free
from my lashings.
   'But after we had left the island behind, the next thing
we saw was smoke, and a heavy surf, and we heard it
thundering.
The men were terrified, and they let the oars fall out of
their hands, and these banged all about in the wash. The
ship stopped
still, with the men no longer rowing to keep way on her.
Then I going up and down the ship urged on my
companions,
standing beside each man and speaking to him in kind
words:
"Dear friends, surely we are not unlearned in evils.
This is no greater evil now than it was when the Cyclops
had us cooped in his hollow cave by force and violence,
but even there, by my courage and counsel and my
intelligence,
we escaped away. I think that all this will be remembered
some day too. Then do as I say, let us all be won over.
Sit well, all of you, to your oarlocks, and dash your oars
deep
into the breaking surf of the water, so in that way Zeus
might grant that we get clear of this danger and flee
away from it.

For you, steersman, I have this order; so store it deeply
in your mind, as you control the steering oar of this
hollow
ship; you must keep her clear from where the smoke
and the breakers
are, and make hard for the sea rock lest, without your
knowing,
she might drift that way, and you bring all of us into
disaster."
   'So I spoke, and they quickly obeyed my words. I had not
spoken yet of Skylla, a plague that could not be dealt
with,
for fear my companions might be terrified and give over
their rowing, and take cover inside the ship. For my part,
I let go from my mind the difficult instruction that Circe
had given me, for she told me not to be armed for
combat;
but I put on my glorious armor and, taking up two long
spears in my hands, I stood bestriding the vessel's
foredeck
at the prow, for I expected Skylla of the rocks to appear first
from that direction, she who brought pain to my
companions.
I could not make her out anywhere, and my eyes grew
weary
from looking everywhere on the misty face of the sea rock.
   'So we sailed up the narrow strait lamenting. On one
side
was Skylla, and on the other side was shining Charybdis,
who made her terrible ebb and flow of the sea's water.
When she vomited it up, like a caldron over a strong fire,
the whole sea would boil up in turbulence, and the foam
flying
spattered the pinnacles of the rocks in either direction;
but when in turn again she sucked down the sea's salt
water,
the turbulence showed all the inner sea, and the rock
around it
groaned terribly, and the ground showed at the sea's
bottom,
black with sand; and green fear seized upon my
companions.
We in fear of destruction kept our eyes on Charybdis,
but meanwhile Skylla out of the hollow vessel snatched six
of my companions, the best of them for strength and
hands' work,
and when I turned to look at the ship, with my other
companions,
I saw their feet and hands from below, already lifted
high above me, and they cried out to me and called me
by name, the last time they ever did it, in heart's sorrow.
And as a fisherman with a very long rod, on a jutting
rock, will cast his treacherous bait for the little fishes,
and sinks the horn of a field-ranging ox into the water,
then hauls them up and throws them on the dry land,
gasping
and struggling, so they gasped and struggled as they
were hoisted
up the cliff. Right in her doorway she ate them up. They
were screaming

and reaching out their hands to me in this horrid
    encounter.
That was the most pitiful scene that these eyes have
    looked on
in my sufferings as I explored the routes over the water.
  'Now when we had fled away from the rocks and
    dreaded Charybdis
and Skylla, next we made our way to the excellent island
of the god, where ranged the handsome wide-browed
    oxen, and many
fat flocks of sheep, belonging to the Sun God, Hyperion.
While I was on the black ship, still out on the open
    water,
I heard the lowing of the cattle as they were driven
home, and the bleating of sheep, and my mind was
    struck by the saying
of the blind prophet, Teiresias the Theban, and also
Aiaian Circe. Both had told me many times over
to avoid the island of Helios who brings joy to mortals.
Then sorrowful as I was I spoke and told my companions:
"Listen to what I say, my companions, though you are
    suffering
evils, while I tell you the prophecies of Teiresias
and Aiaian Circe. Both have told me many times over
to avoid the island of Helios who brings joy to mortals,
for there they spoke of the most dreadful disaster that
    waited
for us. So drive the black ship onward, and pass the island."
  'So I spoke, and the inward heart in them was broken.
At once Eurylochos answered me with a bitter saying:
"You are a hard man, Odysseus. Your force is greater,
your limbs never wear out. You must be made all of iron,
when you will not let your companions, worn with hard
    work and wanting
sleep, set foot on this land, where if we did, on the seagirt
island we could once more make ready a greedy dinner;
but you force us to blunder along just as we are through
    the running
night, driven from the island over the misty face of the
    water.
In the nights the hard stormwinds arise, and they bring
    damage
to ships. How could any of us escape sheer destruction,
if suddenly there rises the blast of a storm from the bitter
blowing of the South Wind or the West Wind, who
    beyond others
hammer a ship apart, in despite of the gods, our masters?
But now let us give way to black night's persuasion; let us
make ready our evening meal, remaining close by our
    fast ship,
and at dawn we will go aboard and put forth onto the
    wide sea."
  'So spoke Eurylochos, and my other companions
    assented.
I saw then what evil the divinity had in mind for us,
and so I spoke aloud to him and addressed him in
    winged words:
"Eurylochos, I am only one man. You force me to it.
But come then all of you, swear a strong oath to me, that if
we come upon some herd of cattle or on some great flock

of sheep, no one of you in evil and reckless action
will slaughter any ox or sheep. No, rather than this, eat
at your pleasure of the food immortal Circe provided."
  'So I spoke, and they all swore me the oath that I
    asked them.
But after they had sworn me the oath and made an end
    of it,
we beached the well-made ship inside of the hollow
    harbor,
close to sweet water, and my companions disembarked
    also
from the ship, and expertly made the evening meal ready.
But when they had put away their desire for eating and
    drinking,
they remembered and they cried for their beloved
    companions
whom Skylla had caught out of the hollow ship and
    eaten,
and on their crying a quiet sleep descended; but after
the third part of the night had come, and the star changes,
Zeus the cloud gatherer let loose on us a gale that
    blustered
in a supernatural storm, and huddled under the cloud
    scuds
land alike and the great water. Night sprang from heaven.
But when the young Dawn showed again with her rosy
    fingers,
we berthed our ship, dragging her into a hollow sea cave
where the nymphs had their beautiful dancing places
    and sessions.
Then I held an assembly and spoke my opinion before them:
"Friends, since there is food and drink stored in the fast
    ship,
let us then keep our hands off the cattle, for fear that
    something
may befall us. These are the cattle and fat sheep of a
    dreaded
god, Helios, who sees all things and listens to all things."
  'So I spoke, and the proud heart in them was persuaded.
But the South Wind blew for a whole month long, nor
    did any other
wind befall after that, but only the South and the East
    Wind.
As long as they still had food to eat and red wine, the
    men kept
their hands off the cattle, striving as they were for
    sustenance. Then, when
all the provisions that had been in the ship had given
out, they turned to hunting, forced to it, and went
    ranging
after fish and birds, anything that they could lay hands on,
and with curved hooks, for the hunger was exhausting
    their stomachs.
Then I went away along the island in order
to pray to the gods, if any of them might show me some
    course
to sail on, but when, crossing the isle, I had left my
    companions
behind, I washed my hands, where there was a place
    sheltered

from the wind, and prayed to all the gods whose hold is
    Olympos;
but what they did was to shed a sweet sleep on my
    eyelids,
and Eurylochos put an evil counsel before his companions:
"Listen to what I say, my companions, though you are
    suffering
evils. All deaths are detestable for wretched mortals,
but hunger is the sorriest way to die and encounter
fate. Come then, let us cut out the best of Helios' cattle,
and sacrifice them to the immortals who hold wide
    heaven,
and if we ever come back to Ithaka, land of our fathers,
presently we will build a rich temple to the Sun God Helios
Hyperion, and store it with dedications, many
and good. But if, in anger over his high-horned cattle,
he wishes to wreck our ship, and the rest of the gods
    stand by him,
I would far rather gulp the waves and lose my life in them
once for all, than be pinched to death on this desolate
    island."
    'So spoke Eurylochos, and the other companions
        assented.
At once, cutting out from near at hand the best of Helios'
cattle; for the handsome broad-faced horn-curved oxen
were pasturing there, not far from the dark-prowed ship;
    driving
these, they stationed themselves around them, and made
    their prayers
to the gods, pulling tender leaves from a deep-leaved oak
    tree;
for they had no white barley left on the strong-benched
    vessel.
When they had made their prayer and slaughtered the
    oxen and skinned them,
they cut away the meat from the thighs and wrapped
    them in fat,
making a double fold, and laid shreds of flesh upon them;
and since they had no wine to pour on the burning
    offerings,
they made a libation of water, and roasted all of the entrails;
but when they had burned the thigh pieces and tasted
    the vitals,
they cut all the remainder into pieces and spitted them.
    'At that time the quiet sleep was lost from my eyelids,
and I went back down to my fast ship and the sand of
    the seashore,
but on my way, as I was close to the oar-swept vessel,
the pleasant savor of cooking meat came drifting around me,
and I cried out my grief aloud to the gods immortal:
"Father Zeus, and you other everlasting and blessed
gods, with a pitiless sleep you lulled me, to my confusion,
and my companions staying here dared a deed that was
    monstrous."
    'Lampetia of the light robes ran swift with the message
to Hyperion the Sun God, that we had killed his cattle,
and angered at the heart he spoke forth among the
    immortals:
"Father Zeus, and you other everlasting and blessed
gods, punish the companions of Odysseus, son of Laertes;

for they outrageously killed my cattle, in whom I always
delighted, on my way up into the starry heaven,
or when I turned back again from heaven toward earth.
    Unless
these are made to give me just recompense for my cattle,
I will go down to Hades' and give my light to the dead
    men."
    'Then in turn Zeus who gathers the clouds answered
        him:
"Helios, shine on as you do, among the immortals
and mortal men, all over the grain-giving earth. For my
    part
I will strike these men's fast ship midway on the open
wine-blue sea with a shining bolt and dash it to pieces."
    'All this I heard afterward from fair-haired Kalypso,
and she told me she herself had heard it from the guide,
    Hermes.
    'But when I came back again to the ship and the
        seashore,
they all stood about and blamed each other, but we were
    not able
to find any remedy, for the oxen were already dead. The
    next thing
was that the gods began to show forth portents before us.
The skins crawled, and the meat that was stuck on the
    spits bellowed,
both roast and raw, and the noise was like the lowing of
    cattle.
    'Six days thereafter my own eager companions feasted
on the cattle of Helios the Sun God, cutting the best ones
out; but when Zeus the son of Kronos established the
    seventh
day, then at last the wind ceased from its stormy blowing,
and presently we went aboard and put forth on the
    wide sea,
and set the mast upright and hoisted the white sails on it.
    'But after we had left the island and there was no more
land in sight, but only the sky and the sea, then Kronian
Zeus drew on a blue-black cloud, and settled it over
the hollow ship, and the open sea was darkened beneath it;
and she ran on, but not for a very long time, as suddenly
a screaming West Wind came upon us, stormily blowing,
and the blast of the stormwind snapped both the
    forestays that were holding
the mast, and the mast went over backwards, and all the
    running gear
collapsed in the wash; and at the stern of the ship the
    mast pole
crashed down on the steersman's head and pounded to
    pieces
all the bones of his head, so that he like a diver
dropped from the high deck, and the proud life left his
    bones there.
Zeus with thunder and lightning together crashed on our
    vessel,
and, struck by the thunderbolt of Zeus, she spun in a circle,
and all was full of brimstone. My men were thrown in
    the water,
and bobbing like sea crows they were washed away on
    the running

waves all around the black ship, and the god took away
   their homecoming.
  'But I went on my way through the vessel, to where
   the high seas
had worked the keel free out of the hull, and the bare
   keel floated
on the swell, which had broken the mast off at the keel;
   yet
still there was a backstay made out of oxhide fastened
to it. With this I lashed together both keel and mast, then
rode the two of them, while the deadly stormwinds
   carried me.
  'After this the West Wind ceased from its stormy blowing,
and the South Wind came swiftly on, bringing to my
   spirit
grief that I must measure the whole way back to Charybdis.
All that night I was carried along, and with the sun
   rising
I came to the sea rock of Skylla, and dreaded Charybdis.
At this time Charybdis sucked down the sea's salt water,
but I reached high in the air above me, to where the tall
   fig tree
grew, and caught hold of it and clung like a bat; there
   was no
place where I could firmly brace my feet, or climb up it,
for the roots of it were far from me, and the branches
   hung out

far, big and long branches that overshadowed Charybdis.
Inexorably I hung on, waiting for her to vomit
the keel and mast back up again. I longed for them, and
   they came
late; at the time when a man leaves the law court, for
   dinner,
after judging the many disputes brought him by litigious
   young men;
that was the time it took the timbers to appear from
   Charybdis.
Then I let go my hold with hands and feet, and dropped off,
and came crashing down between and missing the two
   long timbers,
but I mounted these, and with both hands I paddled my
   way out.
But the Father of Gods and men did not let Skylla see me
again, or I could not have escaped from sheer destruction.
  'From there I was carried along nine days, and on the
   tenth night
the gods brought me to the island Ogygia, home of Kalypso
with the lovely hair, a dreaded goddess who talks with
   mortals.
She befriended me and took care of me. Why tell the
   rest of
this story again, since yesterday in your house I told it
to you and your majestic wife? It is hateful to me
to tell a story over again, when it has been well told.'

SAPPHO

To Anaktoria

Some say cavalry and others claim
infantry or a fleet of long oars
is the supreme sight on the black earth.
I say it is

the one you love. And easily proved.
Didn't Helen—who far surpassed all
mortals in beauty—desert the best
of men, her king,

and sail off to Troy and forget
her daughter and dear kinsmen? Merely
the Kyprian's gaze made her bend and led
her from her path;

these things remind me now
of Anaktoria who is far,
and I
for one

would rather see her warm supple step
and the sparkle of her face—than watch all the
dazzling chariots and armored hoplites of Lydia.

Seizure

To me he seems like a god
as he sits facing you and
hears you near as you speak
softly and laugh

in a sweet echo that jolts
the heart in my ribs. For now
as I look at you my voice
is empty and

can say nothing as my tongue
cracks and slender fire is quick
under my skin. My eyes are dead
to light, my ears

pound, and sweat pours over me.
I convulse, greener than grass,
and feel my mind slip as I
go close to death,

yet, being poor, must suffer
everything.

Age and Light

Here are fine gifts, children.
O friend, singer on the clear tortoise lyre,

all my flesh is wrinkled with age,
my black hair has faded to white,

my legs can no longer carry me,
once nimble like a fawn's,

but what can I do?
It cannot be undone,

no more than can pink-armed Dawn
not end in darkness on earth,

or keep her love for Tithonos,
who must waste away;

yet I love refinement, and beauty and light
are for me the same as desire for the sun.

Chapter

3

Classical Greek Civilization:
The Hellenic Age

ARISTOPHANES

from *Lysistrata*

• • •

MAGISTRATE: Well then, first of all I wish to ask her this: for what purpose have you barred us from the Acropolis?

LYSISTRATA: To keep the treasure safe, so you won't make war on account of it.

MAGISTRATE: What? Do we make war on account of the treasure?

LYSISTRATA: Yes, and you cause all our other troubles for it, too. Peisander and those greedy office-seekers keep things stirred up so they can find occasions to steal. Now let them do what they like: they'll never again make off with any of this money.

MAGISTRATE: What will you do?

LYSISTRATA: What a question! We'll administer it ourselves.

MAGISTRATE: *You* will administer the treasure?

LYSISTRATA: What's so strange in that? Don't we administer the household money for you?

MAGISTRATE: That's different.

LYSISTRATA: How is it different?

MAGISTRATE: We've got to make war with this money.

LYSISTRATA: But that's the very first thing: you mustn't make war.

MAGISTRATE: How else can we be saved?

LYSISTRATA: We'll save you.

MAGISTRATE: *You?*

LYSISTRATA: Yes, we!

MAGISTRATE: God forbid!

LYSISTRATA: We'll save you, whether you want it or not.

MAGISTRATE: Oh! This is terrible!

LYSISTRATA: You don't like it, but we're going to do it none the less.

MAGISTRATE: Good God! it's illegal!

LYSISTRATA: We *will* save you, my little man!

MAGISTRATE: Suppose I don't want you to?

LYSISTRATA: That's all the more reason.

MAGISTRATE: What business have you with war and peace?

LYSISTRATA: I'll explain.

MAGISTRATE: (*shaking his fist*): Speak up, or you'll smart for it.

LYSISTRATA: Just listen, and try to keep your hands still.

MAGISTRATE: I can't. I'm so mad I can't stop them.

FIRST WOMAN: Then you'll be the one to smart for it.

MAGISTRATE: Croak to yourself, old hag! (*to* LYSISTRATA) Now then, speak up.

LYSISTRATA: Very well. Formerly we endured the war for a good long time with our usual restraint, no matter what you men did. You wouldn't let us say "boo," although nothing you did suited us. But we watched you well, and though we stayed at home we'd often hear of some terribly stupid measure you'd proposed. Then, though grieving at heart, we'd smile sweetly and say, "What was passed in the Assembly today about writing on the treaty-stone?" "What's that to you?" my husband would say. "Hold your tongue!" and I held my tongue.

FIRST WOMAN: But I wouldn't have—not I!

MAGISTRATE: You'd have been soundly smacked, if you hadn't kept still.

LYSISTRATA: So I kept still at home. Then we'd hear of some plan still worse than the first; we'd say, "Husband, how could you pass such a stupid proposal!" He'd scowl at me and say, "If you don't mind your spinning, your head will be sore for weeks. *War shall be the concern of men.*"

MAGISTRATE: And he was right, upon my word!

LYSISTRATA: Why right, you confounded fool, when your proposals were so stupid and we weren't allowed to make any suggestions?

"There's not a *man* left in the country," says one. "No, not one," says another. Therefore all we women have decided in council to make a common effort to save Greece. How long should we have waited? Now, if you're willing to listen to our excellent proposals and keep silence for us in your turn, we still may save you.

MAGISTRATE: We men keep silence for you? That's terrible; I won't endure it!

LYSISTRATA: Silence!

MAGISTRATE: Silence for *you*, you wench, when you're wearing a snood? I'd rather die!

LYSISTRATA: Well, if that's all that bothers you—here! Take my snood and tie it round your head. (*During the following words the* WOMEN *dress up the* MAGISTRATE *in women's garments.*) And *now* keep quiet! Here, take this spinning-basket, too, and card your wool with robes tucked up, munching on beans. *War shall be the concern of Women!*

LEADER OF WOMEN: Arise and leave your pitchers, girls; no time is this to falter.
We too must aid our loyal friends; our turn has come for action.

CHORUS OF WOMEN (*singing*):
I'll never tire of aiding them with song and dance; never may
Faintness keep my legs from moving to and fro endlessly.
  For I yearn to do all for my friends;
    They have charm, they have wit, they have grace,
      With courage, brains, and best of virtues—Patriotic
sapience.

LEADER OF WOMEN: Come, child of manliest ancient dames, offspring of stinging nettles,
Advance with rage unsoftened; for fair breezes speed you onward.

LYSISTRATA: If only sweet Eros and the Cyprian Queen of Love shed charm over our breasts and limbs and inspire our men with amorous longing and priapic spasms, I think we may soon be called Peacemakers among the Greeks.

• • •

SOPHOCLES

Oedipus the King

Characters

OEDIPUS *king of Thebes*

A PRIEST *of Zeus*

CREON *brother of Jocasta*

A CHORUS *of Theban citizens and their* LEADER

TIRESIAS *a blind prophet*

JOCASTA *the queen, wife of Oedipus*

A MESSENGER *from Corinth*

A SHEPHERD

A MESSENGER *from inside the palace*

ANTIGONE, ISMENE *daughters of Oedipus and Jocasta*

Guards and attendants

Priests of Thebes

TIME AND SCENE: *The royal house of Thebes. Double doors dominate the façade; a stone altar stands at the center of the stage.*

Many years have passed since OEDIPUS *solved the riddle of the Sphinx and ascended the throne of Thebes, and now a plague has struck the city. A procession of priests enters; suppliants, broken and despondent, they carry branches wound in wool and lay them on the altar.*

The doors open. Guards assemble. OEDIPUS *comes forward, majestic but for a telltale limp, and slowly views the condition of his people.*

OEDIPUS:

Oh my children, the new blood of ancient Thebes,
why are you here? Huddling at my altar,
praying before me, your branches wound in wool.

Our city reeks with the smoke of burning incense,
rings with cries for the Healer and wailing for the dead.
I thought it wrong, my children, to hear the truth
from others, messengers. Here I am myself—
you all know me, the world knows my fame:
I am Oedipus.

Helping a Priest to his feet.

Speak up, old man. Your years,
your dignity—you should speak for the others.
Why here and kneeling, what preys upon you so?
Some sudden fear? some strong desire?
You can trust me. I am ready to help,
I'll do anything. I would be blind to misery
not to pity my people kneeling at my feet.

PRIEST:

Oh Oedipus, king of the land, our greatest power!
You see us before you now, men of all ages
clinging to your altars. Here are boys,
still too weak to fly from the nest,
and here the old, bowed down with the years,
the holy ones—a priest of Zeus myself—and here
the picked, unmarried men, the young hope of Thebes.
And all the rest, your great family gathers now,
branches wreathed, massing in the squares,
kneeling before the two temples of queen Athena
or the river-shrine where the embers glow and die
and Apollo sees the future in the ashes.

Our city—
look around you, see with your own eyes—
our ship pitches wildly, cannot lift her head
from the depths, the red waves of death . . .
Thebes is dying. A blight on the fresh crops
and the rich pastures, cattle sicken and die,
and the women die in labor, children stillborn,
and the plague, the fiery god of fever hurls down
on the city, his lightning slashing through us—
raging plague in all its vengeance, devastating
the house of Cadmus! And black Death luxuriates
in the raw, wailing miseries of Thebes.

Now we pray to you. You cannot equal the gods,
your children know that, bending at your altar.
But we do rate you first of men,
both in the common crises of our lives
and face-to-face encounters with the gods.
You freed us from the Sphinx, you came to Thebes
and cut us loose from the bloody tribute we had paid
that harsh, brutal singer. We taught you nothing,
no skill, no extra knowledge, still you triumphed.
A god was with you, so they say, and we believe it—
you lifted up our lives.
So now again,
Oedipus, king, we bend to you, your power—
we implore you, all of us on our knees:
find us strength, rescue! Perhaps you've heard
the voice of a god or something from other men,
Oedipus . . . what do you know?

The man of experience—you see it every day—
his plans will work in a crisis, his first of all.

Act now—we beg you, best of men, raise up our city!
Act, defend yourself, your former glory!
Your country calls you savior now
for your zeal, your action years ago.
Never let us remember of your reign:
you helped us stand, only to fall once more.
Oh raise up our city, set us on our feet.
The omens were good that day you brought us joy—
be the same man today!
Rule our land, you know you have the power,
but rule a land of the living, not a wasteland.
Ship and towered city are nothing, stripped of men
alive within it, living all as one.

OEDIPUS:

My children,
I pity you. I see—how could I fail to see
what longings bring you here? Well I know
you are sick to death, all of you,
but sick as you are, not one is sick as I.
Your pain strikes each of you alone, each
in the confines of himself, no other. But my spirit
grieves for the city, for myself and all of you.
I wasn't asleep, dreaming. You haven't wakened me—
I have wept through the nights, you must know that,
groping, laboring over many paths of thought.
After a painful search I found one cure:
I acted at once. I sent Creon,
my wife's own brother, to Delphi—
Apollo the Prophet's oracle—to learn
what I might do or say to save our city.

Today's the day. When I count the days gone by
it torments me . . . what is he doing?
Strange, he's late, he's gone too long.
But once he returns, then, then I'll be a traitor
if I do not do all the god makes clear.

PRIEST:

Timely words. The men over there
are signaling—Creon's just arriving.

OEDIPUS:

Sighting CREON, *then turning to the altar.*

Lord Apollo,
let him come with a lucky word of rescue,
shining like his eyes!

PRIEST:

Welcome news, I think—he's crowned, look,
and the laurel wreath is bright with berries.

OEDIPUS:

We'll soon see. He's close enough to hear—

Enter CREON *from the side; his face is shaded with
a wreath.*

Creon, prince, my kinsman, what do you bring us?
What message from the god?

CREON:

Good news.
I tell you even the hardest things to bear,
if they should turn out well, all would be well.

OEDIPUS:

Of course, but what were the god's *words*? There's no hope
and nothing to fear in what you've said so far.

CREON:

If you want my report in the presence of these people . . .

Pointing to the priests while drawing OEDIPUS *toward
the palace.*

I'm ready now, or we might go inside.

OEDIPUS:

Speak out,
speak to us all. I grieve for these, my people,
far more than I fear for my own life.

CREON:

Very well,
I will tell you what I heard from the god.
Apollo commands us—he was quite clear—
"Drive the corruption from the land,
don't harbor it any longer, past all cure,
don't nurse it in your soil—root it out!"

OEDIPUS:

How can we cleanse ourselves—what rites?
What's the source of the trouble?

CREON:

Banish the man, or pay back blood with blood.
Murder sets the plague-storm on the city.

OEDIPUS:

Whose murder?
Whose fate does Apollo bring to light?

CREON:

Our leader,
my lord, was once a man named Laius,
before you came and put us straight on course.

OEDIPUS:

I know—
or so I've heard. I never saw the man myself.

CREON:

Well, he was killed, and Apollo commands us now—
he could not be more clear,
"Pay the killers back—whoever is responsible."

OEDIPUS:

Where on earth are they? Where to find it now,
the trail of the ancient guilt so hard to trace?

CREON:

"Here in Thebes," he said.
Whatever is sought for can be caught, you know,
whatever is neglected slips away.

OEDIPUS:

But where,
in the palace, the fields or foreign soil,
where did Laius meet his bloody death?

CREON:

He went to consult an oracle, Apollo said,
and he set out and never came home again.

OEDIPUS:

No messenger, no fellow-traveler saw what happened?
Someone to cross-examine?

CREON:

No,
they were all killed but one. He escaped,
terrified, he could tell us nothing clearly,
nothing of what he saw—just one thing.

OEDIPUS:

What's that?
One thing could hold the key to it all,
a small beginning give us grounds for hope.

CREON:

He said thieves attacked them—a whole band,
not single-handed, cut King Laius down.

OEDIPUS:

A thief,
so daring, so wild, he'd kill a king? Impossible,
unless conspirators paid him off in Thebes.

CREON:

We suspected as much. But with Laius dead
no leader appeared to help us in our troubles.

OEDIPUS:

Trouble? Your *king* was murdered—royal blood!
What stopped you from tracking down the killer
then and there?

CREON:

The singing, riddling Sphinx.
She . . . persuaded us to let the mystery go
and concentrate on what lay at our feet.

OEDIPUS:

                         No,
I'll start again—I'll bring it all to light myself!
Apollo is right, and so are you, Creon,
to turn our attention back to the murdered man.
Now you have *me* to fight for you, you'll see:
I am the land's avenger by all rights,
and Apollo's champion too.
But not to assist some distant kinsman, no,
for my own sake I'll rid us of this corruption.
Whoever killed the king may decide to kill me too,
with the same violent hand—by avenging Laius
I defend myself.

To the priests.

              Quickly, my children.
Up from the steps, take up your branches now.

To the guards.

One of you summon the city here before us,
tell them I'll do everything. God help us,
we will see our triumph—or our fall.

OEDIPUS *and* CREON *enter the palace, followed by the guards.*

PRIEST:

Rise, my sons. The kindness we came for
Oedipus volunteers himself.
Apollo has sent his word, his oracle—
Come down, Apollo, save us, stop the plague.

The priests rise, remove their branches and exit to the side.

Enter a CHORUS, *the citizens of Thebes, who have not heard the news that* CREON *brings. They march around the altar, chanting.*

CHORUS:

                       Zeus!
Great welcome voice of Zeus, what do you bring?
What word from the gold vaults of Delphi
comes to brilliant Thebes? Racked with terror—
                terror shakes my heart
and I cry your wild cries, Apollo, Healer of Delos
I worship you in dread . . . what now, what is your price?
some new sacrifice? some ancient rite from the past
come round again each spring?—
           what will you bring to birth?
Tell me, child of golden Hope
      warm voice that never dies!

You are the first I call, daughter of Zeus
deathless Athena—I call your sister Artemis,
heart of the market place enthroned in glory,
              guardian of our earth—
I call Apollo, Archer astride the thunderheads of heaven—
O triple shield against death, shine before me now!
If ever, once in the past, you stopped some ruin
launched against our walls
         you hurled the flame of pain
far, far from Thebes—you gods
      come now, come down once more!

                    No, no
the miseries numberless, grief on grief, no end—
too much to bear, we are all dying
O my people . . .
  Thebes like a great army dying
and there is no sword of thought to save us, no
and the fruits of our famous earth, they will not ripen
no and the women cannot scream their pangs to birth—
screams for the Healer, children dead in the womb
         and life on life goes down
                you can watch them go
  like seabirds winging west, outracing the day's fire
down the horizon, irresistibly
        streaking on to the shores of Evening
                      Death
so many deaths, numberless deaths on deaths, no end—
Thebes is dying, look, her children
stripped of pity . . .
  generations strewn on the ground
unburied, unwept, the dead spreading death
and the young wives and gray-haired mothers with them
cling to the altars, trailing in from all over the city—
Thebes, city of death, one long cortege
        and the suffering rises
             wails for mercy rise
  and the wild hymn for the Healer blazes out
clashing with our sobs our cries of mourning—
  O golden daughter of god, send rescue
radiant as the kindness in your eyes!

Drive him back!—the fever, the god of death
              that raging god of war
not armored in bronze, not shielded now, he burns me,
battle cries in the onslaught burning on—
O rout him from our borders!
Sail him, blast him out to the Sea-queen's chamber
             the black Atlantic gulfs
or the northern harbor, death to all
where the Thracian surf comes crashing.
Now what the night spares he comes by day and kills—
the god of death.

        O lord of the stormcloud,
you who twirl the lightning, Zeus, Father,
thunder Death to nothing!

Apollo, lord of the light, I beg you—
      whip your longbow's golden cord
showering arrows on our enemies—shafts of power
champions strong before us rushing on!

Artemis, Huntress,
torches flaring over the eastern ridges—
                    ride Death down in pain!

God of the headdress gleaming gold, I cry to you—
your name and ours are one, Dionysus—
        come with your face aflame with wine
                        your raving women's cries
        your army on the march! Come with the lightning
come with torches blazing, eyes ablaze with glory!
Burn that god of death that all gods hate!

OEDIPUS *enters from the palace to address the* CHORUS,
as if addressing the entire city of Thebes.

OEDIPUS:

You pray to the gods? Let me grant your prayers.
Come, listen to me—do what the plague demands:
you'll find relief and lift your head from the depths.

I will speak out now as a stranger to the story,
a stranger to the crime. If I'd been present then,
there would have been no mystery, no long hunt
without a clue in hand. So now, counted
a native Theban years after the murder,
to all of Thebes I make this proclamation:
if any one of you knows who murdered Laius,
the son of Labdacus, I order him to reveal
the whole truth to me. Nothing to fear,
even if he must denounce himself,
let him speak up
and so escape the brunt of the charge—
he will suffer no unbearable punishment,
nothing worse than exile, totally unharmed.

OEDIPUS *pauses, waiting for a reply.*

                                    Next,
if anyone knows the murderer is a stranger,
a man from alien soil, come, speak up.
I will give him a handsome reward, and lay up
gratitude in my heart for him besides.

Silence again, no reply.

But if you keep silent, if anyone panicking,
trying to shield himself or friend or kin,
rejects my offer, then hear what I will do.
I order you, every citizen of the state
where I hold throne and power: banish this man—
whoever he may be—never shelter him, never
speak a word to him, never make him partner
to your prayers, your victims burned to the gods.
Never let the holy water touch his hands.
Drive him out, each of you, from every home.
He is the plague, the heart of our corruption,
as Apollo's oracle has just revealed to me.
So I honor my obligations:
I fight for the god and for the murdered man.

Now my curse on the murderer. Whoever he is,
a lone man unknown in his crime

or one among many, let that man drag out
his life in agony, step by painful step—
I curse myself as well . . . if by any chance
he proves to be an intimate of our house,
here at my hearth, with my full knowledge,
may the curse I just called down on him strike me!

These are your orders: perform them to the last.
I command you, for my sake, for Apollo's, for this country
blasted root and branch by the angry heavens.
Even if god had never urged you on to act,
how could you leave the crime uncleansed so long?
A man so noble—your king, brought down in blood—
you should have searched. But I am the king now,
I hold the throne that he held then, possess his bed
and a wife who shares our seed . . . why, our seed
might be the same, children born of the same mother
might have created blood-bonds between us
if his hope of offspring had not met disaster—
but fate swooped at his head and cut him short.
So I will fight for him as if he were my father,
stop at nothing, search the world
to lay my hands on the man who shed his blood,
the son of Labdacus descended of Polydorus,
Cadmus of old and Agenor, founder of the line:
their power and mine are one.

                        Oh dear gods,
my curse on those who disobey these orders!
Let no crops grow out of the earth for them—
shrivel their women, kill their sons,
burn them to nothing in this plague
that hits us now, or something even worse.
But you, loyal men of Thebes who approve my actions,
may our champion, Justice, may all the gods
be with us, fight beside us to the end!

LEADER:

In the grip of your curse, my king, I swear
I'm not the murderer, I cannot point him out.
As for the search, Apollo pressed it on us—
he should name the killer.

OEDIPUS:

                        Quite right,
but to force the gods to act against their will—
no man has the power.

LEADER:

                        Then if I might mention
the next best thing . . .

OEDIPUS:

                        The third best too—
don't hold back, say it.

LEADER:

                              I still believe . . .
Lord Tiresias sees with the eyes of Lord Apollo.
Anyone searching for the truth, my king,
might learn it from the prophet, clear as day.

OEDIPUS:

I've not been slow with that. On Creon's cue
I sent the escorts, twice, within the hour.
I'm surprised he isn't here.

LEADER:

                         We need him—
without him we have nothing but old, useless rumors.

OEDIPUS:

Which rumors? I'll search out every word.

LEADER:

Laius was killed, they say, by certain travelers.

OEDIPUS:

I know—but no one can find the murderer.

LEADER:

If the man has a trace of fear in him
he won't stay silent long,
not with your curses ringing in his ears.

OEDIPUS:

He didn't flinch at murder,
he'll never flinch at words.

Enter TIRESIAS, *the blind prophet, led by a boy with
escorts in attendance. He remains at a distance.*

LEADER:

Here is the one who will convict him, look,
they bring him on at last, the seer, the man of god.
The truth lives inside him, him alone.

OEDIPUS:

                              O Tiresias,
master of all the mysteries of our life,
all you teach and all you dare not tell,
signs in the heavens, signs that walk the earth!
Blind as you are, you can feel all the more
what sickness haunts our city. You, my lord,
are the one shield, the one savior we can find.

We asked Apollo—perhaps the messengers
haven't told you—he sent his answer back:
"Relief from the plague can only come one way.
Uncover the murderers of Laius,
put them to death or drive them into exile."
So I beg you, grudge us nothing now, no voice,
no message plucked from the birds, the embers
or the other mantic ways within your grasp.
Rescue yourself, your city, rescue me—

rescue everything infected by the dead.
We are in your hands. For a man to help others
with all his gifts and native strength:
that is the noblest work.

TIRESIAS:

                    How terrible—to see the truth
when the truth is only pain to him who sees!
I knew it well, but I put it from my mind,
else I never would have come.

OEDIPUS:

What's this? Why so grim, so dire?

TIRESIAS:

Just send me home. You bear your burdens,
I'll bear mine. It's better that way,
please believe me.

OEDIPUS:

                    Strange response . . . unlawful,
unfriendly too to the state that bred and reared you—
you withhold the word of god.

TIRESIAS:

                         I fail to see
that your own words are so well-timed.
I'd rather not have the same thing said of me . . .

OEDIPUS:

For the love of god, don't turn away,
not if you know something. We beg you,
all of us on our knees.

TIRESIAS:

                    None of you knows—
and I will never reveal my dreadful secrets,
not to say your own.

OEDIPUS:

What? You know and you won't tell?
You're bent on betraying us, destroying Thebes?

TIRESIAS:

I'd rather not cause pain for you or me.
So why this . . . useless interrogation?
You'll get nothing from me.

OEDIPUS:

                         Nothing! You,
you scum of the earth, you'd enrage a heart of stone!
You won't talk? Nothing moves you?
Out with it, once and for all!

TIRESIAS:

You criticize my temper . . . unaware
of the one *you* live with, you revile me.

OEDIPUS:

Who could restrain his anger hearing you?
What outrage—you spurn the city!

TIRESIAS:

What will come will come.
Even if I shroud it all in silence.

OEDIPUS:

What will come? You're bound to *tell* me that.

TIRESIAS:

I will say no more. Do as you like, build your anger
to whatever pitch you please, rage your worst—

OEDIPUS:

Oh I'll let loose, I have such fury in me—
now I see it all. You helped hatch the plot,
you did the work, yes, short of killing him
with your own hands—and given eyes I'd say
you did the killing single-handed!

TIRESIAS:

                              Is that so!
I charge you, then, submit to that decree
you just laid down: from this day onward
speak to no one, not these citizens, not myself.
You are the curse, the corruption of the land!

OEDIPUS:

You, shameless—
aren't you appalled to start up such a story?
You think you can get away with this?

TIRESIAS:

                              I have already.
The truth with all its power lives inside me.

OEDIPUS:

Who primed you for this? Not your prophet's trade.

TIRESIAS:

You did, you forced me, twisted it out of me.

OEDIPUS:

What? Say it again—I'll understand it better.

TIRESIAS:

Didn't you understand, just now?
Or are you tempting me to talk?

OEDIPUS:

No, I can't say I grasped your meaning.
Out with it, again!

TIRESIAS:

I say you are the murderer you hunt.

OEDIPUS:

That obscenity, twice—by god, you'll pay.

TIRESIAS:

Shall I say more, so you can really rage?

OEDIPUS:

Much as you want. Your words are nothing—
futile.

TIRESIAS:

          You cannot imagine . . . I tell you,
you and your loved ones live together in infamy,
you cannot see how far you've gone in guilt.

OEDIPUS:

You think you can keep this up and never suffer?

TIRESIAS:

Indeed, if the truth has any power.

OEDIPUS:

                              It does
but not for you, old man. You've lost your power,
stone-blind, stone-deaf—senses, eyes blind as stone!

TIRESIAS:

I pity you, flinging at me the very insults
each man here will fling at you so soon.

OEDIPUS:

                              Blind,
lost in the night, endless night that nursed you!
You can't hurt me or anyone else who sees the light—
you can never touch me.

TIRESIAS:

                    True, it is not your fate
to fall at my hands. Apollo is quite enough,
and he will take some pains to work this out.

OEDIPUS:

Creon! Is this conspiracy his or yours?

TIRESIAS:

Creon is not your downfall, no, you are your own.

OEDIPUS:

                                   O power—
wealth and empire, skill outstripping skill
in the heady rivalries of life,
what envy lurks inside you! Just for this,
the crown the city gave me—I never sought it,
they laid it in my hands—for this alone, Creon,
the soul of trust, my loyal friend from the start
steals against me . . . so hungry to overthrow me

he sets this wizard on me, this scheming quack,
this fortune-teller peddling lies, eyes peeled
for his own profit—seer blind in his craft!

Come here, you pious fraud. Tell me,
when did you ever prove yourself a prophet?
When the Sphinx, that chanting Fury kept her
deathwatch here,
why silent then, not a word to set our people free?
There was a riddle, not for some passer-by to solve—
it cried out for a prophet. Where were you?
Did you rise to the crisis? Not a word,
you and your birds, your gods—nothing.
No, but I came by, Oedipus the ignorant,
I stopped the Sphinx! With no help from the birds,
the flight of my own intelligence hit the mark.

And this is the man you'd try to overthrow?
You think you'll stand by Creon when he's king?
You and the great mastermind—
you'll pay in tears, I promise you, for this,
this witch-hunt. If you didn't look so senile
the lash would teach you what your scheming means!

LEADER:

I would suggest his words were spoken in anger,
Oedipus . . . yours too, and it isn't what we need.
The best solution to the oracle, the riddle
posed by god—we should look for that.

TIRESIAS:

You are the king no doubt, but in one respect,
at least, I am your equal: the right to reply.
I claim that privilege too.
I am not your slave. I serve Apollo.
I don't need Creon to speak for me in public.
                                        So,
you mock my blindness? Let me tell you this.
You with your precious eyes,
you're blind to the corruption of your life,
to the house you live in, those you live with—
who *are* your parents? Do you know? All unknowing
you are the scourge of your own flesh and blood,
the dead below the earth and the living here above,
and the double lash of your mother and your father's curse
will whip you from this land one day, their footfall
treading you down in terror, darkness shrouding
your eyes that now can see the light!
                                Soon, soon
you'll scream aloud—what haven won't reverberate?
What rock of Cithaeron won't scream back in echo?
That day you learn the truth about your marriage,
the wedding-march that sang you into your halls,
the lusty voyage home to the fatal harbor!
And a crowd of other horrors you'd never dream
will level you with yourself and all your children.

There. Now smear us with insults—Creon, myself
and every word I've said. No man will ever
be rooted from the earth as brutally as you.

OEDIPUS:

Enough! Such filth from him? Insufferable—
what, still alive? Get out—
faster, back where you came from—vanish!

TIRESIAS:

I would never have come if you hadn't called me here.

OEDIPUS:

If I thought you would blurt out such absurdities,
you'd have died waiting before I'd had you summoned.

TIRESIAS:

Absurd, am I! To you, not to your parents:
the ones who bore you found me sane enough.

OEDIPUS:

Parents—who? Wait . . . who is my father?

TIRESIAS:

This day will bring your birth and your destruction.

OEDIPUS:

Riddles—all you can say are riddles, murk and darkness.

TIRESIAS:

Ah, but aren't you the best man alive at solving riddles?

OEDIPUS:

Mock me for that, go on, and you'll reveal my greatness.

TIRESIAS:

Your great fortune, true, it was your ruin.

OEDIPUS:

Not if I saved the city—what do I care?

TIRESIAS:

Well then, I'll be going.

To his attendant.

                        Take me home, boy.

OEDIPUS:

Yes, take him away. You're a nuisance here.
Out of the way, the irritation's gone.

Turning his back on TIRESIAS, *moving toward the palace.*

TIRESIAS:

                                I will go,
once I have said what I came here to say.
I will never shrink from the anger in your eyes—
you can't destroy me. Listen to me closely:
the man you've sought so long, proclaiming,
cursing up and down, the murderer of Laius—
he is here. A stranger,

you may think, who lives among you,
he soon will be revealed a native Theban
but he will take no joy in the revelation.
Blind who now has eyes, beggar who now is rich,
he will grope his way toward a foreign soil,
a stick tapping before him step by step.

OEDIPUS *enters the palace.*

Revealed at last, brother and father both
to the children he embraces, to his mother
son and husband both—he sowed the loins
his father sowed, he spilled his father's blood!

Go in and reflect on that, solve that.
And if you find I've lied
from this day onward call the prophet blind.

TIRESIAS *and the boy exit to the side.*
CHORUS:

                                              Who—
who is the man the voice of god denounces
resounding out of the rocky gorge of Delphi?
    The horror too dark to tell,
whose ruthless bloody hands have done the work?
His time has come to fly
    to outrace the stallions of the storm
                        his feet a streak of speed—
Cased in armor, Apollo son of the Father
lunges on him, lightning-bolts afire!
And the grim unerring Furies
                        closing for the kill.
                                    Look,
the word of god has just come blazing
flashing off Parnassus' snowy heights!
    That man who left no trace—
after him, hunt him down with all our strength!
Now under bristling timber
    up through rocks and caves he stalks
                        like the wild mountain bull—
cut off from men, each step an agony, frenzied, racing blind
but he cannot outrace the dread voices of Delphi
ringing out of the heart of Earth,
    the dark wings beating around him shrieking doom
                        the doom that never dies, the terror—
The skilled prophet scans the birds and shatters me
    with terror!
I can't accept him, can't deny him, don't know what to say,
I'm lost, and the wings of dark foreboding beating—
I cannot see what's come, what's still to come . . .
and what could breed a blood feud between
    Laius' house and the son of Polybus?
I know of nothing, not in the past and not now,
no charge to bring against our king, no cause
to attack his fame that rings throughout Thebes—
    not without proof—not for the ghost of Laius,
    not to avenge a murder gone without a trace.

Zeus and Apollo know, they know, the great masters
    of all the dark and depth of human life.

But whether a mere man can know the truth,
whether a seer can fathom more than I—
there is no test, no certain proof
    though matching skill for skill
a man can outstrip a rival. No, not till I see
these charges proved will I side with his accusers.
We saw him then, when the she-hawk swept against him,
saw with our own eyes his skill, his brilliant triumph—
    there was the test—he was the joy of Thebes!
    Never will I convict my king, never in my heart.

Enter CREON *from the side.*
CREON:

My fellow-citizens, I hear King Oedipus
levels terrible charges at me. I had to come.
I resent it deeply. If, in the present crisis,
he thinks he suffers any abuse from me,
anything I've done or said that offers him
the slightest injury, why, I've no desire
to linger out this life, my reputation in ruins.
The damage I'd face from such an accusation
is nothing simple. No, there's nothing worse:
branded a traitor in the city, a traitor
to all of you and my good friends.

LEADER:

                                              True,
but a slur might have been forced out of him,
by anger perhaps, not any firm conviction.

CREON:

The charge was made in public, wasn't it?
I put the prophet up to spreading lies?

LEADER:

Such things were said . . .
I don't know with what intent, if any.

CREON:

Was his glance steady, his mind right
when the charge was brought against me?

LEADER:

I really couldn't say. I never look
to judge the ones in power.

The doors open. OEDIPUS *enters.*

                                              Wait,
here's Oedipus now.

OEDIPUS:

                        You—here? You have the gall
to show your face before the palace gates?
You, plotting to kill me, kill the king—
I see it all, the marauding thief himself
scheming to steal my crown and power!

                                        Tell me,
in god's name, what did you take me for,
coward or fool, when you spun out your plot?
Your treachery—you think I'd never detect it
creeping against me in the dark? Or sensing it,
not defend myself? Aren't you the fool,
you and your high adventure. Lacking numbers,
powerful friends, out for the big game of empire—
you need riches, armies to bring that quarry down!

CREON:

Are you quite finished? It's your turn to listen
for just as long as you've . . . instructed me.
Hear me out, then judge me on the facts.

OEDIPUS:

You've a wicked way with words, Creon,
but I'll be slow to learn—from you.
I find you a menace, a great burden to me.

CREON:

Just one thing, hear me out in this.

OEDIPUS:

                                Just one thing,
don't tell *me* you're not the enemy, the traitor.

CREON:

Look, if you think crude, mindless stubbornness
such a gift, you've lost your sense of balance.

OEDIPUS:

If you think you can abuse a kinsman,
then escape the penalty, you're insane.

CREON:

Fair enough, I grant you. But this injury
you say I've done you, what is it?

OEDIPUS:

Did you induce me, yes or no,
to send for that sanctimonious prophet?

CREON:

I did. And I'd do the same again.

OEDIPUS:

All right then, tell me, how long is it now
since Laius . . .

CREON:

                Laius—what did *he* do?

OEDIPUS:

                                Vanished,
swept from sight, murdered in his tracks.

CREON:

The count of the years would run you far back . . .

OEDIPUS:

And that far back, was the prophet at his trade?

CREON:

Skilled as he is today, and just as honored.

OEDIPUS:

Did he ever refer to me then, at that time?

CREON:

                                        No,
never, at least, when I was in his presence.

OEDIPUS:

But you did investigate the murder, didn't you?

CREON:

We did our best, of course, discovered nothing.

OEDIPUS:

But the great seer never accused me then—why not?

CREON:

I don't know. And when I don't, *I* keep quiet.

OEDIPUS:

You do know this, you'd tell it too—
if you had a shred of decency.

CREON:

                                What?
If I know, I won't hold back.

OEDIPUS:

                                Simply this:
if the two of you had never put heads together,
we would never have heard about *my* killing Laius.

CREON:

If that's what he says . . . well, you know best.
But now I have a right to learn from you
as you just learned from me.

OEDIPUS:

                                Learn your fill,
you never will convict me of the murder.

CREON:

Tell me, you're married to my sister, aren't you?

OEDIPUS:

A genuine discovery—there's no denying that.

CREON:

And you rule the land with her, with equal power?

OEDIPUS:

She receives from me whatever she desires.

CREON:

And I am the third, all of us are equals?

OEDIPUS:

Yes, and it's there you show your stripes—
you betray a kinsman.

CREON:

             Not at all.
Not if you see things calmly, rationally,
as I do. Look at it this way first:
who in his right mind would rather rule
and live in anxiety than sleep in peace?
Particularly if he enjoys the same authority.
Not I, I'm not the man to yearn for kingship,
not with a king's power in my hands. Who would?
No one with any sense of self-control.
Now, as it is, you offer me all I need,
not a fear in the world. But if I wore the crown . . .
there'd be many painful duties to perform,
hardly to my taste.
             How could kingship
please me more than influence, power
without a qualm? I'm not that deluded yet,
to reach for anything but privilege outright,
profit free and clear.
Now all men sing my praises, all salute me,
now all who request your favors curry mine.
I am their best hope: success rests in me.
Why give up that, I ask you, and borrow trouble?
A man of sense, someone who sees things clearly
would never resort to treason.
No, I have no lust for conspiracy in me,
nor could I ever suffer one who does.

Do you want proof? Go to Delphi yourself,
examine the oracle and see if I've reported
the message word-for-word. This too:
if you detect that I and the clairvoyant
have plotted anything in common, arrest me,
execute me. Not on the strength of one vote,
two in this case, mine as well as yours.
But don't convict me on sheer unverified surmise.
How wrong it is to take the good for bad,
purely at random, or take the bad for good.
But reject a friend, a kinsman? I would as soon
tear out the life within us, priceless life itself.
You'll learn this well, without fail, in time.
Time alone can bring the just man to light—
the criminal you can spot in one short day.

LEADER:

                          Good advice,
my lord, for anyone who wants to avoid disaster.
Those who jump to conclusions may go wrong.

OEDIPUS:

When my enemy moves against me quickly,
plots in secret, I move quickly too, I must,
I plot and pay him back. Relax my guard a moment,
waiting his next move—he wins his objective,
I lose mine.

CREON:

             What do you want?
You want me banished?

OEDIPUS:

              No, I want you dead.

CREON:

Just to show how ugly a grudge can . . .

OEDIPUS:

                    So,
still stubborn? you don't think I'm serious?

CREON:

I think you're insane.

OEDIPUS:

             Quite sane—in my behalf.

CREON:

Not just as much in mine?

OEDIPUS:

             You—my mortal enemy?

CREON:

What if you're wholly wrong?

OEDIPUS:

             No matter—I must rule.

CREON:

Not if you rule unjustly.

OEDIPUS:

             Hear him, Thebes, my city!

CREON:

My city too, not yours alone!

LEADER:

Please, my lords.

Enter JOCASTA *from the palace.*

             Look, Jocasta's coming,
and just in time too. With her help
you must put this fighting of yours to rest.

JOCASTA:

Have you no sense? Poor misguided men,
such shouting—why this public outburst?
Aren't you ashamed, with the land so sick,
to stir up private quarrels?

To OEDIPUS.

Into the palace now. And Creon, you go home.
Why make such a furor over nothing?

CREON:

My sister, it's dreadful . . . Oedipus, your husband,
he's bent on a choice of punishments for me,
banishment from the fatherland or death.

OEDIPUS:

Precisely. I caught him in the act, Jocasta,
plotting, about to stab me in the back.

CREON:

Never—curse me, let me die and be damned
if I've done you any wrong you charge me with.

JOCASTA:

Oh god, believe it, Oedipus,
honor the solemn oath he swears to heaven.
Do it for me, for the sake of all your people.

The CHORUS *begins to chant.*
CHORUS:

    Believe it, be sensible
        give way, my king, I beg you!

OEDIPUS:

    What do you want from me, concessions?

CHORUS:

    Respect him—he's been no fool in the past
    and now he's strong with the oath he swears to god.

OEDIPUS:

    You know what you're asking?

CHORUS:

                                I do.

OEDIPUS:

                                Then out with it!

CHORUS:

    The man's your friend, your kin, he's under oath—
    don't cast him out, disgraced
    branded with guilt on the strength of hearsay only.

OEDIPUS:

Know full well, if that is what you want
you want me dead or banished from the land.

CHORUS:

                                Never—
    no, by the blazing Sun, first god of the heavens!
        Stripped of the gods, stripped of loved ones,
    let me die by inches if that ever crossed my mind.
    But the heart inside me sickens, dies as the land dies
    and now on top of the old griefs you pile this,
    your fury—both of you!

OEDIPUS:

                                Then let him go,
    even if it does lead to my ruin, my death
    or my disgrace, driven from Thebes for life.
    It's you, not him I pity—your words move me.
    He, wherever he goes, my hate goes with him.

CREON:

    Look at you, sullen in yielding, brutal in your rage—
    you will go too far. It's perfect justice:
    natures like yours are hardest on themselves.

OEDIPUS:

    Then leave me alone—get out!

CREON:

                                I'm going.
    You're wrong, so wrong. These men know I'm right.

Exit to the side. The CHORUS *turns to* JOCASTA.
CHORUS:

    Why do you hesitate, my lady
        why not help him in?

JOCASTA:

    Tell me what's happened first.

CHORUS:

    Loose, ignorant talk started dark suspicions
    and a sense of injustice cut deeply too.

JOCASTA:

    On both sides?

CHORUS:

                                Oh yes.

JOCASTA:

                                What did they say?

CHORUS:

    Enough, please, enough! The land's so racked already
    or so it seems to me . . .
    End the trouble here, just where they left it.

OEDIPUS:

You see what comes of your good intentions now?
And all because you tried to blunt my anger.

CHORUS:

My king,

I've said it once, I'll say it time and again—
    I'd be insane, you know it,
senseless, ever to turn my back on you.
You who set our beloved land—storm-tossed, shattered—
straight on course. Now again, good helmsman,
steer us through the storm!

The CHORUS *draws away, leaving* OEDIPUS *and*
JOCASTA *side by side.*

JOCASTA:

For the love of god,
Oedipus, tell me too, what is it?
Why this rage? You're so unbending.

OEDIPUS:

I will tell you. I respect you, Jocasta,
much more than these men here . . .

Glancing at the CHORUS.

Creon's to blame, Creon schemes against me.

JOCASTA:

Tell me clearly, how did the quarrel start?

OEDIPUS:

He says *I* murdered Laius—I am guilty.

JOCASTA:

How does he know? Some secret knowledge
or simple hearsay?

OEDIPUS:

Oh, he sent his prophet in
to do his dirty work. You know Creon,
Creon keeps his own lips clean.

JOCASTA:

A prophet?
Well then, free yourself of every charge!
Listen to me and learn some peace of mind:
no skill in the world,
nothing human can penetrate the future.
Here is proof, quick and to the point.

An oracle came to Laius one fine day
(I won't say from Apollo himself
but his underlings, his priests) and it declared
that doom would strike him down at the hands of a son,
our son, to be born of our own flesh and blood. But Laius,
so the report goes at least, was killed by strangers,
thieves, at a place where three roads meet . . . my son—
he wasn't three days old and the boy's father
fastened his ankles, had a henchman fling him away
on a barren, trackless mountain.

There, you see?

Apollo brought neither thing to pass. My baby
no more murdered his father than Laius suffered—
his wildest fear—death at his own son's hands.
That's how the seers and all their revelations
mapped out the future. Brush them from your mind.
Whatever the god needs and seeks
he'll bring to light himself, with ease.

OEDIPUS:

Strange,
hearing you just now . . . my mind wandered,
my thoughts racing back and forth.

JOCASTA:

What do you mean? Why so anxious, startled?

OEDIPUS:

I thought I heard you say that Laius
was cut down at a place where three roads meet.

JOCASTA:

That was the story. It hasn't died out yet.

OEDIPUS:

Where did this thing happen? Be precise.

JOCASTA:

A place called Phocis, where two branching roads,
one from Daulia, one from Delphi,
come together—a crossroads.

OEDIPUS:

When? How long ago?

JOCASTA:

The heralds no sooner reported Laius dead
than you appeared and they hailed you king of Thebes.

OEDIPUS:

My god, my god—what have you planned to do to me?

JOCASTA:

What, Oedipus? What haunts you so?

OEDIPUS:

Not yet.
Laius—how did he look? Describe him.
Had he reached his prime?

JOCASTA:

He was swarthy,
and the gray had just begun to streak his temples,
and his build . . . wasn't far from yours.

OEDIPUS:

Oh no no,
I think I've just called down a dreadful curse
upon myself—I simply didn't know!

JOCASTA:

What are you saying? I shudder to look at you.

OEDIPUS:

I have a terrible fear the blind seer can see.
I'll know in a moment. One thing more—

JOCASTA:

                                        Anything,
afraid as I am—ask, I'll answer, all I can.

OEDIPUS:

Did he go with a light or heavy escort,
several men-at-arms, like a lord, a king?

JOCASTA:

There were five in the party, a herald among them,
and a single wagon carrying Laius.

OEDIPUS:

                          Ai—
now I can see it all, clear as day.
Who told you all this at the time, Jocasta?

JOCASTA:

A servant who reached home, the lone survivor.

OEDIPUS:

So, could he still be in the palace—even now?

JOCASTA:

No indeed. Soon as he returned from the scene
and saw you on the throne with Laius dead and gone,
he knelt and clutched my hand, pleading with me
to send him into the hinterlands, to pasture,
far as possible, out of sight of Thebes.
I sent him away. Slave though he was,
he'd earned that favor—and much more.

OEDIPUS:

Can we bring him back, quickly?

JOCASTA:

Easily. Why do you want him so?

OEDIPUS:

                          I am afraid,
Jocasta, I have said too much already.
That man—I've got to see him.

JOCASTA:

                    Then he'll come.
But even I have a right, I'd like to think,
to know what's torturing you, my lord.

OEDIPUS:

And so you shall—I can hold nothing back from you,

now I've reached this pitch of dark foreboding.
Who means more to me than you? Tell me,
whom would I turn toward but you
as I go through all this?

My father was Polybus, king of Corinth.
My mother, a Dorian, Merope. And I was held
the prince of the realm among the people there,
till something struck me out of nowhere,
something strange . . . worth remarking perhaps,
hardly worth the anxiety I gave it.
Some man at a banquet who had drunk too much
shouted out—he was far gone, mind you—
that I am not my father's son. Fighting words!
I barely restrained myself that day
but early the next I went to mother and father,
questioned them closely, and they were enraged
at the accusation and the fool who let it fly.
So as for my parents I was satisfied,
but still this thing kept gnawing at me,
the slander spread—I had to make my move.

                                        And so,
unknown to mother and father I set out for Delphi,
and the god Apollo spurned me, sent me away
denied the facts I came for,
but first he flashed before my eyes a future
great with pain, terror, disaster—I can hear him cry,
"You are fated to couple with your mother, you will bring
a breed of children into the light no man can bear to see—
you will kill your father, the one who gave you life!"
I heard all that and ran. I abandoned Corinth,
from that day on I gauged its landfall only
by the stars, running, always running
toward some place where I would never see
the shame of all those oracles come true.
And as I fled I reached that very spot
where the great king, you say, met his death.

Now, Jocasta, I will tell you all.
Making my way toward this triple crossroad
I began to see a herald, then a brace of colts
drawing a wagon, and mounted on the bench . . . a man,
just as you've described him, coming face-to-face,
and the one in the lead and the old man himself
were about to thrust me off the road—brute force—
and the one shouldering me aside, the driver,
I strike him in anger!—and the old man, watching me
coming up along his wheels—he brings down
his prod, two prongs straight at my head!
I paid him back with interest!
Short work, by god—with one blow of the staff
in this right hand I knock him out of his high seat,
roll him out of the wagon, sprawling headlong—
I killed them all—every mother's son!

Oh, but if there is any blood-tie
between Laius and this stranger . . .
what man alive more miserable than I?
More hated by the gods? *I* am the man
no alien, no citizen welcomes to his house,

law forbids it—not a word to me in public,
driven out of every hearth and home.
And all these curses I—no one but I
brought down these piling curses on myself!
And you, his wife, I've touched your body with these,
the hands that killed your husband cover you with blood.

Wasn't I born for torment? Look me in the eyes!
I am abomination—heart and soul!
I must be exiled, and even in exile
never see my parents, never set foot
on native ground again. Else I am doomed
to couple with my mother and cut my father down . . .
Polybus who reared me, gave me life.
                                        But why, why?
Wouldn't a man of judgment say—and wouldn't he be right—
some savage power has brought this down upon my head?

Oh no, not that, you pure and awesome gods,
never let me see that day! Let me slip
from a world of men, vanish without a trace
before I see myself stained with such corruption,
stained to the heart.

LEADER:

My lord, you fill our hearts with fear.
But at least until you question the witness,
do take hope.

OEDIPUS:

                    Exactly. He is my last hope—
I am waiting for the shepherd. He is crucial.

JOCASTA:

And once he appears, what then? Why so urgent?

OEDIPUS:

I will tell you. If it turns out that his story
matches yours, I've escaped the worst.

JOCASTA:

What did I say? What struck you so?

OEDIPUS:

                    You said *thieves*—
he told you a whole band of them murdered Laius.
So, if he still holds to the same number,
I cannot be the killer. One can't equal many.
But if he refers to one man, one alone,
clearly the scales come down on me:
I am guilty.

JOCASTA:

                    Impossible. Trust me,
I told you precisely what he said,
and he can't retract it now;
the whole city heard it, not just I.
And even if he should vary his first report

by one man more or less, still, my lord,
he could never make the murder of Laius
truly fit the prophecy. Apollo was explicit:
my son was doomed to kill my husband . . . my son,
poor defenseless thing, he never had a chance
to kill his father. They destroyed him first.

So much for prophecy. It's neither here nor there.
From this day on, I wouldn't look right or left.

OEDIPUS:

True, true. Still, that shepherd,
someone fetch him—now!

JOCASTA:

I'll send at once. But do let's go inside.
I'd never displease you, least of all in this.

OEDIPUS *and* JOCASTA *enter the palace.*

CHORUS:

> Destiny guide me always
> Destiny find me filled with reverence
>   pure in word and deed.
> Great laws tower above us, reared on high
> born for the brilliant value of heaven—
>   Olympian Sky their only father,
> nothing mortal, no man gave them birth,
> their memory deathless, never lost in sleep:
> within them lives a mighty god, the god does not
>   grow old.
>
> Pride breeds the tyrant
> violent pride, gorging, crammed to bursting
>   with all that is overripe and rich with ruin—
> clawing up to the heights, headlong pride
> crashes down the abyss—sheer doom!
>   No footing helps, all foothold lost and gone.
> But the healthy strife that makes the city strong—
> I pray that god will never end that wrestling:
> god, my champion, I will never let you go.
>
> But if any man comes striding, high and mighty
>   in all he says and does,
> no fear of justice, no reverence
> for the temples of the gods—
>   let a rough doom tear him down,
> repay his pride, breakneck, ruinous pride!
> If he cannot reap his profits fairly
>   cannot restrain himself from outrage—
> mad, laying hands on the holy things untouchable!
>
>   Can such a man, so desperate, still boast
>   he can save his life from the flashing bolts of god?
>   If all such violence goes with honor now
>   why join the sacred dance?
>
> Never again will I go reverent to Delphi,
>   the inviolate heart of Earth
> or Apollo's ancient oracle at Abae

or Olympia of the fires—
  unless these prophecies all come true
for all mankind to point toward in wonder.
King of kings, if you deserve your titles
  Zeus, remember, never forget!
You and your deathless, everlasting reign.

  They are dying, the old oracles sent to Laius,
  now our masters strike them off the rolls.
  Nowhere Apollo's golden glory now—
    the gods, the gods go down.

Enter JOCASTA *from the palace, carrying a suppliant's branch wound in wool.*

JOCASTA:

Lords of the realm, it occurred to me,
just now, to visit the temples of the gods,
so I have a branch in hand and incense too.

Oedipus is beside himself. Racked with anguish,
no longer a man of sense, he won't admit
the latest prophecies are hollow as the old—
he's at the mercy of every passing voice
if the voice tells of terror.
I urge him gently, nothing seems to help,
so I turn to you, Apollo, you are nearest.

Placing her branch on the altar, while an old herdsman enters from the side, not the one just summoned by the King but an unexpected MESSENGER *from Corinth.*

I come with prayers and offerings . . . I beg you,
cleanse us, set us free of defilement!
Look at us, passengers in the grip of fear,
watching the pilot of the vessel go to pieces.

MESSENGER:

Approaching JOCASTA *and the* CHORUS.

Strangers, please, I wonder if you could lead us
to the palace of the king . . . I think it's Oedipus.
Better, the man himself—you know where he is?

LEADER:

This is his palace, stranger. He's inside.
But here is his queen, his wife and mother
of his children.

MESSENGER:

        Blessings on you, noble queen,
queen of Oedipus crowned with all your family—
blessings on you always!

JOCASTA:

And the same to you, stranger, you deserve it . . .
such a greeting. But what have you come for?
Have you brought us news?

MESSENGER:

        Wonderful news—
for the house, my lady, for your husband too.

JOCASTA:

Really, what? Who sent you?

MESSENGER:

        Corinth.
I'll give you the message in a moment.
You'll be glad of it—how could you help it?—
though it costs a little sorrow in the bargain.

JOCASTA:

What can it be, with such a double edge?

MESSENGER:

The people there, they want to make your Oedipus
king of Corinth, so they're saying now.

JOCASTA:

Why? Isn't old Polybus still in power?

MESSENGER:

No more. Death has got him in the tomb.

JOCASTA:

What are you saying? Polybus, dead?—dead?

MESSENGER:

        If not,
if I'm not telling the truth, strike me dead too.

JOCASTA:

To a servant.

Quickly, go to your master, tell him this!

You prophecies of the gods, where are you now?
This is the man that Oedipus feared for years,
he fled him, not to kill him—and now he's dead,
quite by chance, a normal, natural death,
not murdered by his son.

OEDIPUS:

Emerging from the palace.

        Dearest,
what now? Why call me from the palace?

JOCASTA:

Bringing the MESSENGER *closer.*

Listen to *him*, see for yourself what all
those awful prophecies of god have come to.

OEDIPUS:

And who is he? What can he have for me?

JOCASTA:

He's from Corinth, he's come to tell you
your father is no more—Polybus—he's dead!

OEDIPUS:

Wheeling on the MESSENGER.

What? Let me have it from your lips.

MESSENGER:

Well,

if that's what you want first, then here it is:
make no mistake, Polybus is dead and gone.

OEDIPUS:

How—murder? sickness?—what? what killed him?

MESSENGER:

A light tip of the scales can put old bones to rest.

OEDIPUS:

Sickness then—poor man, it wore him down.

MESSENGER:

That,

and the long count of years he'd measured out.

OEDIPUS:

So!

Jocasta, why, why look to the Prophet's hearth,
the fires of the future? Why scan the birds
that scream above our heads? They winged me on
to the murder of my father, did they? That was my doom?
Well look, he's dead and buried, hidden under the earth,
and here I am in Thebes, I never put hand to sword—
unless some longing for me wasted him away,
then in a sense you'd say I caused his death.
But now, all those prophecies I feared—Polybus
packs them off to sleep with him in hell!
They're nothing, worthless.

JOCASTA:

There.

Didn't I tell you from the start?

OEDIPUS:

So you did. I was lost in fear.

JOCASTA:

No more, sweep it from your mind forever.

OEDIPUS:

But my mother's bed, surely I must fear—

JOCASTA:

Fear?

What should a man fear? It's all chance,
chance rules our lives. Not a man on earth
can see a day ahead, groping through the dark.
Better to live at random, best we can.
And as for this marriage with your mother—
have no fear. Many a man before you,

in his dreams, has shared his mother's bed.
Take such things for shadows, nothing at all—
Live, Oedipus,
as if there's no tomorrow!

OEDIPUS:

Brave words,

and you'd persuade me if mother weren't alive.
But mother lives, so for all your reassurances
I live in fear, I must.

JOCASTA:

But your father's death,

that, at least, is a great blessing, joy to the eyes!

OEDIPUS:

Great, I know . . . but I fear *her*—she's still alive.

MESSENGER:

Wait, who is this woman, makes you so afraid?

OEDIPUS:

Merope, old man. The wife of Polybus.

MESSENGER:

The queen? What's there to fear in her?

OEDIPUS:

A dreadful prophecy, stranger, sent by the gods.

MESSENGER:

Tell me, could you? Unless it's forbidden
other ears to hear.

OEDIPUS:

Not at all.

Apollo told me once—it is my fate—
I must make love with my own mother,
shed my father's blood with my own hands.
So for years I've given Corinth a wide berth,
and it's been my good fortune too. But still,
to see one's parents and look into their eyes
is the greatest joy I know.

MESSENGER:

You're afraid of that?

That kept you out of Corinth?

OEDIPUS:

My *father*, old man—

so I wouldn't kill my father.

MESSENGER:

So that's it.

Well then, seeing I came with such good will, my king,
why don't I rid you of that old worry now?

OEDIPUS:
What a rich reward you'd have for that!

MESSENGER:
What do you think I came for, majesty?
So you'd come home and I'd be better off.

OEDIPUS:
Never, I will never go near my parents.

MESSENGER:
My boy, it's clear, you don't know what you're doing.

OEDIPUS:
What do you mean, old man? For god's sake, explain.

MESSENGER:
If you ran from *them*, always dodging home . . .

OEDIPUS:
Always, terrified Apollo's oracle might come true—

MESSENGER:
And you'd be covered with guilt, from both your parents.

OEDIPUS:
That's right, old man, that fear is always with me.

MESSENGER:
Don't you know? You've really nothing to fear.

OEDIPUS:
But why? If I'm their son—Merope, Polybus?

MESSENGER:
Polybus was nothing to you, that's why, not in blood.

OEDIPUS:
What are you saying—Polybus was not my father?

MESSENGER:
No more than I am. He and I are equals.

OEDIPUS:
                              My father—
how can my father equal nothing? You're nothing to me!

MESSENGER:
Neither was he, no more your father than I am.

OEDIPUS:
Then why did he call me his son?

MESSENGER:
                              You were a gift,
years ago—know for a fact he took you
from my hands.

OEDIPUS:
                    No, from another's hands?
Then how could he love me so? He loved me, deeply . . .

MESSENGER:
True, and his early years without a child
made him love you all the more.

OEDIPUS:
                         And you, did you . . .
buy me? find me by accident?

MESSENGER:
                         I stumbled on you,
down the woody flanks of Mount Cithaeron.

OEDIPUS:
                              So close,
what were you doing here, just passing through?

MESSENGER:
Watching over my flocks, grazing them on the slopes.

OEDIPUS:
A herdsman, were you? A vagabond, scraping for wages?

MESSENGER:
Your savior too, my son, in your worst hour.

OEDIPUS:
                                   Oh—
when you picked me up, was I in pain? What exactly?

MESSENGER:
Your ankles . . . they tell the story. Look at them.

OEDIPUS:
Why remind me of that, that old affliction?

MESSENGER:
Your ankles were pinned together. I set you free.

OEDIPUS:
That dreadful mark—I've had it from the cradle.

MESSENGER:
And you got your name from that misfortune too,
the name's still with you.

SOPHOCLES | *Oedipus the King*   **55**

OEDIPUS:

Dear god, who did it?—
mother? father? Tell me.

MESSENGER:

I don't know.
The one who gave you to me, he'd know more.

OEDIPUS:

What? You took me from someone else?
You didn't find me yourself?

MESSENGER:

No sir,
another shepherd passed you on to me.

OEDIPUS:

Who? Do you know? Describe him.

MESSENGER:

He called himself a servant of . . .
if I remember rightly—Laius.

JOCASTA *turns sharply.*

OEDIPUS:

The king of the land who ruled here long ago?

MESSENGER:

That's the one. That herdsman was *his* man.

OEDIPUS:

Is he still alive? Can I see him?

MESSENGER:

They'd know best, the people of these parts.

OEDIPUS *and the* MESSENGER *turn to the* CHORUS.

OEDIPUS:

Does anyone know that herdsman,
the one he mentioned? Anyone seen him
in the fields, here in the city? Out with it!
The time has come to reveal this once for all.

LEADER:

I think he's the very shepherd you wanted to see,
a moment ago. But the queen, Jocasta,
she's the one to say.

OEDIPUS:

Jocasta,
you remember the man we just sent for?
Is *that* the one he means?

JOCASTA:

That man . . .

why ask? Old shepherd, talk, empty nonsense,
don't give it another thought, don't even think—

OEDIPUS:

What—give up now, with a clue like this?
Fail to solve the mystery of my birth?
Not for all the world!

JOCASTA:

Stop—in the name of god,
if you love your own life, call off this search!
My suffering is enough.

OEDIPUS:

Courage!
Even if my mother turns out to be a slave,
and I a slave, three generations back,
you would not seem common.

JOCASTA:

Oh no,
listen to me, I beg you, don't do this.

OEDIPUS:

Listen to you? No more. I must know it all,
must see the truth at last.

JOCASTA:

No, please—
for your sake—I want the best for you!

OEDIPUS:

Your best is more than I can bear.

JOCASTA:

You're doomed—
may you never fathom who you are!

OEDIPUS:

To a servant.

Hurry, fetch me the herdsman, now!
Leave her to glory in her royal birth.

JOCASTA:

Aieeeeee—
man of agony—
that is the only name I have for you,
that, no other—ever, ever, ever!

*Flinging through the palace doors. A long, tense silence
follows.*

LEADER:

Where's she gone, Oedipus?
Rushing off, such wild grief . . .
I'm afraid that from this silence
something monstrous may come bursting forth.

OEDIPUS:

Let it burst! Whatever will, whatever must!
I must know my birth, no matter how common
it may be—I must see my origins face-to-face.
She perhaps, she with her woman's pride
may well be mortified by my birth,
but I, I count myself the son of Chance,
the great goddess, giver of all good things—
I'll never see myself disgraced. She is my mother!
And the moons have marked me out, my blood-brothers,
one moon on the wane, the next moon great with power.
That is my blood, my nature—I will never betray it,
never fail to search and learn my birth!

CHORUS:

Yes—if I am a true prophet
        if I can grasp the truth,
    by the boundless skies of Olympus,
at the full moon of tomorrow, Mount Cithaeron
you will know how Oedipus glories in you—
you, his birthplace, nurse, his mountain-mother!
And we will sing you, dancing out your praise—
you lift our monarch's heart!
    Apollo, Apollo, god of the wild cry
            may our dancing please you!
                            Oedipus—
            son, dear child, who bore you?
Who of the nymphs who seem to live forever
mated with Pan, the mountain-striding Father?
Who was your mother? who, some bride of Apollo
the god who loves the pastures spreading toward the sun?
    Or was it Hermes, king of the lightning ridges?
Or Dionysus, lord of frenzy, lord of the barren peaks—
did he seize you in his hands, dearest of all his lucky finds?—
    found by the nymphs, their warm eyes dancing, gift
to the lord who loves them dancing out his joy!

OEDIPUS *strains to see a figure coming from the distance.*
Attended by palace guards, an old SHEPHERD *enters*
slowly, reluctant to approach the king.

OEDIPUS:

I never met the man, my friends . . . still,
if I had to guess, I'd say that's the shepherd,
the very one we've looked for all along.
Brothers in old age, two of a kind,
he and our guest here. At any rate
the ones who bring him in are my own men,
I recognize them.

Turning to the LEADER.

                But you know more than I,
you should, you've seen the man before.

LEADER:

I know him, definitely. One of Laius' men,
a trusty shepherd, if there ever was one.

OEDIPUS:

You, I ask you first, stranger,
you from Corinth—is this the one you mean?

MESSENGER:

You're looking at him. He's your man.

OEDIPUS:

To the SHEPHERD.

You, old man, come over here—
look at me. Answer all my questions.
Did you ever serve King Laius?

SHEPHERD:

                        So I did . . .
a slave, not bought on the block though,
born and reared in the palace.

OEDIPUS:

Your duties, your kind of work?

SHEPHERD:

Herding the flocks, the better part of my life.

OEDIPUS:

Where, mostly? Where did you do your grazing?

SHEPHERD:

                                Well,
Cithaeron sometimes, or the foothills round about.

OEDIPUS:

This man—you know him? ever see him there?

SHEPHERD:

Confused, glancing from the MESSENGER *to the King.*
Doing what?—what man do you mean?

OEDIPUS:

Pointing to the MESSENGER.
This one here—ever have dealings with him?

SHEPHERD:

Not so I could say, but give me a chance,
my memory's bad . . .

MESSENGER:

No wonder he doesn't know me, master.
But let me refresh his memory for him.
I'm sure he recalls old times we had
on the slopes of Mount Cithaeron;
he and I, grazing our flocks, he with two
and I with one—we both struck up together,
three whole seasons, six months at a stretch
from spring to the rising of Arcturus in the fall,
then with winter coming on I'd drive my herds
to my own pens, and back he'd go with his
to Laius' folds.

To the SHEPHERD.

                Now that's how it was,
wasn't it—yes or no?

SHEPHERD:

                Yes, I suppose . . .
it's all so long ago.

MESSENGER:

                Come, tell me,
you gave me a child back then, a boy, remember?
A little fellow to rear, my very own.

SHEPHERD:

What? Why rake up that again?

MESSENGER:

Look, here he is, my fine old friend—
the same man who was just a baby then.

SHEPHERD:

Damn you, shut your mouth—quiet!

OEDIPUS:

Don't lash out at him, old man—
you need lashing more than he does.

SHEPHERD:

                    Why,
master, majesty—what have I done wrong?

OEDIPUS:

You won't answer his question about the boy.

SHEPHERD:

He's talking nonsense, wasting his breath.

OEDIPUS:

So, you won't talk willingly—
then you'll talk with pain.

The guards seize the SHEPHERD.

SHEPHERD:

No, dear god, don't torture an old man!

OEDIPUS:

Twist his arms back, quickly!

SHEPHERD:

                God help us, why?—
what more do you need to know?

OEDIPUS:

Did you give him that child? He's asking.

SHEPHERD:

I did . . . I wish to god I'd died that day.

OEDIPUS:

You've got your wish if you don't tell the truth.

SHEPHERD:

The more I tell, the worse the death I'll die.

OEDIPUS:

Our friend here wants to stretch things out, does he?

Motioning to his men for torture.

SHEPHERD:

No, no, I gave it to him—I just said so.

OEDIPUS:

Where did you get it? Your house? Someone else's?

SHEPHERD:

It wasn't mine, no, I got it from . . . someone.

OEDIPUS:

Which one of them?

Looking at the citizens.

                Whose house?

SHEPHERD:

                    No—
god's sake, master, no more questions!

OEDIPUS:

You're a dead man if I have to ask again.

SHEPHERD:

Then—the child came from the house . . .
of Laius.

OEDIPUS:

          A slave? or born of his own blood?

SHEPHERD:

                Oh no,
I'm right at the edge, the horrible truth—I've got to say it!

OEDIPUS:

And I'm at the edge of hearing horrors, yes, but I must hear!

SHEPHERD:

All right! His son, they said it was—his son!
But the one inside, your wife,
she'd tell it best.

OEDIPUS:

My wife—
she gave it to you?

SHEPHERD:

Yes, yes, my king.

OEDIPUS:

Why, what for?

SHEPHERD:

To kill it.

OEDIPUS:

Her own child,
how could she?

SHEPHERD:

She was afraid—
frightening prophecies.

OEDIPUS:

What?

SHEPHERD:

They said—
he'd kill his parents.

OEDIPUS:

But you gave him to this old man—why?

SHEPHERD:

I pitied the little baby, master,
hoped he'd take him off to his own country,
far away, but he saved him for this, this fate.
If you are the man he says you are, believe me,
you were born for pain.

OEDIPUS:

O god—
all come true, all burst to light!
O light—now let me look my last on you!
I stand revealed at last—
cursed in my birth, cursed in marriage,
cursed in the lives I cut down with these hands!

*Rushing through the doors with a great cry. The
Corinthian* MESSENGER, *the* SHEPHERD *and
attendants exit slowly to the side.*

CHORUS:

O the generations of men
the dying generations—adding the total
of all your lives I find they come to nothing . . .
does there exist, is there a man on earth
who seizes more joy than just a dream, a vision?
And the vision no sooner dawns than dies
blazing into oblivion.

You are my great example, you, your life
your destiny, Oedipus, man of misery—
I count no man blest.

You outranged all men!
Bending your bow to the breaking-point
you captured priceless glory, O dear god,
and the Sphinx came crashing down,
the virgin, claws hooked

like a bird of omen singing, shrieking death—
like a fortress reared in the face of death
you rose and saved our land.

From that day on we called you king
we crowned you with honors, Oedipus, towering over all—
mighty king of the seven gates of Thebes.
But now to hear your story—is there a man more agonized?
More wed to pain and frenzy? Not a man on earth,
the joy of your life ground down to nothing
O Oedipus, name for the ages—
one and the same wide harbor served you
son and father both
son and father came to rest in the same bridal chamber.
How, how could the furrows your father plowed
bear you, your agony, harrowing on
in silence O so long?

But now for all your power
Time, all-seeing Time has dragged you to the light,
judged your marriage monstrous from the start—
the son and the father tangling, both one—
O child of Laius, would to god
I'd never seen you, never never!
Now I weep like a man who wails the dead
and the dirge comes pouring forth with all my heart!
I tell you the truth, you gave me life
my breath leapt up in you
and now you bring down night upon my eyes.

Enter a MESSENGER *from the palace.*

MESSENGER:

Men of Thebes, always first in honor,
what horrors you will hear, what you will see,
what a heavy weight of sorrow you will shoulder . . .
if you are true to your birth, if you still have
some feeling for the royal house of Thebes.
I tell you neither the waters of the Danube
nor the Nile can wash this palace clean.
Such things it hides, it soon will bring to light—
terrible things, and none done blindly now,
all done with a will. The pains
we inflict upon ourselves hurt most of all.

LEADER:

God knows we have pains enough already.
What can you add to them?

MESSENGER:

The queen is dead.

LEADER:

Poor lady—how?

MESSENGER:

By her own hand. But you are spared the worst,
you never had to watch . . . I saw it all,
and with all the memory that's in me
you will learn what that poor woman suffered.

Once she'd broken in through the gates
dashing past us, frantic, whipped to fury,
ripping her hair out with both hands—
straight to her rooms she rushed, flinging herself
across the bridal-bed, doors slamming behind her—
once inside, she wailed for Laius, dead so long,
remembering how she bore his child long ago,
the life that rose up to destroy him, leaving
its mother to mother living creatures
with the very son she'd borne.
Oh how she wept, mourning the marriage-bed
where she let loose that double brood—monsters—
husband by her husband, children by her child.
                                        And then—
but how she died is more than I can say. Suddenly
Oedipus burst in, screaming, he stunned us so
we couldn't watch her agony to the end,
our eyes were fixed on him. Circling
like a maddened beast, stalking, here, there,
crying out to us—
                        Give him a sword! His wife,
no wife, his mother, where can he find the mother earth
that cropped two crops at once, himself and all his children?
He was raging—one of the dark powers pointing the way,
none of us mortals crowding around him, no,
with a great shattering cry—someone, something leading
him on—
he hurled at the twin doors and bending the bolts back
out of their sockets, crashed through the chamber.
And there we saw the woman hanging by the neck,
cradled high in the woven noose, spinning,
swinging back and forth. And when he saw her,
giving a low, wrenching sob that broke our hearts,
slipping the halter from her throat, he eased her down,
in a slow embrace he laid her down, poor thing . . .
then, what came next, what horror we beheld!

He rips off her brooches, the long gold pins
holding her robes—and lifting them high,
looking straight up into the points,
he digs them down the sockets of his eyes, crying, "You,
you'll see no more the pain I suffered, all the pain I caused!
Too long you looked on the bones you never should have seen,
blind to the ones you longed to see, to know! Blind
from this hour on! Blind in the darkness—blind!"
His voice like a dirge, rising, over and over
raising the pins, raking them down his eyes.
And at each stroke blood spurts from the roots,
splashing his beard, a swirl of it, nerves and clots—
black hail of blood pulsing, gushing down.

These are the griefs that burst upon them both,
coupling man and woman. The joy they had so lately,
the fortune of their old ancestral house
was deep joy indeed. Now, in this one day,
wailing, madness and doom, death, disgrace,
all the griefs in the world that you can name,
all are theirs forever.

LEADER:
                        Oh poor man, the misery—
has he any rest from pain now?

A voice within, in torment.
MESSENGER:
                        He's shouting,
"Loose the bolts, someone, show me to all of Thebes!
My father's murderer, my mother's—"
No, I can't repeat it, it's unholy.
Now he'll tear himself from his native earth,
not linger, curse the house with his own curse.
But he needs strength, and a guide to lead him on.
This is sickness more than he can bear.

The palace doors open.
                        Look,
he'll show you himself. The great doors are opening—
you are about to see a sight, a horror
even his mortal enemy would pity.

Enter OEDIPUS, *blinded, led by a boy. He stands at the
palace steps, as if surveying his people once again.*
CHORUS:
                        O the terror—
the suffering, for all the world to see,
the worst terror that ever met my eyes.
What madness swept over you? What god,
what dark power leapt beyond all bounds,
beyond belief, to crush your wretched life?—
godforsaken, cursed by the gods!
I pity you but I can't bear to look.
I've much to ask, so much to learn,
so much fascinates my eyes,
but you . . . I shudder at the sight.

OEDIPUS:
                        Oh, Ohh—
the agony! I am agony—
where am I going? where on earth?
    where does all this agony hurl me?
where's my voice—
    winging, swept away on a dark tide—
My destiny, my dark power, what a leap you made!

CHORUS:
To the depths of terror, too dark to hear, to see.

OEDIPUS:
    Dark, horror of darkness
    my darkness, drowning, swirling around me
    crashing wave on wave—unspeakable, irresistible
        headwind, fatal harbor! Oh again,
    the misery, all at once, over and over
    the stabbing daggers, stab of memory
raking me insane.

CHORUS:

No wonder you suffer
twice over, the pain of your wounds,
the lasting grief of pain.

OEDIPUS:

Dear friend, still here?
Standing by me, still with a care for me,
the blind man? Such compassion,
    loyal to the last. Oh it's you,
I know you're here, dark as it is
I'd know you anywhere, your voice—
it's yours, clearly yours.

CHORUS:

Dreadful, what you've done . . .
how could you bear it, gouging out your eyes?
What superhuman power drove you on?

OEDIPUS:

Apollo, friends, Apollo—
he ordained my agonies—these, my pains on pains!
But the hand that struck my eyes was mine,
mine alone—no one else—
    I did it all myself!
What good were eyes to me?
Nothing I could see could bring me joy.

CHORUS:

No, no, exactly as you say.

OEDIPUS:

What can I ever see?
What love, what call of the heart
can touch my ears with joy? Nothing, friends.
    Take me away, far, far from Thebes,
    quickly, cast me away, my friends—
this great murderous ruin, this man cursed to heaven,
    the man the deathless gods hate most of all!

CHORUS:

Pitiful, you suffer so, you understand so much . . .
I wish you had never known.

OEDIPUS:

Die, die—
whoever he was that day in the wilds
who cut my ankles free of the ruthless pins,
he pulled me clear of death, he saved my life
for this, this kindness—
    Curse him, kill him!
If I'd died then, I'd never have dragged myself,
my loved ones through such hell.

CHORUS:

Oh if only . . . would to god.

OEDIPUS:

I'd never have come to this,
my father's murderer—never been branded
mother's husband, all men see me now! Now,
loathed by the gods, son of the mother I defiled
coupling in my father's bed, spawning lives in the loins
that spawned my wretched life. What grief can crown
    this grief?
    It's mine alone, my destiny—I am Oedipus!

CHORUS:

How can I say you've chosen for the best?
Better to die than be alive and blind.

OEDIPUS:

What I did was best—don't lecture me,
no more advice. I, with *my* eyes,
how could I look my father in the eyes
when I go down to death? Or mother, so abused . . .
I have done such things to the two of them,
crimes too huge for hanging.
    Worse yet,
the sight of my children, born as they were born,
how could I long to look into their eyes?
No, not with these eyes of mine, never.
Not this city either, her high towers,
the sacred glittering images of her gods—
I am misery! I, her best son, reared
as no other son of Thebes was ever reared,
I've stripped myself, I gave the command myself.
All men must cast away the great blasphemer,
the curse now brought to light by the gods,
the son of Laius—I, my father's son!

Now I've exposed my guilt, horrendous guilt,
could I train a level glance on you, my countrymen?
Impossible! No, if I could just block off my ears,
the springs of hearing, I would stop at nothing—
I'd wall up my loathsome body like a prison,
blind to the sound of life, not just the sight.
Oblivion—what a blessing . . .
for the mind to dwell a world away from pain.

O Cithaeron, why did you give me shelter?
Why didn't you take me, crush my life out on the spot?
I'd never have revealed my birth to all mankind.

O Polybus, Corinth, the old house of my fathers,
so I believed—what a handsome prince you raised—
under the skin, what sickness to the core.
Look at me! Born of outrage, outrage to the core.
O triple roads—it all comes back, the secret,
dark ravine, and the oaks closing in
where the three roads join . . .
You drank my father's blood, my own blood
spilled by my own hands—you still remember me?
What things you saw me do? Then I came here
and did them all once more!

Marriages! O marriage,
you gave me birth, and once you brought me into the world
you brought my sperm rising back, springing to light
fathers, brothers, sons—one murderous breed—
brides, wives, mothers. The blackest things
a man can do, I have done them all!
                                    No more—
it's wrong to name what's wrong to do. Quickly,
for the love of god, hide me somewhere,
kill me, hurl me into the sea
where you can never look on me again.

Beckoning to the CHORUS *as they shrink away.*
                                    Closer,
it's all right. Touch the man of grief.
Do. Don't be afraid. My troubles are mine
and I am the only man alive who can sustain them.

Enter CREON *from the palace, attended by palace guards.*

LEADER:

Put your requests to Creon. Here he is,
just when we need him. He'll have a plan, he'll act.
Now that he's the sole defense of the country
in your place.

OEDIPUS:

                    Oh no, what can I say to him?
How can I ever hope to win his trust?
I wronged him so, just now, in every way.
You must see that—I was so wrong, so wrong.

CREON:

I haven't come to mock you, Oedipus,
or to criticize your former failings.

Turning to the guards.

                                    You there,
have you lost all respect for human feelings?
At least revere the Sun, the holy fire
that keeps us all alive. Never expose a thing
of guilt and holy dread so great it appalls
the earth, the rain from heaven, the light of day!
Get him into the halls—quickly as you can.
Piety demands no less. Kindred alone
should see a kinsman's shame. This is obscene.

OEDIPUS:

Please, in god's name . . . you wipe my fears away,
coming so generously to me, the worst of men.
Do one thing more, for your sake, not mine.

CREON:

What do you want? Why so insistent?

OEDIPUS:

Drive me out of the land at once, far from sight,
where I can never hear a human voice.

CREON:

I'd have done that already, I promise you.
First I wanted the god to clarify my duties.

OEDIPUS:

The god? His command was clear, every word:
death for the father-killer, the curse—
he said destroy me!

CREON:

So he did. Still in such a crisis
it's better to ask precisely what to do.

OEDIPUS:

                                    So miserable—
you would consult the god about a man like me?

CREON:

By all means. And this time, I assume,
even you will obey the god's decrees.

OEDIPUS:

                                    I will,
I will. And you, I command you—I beg you . . .
the woman inside, bury her as you see fit.
It's the only decent thing,
to give your own the last rites. As for me,
never condemn the city of my fathers
to house my body, not while I'm alive, no,
let me live on the mountains, on Cithaeron,
my favorite haunt, I have made it famous.
Mother and father marked out that rock
to be my everlasting tomb—buried alive.
Let me die there, where they tried to kill me.

Oh but this I know: no sickness can destroy me,
nothing can. I would never have been saved
from death—I have been saved
for something great and terrible, something strange.
Well let my destiny come and take me on its way!
About my children, Creon, the boys at least,
don't burden yourself. They're men,
wherever they go, they'll find the means to live.
But my two daughters, my poor helpless girls,
clustering at our table, never without me
hovering near them . . . whatever I touched,
they always had their share. Take care of them,
I beg you. Wait, better—permit me, would you?
Just to touch them with my hands and take
our fill of tears. Please . . . my king.
Grant it, with all your noble heart.
If I could hold them, just once, I'd think
I had them with me, like the early days
when I could see their eyes.

ANTIGONE *and* ISMENE, *two small children, are led in
from the palace by a nurse.*

What's that?
O god! Do I really hear you sobbing?—
my two children. Creon, you've pitied me?
Sent me my darling girls, my own flesh and blood!
Am I right?

CREON:

Yes, it's my doing.
I know the joy they gave you all these years,
the joy you must feel now.

OEDIPUS:

Bless you, Creon!
May god watch over you for this kindness,
better than he ever guarded me.
Children, where are you?
Here, come quickly—

Groping for ANTIGONE *and* ISMENE, *who approach their
father cautiously, then embrace him.*

Come to these hands of mine,
your brother's hands, your own father's hands
that served his once bright eyes so well—
that made them blind. Seeing nothing, children,
knowing nothing. I became your father,
I fathered you in the soil that gave me life.

How I weep for you—I cannot see you now . . .
just thinking of all your days to come, the bitterness,
the life that rough mankind will thrust upon you.
Where are the public gatherings you can join,
the banquets of the clans? Home you'll come,
in tears, cut off from the sight of it all,
the brilliant rites unfinished.
And when you reach perfection, ripe for marriage,
who will he be, my dear ones? Risking all
to shoulder the curse that weighs down my parents,
yes and you too—that wounds us all together.
What more misery could you want?
Your father killed his father, sowed his mother,
one, one and the selfsame womb sprang you—
he cropped the very roots of his existence.

Such disgrace, and you must bear it all!
Who will marry you then? Not a man on earth.
Your doom is clear: you'll wither away to nothing,
single, without a child.

Turning to CREON.

Oh Creon,
you are the only father they have now . . .
we who brought them into the world
are gone, both gone at a stroke—
Don't let them go begging, abandoned,
women without men. Your own flesh and blood!
Never bring them down to the level of my pains.
Pity them. Look at them, so young, so vulnerable,
shorn of everything—you're their only hope.
Promise me, noble Creon, touch my hand!

Reaching toward CREON, *who draws back.*

You, little ones, if you were old enough
to understand, there is much I'd tell you.
Now, as it is, I'd have you say a prayer.
Pray for life, my children,
live where you are free to grow and season.
Pray god you find a better life than mine,
the father who begot you.

CREON:

Enough.
You've wept enough. Into the palace now.

OEDIPUS:

I must, but I find it very hard.

CREON:

Time is the great healer, you will see.

OEDIPUS:

I am going—you know on what condition?

CREON:

Tell me. I'm listening.

OEDIPUS:

Drive me out of Thebes, in exile.

CREON:

Not I. Only the gods can give you that.

OEDIPUS:

Surely the gods hate me so much—

CREON:

You'll get your wish at once.

OEDIPUS:

You consent?

CREON:

I try to say what I mean; it's my habit.

OEDIPUS:

Then take me away. It's time.

CREON:

Come along, let go of the children.

OEDIPUS:

No—
don't take them away from me, not now! No no no!

*Clutching his daughters as the guards wrench them
loose and take them through the palace doors.*

CREON:

Still the king, the master of all things?
No more: here your power ends.
None of your power follows you through life.

Exit OEDIPUS *and* CREON *to the palace. The* CHORUS
comes forward to address the audience directly.

CHORUS:

People of Thebes, my countrymen, look on Oedipus.
He solved the famous riddle with his brilliance,

he rose to power, a man beyond all power.
Who could behold his greatness without envy?
Now what a black sea of terror has overwhelmed him.
Now as we keep our watch and wait the final day,
count no man happy till he dies, free of pain at last.

Exit in procession.

THUCYDIDES

from *History of the Peloponnesian War*

Book II (Pericles' Funeral Oration)

• • •

'Many of those who have spoken here in the past have praised the institution of this speech at the close of our ceremony. It seemed to them a mark of honour to our soldiers who have fallen in war that a speech should be made over them. I do not agree. These men have shown themselves valiant in action, and it would be enough, I think, for their glories to be proclaimed in action, as you have just seen it done at this funeral organized by the state. Our belief in the courage and manliness of so many should not be hazarded on the goodness or badness of one man's speech. Then it is not easy to speak with a proper sense of balance, when a man's listeners find it difficult to believe in the truth of what one is saying. The man who knows the facts and loves the dead may well think that an oration tells less than what he knows and what he would like to hear: others who do not know so much may feel envy for the dead, and think the orator over-praises them, when he speaks of exploits that are beyond their own capacities. Praise of other people is tolerable only up to a certain point, the point where one still believes that one could do oneself some of the things one is hearing about. Once you get beyond this point, you will find people becoming jealous and incredulous. However, the fact is that this institution was set up and approved by our forefathers, and it is my duty to follow the tradition and do my best to meet the wishes and the expectations of every one of you.

'I shall begin by speaking about our ancestors, since it is only right and proper on such an occasion to pay them the honour of recalling what they did. In this land of ours there have always been the same people living from generation to generation up till now, and they, by their courage and their virtues, have handed it on to us, a free country. They certainly deserve our praise. Even more so do our fathers deserve it. For to the inheritance they had received they added all the empire we have now, and it was not without blood and toil that they handed it down to us of the present generation. And then we ourselves, assembled here today, who are mostly in the prime of life, have, in most directions, added to the power of our empire and have organized our State in such a way that it is perfectly well able to look after itself both in peace and in war.

'I have no wish to make a long speech on subjects familiar to you all: so I shall say nothing about the warlike deeds by which we acquired our power or the battles in which we or our fathers gallantly resisted our enemies, Greek or foreign. What I want to do is, in the first place, to discuss the spirit in which we faced our trials and also our constitution and the way of life which has made us great. After that I shall speak in praise of the dead, believing that this kind of speech is not inappropriate to the present occasion, and that this whole assembly, of citizens and foreigners, may listen to it with advantage.

'Let me say that our system of government does not copy the institutions of our neighbours. It is more the case of our being a model to others, than of our imitating anyone else. Our constitution is called a democracy because power is in the hands not of a minority but of the whole people. When it is a question of settling private disputes, everyone is equal before the law; when it is a question of putting one person before another in positions of public responsibility, what counts is not membership of a particular class, but the actual ability which the man possesses. No one, so long as he has it in him to be of service to the state, is kept in political obscurity because of poverty. And, just as our political life is free and open, so is our day-to-day life in our relations with each other. We do not get into a state with our next-door neighbour if he enjoys himself in his own way, nor do we give him the kind of black looks which, though they do no real harm, still do hurt people's feelings. We are free and tolerant in our private lives; but in public affairs we keep to the law. This is because it commands our deep respect.

'We give our obedience to those whom we put in positions of authority, and we obey the laws themselves, especially those which are for the protection of the oppressed, and those unwritten laws which it is an acknowledged shame to break.

'And here is another point. When our work is over, we are in a position to enjoy all kinds of recreation for our spirits. There are various kinds of contests and sacrifices regularly throughout the year; in our own homes we find a beauty and a good taste which delight us every day and which drive away our cares. Then the greatness of our city brings it about that all the good things from all over the world flow in to us, so that to us it seems just as natural to enjoy foreign goods as our own local products.

'Then there is a great difference between us and our opponents, in our attitude towards military security. Here are some examples: Our city is open to the world, and we have no periodical deportations in order to prevent people observing or finding out secrets which might be of military advantage to the enemy. This is because we rely, not on secret weapons, but on our own real courage and loyalty. There is a difference, too, in our educational systems. The Spartans, from their earliest boyhood, are submitted to the most laborious training in courage; we pass our lives without all these restrictions, and yet are just as ready to face the same dangers as they are. Here is a proof of this: When the Spartans invade our land, they do not come by themselves, but bring all their allies with them; whereas we, when we launch an attack abroad, do the job by ourselves, and, though fighting on foreign soil, do not often fail to defeat opponents who are fighting for their own hearths and homes. As a matter of fact none of our enemies has ever yet been confronted with our total strength, because we have to divide our attention between our navy and the many missions on which our troops are sent on land. Yet, if our enemies engage a detachment of our forces and defeat it, they give themselves credit for having thrown back our entire army; or, if they lose, they claim that they were beaten by us in full strength. There are certain advantages, I think, in our way of meeting danger voluntarily, with an easy mind, instead of with a laborious training, with natural rather than with state-induced courage. We do not have to spend our time practising to meet sufferings which are still in the future; and when they are actually upon us we show ourselves just as brave as these others who are always in strict training. This is one point in which, I think, our city deserves to be admired. There are also others:

'Our love of what is beautiful does not lead to extravagance; our love of the things of the mind does not make us soft. We regard wealth as something to be properly used, rather than as something to boast about. As for poverty, no one need be ashamed to admit it: the real shame is in not taking practical measures to escape from it. Here each individual is interested not only in his own affairs but in the affairs of the state as well: even those who are mostly occupied with their own business are extremely well-informed on general politics—this is a peculiarity of ours: we do not say that a man who takes no interest in politics is a

man who minds his own business; we say that he has no business here at all. We Athenians, in our own persons, take our decisions on policy or submit them to proper discussions: for we do not think that there is an incompatibility between words and deeds; the worst thing is to rush into action before the consequences have been properly debated. And this is another point where we differ from other people. We are capable at the same time of taking risks and of estimating them beforehand. Others are brave out of ignorance; and, when they stop to think, they begin to fear. But the man who can most truly be accounted brave is he who best knows the meaning of what is sweet in life and of what is terrible, and then goes out undeterred to meet what is to come.

'Again, in questions of general good feeling there is a great contrast between us and most other people. We make friends by doing good to others, not by receiving good from them. This makes our friendship all the more reliable, since we want to keep alive the gratitude of those who are in our debt by showing continued goodwill to them: whereas the feelings of one who owes us something lack the same enthusiasm, since he knows that, when he repays our kindness, it will be more like paying back a debt than giving something spontaneously. We are unique in this. When we do kindnesses to others, we do not do them out of any calculations of profit or loss: we do them without afterthought, relying on our free liberality. Taking everything together then, I declare that our city is an education to Greece, and I declare that in my opinion each single one of our citizens, in all the manifold aspects of life, is able to show himself the rightful lord and owner of his own person, and do this, moreover, with exceptional grace and exceptional versatility. And to show that this is no empty boasting for the present occasion, but real tangible fact, you have only to consider the power which our city possesses and which has been won by those very qualities which I have mentioned. Athens, alone of the states we know, comes to her testing time in a greatness that surpasses what was imagined of her. In her case, and in her case alone, no invading enemy is ashamed at being defeated, and no subject can complain of being governed by people unfit for their responsibilities. Mighty indeed are the marks and monuments of our empire which we have left. Future ages will wonder at us, as the present age wonders at us now. We do not need the praises of a Homer, or of anyone else whose words may delight us for the moment, but whose estimation of facts will fall short of what is really true. For our adventurous spirit has forced an entry into every sea and into every land; and everywhere we have left behind us everlasting memorials of good done to our friends or suffering inflicted on our enemies.

'This, then, is the kind of city for which these men, who could not bear the thought of losing her, nobly fought and nobly died. It is only natural that every one of us who survive them should be willing to undergo hardships in her service. And it was for this reason that I have spoken at such length about our city, because I wanted to make it clear that for us there is more at stake than there is for others who lack our advantages; also I wanted my words of praise for the dead to be set in the bright light of evidence. And now the most important of these words has been spoken. I have sung the praises of our city; but it was the courage and gallantry of these men, and of people like them, which made her splendid. Nor would you find it true in the case of many of the Greeks, as it is true of them, that no words can do more than justice to their deeds.

'To me it seems that the consummation which has overtaken these men shows us the meaning of manliness in its first revelation and in its final proof. Some of them, no doubt, had their faults; but what we ought to remember first is their gallant conduct against the enemy in defence of their native land. They have blotted out evil with good, and done more service to the commonwealth than they ever did harm in their private lives. No one of these men weakened because he wanted to go on enjoying his wealth: no one put off the awful day in the hope that he might live to escape his poverty and grow rich. More to be desired than such things, they chose to check the enemy's pride. This, to them, was a risk most glorious, and they accepted it, willing to strike down the enemy and relinquish everything else. As for success or failure, they left that in the doubtful hands of Hope, and when the reality of battle was before their faces, they put their trust in their own selves. In the fighting, they thought it more honourable to stand their ground and suffer death than to give in and save their lives. So they fled from the reproaches of men, abiding with life and limb the brunt of battle; and, in a small moment of time, the climax of their lives, a culmination of glory, not of fear, were swept away from us.

'So and such they were, these men—worthy of their city. We who remain behind may hope to be spared their fate, but must resolve to keep the same daring spirit against the foe. It is not simply a question of estimating the advantages in theory. I could tell you a long story (and you know it as well as I do) about what is to be gained by beating the enemy back. What I would prefer is that you should fix your eyes every day on the greatness of Athens as she really is, and should fall in love with her. When you realize her greatness, then reflect that what made her great was men with a spirit of adventure, men who knew their duty, men who were ashamed to fall below a certain standard. If they ever failed in an enterprise, they made up their minds that at any rate the city should not find their courage lacking to her, and they gave to her the best contribution that they could. They gave her their lives, to her and to all of us, and for their own selves they won praises that never grow old, the most splendid of sepulchres—not the sepulchre in which their bodies are laid, but where their glory remains eternal in men's minds, always there on the right occasion to stir others to speech or to action. For famous men have the whole earth as their memorial: it is not only the inscriptions on their graves in their own country that mark them out; no, in foreign lands also, not in any visible form but in people's hearts, their memory abides and grows. It is for you to try to be like them. Make up your minds that happiness depends on being free, and freedom depends on being courageous. Let there be no relaxation in face of the perils of the war. The people who have most excuse for despising death are not the wretched and unfortunate, who have no hope of doing well for themselves, but those who run the risk of a complete reversal in their lives, and who would feel the difference most intensely, if things went wrong for them. Any intelligent man would find a humiliation caused by his own slackness more painful to bear than death, when death comes to him unperceived, in battle, and in the confidence of his patriotism.'

PLATO

from *The Republic*

Book VII (The Allegory of the Cave)

"Next, then," I said, "take the following parable of education and ignorance as a picture of the condition of our nature. Imagine mankind as dwelling in an underground cave with a long entrance open to the light across the whole width of the cave; in this they have been from childhood, with necks and legs fettered, so they have to stay where they are. They cannot move their heads round because of the fetters, and they can only look forward, but light comes to them from fire burning behind them higher up at a distance. Between the fire and the prisoners is a road above their level, and along it imagine a low wall has been built, as puppet showmen have screens in front of their people over which they work their puppets.''

"I see," he said.

"See, then, bearers carrying along this wall all sorts of articles which they hold projecting above the wall, statues of men and other living things, made of stone or wood and all kinds of stuff, some of the bearers speaking and some silent, as you might expect."

"What a remarkable image," he said, "and what remarkable prisoners!"

"Just like ourselves," I said. "For, first of all, tell me this: What do you think such people would have seen of themselves and each other except their shadows, which the fire cast on the opposite wall of the cave?"

"I don't see how they could see anything else," said he, "if they were compelled to keep their heads unmoving all their lives!"

"Very well, what of the things being carried along? Would not this be the same?"

"Of course it would."

"Suppose the prisoners were able to talk together, don't you think that when they named the shadows which they saw passing they would believe they were naming things?"

"Necessarily."

"Then if their prison had an echo from the opposite wall, whenever one of the passing bearers uttered a sound, would they not suppose that the passing shadow must be making the sound? Don't you think so?"

"Indeed I do," he said.

"If so," said I, "such persons would certainly believe that there were no realities except those shadows of handmade things."

"So it must be," said he.

"Now consider," said I, "what their release would be like, and their cure from these fetters and their folly; let us imagine whether it might naturally be something like this. One might be released, and compelled suddenly to stand up and turn his neck round, and to walk and look towards the firelight; all this would hurt him, and he would be too much dazzled to see distinctly those things whose shadows he had seen before. What do you think he would say, if someone told him that what he saw before was foolery, but now he saw more rightly, being a bit nearer reality and turned towards what was a little more real? What if he were shown each of the passing things, and compelled by questions to answer what each one was? Don't you think he would be puzzled, and believe what he saw before was more true than what was shown to him now?"

"Far more," he said.

"Then suppose he were compelled to look towards the real light, it would hurt his eyes, and he would escape by turning them away to the things which he was able to look at, and these he would believe to be clearer than what was being shown to him."

"Just so," said he.

"Suppose, now," said I, "that someone should drag him thence by force, up the rough ascent, the steep way up, and never stop until he could drag him out into the light of the sun, would he not be distressed and furious at being dragged; and when he came into the light, the brilliance would fill his eyes and he would not be able to see even one of the things now called real?"

"That he would not," said he, "all of a sudden."

"He would have to get used to it, surely, I think, if he is to see the things above. First he would most easily look at shadows, after that images of mankind and the rest in water, lastly the things themselves. After this he would find it easier to survey by night the heavens themselves and all that is in them, gazing at the light of the stars and moon, rather than by day the sun and the sun's light."

"Of course."

"Last of all, I suppose, the sun; he could look on the sun itself by itself in its own place, and see what it is like, not reflections of it in water or as it appears in some alien setting."

"Necessarily," said he.

"And only after all this he might reason about it, how this is he who provides seasons and years, and is set over all there is in the visible region, and he is in a manner the cause of all things which they saw."

"Yes, it is clear," said he, "that after all that, he would come to this last."

"Very good. Let him be reminded of his first habitation, and what was wisdom in that place, and of his fellow-prisoners there; don't you think he would bless himself for the change, and pity them?"

"Yes, indeed."

"And if there were honours and praises among them and prizes for the one who saw the passing things most sharply and remembered best which of them used to come before and which after and which together, and from these was best able to prophesy accordingly what was going to come—do you believe he would set his desire on that, and envy those who were honoured men or potentates among them? Would he not feel as Homer says, and heartily desire rather to be serf of some landless man on earth and to endure anything in the world, rather than to opine as they did and to live in that way?"

"Yes, indeed," said he, "he would rather accept anything than live like that."

"Then again," I said, "just consider; if such a one should go down again and sit on his old seat, would he not get his eyes full of darkness coming in suddenly out of the sun?"

"Very much so," said he.

"And if he should have to compete with those who had been always prisoners, by laying down the law about those shadows while he was blinking before his eyes were settled down—and it would take a good long time to get used to things—wouldn't they all laugh at him and say he had spoiled his eyesight by going up there, and it was not worth-while so much as to try to go up? And would they not kill anyone who tried to release them and take them up, if they could somehow lay hands on him and kill him?"

"That they would!" said he.

"Then we must apply this image, my dear Glaucon," said I, "to all we have been saying. The world of our sight is like the habitation in prison, the firelight there to the sunlight here, the ascent and the view of the upper world is the rising of the soul into the world of mind; put it so and you will not be far from my own surmise, since that is what you want to hear; but God knows if it is really true. At least, what appears to me is, that in the world of the known, last of all, is the idea of the good, and with what toil to be seen! And seen, this must be inferred to be the cause of all right and beautiful things for all, which gives birth to light and the king of light in the world of sight, and, in the world of mind, herself the queen produces truth and reason; and she must be seen by one who is to act with reason publicly or privately."

PLATO
from *Phaedo*

[Socrates is speaking.] "Now then, I want to give the proof at once, to you as my judges, why I think it likely that one who has spent his life in philosophy should be confident when he is going to die, and have good hopes that he will win the greatest blessings in the next world when he has ended: so Simmias and Cebes my judges, I will try to show how this could be true.

"The fact is, those who tackle philosophy aright are simply and solely practising dying, practising death, all the time, but nobody sees it. If this is true, then it would surely be unreasonable that they should earnestly do this and nothing else all their lives, yet when death comes they should object to what they had been so long earnestly practising."

Simmias laughed at this, and said, "I don't feel like laughing just now, Socrates, but you have made me laugh. I think the many if they heard that would say, 'That's a good one for the philosophers!' And other people in my city would heartily agree that philosophers are really suffering from a wish to die, and now they have found them out, that they richly deserve it!"

"That would be true, Simmias," said Socrates, "except the words 'found out.' For they have not found out in what sense the real philosophers wish to die and deserve to die, and what kind of death it is. Let us say good-bye to them," he went on, "and ask ourselves: Do we think there is such a thing as death?"

"Certainly," Simmias put in.

"Is it anything more than the separation of the soul from the body?" said Socrates. "Death is, that the body separates from the soul, and remains by itself apart from the soul, and the soul, separated from the body, exists by itself apart from the body. Is death anything but that?"

"No," he said, "that is what death is."

"Then consider, my good friend, if you agree with me here, for I think this is the best way to understand the question we are examining. Do you think it the part of a philosopher to be earnestly concerned with what are called pleasures, such as these—eating and drinking, for example?"

"Not at all," said Simmias.

"The pleasures of love, then?"

"Oh no."

"Well, do you suppose a man like that regards the other bodily indulgences as precious? Getting fine clothes and shoes and other bodily adornments—ought he to price them high or low, beyond whatever share of them it is absolutely necessary to have?"

"Low, I think," he said, "if he is a true philosopher."

"Then in general," he said, "do you think that such a man's concern is not for the body, but as far as he can he stands aloof from that and turns towards the soul?"

"I do."

"Then firstly, is it not clear that in such things the philosopher as much as possible sets free the soul from communion with the body, more than other men?"

"So it appears."

"And I suppose, Simmias, it must seem to most men that he who has no pleasure in such things and takes no share in them does not deserve to live, but he is getting pretty close to death if he does not care about pleasures which he has by means of the body."

"Quite true, indeed."

"Well then, what about the actual getting of wisdom? Is the body in the way or not, if a man takes it with him as companion in the search? I mean, for example, is there any truth for men in their sight and hearing? Or as poets are forever dinning into our ears, do we hear nothing and see nothing exactly? Yet if these of our bodily senses are not exact and clear, the others will hardly be, for they are all inferior to these, don't you think so?"

"Certainly," he said.

"Then," said he, "when does the soul get hold of the truth? For whenever the soul tries to examine anything in company with the body, it is plain that it is deceived by it."

"Quite true."

"Then is it not clear that in reasoning, if anywhere, something of the realities becomes visible to it?"

"Yes."

"And I suppose it reasons best when none of these senses disturbs it, hearing or sight, or pain, or pleasure indeed, but when it is completely by itself and says good-bye to the body, and so far as possible has no dealings with it, when it reaches out and grasps that which really is."

"That is true."

"And is it not then that the philosopher's soul chiefly holds the body cheap and escapes from it, while it seeks to be by itself?"

"So it seems."

"Let us pass on, Simmias. Do we say there is such a thing as justice by itself, or not?"

"We do say so, certainly!"

"Such a thing as the good and beautiful?"

"Of course!"

"And did you ever see one of them with your eyes?"

"Never," said he.

"By any other sense of those the body has did you ever grasp them? I mean all such things, greatness, health, strength, in short everything that really is the nature of things whatever they are: Is it through the body that the real truth is perceived? Or is this better—whoever of us prepares himself most completely and most exactly to comprehend each thing which he examines would come nearest to knowing each one?"

"Certainly."

"And would he do that most purely who should approach each with his intelligence alone, not adding sight to intelligence, or dragging in any other sense along with reasoning, but using the intelligence uncontaminated alone by itself, while he tries to hunt out each essence uncontaminated, keeping clear of eyes and ears and, one might say, of the whole body, because he thinks the body disturbs him and hinders the soul from getting possession of truth and wisdom when body and soul are companions—is not this the man, Simmias, if anyone, who will hit reality?"

"Nothing could be more true, Socrates," said Simmias.

"Then from all this," said Socrates, "genuine philosophers must come to some such opinion as follows, so as to make to one another statements such as these: 'A sort of direct path, so to speak, seems to take us to the conclusion that so long as we have the body with us in our enquiry, and our soul is mixed up with so great an evil, we shall never attain sufficiently what we desire, and that, we say, is the truth. For the body provides thousands of busy distractions because of its necessary food; besides, if diseases fall upon us, they hinder us from the pursuit of the real. With loves and desires and fears and all kinds of fancies and much rubbish, it infects us, and really and truly makes us, as they say, unable to think one little bit about anything at any time. Indeed, wars and factions and battles all come from the body and its desires, and from nothing else. For the desire of getting wealth causes all wars, and we are compelled to desire wealth by the body, being slaves to its culture; therefore we have no leisure for philosophy, from all these reasons. Chief of all is that if we do have some leisure, and turn away from the body to speculate on something, in our searches it is everywhere interfering, it causes confusion and disturbance, and dazzles us so that it will not let us see the truth; so in fact we see that if we are ever to know anything purely we must get rid of it, and examine the real things by the soul alone; and then, it seems, after we are dead, as the reasoning shows, not while we live, we shall possess that which we desire, lovers of which we say we are, namely wisdom. For if it is impossible in company with the body to know anything purely, one thing of two follows: either knowledge is possible nowhere, or only after death; for then alone the soul will be quite by itself apart from the body, but not before. And while we are alive, we shall be nearest to knowing, as it seems, if as far as possible we have no commerce or communion with the body which is not absolutely necessary, and if we are not infected with its nature, but keep ourselves pure from it, until God himself shall set us free. And so, pure and rid of the body's foolishness, we shall probably be in the company of those like ourselves, and shall know through our own selves complete incontamination, and that is perhaps the truth. But for the impure to grasp the pure is not, it seems, allowed.' So we must think, Simmias, and so we must say to one another, all who are rightly lovers of learning; don't you agree?"

"Assuredly, Socrates."

"Then," said Socrates, "if this is true, my comrade, there is great hope that when I arrive where I am travelling, there if anywhere I shall sufficiently possess that for which all our study has been pursued in this past life. So the journey which has been commanded for me is made with good hope, and

the same for any other man who believes he has got his mind purified, as I may call it."

"Certainly," replied Simmias.

"And is not purification really that which has been mentioned so often in our discussion, to separate as far as possible the soul from the body, and to accustom it to collect itself together out of the body in every part, and to dwell alone by itself as far as it can, both at this present and in the future, being freed from the body as if from a prison?"

"By all means," said he.

"Then is not this called death—a freeing and separation of soul from body?"

"Not a doubt of that," said he.

"But to set it free, as we say, is the chief endeavour of those who rightly love wisdom, nay of those alone, and the very care and practice of the philosophers is nothing but the freeing and separation of soul from body, don't you think so?"

"It appears to be so."

"Then, as I said at first, it would be absurd for a man preparing himself in his life to be as near as possible to death, so to live, and then when death came, to object?"

"Of course."

"Then in fact, Simmias," he said, "those who rightly love wisdom are practising dying, and death to them is the least terrible thing in the world. Look at it in this way: If they are everywhere at enmity with the body, and desire the soul to be alone by itself, and if, when this very thing happens, they shall fear and object—would not that be wholly unreasonable? Should they not willingly go to a place where there is good hope of finding what they were in love with all through life (and they loved wisdom), and of ridding themselves of the companion which they hated? When human favourites and wives and sons have died, many have been willing to go down to the grave, drawn by the hope of seeing there those they used to desire, and of being with them; but one who is really in love with wisdom and holds firm to this same hope, that he will find it in the grave, and nowhere else worth speaking of—will he then fret at dying and not go thither rejoicing? We must surely think, my comrade, that he will go rejoicing, if he is really a philosopher; he will surely believe that he will find wisdom in its purity there and there alone. If this is true, would it not be most unreasonable, as I said just now, if such a one feared death?"

"Unreasonable, I do declare," said he. . . .

With these words, he got up and retired into another room for the bath, and Criton went after him, telling us to wait. So we waited discussing and talking together about what had been said, or sometimes speaking of the great misfortune which had befallen us, for we felt really as if we had lost a father and had to spend the rest of our lives as orphans. When he had bathed, and his children had been brought to see him—for he had two little sons, and one big—and when the women of his family had come, he talked to them before Criton and gave what instructions he wished. Then he asked the women and children to go, and came back to us. It was now near sunset, for he had spent a long time within. He came and sat down after his bath, and he had not talked long after this when the servant of the Eleven came in, and standing by him said, "O Socrates! I have not to complain of you as I do of others, that they are angry with me, and curse me, because I bring them word to drink their potion, which my officers make me do! But I have always found you in this time most generous and gentle, and the best man who ever came here. And now too, I know well you are not angry with me, for you know who are responsible, and you keep it for them. Now you know what I came to tell you, so farewell, and try to bear as well as you can what can't be helped."

Then he turned and was going out, with tears running down his cheeks. And Socrates looked up at him and said, "Farewell to you also, I will do so." Then, at the same time turning to us, "What a nice fellow!" he said. "All the time he has been coming and talking to me, a real good sort, and now how generously he sheds tears for me! Come along, Criton, let's obey him. Someone bring the potion, if the stuff has been ground; if not, let the fellow grind it."

Then Criton said, "But Socrates, I think the sun is still over the hills, it has not set yet. Yes, and I know of others who, having been told to drink the poison, have done it very late; they had dinner first and a good one, and some enjoyed the company of any they wanted. Please don't be in a hurry, there is time to spare."

But Socrates said, "Those you speak of have very good reason for doing that, for they think they will gain by doing it; and I have good reasons why I won't do it. For I think I shall gain nothing by drinking a little later, only that I shall think myself a fool for clinging to life and sparing when the cask's empty. Come along," he said, "do what I tell you, if you please."

And Criton, hearing this, nodded to the boy who stood near. The boy went out, and after spending a long time, came in with the man who was to give the poison carrying it ground ready in a cup. Socrates caught sight of the man and said, "Here, my good man, you know about these things; what must I do?"

"Just drink it," he said, "and walk about till your legs get heavy, then lie down. In that way the drug will act of itself."

At the same time, he held out the cup to Socrates, and he took it quite cheerfully, Echecrates, not a tremble, not a change in colour or looks; but looking full at the man under his brows, as he used to do, he asked him, "What do you say about this drink? What of a libation to someone? Is that allowed, or not?"

He said, "We only grind so much as we think enough for a moderate potion."

"I understand," he said, "but at least, I suppose, it is allowed to offer a prayer to the gods and that must be done, for good luck in the migration from here to there. Then that is my prayer, and so may it be!"

With these words he put the cup to his lips and, quite easy and contented, drank it up. So far most of us had been able to hold back our tears pretty well; but when we saw him begin drinking and end drinking, we could no longer. I burst into a flood of tears for all I could do, so I wrapped up my face and cried myself out; not for him indeed, but for my own misfortune in losing such a man and such a comrade. Criton had got up and gone out even before I did, for he could not hold the tears in. Apollodoros had never ceased weeping all this time, and now he burst out into loud sobs, and by his weeping and lamentations completely broke down every man there except Socrates himself. He only said, "What a scene! You amaze me. That's just why I sent the women away, to keep them from making a scene like this. I've heard that one ought to make an end in decent silence. Quiet yourselves and endure."

When we heard him we felt ashamed and restrained our tears. He walked about, and when he said that his legs were feeling heavy, he lay down on his back, as the man told him to do; at the same time the one who gave him the potion felt him, and after a while examined his feet and legs; then pinching a foot hard, he asked if he felt anything; he said no. After this, again, he pressed the shins; and, moving up like this, he showed us that he was growing cold and stiff. Again he felt him, and told us that when it came to his heart, he would be gone. Already the cold had come nearly as far as the abdomen, when Socrates threw off the covering from his face—for he had covered it over—and said, the last words he uttered, "Criton," he said, "we owe a cock to Asclepios; pay it without fail."

"That indeed shall be done," said Criton. "Have you anything more to say?"

When Criton had asked this, Socrates gave no further answer, but after a little time, he stirred, and the man uncovered him, and his eyes were still. Criton, seeing this, closed the mouth and eyelids.

This was the end of our comrade, Echecrates, a man, as we would say, of all then living we had ever met, the noblest and the wisest and most just.

ARISTOTLE
from *On the Art of Poetry*

The Objects of Poetic Imitation

Since imitative artists represent men in action, and men who are necessarily either of good or of bad character (for as all people differ in their moral nature according to the degree of their goodness or badness, characters almost always fall into one or other of these types), these men must be represented either as better than we are, or worse, or as the same kind of people as ourselves. Thus among the painters Polygnotus represented his subjects as better, and Pauson as worse, while Dionysius painted them just as they were. It is clear that each of the kinds of imitation I have referred to will admit of these variations, and they will differ in this way according to the differences in the objects they represent. Such diversities may occur even in dancing, and in music, for the flute and the lyre; they occur also in the art that is based on language, whether it uses prose or verse unaccompanied by music. Homer, for example, depicts the better types of men, and Cleophon normal types, while Hegemon of Thasos, the first writer of parodies, and Nicochares, the author of the *Deiliad*, show them in a bad light. The same thing happens in dithyrambic and nomic poetry; for instance, the Cyclops might be represented in different ways, as was done by Timotheus and Philoxenus. This is the difference that marks the distinction between comedy and tragedy; for comedy aims at representing men as worse than they are nowadays, tragedy as better. . . .

The Rise of Comedy. Epic Compared with Tragedy

As I have remarked, comedy represents the worse types of men; worse, however, not in the sense that it embraces any and every kind of badness, but in the sense that the ridiculous is a species of ugliness or badness. For the ridiculous consists in some form of error or ugliness that is not painful or injurious; the comic mask, for example, is distorted and ugly, but causes no pain. . . .

Unity of Plot

A plot does not possess unity, as some people suppose, merely because it is about one man. Many things, countless things indeed, may happen to one man, and some of them will not contribute to any kind of unity; and similarly he may carry out many actions from which no single unified action will emerge. It seems, therefore, that all those poets have been on the wrong track who have written a *Heracleid*, or a *Theseid*, or some other poem of this kind, in the belief that, Heracles being a single person, his story must necessarily possess unity. Homer, exceptional in this as in all other respects, seems, whether by art or by instinct, to have been well aware of what was required. In writing his *Odyssey* he did not put in everything that happened to Odysseus, that he was wounded on Mount Parnassus, for example, or that he feigned madness at the time of the call to arms, for it was not a matter of necessity or probability that either of these incidents should have led to the other; on the contrary, he constructed the *Odyssey* round a single action of the kind I have spoken of, and he did this with the *Iliad* too. Thus, just as in the other imitative arts each individual representation is the presentation of a single object, so too the plot of a play, being the representation of an action, must present it as a unified whole; and its various incidents must be so arranged that if any one of them is differently placed or taken away the effect of wholeness will be seriously disrupted. For if the presence or absence of something makes no apparent difference, it is no real part of the whole.

Poetic Truth and Historical Truth

It will be clear from what I have said that it is not the poet's function to describe what has actually happened, but the kinds of thing that might happen, that is, that could happen because they are, in the circumstances, either probable or necessary. The difference between the historian and the poet is not that the one writes in prose and the other in verse; the work of Herodotus might be put into verse, and in this metrical form it would be no less a kind of history than it is without metre. The difference is that the one tells of what has happened, the other of the kinds of things that might happen. For this reason poetry is something more philosophical and more worthy of serious attention than history; for while poetry is concerned with universal truths, history treats of particular facts.

By universal truths are to be understood the kinds of thing a certain type of person will probably or necessarily say or do in a given situation; and this is the aim of poetry, although it gives individual names to its characters. The particular facts of the historian are what, say, Alcibiades did, or what happened to him. By now this distinction has become clear where comedy is concerned, for comic poets build up their plots out of probable occurrences, and then add any names that occur to them: they do not, like the iambic poets, write about actual people. In tragedy, on the other hand, the authors keep to the names of real people, the reason being that what is possible is credible. Whereas we cannot be certain of the possibility of something that has not happened, what has happened is obviously possible, for it would not have happened if this had not been so. Nevertheless, even in some tragedies only one or two of the names are well known, and the rest are fictitious; and indeed there are some in which nothing is familiar, Agathon's *Antheus*, for example, in which both the incidents and the names are fictitious, and the play is none the less well liked for that. It is not necessary, therefore, to keep entirely to the traditional stories which form the subjects of our tragedies. Indeed it would be absurd to do so, since even the familiar stories are familiar only to a few, and yet they please everybody.

What I have said makes it obvious that the poet must be a maker of plots rather than of verses, since he is a poet by virtue of his representation, and what he represents is actions. And even if he writes about things that have actually happened, that does not make him any the less a poet, for there is nothing to prevent some of the things that have happened from being in accordance with the laws of possibility and probability, and thus he will be a poet in writing about them.

Of simple plots and actions those that are episodic are the worst. By an episodic plot I mean one in which the sequence of the episodes is neither probable nor necessary. Plays of this kind are written by bad poets because they cannot help it, and by good poets because of the actors; writing for the dramatic competitions, they often strain a plot beyond the bounds of possibility, and are thus obliged to dislocate the continuity of events.

However, tragedy is the representation not only of a complete action, but also of incidents that awaken fear and pity, and effects of this kind are heightened when things happen unexpectedly as well as logically, for then they will be more remarkable than if they seem merely mechanical or accidental. Indeed, even chance occurrences seem most remarkable when they have the appearance of having been brought about by design—when, for example, the statue of Mitys at Argos killed the man who had caused Mitys's death by falling down on him at a public entertainment. Things like this do not seem mere chance occurrences. Thus plots of this type are necessarily better than others.

Simple and Complex Plots

Some plots are simple, and some complex, for the obvious reason that the actions of which they are representations are of one or other of these kinds. By a simple action I refer to one which is single and continuous in the sense of my earlier definition, and in which the change of fortune comes about without a reversal or a discovery. A complex action is one in which the change is accompanied by a discovery or a reversal, or both. These should develop out of the very structure of the plot, so that they are the inevitable or probable consequence of what has gone before, for there is a big difference between what happens as a result of something else and what merely happens after it.

====

Reversal, Discovery, and Calamity

As has already been noted, a reversal is a change from one state of affairs to its opposite, one which conforms, as I have said, to probability or necessity. In *Oedipus*, for example, the Messenger who came to cheer Oedipus and relieve him of his fear about his mother did the very opposite by revealing to him who he was. In the *Lynceus*, again, Lynceus is being led off to execution, followed by Danaus who is to kill him, when, as a result of events that occurred earlier, it comes about that he is saved and it is Danaus who is put to death.

As the word itself indicates, a discovery is a change from ignorance to knowledge, and it leads either to love or to hatred between persons destined for good or ill fortune. The most effective form of discovery is that which is accompanied by reversals, like the one in *Oedipus*. There are of course other forms of discovery, for what I have described may happen in relation to inanimate and trifling objects, and moreover it is possible to discover whether a person has done something or not. But the form of discovery most essentially related to the plot and action of the play is the one described above,

for a discovery of this kind in combination with a reversal will carry with it either pity or fear, and it is such actions as these that, according to my definition, tragedy represents; and further, such a combination is likely to lead to a happy or an unhappy ending.

As it is persons who are involved in the discovery, it may be that only one person's identity is revealed to another, that of the second being already known. Sometimes, however, a natural recognition of two parties is necessary, as for example, when the identity of Iphigenia was made known to Orestes by the sending of the letter, and a second discovery was required to make him known to Iphigenia.

Two elements of plot, then, reversal and discovery, turn upon such incidents as these. A third is suffering, or calamity. Of these three, reversal and discovery have already been defined. A calamity is an action of a destructive or painful nature, such as death openly represented, excessive suffering, wounding, and the like. . . .

====

Tragic Action

Following upon the points I have already made, I must go on to say what is to be aimed at and what guarded against in the construction of plots, and what are the sources of the tragic effect.

We saw that the structure of tragedy at its best should be complex, not simple, and that it should represent actions capable of awakening fear and pity—for this is a characteristic function of representations of this type. It follows in the first place that good men should not be shown passing from prosperity to misery, for this does not inspire fear or pity, it merely disgusts us. Nor should evil men be shown progressing from misery to prosperity. This is the most untragic of all plots, for it has none of the requisites of tragedy; it does not appeal to our humanity, or awaken pity or fear in us. Nor again should an utterly worthless man be seen falling from prosperity into misery. Such a course might indeed play upon our humane feelings, but it would not arouse either pity or fear; for our pity is awakened by undeserved misfortune, and our fear by that of someone just like ourselves—pity for the undeserving sufferer and fear for the man like ourselves—so that the situation in question would have nothing in it either pitiful or fearful.

There remains a mean between these extremes. This is the sort of man who is not conspicuous for virtue and justice,

and whose fall into misery is not due to vice and depravity, but rather to some error, a man who enjoys prosperity and a high reputation, like Oedipus and Thyestes and other famous members of families like theirs.

Inevitably, then, the well-conceived plot will have a single interest, and not, as some say, a double. The change in fortune will be, not from misery to prosperity, but the reverse, from prosperity to misery, and it will be due, not to depravity, but to some great error either in such a man as I have described or in one better than this, but not worse. This is borne out by existing practice. For at first the poets treated any stories that came to hand, but nowadays the best tragedies are written about a handful of families, those of Alcmaeon, for example, and Oedipus and Orestes and Meleager and Thyestes and Telephus, and others whom it has befallen to suffer or inflict terrible experiences.

The best tragedies in the technical sense are constructed in this way. Those critics are on the wrong tack, therefore, who criticize Euripides for following such a procedure in his tragedies, and complain that many of them end in misfortune; for, as I have said, this is the right ending. The strongest evidence of this is that on the stage and in the dramatic competitions plays of this kind, when properly worked out, are the most tragic of all, and Euripides, faulty as is his management of other points, is nevertheless regarded as the most tragic of our dramatic poets.

The next best type of structure, ranked first by some critics, is that which, like the *Odyssey*, has a double thread of plot, and ends in opposite ways for the good and the bad characters. It is considered the best only because of the feeble judgement of the audience, for the poets pander to the taste of the spectators. But this is not the pleasure that is proper to tragedy. It belongs rather to comedy, where those who have been the bitterest of enemies in the original story, Orestes and Aegisthus, for example, go off at the end as friends, and nobody is killed by anybody.

Fear and Pity

Fear and pity may be excited by means of spectacle; but they can also take their rise from the very structure of the action, which is the preferable method and the mark of a better dramatic poet. For the plot should be so ordered that even without seeing it performed anyone merely hearing what is afoot will shudder with fear and pity as a result of what is happening—as indeed would be the experience of anyone hearing the story of Oedipus. To produce this effect by means of stage-spectacle is less artistic, and requires the cooperation of the producer. Those who employ spectacle to produce an effect, not of fear, but of something merely monstrous, have nothing to do with tragedy, for not every kind of pleasure should be demanded of tragedy, but only that which is proper to it; and since the dramatic poet has by means of his representation to produce the tragic pleasure that is associated with pity and fear, it is obvious that this effect is bound up with the events of the plot.

Let us now consider what kinds of incident are to be regarded as fearful or pitiable. Deeds that fit this description must of course involve people who are either friends to one another, or enemies, or neither. Now if a man injures his enemy, there is nothing pitiable either in his act or in his intention, except in so far as suffering is inflicted; nor is there if they are indifferent to each other. But when the sufferings involve those who are near and dear to one another, when for example brother kills brother, son father, mother son, or son mother, or if such a deed is contemplated, or something else of the kind is actually done, then we have a situation of the kind to be aimed at. Thus it will not do to tamper with the traditional stories, the murder of Clytemnestra by Orestes, for instance, and that of Eriphyle by Alcmaeon; on the other hand, the poet must use his imagination and handle the traditional material effectively.

I must explain more clearly what I mean by 'effectively.' The deed may be done by characters acting consciously and in full knowledge of the facts, as was the way of the early dramatic poets, when for instance Euripides made Medea kill her children. Or they may do it without realizing the horror of the deed until later, when they discover the truth; this is what Sophocles did with Oedipus. Here indeed the relevant incident occurs outside the action of the play; but it may be a part of the tragedy, as with Alcmaeon in Astydamas's play, or Telegonus in *The Wounded Odysseus*. A third alternative is for someone who is about to do a terrible deed in ignorance of the relationship to discover the truth before he does it. These are the only possibilities, for the deed must either be done or not done, and by someone either with or without knowledge of the facts.

The least acceptable of these alternatives is when someone in possession of the facts is on the point of acting but fails to do so, for this merely shocks us, and, since no suffering is involved, it is not tragic. Hence nobody is allowed to behave like this, or only seldom, as when Haemon fails to kill Creon in the *Antigone*. Next in order of effectiveness is when the deed is actually done, and here it is better that the character should act in ignorance and only learn the truth afterwards, for there is nothing in this to outrage our feelings, and the revelation comes as a surprise. However, the best method is the last, when, for example, in the *Cresphontes* Merope intends to kill her son, but recognizes him and does not do so; or when the same thing happens with brother and sister in *Iphigenia in Tauris*; or when, in the *Helle*, the son recognizes his mother when he is just about to betray her.

This then is the reason why, as I said before, our tragedies keep to a few families. For in their search for dramatic material it was by chance rather than by technical knowledge that the poets discovered how to gain tragic effects in their plots. And they are still obliged to have recourse to those families in which sufferings of the kind I have described have been experienced.

I have said enough now about the arrangement of the incidents in a tragedy and the type of plot it ought to have.

The Characters of Tragedy

In characterization there are four things to aim at. First and foremost, the characters should be good. Now character will be displayed, as I have pointed out, if some preference is revealed in speech or action, and if it is a preference for what is good the character will be good. There can be goodness in every class of person; for instance, a woman or a slave may be good, though the one is possibly an inferior being and the other in general an insignificant one.

In the second place the portrayal should be appropriate. For example, a character may possess manly qualities, but it is not appropriate that a female character should be given manliness or cleverness.

Thirdly, the characters should be lifelike. This is not the same thing as making them good, or appropriate in the sense in which I have used the word.

And fourthly, they should be consistent. Even if the person who is being represented is inconsistent, and this trait is the basis of his character, he must nevertheless be portrayed as consistently inconsistent.

As an example of unnecessary badness of character, there is Menelaus in the *Orestes.* The character who behaves in an unsuitable and inappropriate way is exemplified in Odysseus' lament in the *Scylla,* and in Melanippe's speech. An inconsistent character is shown in *Iphigenia at Aulis,* for Iphigenia as a suppliant is quite unlike what she is later.

As in the arrangement of the incidents, so too in characterization one must always bear in mind what will be either necessary or probable; in other words, it should be necessary or probable that such and such a person should say or do such and such a thing, and similarly that this particular incident should follow on that.

Furthermore, it is obvious that the unravelling of the plot should arise from the circumstances of the plot itself, and not be brought about *ex machina,* as is done in the *Medea* and in the episode of the embarkation in the *Iliad.* The *deus ex machina* should be used only for matters outside the play proper, either for things that happened before it and that cannot be known by the human characters, or for things that are yet to come and that require to be foretold prophetically—for we allow to the gods the power to see all things. However, there should be nothing inexplicable about what happens, or if there must be, it should be kept outside the tragedy, as is done in Sophocles's *Oedipus.*

Since tragedy is a representation of people who are better than average, we must copy the good portrait-painters. These, while reproducing the distinctive appearance of their sitters and making likenesses, paint them better-looking than they are. In the same way the poet, in portraying men who are hot-tempered, or phlegmatic, or who have other defects of character, must bring out these qualities in them, and at the same time show them as decent people, as Agathon and Homer have portrayed Achilles.

These points must be carefully watched, as too must those means used to appeal to the eye, which are necessarily dependent on the poet's art; for here too it is often possible to make mistakes. However, enough has been said about these matters in my published works.

Chapter

4

Classical Greek Civilization:
The Hellenistic Age

MENANDER

from *The Woman of Samos*

Act III

[Demeas is preparing for his son Moschion's wedding. Moschion is marrying the woman he accidentally impregnated. The child was born while his father was travelling. Fearing parental wrath at his premarital indiscretions, Moschion has concocted a scheme with Chrysis (Demeas's consort) to convince Demeas the baby is really his, by Chrysis. However, the plot thickens when Demeas overhears a conversation, as he relates here.—Ed.]

(Demeas comes out of his house with an elaborate show of being casual, and walks downstage. Suddenly shedding his casual air, he addresses the audience in great perturbation. His opening words have been lost.)

DEMEAS . . . the hurricane that suddenly comes out of the blue during a calm voyage—you're sailing along under clear skies, and it smashes right into you and over you go. Sometimes like that is what I'm going through right now. I'm the one who's holding the wedding, who's appeasing all the gods, who just a while ago was having things go exactly the way I wanted—my god, right now I'm not sure any longer whether I can see straight! I'm here before you with a sudden aching hurt in my heart. (*Shaking his head in bewilderment*) It's incredible! Look here. Am I in my right mind? Or am I crazy and, because I jumped to all the wrong conclusions a moment ago, heading for disaster for no good reason?

(*Visibly getting hold of himself, in calmer tones*) As soon as I went inside, since I was very anxious to get on with the wedding, I simply announced to the servants what was going to happen and ordered them to make all the necessary preparations—clean up, do the baking, get everything set for the ceremony. Things were getting done, all right, but naturally, there was some confusion because of the rush. The baby had been sort of left on a couch out of the way and was screaming its head off. And everybody was hollering at the same time: (*imitating the voices*) "Bring some flour. Bring some water. Bring some oil. Bring some charcoal." I pitched in myself and helped hand things out. That's how I happened to go into the pantry and, since I was busy there picking out extra supplies and looking things over, I didn't come right out. Well, while I was in there, one of the women came down from the second floor into the room in front of the pantry. We do our weaving there, and you have to go through it either to get to the staircase or the pantry. It was an old woman who used to be Moschion's nanny; she was one of my slaves until I freed her. She saw the baby screaming away because nobody was minding it and, having no idea that I was inside and that she ought to watch out what she was saying, she goes up to it and starts to talk to it the way they do (*imitating her*): "Sweet little baby," and "My precious, where's your mommy?" And she kissed it and rocked it and, when it stopped crying, she says to herself, "Dear me! It seems just yesterday that I was petting and nursing Moschion when he was no bigger than this, and now he's got a baby of his own." [Two or three lines are lost here.]

While she was prattling on, one of the serving girls came running in, and the old one shouts at her: "Here you! Give this baby a bath! What is this? His own father's getting married, and you're not giving his little one the least bit of attention! Right away the other one whispers to her (*dropping his voice and imitating her*), "What are you talking so loud for, you poor fool? *He's in there.*" "No! Where?" "In the pantry!" And then, speaking in her natural voice, she says (*raising his voice*), "Nurse, Chrysis is calling for you" and "Hurry, run along," and then (*lowering it again*), "We're in luck, he hasn't heard anything." So the old one scuttled off somewhere

mumbling to herself (*mimicking her*), "Dear me, this big mouth of mine!"

Then I came out, very calmly, just as you saw me come out a moment ago, acting as if I hadn't heard or didn't know a thing. And, right outside, what do I see? Chrysis herself with the baby, nursing it. So one thing we know for certain: it's her baby. But who the father is, I or—no, gentlemen, I'm not going to say it to you, I'm not even going to suspect it. I'm reporting the facts, what I heard with my own ears. I'm not angry with anybody—not yet. (*As the calm he has been struggling to maintain starts to desert him, emphatically*) Good god, I know that boy of mine; he's always been thoroughly decent, always been as considerate toward me as any son could be. (*Shakes his head worriedly.*) Yet, when I consider that it was his old nanny who said it and that it was something I wasn't supposed to hear, and when I look back at the way that woman of mine fondled the child and forced me to let her keep it against my will—I can go out of my mind! (*Looks toward the wings, stage left, and sees someone approaching.*) Good—here comes Parmeno back from the market just in time. But first I've got to let him take in the help he's brought back with him. . . .

THEOCRITUS

from *The Idylls*

The Cyclops

I have learnt that there can be no remedy for love,
No special herb or ointment to soothe the heart
Except the Muses. It is light and quick, their drug,
And works for all, but is very hard to find.
I think you know this, Nicias, without my saying,
Since you are doctor and poet, a child of the Nine.
My simple countryman, Polyphemus the Cyclops,
Discovered this long ago when he loved Galatea
And down spread over his cheeks and round his mouth.
His was no game of love-locks and little gifts
But a pure madness that shut out all other thoughts.
His flock would come home to the cave unshepherded
From the green pasture, while he would be off by himself
All day, singing up the dawn on the weedstrewn shore
And pining for Galatea as he nursed the wound
Which the dart from Cypris had cut into his bowels.
Gazing seaward from the high rock where he sat
He found and applied the one remedy.

This was his song:

* * *

Galatea, why do you treat your lover harshly?
You are whiter than ricotta, gentler than a lamb,

Livelier than a calf, firmer than an unripe grape.
You wait until sleep takes hold of me to come here
And when sleep lets me go, then you slip away
As if you were a sheep and I the great grey wolf.
I fell in love with you, girl, on your first visit.
You came with my mother, wanting to gather orchids
In the hill-meadows. It was I who showed the way.
To you it meant nothing at all. But to me the moment
When I set eyes on you lasts from that day to this.
You slip away from me, girl, unreachably graceful.
No need to say the reason: this shaggy eyebrow
Which stretches from ear to ear across my forehead;
This single eye and flattened nose, these lips.
But fine looks could not buy me the flock I graze,
A thousand strong, nor the milk I draw and drink
Nor the cheese which lasts through summer into autumn
And loads the racks down even to winter's end.
No other Cyclops plays the pipe as I can,
Singing far into the night, my silver pippin,
Of you and me. For your amusement I rear
Four bear-cubs and eleven fawns with dappled coats.
Come to me then. You will never wish yourself back.
Let the green sea waste its anger on the shore:

Night spent in the cave beside me is far more sweet.
Baytrees and slender cypresses grow there, ivy
With its dark leaves and vines with sugary grapes.
Fresh water flows there, which forest-sided Etna
Sends down for me, cold fruit of her white snow.
Who could refuse such things for the cheerless sea?
And if I seem shaggy, I keep in my heart's cave
A fire of oaklogs glowing beneath the cinders.
Let it blaze: I shall not mind how it sears my life
Or shrivels this treasure of treasures, my single eye.
If Mother had only borne me with fish's gills!
I might have dived and found you and kissed your hand
(If you would not give your lips); I might have brought you
Delicate poppies with broad red petals, or snowdrops;
A posy for summer or winter, each in its time.
I could not bring you their white and scarlet together.
I must learn to swim at once; but perhaps if I wait
Some kindly stranger will come in a ship to teach me.
Then I may fathom what pleasure lives in the depths.
Come up from the sea, Galatea. Forget to go home.

I will teach you by my example, sitting her late.
Follow the flocks with me and help me to milk them,
Help me to set the cheese with a dribble of rennet.
Mother is to blame. Though she might have won you
By speaking for me, she said not a single word.
Doesn't she see me grow thinner day by day?
I will tell her my head and feet ache fit to burst,
To make her sicken with worry and suffer like me.
O Cyclops, Cyclops, have you gone out of your mind?
You should be gathering browse to feed your lambs
Or plaiting baskets for cheese; that would show more sense.
Milk the beast you can catch; let the others range.
You will find a new Galatea with lovelier looks.
The girls call after me, "Shall I see you tonight?"
And laugh in a huddle as soon as I turn my head.
On land, I clearly have something to show for myself.

* * *

So Polyphemus shepherded his love by singing
And found more relief than if he had paid out gold.

The Graces

The proper task of Zeus's daughters and of poets
Is to celebrate the gods and great men's lives.
The Muses are heavenly beings; they sing of heaven.
We are earthbound creatures; we too should sing our own.

Where does he live, beneath what glittering sky,
The man who will open his house to receive our Graces,
Not turn them away unrecognized, unrewarded?
They come home sulky, trailing their bare feet
And blame me for sending them on a wasted journey;
Then they crouch at the bottom of a wooden coffer,
Their heads on their cold knees, their confidence gone.
Where can they turn, when every door is closed?
Show me the man with a proper sense of glory,
Who knows the praiser's worth. Can he still be found?
Now the cry is, "Give me the money, keep the praise",
And each man cradles silver under his shirt,
Jealous even of its tarnish, with greed in his eyes
And a smug rebuff on his lips: "It's all in Homer";
"The gods will look after the poets—that's their job";
"Charity begins at home"—and goes no further;
"The poet I like is the one who costs me nothing".

But, gentlemen, how does it help you to lock away
Your wealth? A wise man, putting his money to use,
Takes care of himself, but does not forget the poet.
A crowd of dependents and family count on his help;
He provides the altars with offerings for the gods;
He welcomes guests to his table, a generous host,
And sends them away cheered when they choose to leave;

But the Muses' servants receive his special care.
That way you shall be rewarded when death hides you,
Not loiter by cold Acheron, shorn of your fame,
No better than a poor labourer with callused hands
Who swings a mattock and hoards a birthright of tears.
In the halls of Antiochus and kingly Aleuas
An army of bondsmen gathered for a monthly dole;
At nightfall the pens of the Scopadae were crowded
With wide-horned cattle lowing to meet their young;
The shepherds who served the hospitable Creondae
Ranged Crannon's open ground with numberless flocks:
All joy of possession vanished when once their souls
Were emptied into the sour old ferryman's barge
And they went down into darkness with the common ghosts,
Severed from their fortunes; they would be clean forgotten
If the subtle music and bright-emblazoning voice
Of the Cean poet had not named and made them known
In times to come. We remember even their horses,
Honoured creatures who brought them prizes from the
    games.
What would they mean to us, Cycnus with womanly skin
Or the Lycian chiefs or Priam's long-haired sons,
If poetry did not ring with their ancient war-cries?
Or Odysseus? For ten years he wandered the wide world;
He came alive to Hades, he entered the cave
Of the deadly Cyclops and lived to tell the tale,
While Eumaeus watched the pigs and Philoetius the cows
And noble Laertes tended his patch of ground:
Great names, but they would have vanished all alike
If the blind Ionian had not come to their rescue.

Though living men make free with a dead man's goods,
The Muses' gift of fame can never be taken.
But to sit and count the waves which wind and sea
Drive shoreward in grey succession, or fetch clear water
To wash a mudbrick clean, is the game of a fool;
And you will as soon heal a miser's damaged heart.
Goodbye to the miser! Let him keep his silver;
With all his useless wealth, let him pine for more.
I think goodwill and honour are truer possessions
Than the mules and horses in a rich man's stable.
I look for a patron eager to take me in,
And the Muses with me. The roads are not safe for
    poets
Unless wise Zeus's daughters are there to guide them.
Untiringly heaven brings the months and years;
The horses stir, and day's bright wheel lifts high:
I will find the Achilles, the Ajax of our age,
And celebrate exploits great as those performed
Where Simois runs by the tomb of Phrygian Ilus.
Now the Phoenicians, dwellers on the hot shore
Of Africa, shiver with fear; their sun sinks low.
The men of Syracuse grip their spears for battle,
They shoulder their heavy wicker shields; among them
Hiero stands, armed and ready, a pattern of valour,
His gleaming helmet shadowed by a horsehair crest.

I beg you, Father Zeus and Lady Athena,
And you who watch over Syracuse, the great city
By the Lake of Lysimeleia, you and your mother:
Let violence clear our enemies from this island,
Allowing a handful only to sail back home
To bring their women and children news of slaughter.
May the old inhabitants repossess their cities,
Build on ruins and restore what has been spoiled.
May the fields be worked and bring forth crops once
    more
While bleating flocks, too many to count, grow fat
On the grassy plains. May the passer-by at nightfall
Quicken his steps as the cattle are driven home.
Let fallows be ploughed for sowing while the cicada,
The shepherd's sentinel, high among branches, rasps
The midday silence. Let the armoury be shrouded
In cobwebs, the war-cry become a forgotten sound.
Let poetry carry Hiero's fame through the world
From Scythian waters to where the asphalt rampart
Raised by Semiramis guards her ancient kingdom.
I am one among many poets, each with a claim
On the Muses, each ready to celebrate Arethusa,
Her brave Sicilians and Hiero, lord of the spear.
O Gracious Goddesses, worshipped by Eteocles,
Who love Orchomenus, Thebes's once loathed rival,
I will not jostle for notice but, if summoned,
Will answer gratefully, gladly—I and my Muses.
You too must accompany me. There is no delight
When once the Graces have gone. Let me not betray
    them.

EPICURUS

Letter to Menoeceus

No one should postpone the study of philosophy when he is young, nor should he weary of it when he becomes mature, because the search for mental health is never untimely or out of season. To say that the time to study philosophy has not yet arrived or that it is past is like saying that the time for happiness is not yet at hand or is no longer present. Thus both the young and the mature should pursue philosophy, the latter in order to be rejuvenated as they age by the blessings that accrue from pleasurable past experience, and the youthful in order to become mature immediately through having no fear of the future. Hence we should make a practice of the things that make for happiness, for assuredly when we have this, we have everything, and we do everything we can to get it when we don't have it.

The Preconditions of Happiness

[1. You should do and practice all the things I constantly recommended to you, with the knowledge that they are the fundamentals of the good life. First of all, you should think of deity as imperishable and blessed being (as delineated in the universal conception of it common to all men), and you should not attribute to it anything foreign to its immortality or inconsistent with its blessedness. On the contrary, you should hold every doctrine that is capable of safeguarding its blessedness in common with its imperishability. The gods do indeed exist, since our knowledge of them is a matter of clear and distinct perception; but they are not like what the masses suppose them to be, because most people do not maintain the pure conception of the gods. The irreligious man is not the person who destroys the gods of the masses but the person who imposes the ideas of the masses on the gods. The opinions held by most people about the gods are not true conceptions of them but fallacious notions, according to which awful penalties are meted out to the evil and the greatest of blessings to the good. The masses, by assimilating the gods in every respect to their own moral qualities, accept deities similar to themselves and regard anything not of this sort as alien.

Second, you should accustom yourself to believing that death means nothing to us, since every good and every evil lies in sensation; but death is the privation of sensation. Hence a correct comprehension of the fact that death means nothing to us makes the mortal aspect of life pleasurable, not be conferring on us a boundless period of time but by removing the yearning for deathlessness. There is nothing fearful in living for the person who has really laid hold of the fact that there is nothing fearful in not living. So it is silly for a person to say that he dreads death—not because it will be painful when it arrives but because it pains him now as a future certainty; for that which makes no trouble for us when it arrives is a meaningless pain when we await it. This, the most horrifying of evils, means nothing to us, then, because so long as we are existent death is not present and whenever it is present we are nonexistent. Thus it is of no concern either to the living or to those who have completed their lives. For the former it is nonexistent, and the latter are themselves nonexistent.

Most people, however, recoil from death as though it were the greatest of evils; at other times they welcome it as the end-all of life's ills. The sophisticated person, on the other hand, neither begs off from living nor dreads not living. Life is not a stumbling block to him, nor does he regard not being alive as any sort of evil. As in the case of food he prefers the most savory dish to merely the larger portion, so in the case of time, he garners to himself the most agreeable moments rather than the longest span.

Anyone who urges the youth to lead a good life but counsels the older man to end his life in good style is silly, not merely because of the welcome character of life but because of the fact that living well and dying well are one and the same discipline. Much worse off, however, is the person who says it were well not to have been born "but once born to pass Hades' portals as swiftly as may be." Now if he says such a thing from inner persuasion why does he not withdraw from life? Everything is in readiness for him once he has firmly resolved on this course. But if he speaks facetiously he is a trifler standing in the midst of men who do not welcome him.

It should be borne in mind, then, that the time to come is neither ours nor altogether not ours. In this way we shall neither expect the future outright as something destined to be, nor despair of it as something absolutely not destined to be.

The Good Life

[2. It should be recognized that within the category of desire certain desires are natural, certain others unnecessary and trivial; that in the case of the natural desires certain ones are necessary, certain others merely natural; and that in the case of necessary desires certain ones are necessary for happiness, others to promote freedom from bodily discomfort, others for the maintenance of life itself. A steady view of these matters shows us how to refer all moral choice and aversion to bodily health and imperturbability of mind, these being the twin goals of happy living. It is on this account that we do everything we do—to achieve freedom from pain and freedom from fear. When once we come to this, the tumult

in the soul is calmed and the human being does not have to go about looking for something that is lacking or to search for something additional with which to supplement the welfare of soul and body. Accordingly we have need of pleasure only when we feel pain because of the absence of pleasure, but whenever we do not feel pain we no longer stand in need of pleasure. And so we speak of pleasure as the starting point and the goal of the happy life because we realize that it is our primary native good, because every act of choice and aversion originates with it, and because we come back to it when we judge every good by using the pleasure feeling as our criterion.

Because of the very fact that pleasure is our primary and congenital good we do not select every pleasure; there are times when we forego certain pleasures, particularly when they are followed by too much unpleasantness. Furthermore, we regard certain states of pain as preferable to pleasures, particularly when greater satisfaction results from our having submitted to discomforts for a long period of time. Thus every pleasure is a good by reason of its having a nature akin to our own, but not every pleasure is desirable. In like manner every state of pain is an evil, but not all pains are uniformly to be rejected. At any rate, it is our duty to judge all such cases by measuring pleasures against pains, with a view to their respective assets and liabilities, inasmuch as we do experience the good as being bad at times and, contrariwise, the bad as being good.

In addition, we consider limitation of the appetites a major good, and we recommend this practice not for the purpose of enjoying just a few things and no more but rather for the purpose of enjoying those few in case we do not have much. We are firmly convinced that those who need expensive fare least are the ones who relish it most keenly and that a natural way of life is easily procured, while trivialities are hard to come by. Plain foods afford pleasure equivalent to that of a sumptuous diet, provided that the pains of penury are wholly eliminated. Barley bread and water yield the peak of pleasure whenever a person who needs them sets them in front of himself. Hence becoming habituated to a simple rather than a lavish way of life provides us with the full complement of health; it makes a person ready for the necessary business of life; it puts us in a position of advantage when we happen upon sumptuous fare at intervals and prepares us to be fearless in facing fortune.

Thus when I say that pleasure is the goal of living I do not mean the pleasures of libertines or the pleasures inherent in positive enjoyment, as is supposed by certain persons who are ignorant of our doctrine or who are not in agreement with it or who interpret it perversely. I mean, on the contrary, the pleasure that consists in freedom from bodily pain and mental agitation. The pleasant life is not the product of one drinking party after another or of sexual intercourse with women and boys or of the sea food and other delicacies afforded by a luxurious table. On the contrary, it is the result of sober thinking—namely, investigation of the reasons for every act of choice and aversion and elimination of those false ideas about the gods and death which are the chief source of mental disturbances.

The starting point of this whole scheme and the most important of its values is good judgment, which consequently is more highly esteemed even than philosophy. All the other virtues stem from sound judgment, which shows us that it is impossible to live the pleasant Epicurean life without also living sensibly, nobly, and justly and, vice versa, that it is impossible to live sensibly, nobly, and justly without living pleasantly. The traditional virtues grow up together with the pleasant life; they are indivisible. Can you think of anyone more moral than the person who has devout beliefs about the gods, who is consistently without fears about death, and who has pondered man's natural end? Or who realizes that the goal of the good life is easily gained and achieved and that the term of evil is brief, both in extent of time and duration of pain? Or the man who laughs at the "decrees of Fate," a deity whom some people have set up as sovereign of all?

The good Epicurean believes that certain events occur deterministically, that others are chance events, and that still others are in our own hands. He sees also that necessity cannot be held morally responsible and that chance is an unpredictable thing, but that what is in our own hands, since it has no master, is naturally associated with blameworthiness and the opposite. (Actually it would be better to subscribe to the popular mythology than to become a slave by accepting the determinism of the natural philosophers, because popular religion underwrites the hope of supplicating the gods by offerings but determinism contains an element of necessity, which is inexorable.) As for chance, the Epicurean does not assume that it is a deity (as in popular belief) because a god does nothing irregular; nor does he regard it as an unpredictable cause of all events. It is his belief that good and evil are not the chance contributions of a deity, donated to mankind for the happy life, but rather that the initial circumstances for great good and evil are sometimes provided by chance. He thinks it preferable to have bad luck rationally than good luck irrationally. In other words, in human action it is better for a rational choice to be unsuccessful than for an irrational choice to succeed through the agency of chance.

Think about these and related matters day and night, by yourself and in company with someone like yourself. If you do, you will never experience anxiety, waking or sleeping, but you will live like a god among men. For a human being who lives in the midst of immortal blessings is in no way like mortal man!

Chapter

5

Roman Civilization:
The Pre-Christian Centuries

CICERO

from *On the Good Life*

The Dream of Scipio

As you know, I was military tribune in the Fourth Legion in Africa under the command of the consul Manius Manilius. When I arrived there I was particularly eager to meet King Masinissa, who for good reason was a close friend of my family. When I came into his presence the old man embraced me and wept. Then, after a moment, he lifted his eyes to heaven and uttered these words.

'Most glorious Sun and other heavenly beings, I offer you my thanks! For before I depart from this life, I am now seeing with my own eyes, within this kingdom of mine and beneath my roof, Publius Cornelius Scipio. The very sound of his name revives my strength. For never a moment has the recollection of his glorious, invincible forbear faded from my memory.'

Then I began asking him questions about his kingdom, and he in turn interrogated me about Rome; and so we spent the whole day in conversation. Afterwards, he entertained me in regal splendour, and we continued our discussion far into the night, as the aged king wanted nothing better than to talk of Africanus. He had not forgotten a single deed the great man had ever done, or a single word he had ever uttered.

When we finally parted and retired to bed, my journey and the lateness of the hour had made me tired, and I fell into a deeper sleep than usual. As I slept I had a dream, prompted no doubt by what we had been talking about. For it frequently happens that the subjects of our meditations and discussions reappear in our dreams. This happened for example to the poet Ennius; he writes of his dream about Homer, who was naturally the constant subject of his thoughts and conversations when he was awake. And so I dreamt that Africanus was with me; his appearance recalled his portrait busts rather than his actual living self.

* * *

I recognized him—and trembled with fear. But he spoke to me; and this is what he said.

'Calm yourself, Scipio. Do not be afraid. But remember carefully the things I am about to tell you. Do you see that city there? It was I who made its people submit to Rome. But now they are starting up the old conflicts once again; they refuse to remain at peace!' And from where he stood amid the bright illumination of radiant stars, he pointed down at

81

Carthage, and began speaking once more. 'This,' he declared, is the city you have come to attack. At present you are not much more than an ordinary soldier. But within the space of two years you will have been elected consul, and then you will overthrow the place utterly. Thereafter the surname, which you now bear as an inheritance from myself, will be yours by your own right. Later on, after you have destroyed Carthage and celebrated a Triumph, after you have held the office of censor and undertaken missions to Egypt, Syria, Asia and Greece, you will be elected to the consulship for the second time, while you are absent, and you will win a very great war and raze Numantia to the ground. But at the time when you yourself are proceeding in Triumph to the Capitol, you will find the government in a state of confusion: for which the machinations of my grandson will be responsible.

'After that, Africanus, it will be your duty to devote to your people the full splendid benefit of all your integrity, talent and wisdom. But at that juncture I see two divergent paths of destiny opening up before you. For when your life has completed seven times eight circuitous revolutions of the sun, and when these two numbers, each of which for a different reason is regarded as possessing some quality of perfection, have in their natural course brought you to your supreme moment of destiny, that is the time when the entire Roman State will turn to you and all that you stand for: the Senate, every right-minded citizen, our subject allies, the entire Latin people. The fate of the whole country, at that juncture, will depend on you and you alone. In other words, it will be your duty to assume the role of dictator, and restore order to our commonwealth—provided only that death does not overtake you at the criminal hands of your own kinsmen!'

At this, Laelius cried out aloud, and a deep groan was heard from all. But the younger Scipio smiled serenely, and went on: 'Hush! Do not, I beg you, awaken me from my sleep. Listen a little longer, and take heed of what my ancestor went on to say next.'

For then he continued speaking. 'But consider this, Africanus,' he said, 'and the thought will make your determination to defend your homeland even greater than it is already. Every man who has preserved or helped his country, or has made its greatness even greater, is reserved a special place in heaven, where he may enjoy an eternal life of happiness. For all things that are done on earth nothing is more acceptable to the Supreme God, who rules the whole universe, than those gatherings and assemblages of men who are bound together by law, the communities which are known as states. Indeed, it is from here in heaven that the rulers and preservers of those states once came; and it is to here that they eventually return.'

By now I was thoroughly alarmed. It was not the idea of death that frightened me so much, but the thought of treachery inside my own family. Nevertheless, I managed to ask Africanus a question. Was he, was my father Paullus, were the other men we think of as having died, really dead? Or were they still alive?

'To be sure they are still living,' he replied, 'seeing that they have escaped from the prison-house of their bodies— that is to say from "life", as you call it, which is, in fact, death. Look: do you not see your father Paullus coming towards you?'

Indeed I now saw him approaching; and I burst into a flood of tears. But my father put his arms round me and kissed me, and told me not to weep. So when I had suppressed my tears and felt able to speak, I cried out, 'Since this, most revered and best of fathers, is true life, as I hear Africanus declare, why must I stay any longer upon earth? Why should I not come and join you, with the utmost possible speed?'

'That must not be,' replied Paullus. 'For unless God, whose sacred domain is all that you see around you here, has freed you from your confinement in the body, you cannot be admitted to this place. For men were brought into existence in order that they should inhabit the globe known as the earth, which you see here at the centre of this holy space. They have been endowed with souls made out of the ever-lasting fires called stars and constellations, consisting of globular, spherical bodies which are animated by the divine mind and move with marvellous speed, each in its own orbit and cycle. Therefore it is destined that you, Publius, and all other righteous men, shall suffer your souls to stay in the custody of the body. You must not abandon human life except at the command of him who gave it to you. For otherwise you would have failed in the duty which you, like the rest of humanity, have to fulfil.

'Instead, then, Scipio, do upon earth as your grandfather has done. Do as I have done, who begot you. Cherish justice and devotion. These qualities in abundance are owed to parents and kinsmen; and most of all they are owed to one's country.

'That is the life which leads to heaven, and to the company of those who, having completed their lives in the world, are now released from their bodies and dwell in that region you see over there, which the Greeks have taught you people on earth to call the Milky Way.' And he pointed to a circle of light, blazing brilliantly among all the other fires.

As I gazed out from where I stood, first in one direction and then another, the whole prospect looked marvellously beautiful. There were stars we never see from the earth, and they were larger than we could possibly have imagined. The smallest was the luminary which is farthest away from heaven and nearest to the earth, and shines with reflected light. These starry spheres were much larger than the earth. Indeed the earth now seemed to me so small that I began to think less of this empire of ours, which only amounts to a pinpoint on its surface.

* * *

While I looked more and more intently down at the earth Africanus checked me. 'How long,' he asked, 'do you propose to keep your eyes fastened down there upon that world of yours? Look up, instead, and look round at the sacred region into which you have now entered.

'The universe is held together by nine concentric spheres. The outermost sphere is heaven itself, and it includes and embraces all the rest. For it is the Supreme God in person, enclosing and comprehending everything that exists, that is to say all the stars which are fixed in the sky yet rotate upon their eternal courses. Within this outermost sphere are eight others. Seven of them contain the planets—a single one in each sphere, all moving in the contrary direction to the great movement of heaven itself. The next sphere to the outermost is occupied by the orb which people on earth name after Saturn. Below Saturn shines the brilliant light of Jupiter, which is benign and healthful to mankind. Then comes the star we call Mars, red and terrible to men upon earth.

'Next, almost midway between heaven and earth, blazes the Sun. He is the prince, lord and ruler of all the other worlds, the mind and guiding principle of the entire universe, so gigantic in size that everything, everywhere, is pervaded and drenched by his light. In attendance upon the Sun are Venus and Mercury, each in its own orbit; and the lowest sphere of all contains the Moon, which takes its light, as it revolves, from the rays of the sun. Above the Moon there is nothing which is not eternal, but beneath that level everything is moral and transient (except only for the souls in human beings, which are a gift to mankind from the gods). For there below the Moon is the earth, the ninth and lowest of the spheres, lying at the centre of the universe. The earth remains fixed and without motion; all things are drawn to it, because the natural force of gravity pulls them down.'

I surveyed the scene in a stupor. But finally I recovered enough to ask: 'What is this sound, so strong and so sweet, which fills my ears?'

'That,' he replied, 'is the music of the spheres. They create it by their own motion as they rush upon their way. The intervals between them, although differing in length, are all measured according to a fixed scheme of proportions; and this arrangement produces a melodious blend of high and low notes, from which emerges a varied harmony. For it cannot be that these vast movements should take place in silence, and nature has ordained that the spheres utter music, those at the summit giving forth high sounds, whereas the sounds of those beneath are low and deep. That is to say, the spheres containing the uppermost stars, comprising those regions of the sky where the movements are speediest, give out a high and piercing sound, whereas the Moon, which lies beneath all the others, sends forth the lowest note.

'The ninth of the spheres, the earth, fixed at the centre of the universe, is motionless and silent. But the other eight spheres produce seven different sounds on the scale—not eight, since two of these orbs move at identical speeds, but seven, a number which is the key to almost all things that exist. Clever men, by imitating these musical effects with their stringed instruments and voices, have given themselves the possibility of eventually returning to this place; and the same chance exists for others too, who during their earthly lives have devoted their outstanding talents to heavenly activities.

'The ears of mankind are filled with this music all the time. But they have become completely deaf to its melody; no other human faculty has become so atrophied as this. The same thing happens where the Nile rushes down from high mountains to the place known as Catadupa. For the sound there is so loud that the people who live nearby have entirely lost their sense of hearing. And that, too, is why the mighty music of the spheres, created by the immeasurably fast rotations of the whole universe, cannot be apprehended by the human ears—any more than you can look at the light of the Sun, which is so intense it blots out your power of vision altogether.'

The scene filled me with awe and delight. And yet all the time I still could not help riveting my eyes upon our own world there below. Africanus noticed this, and spoke again. 'I see,' he said, 'that your gaze is still fastened, even now, upon the places where mortals dwell upon the earth. But can you not understand that the earth is totally insignificant? Contemplate these heavenly regions instead! Scorn what is mortal!

'For the lips of mankind can give you no fame or glory worth the seeking. Note how few and minute are the inhabited portions of the earth, and look upon the vast deserts that divide each one of these patches from the next. See, the inhabitants of the world are so cut off from one another that their different centres cannot even communicate with each other. The place where you yourself dwell, for example, is far removed from certain of the other populated areas, both in latitude and longitude; and some people live in regions that are at the very opposite end of the world from yours. Surely you cannot expect *them* to honour your name.

'Furthermore, you will observe that the surface of the earth is girdled and encompassed by a number of different zones; and that the two which are most widely separated from one another, and lie beneath opposite poles of the heavens, are rigid with icy cold, while the central, broadest zone is burnt up with the heat of the sun. Two others, situated between the hot zones and the cold, are habitable. The zone which lies towards the south has no connexion with yours at all; it represents your antipodes. As to its northern counterpart, where you yourselves live, you will realize, if you look, what a diminutive section of this region can really be regarded as your property. For the territory you occupy is nothing more than a small island, narrow from north to south, somewhat less narrow from east to west, and surrounded by the sea which is known on earth as the Atlantic, or the Great Sea, or the Ocean. In spite of the grand name this stretch of water bears, you can tell from here how tiny it really is.

'And I must disabuse you of any idea that your own fame, or the fame of any one of us, could ever be great enough to extend beyond these known and settled lands. It could never scale the Caucasus mountains (you see them down there); it could never swim the river Ganges. Not one of the inhabitants of all those eastern tracts, or the remote west either, or the far off north and south, will ever so much as hear the sound of your name! And once you leave all these hosts of people out of account, you will have to conclude that the area over which your glory is so eager to extend itself is really of the most trifling dimensions.

'And now about the people who *do* know and speak about us. The point is, how long will this go on? Assume, if you like, that future generations, having inherited our praises from their fathers, will indeed retain the desire to hand them down to their children as well. Even so the deluges and conflagrations which inevitably descend upon the earth at fixed intervals will make it impossible for any glory we may gain in this way to be eternal—or even to last for any length of time. But in any case why do you regard it as so important to be talked about by people who have not yet been born? After all, you were never spoken of by all the multitudes who lived before you—and they were every bit as numerous, and were better men.

'It is also necessary to remind ourselves that even the people who may in fact hear our names mentioned will not retain the recollection even for as much as the space of one year. I am not referring to the year as it is commonly understood, which is measured according to the revolution of the sun, that is to say according the movements of one single star. But when *all* the stars return to the places where they started from, so that after an immense interval has elapsed the entire heavens finally resume their original configuration, then that great period of rotation can truly be called a year—but how many generations of human life it comprises, I should not venture to say.

'Long ago, when the spirit of Romulus ascended into these sacred expanses, it seemed to those living at the time that a shadow suddenly passed over the sun, and its light was blotted out. When, once again, the sun shall go into eclipse in the very same position and at the very same hour, that will signify that all the constellations and stars have returned to their original positions: and then you will know that the Year has been completed. But you must understand that, up to now, not one twentieth part of its course has been run.

* * *

'As for yourself, do not abandon hope of coming back here one day. For this is the place which offers great and eminent men their authentic reward—and, after all, such fame as you are able to win among mere human beings can evidently be disregarded, seeing that it is scarcely capable of enduring even for a small part of one single year. Look upwards, then! Contemplate this place which is a habitation for all eternity! Then you will not need any longer to be at the mercy of what the multitude says about you: then you will not have to put your trust in whatever human rewards your achievements may earn.

'Instead let Virtue herself, by her own unaided allurements, summon you to a glory that is genuine and real. Feel no concern about what other people may say about you. They will say it in any case. Besides, whatever words they may choose to utter will not pass beyond the narrow limits you now see below you. No utterance of man about his fellowmen has ever been lasting. When a person dies his words die with him. Posterity forgets them; and they pass into annihilation.'

He stopped speaking, and I cried out my assent. 'Even when I was only a boy, Africanus,' I declared, 'I was already exerting myself to the utmost to follow in your footsteps, and in those of my father. I longed to be not unworthy of your fame! And if there is really a path leading right to the entrance of heaven for those who have served their country well, the knowledge of this great goal before me will inspire me to redouble my endeavours.'

'Strive on,' he replied. 'And rest assured that it is only your body that is mortal; your true self is nothing of the kind. For the man you outwardly appear to be is not yourself at all. Your real self is not that corporeal, palpable shape, but the spirit inside. *Understand that you are god.* You have a god's capacity of aliveness and sensation and memory and foresight; a god's power to rule and govern and direct the body that is your servant, in the same way as God himself, who reigns over us, directs the entire universe. And this rule exercised by eternal God is mirrored in the dominance of your frail body by your immortal soul.

* * *

'That which is always in motion is eternal; yet that which communicates motion to something else, but is itself moved by another force, must necessarily cease to live when the transmission of this motion to it has ceased. Consequently the only thing that never ceases to move is something which has the power of starting up motion all *on its own*—it can go on moving because its power to achieve motion depends on itself and itself alone. This, therefore, it must be concluded, is the source and first principle of motion for all things that move.

'Being the first principle, it never had a beginning: since the first principle is what everything else has originated from, it cannot possibly have originated from anything else. For if it owed its origin to something else, it could not be described as the first principle.

'And since it never had a beginning it will never have an end. For if the first principle were destroyed it could never be reborn from any other source and would no longer be able to create things on its own account—which is obviously what the first principle has to do.

'The beginning of all movement, then, comes from that which has set itself in motion: which can neither be born nor die. For if that were not so, one would have to envisage the entire heavens and all things that have ever been created crashing down and coming to an end—for that is what would happen if the force generating their motion were taken away from them.

'Since, therefore, it is plain that the self-moving principle is eternal, the same must evidently apply to the human soul. For unlike lifeless objects which can only be set in motion from outside, the soul, by its very essence and nature, is a living thing such as can only derive its life and motion from within itself. And since, uniquely, it possesses this characteristic of self-impulsion, surely it has no beginning, and lives for ever.

* * *

'Use this eternal force, therefore, for the most splendid deeds it is in you to achieve! And the very best deeds are those which serve your country. A soul devoted to such pursuits will find it easiest of all to soar upwards to this place, which is its proper habitation and home. And its flight will be all the more rapid if already during the period of its confinement within the body it has ranged freely abroad, and, by contemplating what lies outside itself, has contrived to detach itself from the body to the greatest possible degree.

'When, on the other hand, a man has failed to do this, and has abandoned himself instead to bodily indulgence and become its slave, letting the passions which serve pleasure impel him to flout the laws both of gods and of men, his soul, after departing from his body, hovers about close to the earth. Nor does it return to this place until many ages of torment have been undergone.'

Then Africanus vanished; and I awoke from my sleep.

CATULLUS
Poems

5

Lesbia
   live with me
& love me so
we'll laugh at all
the sour-faced strict-
ures of the wise.
This sun once set
will rise again,
when our sun sets
follows night &
an endless sleep.
Kiss me now a
thousand times &
now a hundred
more & then a

hundred & a
thousand more again
till with so many
hundred thousand
kisses you & I
shall both lose count
nor any can
from envy of
so much of kissing
put his finger
on the number
of sweet kisses
you of me &
I of you,
darling, have had.

22

I must, Varus, tell you:
   Suffenus, known to us both as
a man of elegance, wit
   & sophistication
is also a poet
   who turns out verse by the yard.
No palimpsest copies
   but new books with new ivories
inscribed on Augustan Royal,
   the lines lead-ruled,
red tabs & red wrappers,
   the ends shaved with pumice.
But unwind the scroll
   & Suffenus
the well-known diner-out
   disappears.
A goatherd
   a country bumpkin

looks at us—
   strangely transmogrified.
What should one think?
   The envy of wits
becomes
   at the touch of the Muses
a bundle of gaucheries. . . .
   and he likes nothing better
fancies himself
   in the role of a poet. . . .
Yet who,
   in his own way,
is not a Suffenus?
   Each has his blind spot.
The mote & the beam.
   As Aesop says,
the pack on our own back
   that we don't see.

51

Godlike the man who
sits at her side, who
watches and catches
    that laughter
which (softly) tears me
to tatters: nothing is
left of me, each time
    I see her,
. . . tongue numbed; arms, legs
melting, on fire; drum

drumming in ears; head-
    lights gone black.

Coda
Her ease is your sloth, Catullus
you itch & roll in her ease:

former kings and cities
lost in the valley of her arm.

72

There was a time, Lesbia, when
you confessed only to Catullus in love:
you would set me above Jupiter himself.
I loved you then
    not as men love their women
but as a father his children—his family.
Today I know you too well

and desire burns deeper in me
and you are more coarse
    more frivolous in my thought.
"How," you may ask, "can this be?"
Such actions as yours excite
    increased violence of love,
Lesbia, but with friendless intention.

75

Reason blinded by sin, Lesbia,
a mind drowned in its own devotion:
come clothed in your excellences—

I cannot think tenderly of you,
sink to what acts you dare—
I can never cut this love.

VIRGIL

from *The Aeneid*

Book VI

· · ·

You gods who rule the world of the spirits, you silent shades, and Chaos, and Phlegethon, you dark and silent wastes, let it be right for me to tell what I have been told, let it be with your divine blessing that I reveal what is hidden deep in the mists beneath the earth.

They walked in the darkness of that lonely night with shadows all about them, through the empty halls of Dis and his desolate kingdom, as men walk in a wood by the sinister light of a fitful moon when Jupiter has buried the sky in shade and black night has robbed all things of their colour. Before the entrance hall of Orcus, in the very throat of hell, Grief and Revenge have made their beds and Old Age lives there in despair, with white faced Diseases and Fear and Hunger, corrupter of men, and squalid Poverty, things dreadful to look upon, and Death and Drudgery besides. Then there are Sleep, Death's sister, perverted Pleasures, murderous War astride the threshold, the iron chambers of the Furies and raving Discord with blood-soaked ribbons binding her viperous hair. In the middle a huge dark elm spreads out its ancient arms, the resting-place, so they say, of flocks of idle dreams, one clinging under every leaf. Here too are all manner of monstrous beasts, Centaurs stabling inside the gate, Scyllas—half dogs, half women—Briareus with his hundred heads, the Hydra of Lerna hissing fiercely, the Chimaera armed in fire, Gorgons and Harpies and the triple phantom of Geryon. Now Aeneas drew his sword in sudden alarm to meet them with naked steel as they came at him, and if his wise companion had not warned him that this was the fluttering of disembodied spirits, a mere semblance of living substance, he would have rushed upon them and parted empty shadows with steel.

Here begins the road that leads to the rolling waters of Acheron, the river of Tartarus. Here is a vast quagmire of boiling whirlpools which belches sand and slime into Cocytus, and these are the rivers and waters guarded by the terrible Charon in his filthy rags. On his chin there grows a thick grey beard, never trimmed. His glaring eyes are lit with fire and a foul cloak hangs from a knot at his shoulder. With his own hands he plies the pole and sees to the sails as he ferries the dead in a boat the colour of burnt iron. He is no longer young but, being a god, enjoys rude strength and a green old age. The whole throng of the dead was rushing to this part of the bank, mothers, men, great-hearted heroes whose lives were ended, boys, unmarried girls and young men laid on the pyre before the faces of their parents, as many as are the leaves that fall in the forest at the first chill of autumn, as many as the birds that flock to land from deep ocean when the cold season of the year drives them over the sea to lands bathed in sun. There they stood begging to be allowed to be the first to cross and stretching out their arms in longing for the further shore. But the grim boatman takes some here and some there, and others he pushes away far back from the sandy shore.

Aeneas, amazed and distressed by all this tumult, cried out: 'Tell me, virgin priestess, what is the meaning of this crowding to the river? What do the spirits want? Why are some pushed away from the bank while others sweep the livid water with their oars?' The aged Sibyl made this brief reply: 'Son of Anchises, beyond all doubt the offspring of the gods, what you are seeing is the deep pools of the Cocytus and the swamp of the Styx, by whose divine power the gods are afraid to swear and lie. The throng you see on this side are the helpless souls of the unburied. The ferryman there is Charon. Those sailing the waters of the Styx have all been buried. No man may be ferried from fearful bank to fearful bank of this roaring current until his bones are laid to rest. Instead they wander for a hundred years, fluttering round these shores until they are at last allowed to return to the pools they have so longed for.' The son of Anchises checked his stride and stood stock still with many thoughts coursing through his mind as he pitied their cruel fate, when there among the sufferers, lacking all honour in death, he caught sight of Leucaspis, and Orontes, the captain of the Lycian fleet, men who had started with him from Troy, sailed the wind-torn seas and been overwhelmed by gales from the south that rolled them in the ocean, ships and crews. . . .

And so they carried on to the end of the road on which they had started, and at last came near the river. When the boatman, now in mid-stream, looked ashore from the waves of the Styx and saw them coming through the silent wood towards the bank, he called out to them and challenged them: 'You there, whoever you are, making for our river with a sword by your side, come tell us why you are here. Speak to us from where you stand. Take not another step. This place belongs to the shades, to Sleep and to Night, the bringer of Sleep. Living bodies may not be carried on the boat that plies the Styx. It gave me little enough pleasure to take even Hercules aboard when he came, or Theseus, or Pirithous, although they said they were born of gods and their strength was irresistible. It was Hercules whose hand put chains on the watchdog of Tartarus and dragged him shivering from the very throne of our king. The others had taken it upon themselves to steal the queen, my mistress, from the chamber of Dis.' The answer of the Amphrysian Sibyl was brief: 'Here there are no such designs. You have no need for alarm. These weapons of his bring no violence. The monstrous keeper of the gate can bark in his cave and frighten the bloodless shades till the end of time and Proserpina can stay chaste behind her uncle's doors. Trojan Aeneas, famous for his devotion and his feats of arms, is going down to his father in the darkest depths of Erebus. If the sight of such devotion does not move you, then look at this branch,' she said, showing the branch that had been hidden in her robes, 'and realize what it is.' At this the swelling anger subsided in his heart. No more words were needed. Seeing it again after a long age, and marvelling at the fateful branch, the holy offering, he turned his dark boat and steered towards the bank. He then drove off the souls who were on board with him sitting all along the cross benches, and cleared the gangways. In the same moment he took the huge Aeneas into the hull of his little boat. Being only sewn together, it groaned under his weight, shipping great volumes of stagnant water through the seams, but in the end it carried priestess and hero safely over and landed them on the foul slime among the grey-green reeds.

The kingdom on this side resounded with barking from the three throats of the huge monster Cerberus lying in a cave in front of them. When the priestess was close enough to see the snakes writhing on his neck, she threw him a honey cake steeped in soporific drugs. He opened his three jaws, each of them rabid with hunger, and snapped it up where it fell. The massive back relaxed and he sprawled full length on the ground, filling his cave. The sentry now sunk in sleep, Aeneas leapt to take command of the entrance and was soon free of the bank of that river which no man may recross.

In that instant they heard voices, a great weeping and wailing of the souls of infants who had lost their share of the sweetness of life on its very threshold, torn from the breast on some black day and drowned in the bitterness of death. Next to them were those who had been condemned to death on false charges, but they did not receive their places without the casting of lots and the appointment of juries. Minos, the president of the court, shakes the lots in the urn, summoning the silent dead to act as jurymen, and holds inquiry into the lives of the accused and the charges against them. Next to them were those unhappy people who had raised their innocent hands against themselves, who had so loathed the light that they had thrown away their own lives. But now how they would wish to be under high heaven, enduring poverty and drudgery, however hard! That cannot be, for they are bound in the coils of the hateful swamp of the waters of death, trapped in the ninefold windings of the river Styx. Not far from here could be seen what they call the Mourning Plains, stretching away in every direction. Here are the victims of unhappy love, consumed by that cruel wasting sickness, hidden in the lonely byways of an encircling wood of myrtle trees, and their suffering does not leave them even in death. Here Aeneas saw Phaedra, and Procris, and Eriphyle in tears as she displayed the wounds her cruel son had given her. Here he saw Evadne and Pasiphae with Laodamia walking by their side, and Caeneus, once a young man, but now a woman restored by destiny to her former shape.

Wandering among them in that great wood was Phoenician Dido with her wound still fresh. When the Trojan hero stopped beside her, recognizing her dim form in the darkness, like a man who sees or thinks he has seen the new moon rising through the clouds at the beginning of the month, in that instant he wept and spoke sweet words of love to her: 'So the news they brought me was true, unhappy Dido? They told me you were dead and had ended your life with the sword. Alas! Alas! Was I the cause of your dying? I swear by the stars, by the gods above, by whatever there is to swear by in the depths of the earth, it was against my will, O queen, that I left your shore. It was the stern authority of the commands of the gods that drove me on, as it drives me now through the shades of this dark night in this foul and mouldering place. I could not have believed that my leaving would cause you such sorrow. Do not move away. Do not leave my sight. Who are you running from? Fate has decreed that I shall not speak to you again.' With these words Aeneas, shedding tears, tried to comfort that burning spirit, but grim-faced she kept her eyes upon the ground and did not look at him. Her features moved no more when he began to speak than if she had been a block of flint or Parian marble quarried on Mount Marpessus. Then at last she rushed away, hating him, into the shadows of the wood where Sychaeus, who had been her husband, answered her grief with grief and her love with love. Aeneas was no less stricken by the injustice of her fate and long did he gaze after her, pitying her as she went.

From here they continued on their appointed road and they were soon on the most distant of these fields, the place set apart for brave warriors. Here Tydeus came to meet him, and Parthenopaeus, famous for his feats of arms, and the pale phantom of Adrastus. Here he saw and groaned to see standing in their long ranks all the sons of Dardanus who had fallen in battle and been bitterly lamented in the upper world, Glaucus, Medon and Thersilochus, the three sons of Antenor, and Polyboetes, the consecrated priest of Ceres, and Idaeus still keeping hold of Priam's chariot, still keeping hold of his armour. The shades crowded round him on the right and on the left and it was not enough just to see him, they wished to delay him, to walk with him, to learn the reasons for his coming. But when the Greek leaders and the soldiers of Agamemnon in their phalanxes saw the hero and his armour gleaming through the shadows, a wild panic seized them. Some turned and ran as they had run once before to get back to their ships, while others lifted up their voices and raised a tiny cry, which started as a shout from mouth wide open, but no shout came.

Here too he saw Deiphobus, son of Priam, his whole body mutilated and his face cruelly torn. The face and both hands were in shreds. The ears had been ripped from the head. He was noseless and hideous. Aeneas, barely recognizing him as he tried frantically to hide the fearsome punishment he had received, went up to him and spoke in the voice he knew so well: 'Deiphobus, mighty warrior, descended from the noble blood of Teucer, who could have wished to inflict such a punishment upon you? And who was able to do this? I was told that on that last night you wore yourself out killing the enemy and fell on a huge pile of Greek and Trojan dead. At that time I did all I could do, raising an empty tomb for you on the shore of Cape Rhoeteum and lifting up my voice to call three times upon your shade. Your name and your arms mark the place but you I could not find, my friend, to bury your body in our native land as I was leaving it.'

To this the son of Priam answered: 'You, my friend, have left nothing undone. You have paid all that is owed to Deiphobus and to his dead shade. It is my own destiny and the crimes of the murderess from Sparta that have brought me to this. These are reminders of Helen. You know how we spent that last night in false joy. It is our lot to remember it only too well. When the horse that was the instrument of Fate, heavy with the brood of armed men in its belly, leapt over the high walls of Pergamum, Helen was pretending to be worshipping Bacchus, leading the women of Phrygia around the city, dancing and shrieking their ritual cries. There she was in the middle of them with a huge torch, signalling to the Greeks from the top of the citadel, and all the time I was sleeping soundly in our accursed bed, worn out by all I had suffered and sunk in a sleep that was sweet and deep and like the peace of death. Meanwhile this excellent wife of mine, after moving all my armour out of the house and taking the good sword from under my head, called in Menelaus and threw open the doors, hoping no doubt that her loving husband would take this as a great favour to wipe out the memory of her past sins. You can guess the rest. They burst into the room, taking with them the man who had incited them to their crimes, their comrade Ulixes—they say he is descended from Aeolus. You gods, if the punishment I ask is just, grant that a fate like mine should strike again and strike Greeks. But come, it is now time for you to tell me what chance has brought you here alive. Is it your sea wanderings that have taken you here? Are you under the instructions of the gods? What fortune is dogging you, that you should come here to our sad and sunless homes in this troubled place?'

While they were speaking to one another, Dawn's rosy chariot had already run its heavenly course past the midpoint of the vault of the sky, and they might have spent all the allotted time in talking but for Aeneas' companion. The Sibyl gave her warning in few words: 'Night is running quickly by, Aeneas, and we waste the hours in weeping. This is where the way divides. On the right it leads up to the walls of great Dis. This is the road we take for Elysium. On the left is the road of punishment for evil-doers, leading to Tartarus, the place of the damned.' 'There is no need for anger, great priestess,' replied Deiphobus. 'I shall go to take my place among the dead and return to darkness. Go, Aeneas, go, great glory of our Troy, and enjoy a better fate than mine.' These were his only words, and as he spoke he turned on his heel and strode away.

Aeneas looked back suddenly and saw under a cliff on his left a broad city encircled by a triple wall and washed all round by Phlegethon, one of the rivers of Tartarus, a torrent of fire and flame, rolling and grinding great boulders in its current. There before him stood a huge gate with columns of solid adamant so strong that neither the violence of men nor of the heavenly gods themselves could ever uproot them in war, and an iron tower rose into the air where Tisiphone sat with her blood-soaked dress girt up, guarding the entrance and never sleeping, night or day. They could hear the groans from the city, the cruel crack of the lash, the dragging and clanking of iron chains. Aeneas stood in terror, listening to the noise. 'What kinds of criminal are here? Tell me, virgin priestess, what punishments are inflicted on them? What is this wild lamentation in the air?' The Sibyl replied: 'Great leader of the Trojans, the chaste may not set foot upon the threshold of that evil place, but when Hecate put me in charge of the groves of Avernus, she herself explained the punishments the gods had imposed and showed me them all. Here Rhadamanthus, king of Cnossus, holds sway with his unbending laws, chastising men, hearing all the frauds they have practised and forcing them to confess the undiscovered crimes they have gloated over in the upper world—foolishly, for they have only delayed the day of atonement till after death. Immediately the avenging Tisiphone leaps upon the guilty and flogs them till they writhe, waving fearful serpents over them in her left hand and calling up the cohorts of her savage sisters, the Furies. Then at last the gates sacred to the gods below shriek in their sockets and open wide. You see what a watch she keeps, sitting in the entrance? What a sight she is guarding the threshold? Inside, more savage still, the huge, black-throated, fifty-headed Hydra has its lair. And then there is Tartarus itself, stretching sheer down into its dark chasm twice as far as we look up to the ethereal Olympus in the sky. Here, rolling in the bottom of the abyss, is the ancient brood of Earth, the army of Titans, hurled down by the thunderbolt. Here too I saw the huge bodies of the twin sons of Aloeus who laid violent hands on the immeasurable sky to wrench it from its place and tear down Jupiter from his heavenly kingdom. I saw too Salmoneus suffering cruel punishment, still miming the flames of Jupiter and the rumblings of Olympus. He it was who, riding his four-horse chariot and brandishing a torch, used to go in glory through the peoples of Greece and the city of Olympia in the heart of Elis, laying claim to divine honours for himself—fool that he was to copy the storm and the inimitable thunderbolt with the rattle of the horn of his horses' hooves on bronze. Through the thick clouds the All-powerful Father hurled his lightning—no smoky light from pitchy torches for him—and sent him spinning deep into the abyss. Tityos too I could see, the nurseling of Earth, mother of all, his body sprawling over nine whole acres while a huge vulture with hooked beak cropped his immortal liver and the flesh that was such a rich supplier of punishment. Deep in his breast it roosts and forages for its dinners, while the filaments of his liver know no rest but are restored as soon as they are consumed. I do not need to speak of the Lapiths, of Ixion or Pirithous, over whose heads the boulder of black flint is always slipping, always seeming to be falling. The gold gleams on the high supports of festal couches and a feast is laid in regal splendour before the eyes of the guilty, but the greatest of the Furies is reclining at table and allows no hand to touch the food, but leaps up brandishing a torch and shouting with a voice of thunder. Immured in this place and waiting for punishment are those who in life hated their brothers, beat their fathers, defrauded their dependants, found wealth and brooded over it alone without setting aside a share for their kinsmen—these are most numerous of all—men caught and killed in adultery, men who took up arms against their own people and did not shrink from abusing their masters' trust. Do not ask to know what their punishments are, what form of pain or what misfortune has engulfed them. Some are rolling huge rocks, or hang spreadeagled on the spokes of wheels. Theseus is sitting there dejected, and there he will sit until the end of time, while Phlegyas, most wretched of them all, shouts this lesson for all men at the top of his voice in the darkness: "Learn to be just and not to slight the gods. You have been warned." Here is the man who has sold his native land for gold, and set a tyrant over it, putting up tablets with new laws for a price and for a price removing them. Here is the man who forced his way into his daughter's bed and a forbidden union. They have all dared to attempt some monstrous crime against the gods and have succeeded in their attempt. If I had a hundred tongues, a hundred mouths and a voice of iron, I could not encompass all their different crimes or speak the names of all their different punishments.'

When the aged priestess of Apollo had finished her answer, she added these words: 'But come now, you must take the road and complete the task you have begun. Let us hasten. I can see the high walls forged in the furnaces of the Cyclopes and the gates there in front of us in the arch. This is where we have been told to lay the gift that is required of us.' After these words they walked the dark road together, soon covering the distance and coming close to the doors. There Aeneas leapt on the threshold, sprinkled his body with fresh water and fixed the bough full in the doorway.

When this rite was at last performed and his duty to the goddess was done, they entered the land of joy, the lovely glades of the fortunate woods and the home of the blest. Here a broader sky clothes the plains in glowing light, and the spirits have their own sun and their own stars. Some take exercise on grassy wrestling-grounds and hold athletic contests and wrestling bouts on the golden sand. Others pound the earth with dancing feet and sing their songs while Orpheus, the priest of Thrace, accompanies their measures on his seven-stringed lyre, plucking the notes sometimes with his fingers, sometimes with his ivory plectrum. Here was the ancient line of Teucer, the fairest of all families, great-hearted heroes born in a better time, Ilus, Assaracus and Dardanus, the founder of Troy. Aeneas admired from a distance their armour and empty chariots. Their swords were planted in the ground and their horses wandered free on the plain cropping the grass. Reposing there below the earth, they took the same joy in their chariots and their armour as when alive, and the same care to feed their sleek horses. Then suddenly he saw others on both sides of him feasting on the grass, singing in a joyful choir their paean to Apollo all through a grove of fragrant laurels where the mighty river Eridanus rolls through the forest to the upper world. Here were armies of men bearing wounds received while fighting for their native land, priests who had been chaste unto death and true prophets whose words were worthy of Apollo; then those who have raised human life to new heights by the skills they have discovered and those whom men remember for what they have done for men. All these with sacred ribbons of white round their foreheads gathered round Aeneas and the Sibyl, and she addressed these words to them, especially to Musaeus, for the whole great throng looked up to him as he stood there in the middle, head and shoulders above them all: 'Tell me, blessed spirits, and you, best of poets, which part of this world holds Anchises? Where is he to be found? It is because of Anchises that we have come here and crossed the great rivers of Erebus.' The hero returned a short answer: 'None of us has a fixed home. We live in these densely wooded groves and rest on the soft couches of the river bank and in the fresh water-meadows. But if that is the desire of your hearts, come climb this ridge and I shall soon set you on an easy path.' So saying, he walked on in front of them to a place from where they could see the plains below them bathed in light, and from that point Aeneas and the Sibyl came down from the mountain tops.

Father Anchises was deep in a green valley, walking among the souls who were enclosed there and eagerly surveying them as they waited to rise into the upper light. It so happened that at that moment he was counting the number of his people, reviewing his dear descendants, their fates and their fortunes, their characters and their courage in war. When he saw Aeneas coming towards him over the grass, he stretched out both hands in eager welcome, with the tears streaming down his cheeks, and these were the words that broke from his mouth: 'You have come at last,' he cried. 'I knew your devotion would prevail over all the rigour of the journey and bring you to your father. Am I to be allowed to look upon your face, my son, to hear the voice I know so well and answer it with my own? I never doubted it. I counted the hours, knowing you would come, and my love has not deceived me. I understand how many lands you have travelled and how many seas you have sailed to come to me here. I know the dangers that have beset you. I so feared the kingdom of Libya would do you harm.' 'It was my vision of you,' replied Aeneas, 'always before my eyes and always stricken with sorrow, that drove me to the threshold of this place. The fleet is moored in the Tyrrhenian sea on the shores of Italy. Give me your right hand, father. Give it me. Do not avoid my embrace.' As he spoke these words his cheeks were washed with tears and three times he tried to put his arms around his father's neck. Three times the phantom melted in his hands, as weightless as the wind, as light as the flight of sleep.

And now Aeneas saw in a side valley a secluded grove with copses of rustling trees where the river Lethe glided along past peaceful dwelling houses. Around it fluttered numberless races and tribes of men, like bees in a meadow on a clear summer day, settling on all the many-coloured flowers and crowding round the gleaming white lilies while the whole plain is loud with their buzzing. Not understanding what he saw, Aeneas shuddered at the sudden sight of them and asked why this was, what was that river in the distance and who were all those companies of men crowding its banks. 'These are the souls to whom Fate owes a second body,' replied Anchises. 'They come to the waves of the river Lethe and drink the waters of serenity and draughts of long oblivion. I have long been eager to tell you who they are, to show them to you face to face and count the generations of my people to you so that you could rejoice the more with me at the finding of Italy.' 'But are we to believe,' replied Aeneas to his dear father, 'that there are some souls who rise from here to go back under the sky and return to sluggish bodies? Why do the poor wretches have this terrible longing for the light?' 'I shall tell you, my son, and leave you no longer in doubt,' replied Anchises, and he began to explain all things in due order.

'In the beginning Spirit fed all things from within, the sky and the earth, the level waters, the shining globe of the moon and the Titan's star, the sun. It was Mind that set all this matter in motion. Infused through all the limbs, it mingled with that great body, and from the union there sprang the families of men and of animals, the living things of the air and the strange creatures born beneath the marble surface of the sea. The living force within them is of fire and its seeds have their source in heaven, but their guilt-ridden bodies make them slow and they are dulled by earthly limbs and dying flesh. It is this that gives them their fears and desires, their griefs and joys. Closed in the blind darkness of this prison they do not see out to the winds of air. Even when life leaves them on their last day of light, they are not wholly freed from all the many ills and miseries of the body which must harden in them over the long years and become ingrained in ways we cannot understand. And so they are put to punishment, to pay the penalty for all their ancient sins. Some are stretched and hung out empty to dry in the winds. Some have the stain of evil washed out of them under a vast tide of water or scorched out by fire. Each of us suffers his own fate in the after-life. From here we are sent over the broad plains of Elysium and some few of us possess these fields of joy until the circle of time is completed and the length of days has removed ingrained corruption and left us pure ethereal sense, the fire of elemental air. All these others whom you see, when they have rolled the wheel for a thousand years, are called out by God to come in great columns to the river of Lethe, so that they may duly go back and see the vault of heaven again remembering nothing, and begin to be willing to return to bodies.' . . .

HORACE

from *Odes*

II.16
Otium divos

Peace, Grosphus, is what the man on the open
Aegean requires of the Gods when black cloud
obscures the moon and no fixed star can
    flash for the sailors.

Peace for the Thracians enraged with war,
peace for the Medes with their stylish quivers,
is not to be bought with gems or gold
    or gleaming fabrics.

Neither Persian treasure nor the consul's
lictor can disperse the wretched mob
of the mind or the cares that flit about
    your coffered ceilings.

He lives well on a little whose family
salt-cellar shines amid a modest
table, whose gentle sleep is not dispelled
    by fear or base greed.

Why do we aim so high, so bravely,
so briefly? Why hanker for countries scorched
by an alien sun? What exile from home
    can avoid himself?

Care clambers aboard the armoured ships,
keeps pace with the cavalry squadrons, comes
swift as East-Wind-driven rain, comes
    swift as any stag.

The soul content with the present
is not concerned with the future and tempers
dismay with an easy laugh. No
    blessing is unmixed.

An early death snatched bright Achilles;
long senility reduced Tithonus:
this hour will offer to me, maybe, the good
    it denies to you.

For you a hundred herds of Sicilian
cattle moo; for you are bred
neighing mares apt for the chariot;
    you dress in twice-dyed

Tyrian purple wool: to me honest Fate
has given a little farm, the delicate breath
of the Grecian Muse, and disdain
    for the jealous mob.

II.18
Non ebur neque aureum

No ivory or gilded
panels gleam in my house; no
  beams from Hymettus
press on columns quarried in Africa's

  heartland; I have not
unexpectedly inherited a palace from Attalus;
  I have no retinue
of ladies trailing Laconian purple

  robes. I am loyal, however,
and of a kindly humour: though poor,
  am courted by the rich. Content
with my Sabine farm, I make no more suits

  to my powerful friend,
seek nothing further from the Gods above.
  Each day drives out the day
before, new moons make haste to wane:

  yet you, on the brink of the grave,
contract for the cutting of marble slabs;
  forgetful of death you fret
to build your mansion out from the coast

  in the roaring sea at Baiac—
the mainland shore will not suffice.
  What do you hope to achieve
by tearing down fences and avidly

  jumping your tenants'
boundaries? Men and women are evicted,
  clutching to their breasts
both household Gods and ragged children.

  And yet no hall more certainly
awaits the rich grandee than does rapacious
  Orcus' predestined
bourne. What more can you need? Earth

  opens impartially for paupers
and the sons of kings, and Charon could not
  be bribed to ferry back
even resourceful Prometheus. He holds

  Tantalus and Tantalus'
progeny, and whether or not invoked
  is alert to disburden
the serf when his labour is done.

III.6
Delicta maiorum

Though innocent you shall atone for the crimes
of your fathers, Roman, until you have restored
the temples and crumbling shrines of the Gods
and their statues grimy with smoke.

Acknowledge the rule of the Gods—and rule:
hence all things begin, to this ascribe the outcome.
Contemned, the Gods have visited many
evils on grieving Hesperia.

Already twice Monaeses and Pacorus' band
have crushed our ill-starred offensive
and preen themselves on having added
Roman spoils to their paltry gauds.

Our city busied with sedition has almost
suffered destruction by Egypt allied to Dacia,
the former renowned for her fleet, the latter
rather for hurtling arrows.

Teeming with sin, the times have sullied
first marriage, our children, our homes:
sprung from that source disaster has whelmed
our fatherland and our people.

The grown girl loves to be taught to be
artful and dance oriental dances,
obsessed to her dainty fingernails
with illicit amours.

She sniffs out young philand'rers at her
husband's feast, nor is she nice to choose
to whom she (hurriedly) grants her favours
when the lamps are removed,

but brazenly stands when called—with her
husband's assent—though some travelling
salesman or Spanish ship's captain
may be the agent of Shame.

The generation that dyed the Punic
sea with blood and laid low Pyrrhus,
Antiochus and Hannibal was not born
of parents such as these,

but of manly comrades, yeoman soldiers
taught to turn the soil with Sabine hoes
and carry cut firewood at a strict
mother's bidding when the Sun

advanced the shadows of the hills
and lifted the yokes from weary steers,
his departing chariot leading in
the hours of comfort.

What does corrupting time not diminish?
Our grandparents brought forth feebler heirs;
we are further degen'rate; and soon will beget
progeny yet more wicked.

OVID

from *Metamorphoses*

Book I (Daphne and Apollo)

• • •

Daphne, the daughter of Peneus, was Phoebus' first love, and it was not blind chance which brought this about, but Cupid's savage spite. Not long before, the Delian god, still exultant over his slaying of the serpent, had seen Cupid bending his taut bow, and had said: 'You naughty boy, what have you to do with a warrior's arms? Weapons such as these are suited to my shoulders: for I can aim my shafts unerringly, to wound wild beast or human foe, as I lately slew the bloated Python with my countless arrows, though it covered so many acres with its pestilential coils. You be content with your torch to excite love, whatever that may be, and do not aspire to praises that are my prerogative.' But Venus' son replied: 'Your bow may pierce everything else, Phoebus, but mine will pierce *you*: and as all animals are inferior to the gods, your glory is to that extent less than mine.'

With these words he swiftly winged his way through the air, till he alighted on the shady summit of Parnassus. From his quiver, full of arrows, he drew two darts, with different properties. The one puts love to flight, the other kindles it. That which kindles love is golden, and shining, sharp-tipped; but that which puts it to flight is blunt, its shaft tipped with lead. With this arrow the god pierced the nymph, Peneus' daughter, but Apollo he wounded with the other, shooting it into the marrow of his bones. Immediately the one fell in love; the other, fleeing the very word 'lover', took her delight in woodland haunts and in the spoils of captured beasts, emulating Diana, the maiden goddess, with her hair carelessly caught back by a single ribbon.

Many a suitor wooed her but, turning away from their entreaties, she roamed the pathless woods, knowing nothing of men, and caring nothing for them, heedless of what marriage or love or wedded life might be. Again and again her father said: 'It is your duty to marry and give me a son-in-law, my child.' Often he repeated: 'My child, it is your duty to give me grandchildren.' But she blushed, hating the thought of marriage as if it were some crime. The modest colour crimsoned her fair face and, throwing her arms round her father's neck, she cried imploringly: 'My dear, dear father, let me enjoy this state of maiden bliss for ever! Diana's father granted her such a boon in days gone by!' Her father did, indeed, yield to her request, but her very loveliness prevented her from being what she desired, and her beauty defeated her own wishes.

As soon as Phoebus saw Daphne, he fell in love with her, and wanted to marry her. His own prophetic powers deceived him and he hoped to achieve his desire. As the light stubble blazes up in a harvested field, or as the hedge is set alight, if a traveller chance to kindle a fire too close, or leaves one smouldering when he goes off at daybreak, so the god was all on fire, his whole heart was aflame, and he nourished his fruitless love on hope. He eyed her hair as it hung carelessly about her neck, and sighed: 'What if it were properly arranged!' He looked at her eyes, sparkling bright as stars, he looked at her lips, and wanted to do more than look at them. He praised her fingers, her hands and arms, bare almost to the shoulder. Her hidden charms he imagined lovelier still.

But Daphne ran off, swifter than the wind's breath, and did not stop to hear his words, though he called her back: 'I implore you, nymph, daughter of Peneus, do not run away! Though I pursue you, I am no enemy. Stay, sweet nymph! You flee as a lamb flees the wolf, or the deer the lion, as doves on fluttering wings fly from an eagle, as all creatures flee their natural foes! But it is love that drives me to follow you. Alas, how I fear lest you trip and fall, lest briars scratch your innocent legs, and I be the cause of your hurting yourself. These are rough places through which you are running—go less swiftly, I beg of you, slow your flight, and I in turn shall pursue less swiftly!

'Yet stay to inquire whose heart you have charmed. I am no peasant, living in a mountain hut, nor am I a shepherd or boorish herdsman who tends his flocks and cattle in these regions. Silly girl, you do not know from whom you are fleeing: indeed, you do not, or else you would not flee. I am lord of Delphi, Claros, and Tenedos, and of the realms of Patara too. I am the son of Jupiter. By my skill, the past, the present, and the future are revealed; thanks to me, the lyre strings thrill with music. My arrow is sure, though there is one surer still, which has wounded my carefree heart. The art of medicine is my invention, and men the world over give me the name of healer. All the properties of herbs are known to me: but alas, there are no herbs to cure love, and the skill which helps others cannot help its master.'

He would have said more, but the frightened maiden fled from him, leaving him with his words unfinished; even then, she was graceful to see, as the wind bared her limbs and its gusts stirred her garments, blowing them out behind her. Her hair streamed in the light breeze, and her beauty was enhanced by her flight. But the youthful god could not endure to waste his time on further blandishments and, as love itself prompted, sped swiftly after her. Even so, when a Gallic hound spies a hare in some open meadow he tries by his swiftness to secure his prey, while the hare, by her swiftness, seeks safety: the dog, seeming just about to fasten on his quarry, hopes at every moment that he has her, and grazes her hind quarters with outstretched muzzle, but the hare, uncertain whether she has not already been caught, snatches herself out of his very jaws, and escapes the teeth which almost touch her.

Thus the god and the nymph sped on, one made swift by hope and one by fear; but he who pursued was swifter, for he was assisted by love's wings. He gave the fleeing maiden no respite, but followed close on her heels, and his breath touched the locks that lay scattered on her neck, till Daphne's strength was spent, and she grew pale and weary with the effort of her swift flight. Then she saw the waters of the Peneus: 'O father,' she cried, 'help me! If you rivers really have divine powers, work some transformation, and destroy this beauty which makes me please all too well!' Her prayer was scarcely ended when a deep languor took hold on her limbs, her soft breast was enclosed in thin bark, her hair grew into leaves, her arms into branches, and her feet that were lately so swift were held fast by sluggish roots, while her face became the treetop. Nothing of her was left, except her shining loveliness.

Even as a tree, Phoebus loved her. He placed his hand against the trunk, and felt her heart still beating under the new bark. Embracing the branches as if they were limbs he kissed the wood: but, even as a tree, she shrank from his kisses. Then the god said: 'Since you cannot be my bride, surely you will at least be my tree. My hair, my lyre, my quivers will always display the laurel. You will accompany the generals of Rome, when the Capitol beholds their long triumphal processions, when joyful voices raise the song of victory. You will stand by Augustus' gateposts too, faithfully guarding his doors, and keeping watch from either side over the wreath of oak leaves that will hang there. Further, as my head is ever young, my tresses never shorn, so do you also, at all times, wear the crowning glory of never-fading foliage.' Paean, the healer, had done: the laurel tree inclined her newmade branches, and seemed to nod her leafy top, as if it were a head, in consent. . . .

JUVENAL
Satire III

Despite the wrench of parting, I applaud my old friend's
Decision to make his home in lonely Cumae—the poor
Sibyl will get at least *one* fellow-citizen now!
It's a charming coastal retreat, and just across the point
From our smartest watering-spot. Myself, I would value
A barren offshore island more than Rome's urban heart:
Squalor and isolation are minor evils compared
To this endless nightmare of fires and collapsing houses,
The cruel city's myriad perils—and poets reciting
Their work in *August*!
                    While his goods were being loaded
On one small waggon, my old friend lingered a while
By the ancient dripping arches of the Capuan Gate,
        where once
King Numa had nightly meetings with his mistress.
    (But today

Egeria's grove and shrine and sacred spring are rented
To Jewish squatters, their sole possession a Sabbath
        haybox.
Each tree must show a profit, the Muses have been
        evicted,
The wood's aswarm with beggars.)
                        From here we strolled down
To the nymph's new, modernized grotto. (What a gain in
        sanctity
And atmosphere there would be if grassy banks
Surrounded the pool, if no flash marble affronted
Our native limestone!) Here Umbricius stood, and
Opened his heart to me.
                    'There's no room in this city,'
He said, 'for the decent professions: they don't show any
        profit.

My resources have shrunk since yesterday, and tomorrow
Will eat away more of what's left. So I am going
Where Daedalus put off his weary wings, while as yet
I'm in vigorous middle age, while active years are left me,
While my white hairs are still few, and I need no stick
To guide my tottering feet. So farewell Rome, I leave you
To sanitary engineers and municipal architects, men
Who by swearing black is white land all the juicy
    contracts
Just like that—a new temple, swamp-drainage,
    harbour-works,
River-clearance, undertaking, the lot—then pocket the
    cash
And fraudulently file their petition in bankruptcy.
Once these fellows were horn-players, stumping the
    provinces
In road-shows, their puffed-out cheeks a familiar sight
To every country village. But now they stage shows
    themselves,
Of the gladiatorial sort, and at the mob's thumbs-down
Will butcher a loser for popularity's sake, and
Pass on from that to erecting public privies. Why not?
These are such men as Fortune, by way of a joke,
Will sometimes raise from the gutter and make Top
    People.
What can I do in Rome? I never learnt how
To lie. If a book is bad, I cannot puff it, or bother
To ask around for a copy; astrological clap-trap
Is not in my stars. I cannot and will not promise
To encompass any man's death by way of obliging his son.
I have never meddled with frogs' guts; the task of
    carrying
Letters and presents between adulterous lovers
I resign to those who know it. I refuse to become
An accomplice in theft—which means that no governor
Will accept me on his staff. It's like being a cripple
With a paralysed right hand. Yet who today is favoured
Above the conspirator, his head externally seething
With confidential matters, never to be revealed?
Harmless secrets carry no obligations, and he
Who shares them with you feels no great call thereafter
To keep you sweet. But if Verres promotes a man
You can safely assume that man has the screws on Verres
And could turn him in tomorrow. Not all the gold
Washed seaward with the silt of tree-lined Tagus
Is worth the price you pay, racked by insomnia, seeing
Your high-placed friends all cringe at your approach—and
For what? Too-transient prizes, unwillingly resigned.
    'Now let me turn to that race which goes down so well
With our millionaires, but remains *my* special pet aversion,
And not mince my words. I cannot, citizens, stomach
A Greek-struck Rome. Yet what fraction of these
    sweepings
Derives, in fact, from Greece? For years now Syrian
Orontes has poured its sewerage into our native Tiber—
Its lingo and manners, its flutes, its outlandish harps
With their transverse strings, its native tambourines,
And the whores who hang out round the race-course.
    (That's where to go
If you fancy a foreign piece in one of those saucy toques.)

Our beloved Founder should see how his homespun
    rustics
Behave today, with their dinner-pumps—*trechedipna*
They call them—not to mention their *niceteria*
(Decorations to you) hung round their *ceromatic* (that's
Well-greased) wrestlers' necks. Here's one from Sicyon,
Another from Macedonia, two from Aegean islands—
Andros, say, or Samos—two more from Caria,
All of them lighting out for the City's classiest districts
And burrowing into great houses, with a long-term plan
For taking them over. Quick wit, unlimited nerve, a gift
Of the gab that outsmarts a professional public speaker—
These are their characteristics. What do you take
That fellow's profession to be? He has brought a whole
    bundle
Of personalities with him—schoolmaster, rhetorician,
Surveyor, artist, masseur, diviner, tightrope-walker,
Magician or quack, your versatile hungry Greekling
Is all by turns. Tell him to fly—he's airborne.
The inventor of wings was no Moor or Slav, remember,
Or Thracian, but born in the very heart of Athens.
    'When such men as these wear the purple, when some
    creature
Blown into Rome along with the figs and damsons
Precedes me at dinner-parties, or for the witnessing
Of manumissions and wills—*me*, who drew my first breath
On these Roman hills, and was nourished on Sabine
    olives!—
Things have reached a pretty pass. What's more, their
    talent
For flattery is unmatched. They praise the conversation
Of their dimmest friends; the ugly they call handsome,
So that your scrag-necked weakling finds himself compared
To Hercules holding the giant Antaeus aloft
Way off the earth. They go into ecstasies over
Some shrill and scrannel voice that sounds like a hen
When the cock gets at her. We can make the same
    compliments, but
It's they who convince. On the stage they remain supreme
In female parts, courtesan, matron or slave-girl,
With no concealing cloak: you'd swear it was a genuine
Woman you saw, and not a masked performer.
Look there, beneath that belly: no bulge, all smooth, a neat
Nothingness—even a hint of the Great Divide. Yet back home
These queens and dames pass unnoticed. Greece is a
    nation
Of actors. Laugh, and they split their sides. At the sight
Of a friend's tears, they weep too—though quite unmoved.
If you ask for a fire in winter, the Greek puts on his cloak;
If you say "I'm hot", *he* starts sweating. So you see
We are not on an equal footing: he has the great advantage
Of being able on all occasions, night and day,
To take his cue, his mask, from others. He's always ready
To throw up his hands and applaud when a friend
    delivers
A really resounding belch, or pisses right on the mark,
With a splendid drumming sound from the upturned
    golden basin.
    'Besides, he holds nothing sacred, not a soul is safe
From his randy urges, the lady of the house, her

Virgin daughter, her daughter's still unbearded
Husband-to-be, her hitherto virtuous son—
And if none of these are to hand, he'll cheerfully lay
His best friend's grandmother. (Anything to ferret
Domestic secrets out, and get a hold over people.)
  'And while we are on the subject of Greeks, let us
    consider
Academics and their vices—not the gymnasium crowd
But big philosophical wheels, like that Stoic greybeard
Who narked on his friend and pupil, and got him
    liquidated.
He was brought up in Tarsus, by the banks of that river
Where Bellerophon fell to earth from the Gorgon's flying
    nag.
No room for honest Romans when Rome's ruled by a
    junta
Of Greek-born secret agents, who—like all their race—
Never share friends or patrons. One small dose of venom
(Half Greek, half personal) dropped in that ready ear
And I'm out, shown the back-door, my years of
    obsequious
Service all gone for nothing. Where can a hanger-on
Be ditched with less fuss than in Rome? Besides (not to
    flatter ourselves)
What use are our poor efforts, where does it all get us,
Dressing up while it's dark still, hurrying along
To pay our morning respects to a couple of wealthy
Maiden aunts? But the praetor's really worked up, his
Colleague may get there before him, the ladies have been
    awake
For hours already, the minions catch it—"Get
A *move* on there, can't you?" Here a citizen, free-born,
Must stand aside on the pavement for some wealthy
    tycoon's slave:
He can afford to squander a senior officer's income
On classy amateur harlots, just for the privilege
Of laying them once or twice. But when *you* fancy
A common-or-garden tart, you dither and hesitate:
Can I afford to accost her? With witnesses in court
The same applies. Their morals may be beyond cavil,
    and yet
If Scipio took the stand (and he was selected
To escort the Mother Goddess on her journey to Rome)
    or Metellus
Who rescued Minerva's image from her blazing shrine,
    or even
King Numa himself, still the first and foremost question
Would be: *"What's he worth?"* His character would
    command
Little if any respect. "How many slaves does he keep?
What's his acreage? What sort of dinner-service
Appears on his table—how many pieces, how big?"
Each man's word is as good as his bond—or rather,
The number of bonds in his strong-box. A pauper can
    swear by every
Altar, and every god between Rome and Samothrace, still
(Though the gods themselves forgive them) he'll pass for
    a perjuror
Defying the wrath of heaven. The poor man's an eternal
Butt for bad jokes, with his torn and dirt-caked top-coat,

His grubby toga, one shoe agape where the leather's
Split—those clumsy patches, that coarse and tell-tale
    stitching
Only a day or two old. The hardest thing to bear
In poverty is the fact that it makes us ridiculous.
"Out of those front-row seats," we're told. "You ought to be
Ashamed of yourselves—your incomes are far too small, and
The law's the law. Make way for some pander's son,
Spawned in an unknown brothel, let your place be occupied
By that natty auctioneer's offspring, with his high-class
    companions
The trainer's brat and the son of the gladiator
Applauding beside him." Such were the fruits of that
    pinhead
Otho's Reserved Seat Act. What prospective son-in-law
Ever passed muster here if he was short on cash
To match the girl's dowry? What poor man ever inherits
A legacy, or is granted that meanest of sinecures—
A job with the Office of Works? All lower-income citizens
Should have marched out of town, in a body, years ago.
Nobody finds it easy to get to the top if meagre
Resources cripple his talent. But in Rome the problem's
    worse
Than anywhere else. Inflation hits the rental
Of your miserable apartment, inflation distends
The ravenous maws of your slaves; your humble dinner
Suffers inflation too. You feel ashamed to eat
Off earthenware dishes—yet if you were transported
To some rural village, you'd be content enough
And happily wear a cloak of coarse blue broadcloth
Complete with hood. Throughout most of Italy—we
Might as well admit it—no one is seen in a toga
Till the day he dies. Even on public holidays,
When the same old shows as last year are cheerfully
    staged
In the grassgrown theatre, when peasant children, sitting
On their mothers' laps, shrink back in terror at the sight
Of those gaping, whitened masks, you will still find the
    whole
Audience—top row or bottom—dressed exactly alike;
Even the magistrates need no better badge of status
Than a plain white tunic. But here in Rome we must toe
The line of fashion, living beyond our means, and
Often on borrowed credit: every man jack of us
Is keeping up with his neighbours. To cut a long story
    short,
Nothing's for free in Rome. How much does it cost you
To salute our noble Cossus (rare privilege!) or extract
One casual, tight-lipped nod from Veiento the
    honours-broker?
X will be having his beard trimmed, Y just offering up
His boy-friend's kiss-curls: the whole house swarms with
    barbers,
Each of them on the make. You might as well swallow
Your bile, and face the fact that we hangers-on
Have to bribe our way, swell some sleek menial's savings.
  'What countryman ever bargained, besides, for his
    house collapsing
About his ears? Such things are unheard-of in cool
Praeneste, or rural Gabii, or Tivoli perched on its hillside,

Or Volsinii, nestling amid its woodland ridges. But here
We live in a city shored up, for the most part, with
    gimcrack
Stays and props: that's how our landlords arrest
The collapse of their property, papering over great cracks
In the ramshackle fabric, reassuring the tenants
They can sleep secure, when all the time the building
Is poised like a house of cards. I prefer to live where
Fires and midnight panics are not quite such common
    events.
By the time the smoke's got up to your third-floor
    apartment
(And you still asleep) your downstairs neighbour is
    roaring
For water, and shifting his bits and pieces to safety.
If the alarm goes at ground-level, the last to fry
Will be the attic tenant, way up among the nesting
Pigeons, with nothing but tiles between himself and the
    weather.
What did friend Cordus own? One truckle bed, too short
For even a midget nympho; one marble-topped sideboard
On which stood six little mugs; beneath it, a pitcher
And an up-ended bust of Chiron; one ancient settle
Crammed with Greek books (though by now
    analphabetic mice
Had gnawed their way well into his texts of the great poets).
Cordus could hardly be called a property-owner, and yet
What little the poor man had, he lost. Today the final
Straw on his load of woe (clothes worn to tatters, reduced
To begging for crusts) is that no one will offer him
    lodging
Or shelter, not even stand him a decent meal. But if
Some millionaire's mansion is gutted, women rend their
    garments,
Top people put on mourning, the courts go into recess:
Then you hear endless complaints about the hazards
Of city life, these deplorable outbreaks of fire;
Then contributions pour in while the shell is still
    ash-hot—
Construction materials, marble, fresh-gleaming sculptured
    nudes.
Up come A with bronzes (genuine antique works
By a real Old Master) acquired, as part of his booty,
From their hallowed niche in some Asiatic temple;
B provides bookshelves, books, and a study bust of
    Minerva;
C a sackful of silver. So it goes on, until
This dandified bachelor's losses are all recouped—
And more than recouped—with even rarer possessions,
And a rumour (well-founded) begins to circulate
That he fired the place himself, a deliberate piece of arson.
    'If you can face the prospect of no more public games
Purchase a freehold house in the country. What it will
    cost you
Is no more than you pay in annual rent for some shabby
And ill-lit garret here. A garden plot's thrown in
With the house itself, and a well with a shallow basin—
No rope-and-bucket work when your seedlings need
    some water!
Learn to enjoy hoeing, work and plant your allotment

Till a hundred vegetarians could feast off its produce.
It's quite an achievement, even out in the backwoods,
To have made yourself master of—well, say one lizard, even.
    'Insomnia causes more deaths amongst Roman invalids
Than any other factor (the most common *complaints*, of
    course,
Are heartburn and ulcers, brought on by over-eating.)
How much sleep, I ask you, can one get in lodgings here?
Unbroken nights—and this is the root of the trouble—
Are a rich man's privilege. The waggons thundering past
Through those narrow twisting streets, the oaths of
    draymen
Caught in a traffic-jam—these alone would suffice
To jolt the doziest sea-cow of an Emperor into
Permanent wakefulness. If a business appointment
Summons the tycoon, *he* gets there fast, by litter,
Tacking above the crowd. There's plenty of room inside:
He can read, or take notes, or snooze as he jogs along—
Those drawn blinds are most soporific. Even so
He outstrips us: however fast we pedestrians hurry
We're blocked by the crowds ahead, while those behind us
Tread on our heels. Sharp elbows buffet my ribs,
Poles poke into me; one lout swings a crossbeam
Down on my skull, another scores with a barrel.
My legs are mud-encrusted, big feet kick me, a hobnailed
Soldier's boot lands squarely on my toes. Do you see
All that steam and bustle? The great man's hangers-on
Are getting their free dinner, each with his own
Kitchen-boy in attendance. Those outsize dixies,
And all the rest of the gear one poor little slave
Must balance on his head, while he trots along
To keep the charcoal glowing, would tax the strength
Of a musclebound general. Recently-patched tunics
Are ripped to shreds. Here's the great trunk of a fir-tree
Swaying along on its waggon, and look, another dray
Behind it, stacked high with pine-logs, a nodding threat
Over the heads of the crowd. If that axle snapped, and a
Cartload of marble avalanched down on them, what
Would be left of their bodies? Who could identify bits
Of ownerless flesh and bone? The poor man's flattened
    corpse
Would vanish along with his soul. And meanwhile, all
    unwitting,
The folk at home are busily scouring dishes,
Blowing the fire to a glow, clattering over greasy
Flesh-scrapers, filling up oil-flasks, laying out clean towels.
But all the time, as his houseboys hasten about their
    chores,
Himself is already sitting—the latest arrival—
By the bank of the Styx, and gawping in holy terror
At its filthy old ferryman. No chance of a passage over
That mud-thick channel for him, poor devil, without so
    much
As a cooper stuck in his mouth to pay for the ride.
    'There are other nocturnal perils, of various sorts,
Which you should consider. It's a long way up to the
    rooftops,
And a falling tile can brain you—not to mention all
Those cracked or leaky pots that people toss out through
    windows.

Look at the way they smash, the weight of them, the
    damage
They do to the pavement! You'll be thought most
    improvident,
A catastrophe-happy fool, if you don't make your will
    before
Venturing out to dinner. Each open upper casement
Along your route at night may prove a death-trap:
So pray and hope (poor you!) that the local housewives
Drop nothing worse on your head than a pailful of slops.
    'Then there's the drunken bully, in an agonized state
For lack of a victim, who lies there tossing and turning
The whole night through, like Achilles after the death
Of his boy-friend Patroclus. [This lout is doomed to
    insomnia
Unless he gets a fight.] Yet however flown with wine
Our young hothead may be, he carefully keeps his
    distance
From the man in a scarlet cloak, the man surrounded
By torches and big brass lamps and a numerous
    bodyguard.
But for me, a lonely pedestrian, trudging home by
    moonlight
Or with hand cupped round the wick of one poor
    guttering candle,
He has no respect whatever. This is the way the wretched
Brawl comes about (if you can term it a brawl
When you do the fighting and I'm just cast as punchbag).
He blocks my way. "Stop," he says. I have no option
But to obey—what else can one do when attacked
By a huge tough, twice one's size and fighting-mad as well?
"Where have *you* sprung from?" he shouts. "Ugh, what a
    stench
Of beans and sour wine! I know your sort, you've been
    round
With some cobbler-crony, scoffing a boiled sheep's head
And a dish of spring leeks. What? Nothing to say for
    yourself?
Speak up, or I'll kick your teeth in! Tell me, where's your
    pitch?

What synagogue do you doss in?" It makes not a jot of
    difference
Whether you try to answer, or back away from him
Without saying a word, you get beaten up just the
    same—
And then your irate "victim" takes *you* to court on a
    charge
Of assault and battery. Such is the poor man's "freedom":
After being slugged to a pulp, he may beg, as a special
Favour, to be left with his last few remaining teeth.
    'Nor is this the sum of your terrors: when every house
Is shut up for the night, when shops stand silent, when
    bolts
Are shot, and doors on the chain, there are still burglars
Lurking around, or maybe some street-apache will settle
Your hash with a knife, the quick way. (Whenever armed
    detachments
Are patrolling the swamps and forests, Rome becomes
A warren for this sort of scum.) Our furnaces glow, our
    anvils
Groan everywhere under their output of chains and fetters:
That's where most of our iron goes nowadays: one wonders
Whether ploughshares, hoes and mattocks may not soon
    be obsolete.
How fortunate they were (you well may think) those early
Forbears of ours, how happy the good old days
Of Kings and Tribunes, when Rome made do with one
    prison only!
    'There are many other arguments I could adduce: but
    the sun
Slants down, my cattle are lowing, I must be on my way—
The muleteer has been signalling me with his whip
For some while now. So goodbye, and don't forget me—
Whenever you go back home for a break from the City,
    invite
Me over too, to share your fields and coverts,
Your country festivals: I'll put on my thickest boots
And make the trip to those chilly uplands—and listen
To your *Satires*, if I am reckoned worthy of that honour.'

Chapter

6

Judaism and the Rise of Christianity

from *The New English Bible*

Psalm 22

My God, my God, why hast thou forsaken me
  and art so far from saving me, from heeding my groans?
O my God, I cry in the day-time but thou dost not answer,
  in the night I cry but get no respite.
And yet thou art enthroned in holiness,
    thou art he whose praises Israel sings.
In thee our fathers put their trust;
    they trusted, and thou didst rescue them.
Unto thee they cried and were delivered;
  in thee they trusted and were not put to shame.
But I am a worm, not a man,
    abused by all men, scorned by the people.
All who see me jeer at me,
make mouths at me and wag their heads:
  'He threw himself on the Lord for rescue;
  let the Lord deliver him, for he holds him dear!'
But thou art he who drew me from the womb,
    who laid me at my mother's breast.
Upon thee was I cast at birth;
  from my mother's womb thou hast been my God.
    Be not far from me,
for trouble is near, and I have no helper.
  A herd of bulls surrounds me,
    great bulls of Bashan beset me.

Ravening and roaring lions
  open their mouths wide against me.
    My strength drains away like water
    and all my bones are loose.
My heart has turned to wax and melts within me.
  My mouth is dry as a potsherd,
  and my tongue sticks to my jaw;
    I am laid low in the dust of death.
    The huntsmen are all about me;
    a band of ruffians rings me round,
  and they have hacked off my hands and my feet.
    I tell my tale of misery,
  while they look on and gloat.
They share out my garments among them
  and cast lots for my clothes.
But do not remain so far away, O Lord;
O my help, hasten to my aid.
Deliver my very self from the sword,
  my precious life from the axe.
    Save me from the lion's mouth,
    my poor body from the horns of the wild ox.

I will declare thy fame to my brethren;
  I will praise thee in the midst of the assembly.

Praise him, you who fear the Lord;
  all you sons of Jacob, do him honour;
stand in awe of him, all sons of Israel.
  For he has not scorned the downtrodden,
  nor shrunk in loathing from his plight,
nor hidden his face from him,
but gave heed to him when he cried out.
Thou dost inspire my praise in the full assembly;
  and I will pay my vows before all who fear thee.
  Let the humble eat and be satisfied.
  Let those who seek the Lord praise him
  and be in good heart for ever.
Let all the ends of the earth remember and turn again to
    the Lord;

let all the families of the nations bow down before him.
  For kingly power belongs to the Lord,
  and dominion over the nations is his.
  How can those buried in the earth do him homage,
  how can those who go down to the grave bow before him?
  But I shall live for his sake,
  my posterity shall serve him.
This shall be told of the Lord to future generations;
  and they shall justify him,
  declaring to a people yet unborn
  that this was his doing.

═══════

Psalm 23

─────────

The Lord is my shepherd; I shall want nothing.
  He makes me lie down in green pastures,
and leads me beside the waters of peace;
  he renews life within me,
and for his name's sake guides me in the right path.
Even though I walk through a valley dark as death
I fear no evil, for thou art with me,
thy staff and thy crook are my comfort.

Thou spreadest a table for me in the sight of my
    enemies;
  thou hast richly bathed my head with oil,
  and my cup runs over.
  Goodness and love unfailing, these will follow me
  all the days of my life,
  and I shall dwell in the house of the Lord
  my whole life long.

═══════

Psalm 24

─────────

The earth is the Lord's and all that is in it,
  the world and those who dwell therein.
For it was he who founded it upon the seas
  and planted it firm upon the waters beneath.

Who may go up the mountain of the Lord?
And who may stand in his holy place?
  He who has clean hands and a pure heart,
who has not set his mind on falsehood,
  and has not committed perjury.
He shall receive a blessing from the Lord,
  and justice from God his saviour.
  Such is the fortune of those who seek him,
  who seek the face of the God of Jacob.

Lift up your heads, you gates,
  lift yourselves up, you everlasting doors,
that the king of glory may come in.
  Who is the king of glory?
  The Lord strong and mighty,
  the Lord mighty in battle.
Lift up your heads, you gates,
  lift them up, you everlasting doors,
  that the king of glory may come in.
Who then is the king of glory?
The king of glory is the Lord of Hosts.

Psalm 104

Bless the Lord, my soul:
O Lord my God, thou art great indeed,
  clothed in majesty and splendour,
  and wrapped in a robe of light.
  Thou hast spread out the heavens like a tent
  and on their waters laid the beams of thy pavilion;
  who takest the clouds for thy chariot,
  riding on the wings of the wind;
  who makest the winds thy messengers
  and flames of fire thy servants;
  thou didst fix the earth on its foundation
  so that it never can be shaken;
  the deep overspread it like a cloak,
  and the waters lay above the mountains.
  At thy rebuke they ran,
  at the sound of thy thunder they rushed away,
  flowing over the hills,
  pouring down into the valleys
  to the place appointed for them.
Thou didst fix a boundary which they might not pass;
  they shall not return to cover the earth.

Thou dost make springs break out in the gullies,
  so that their water runs between the hills.
  The wild beasts all drink from them,
  the wild asses quench their thirst;
  the birds of the air nest on their banks
  and sing among the leaves.

From thy high pavilion thou dost water the hills;
  the earth is enriched by thy provision.
  Thou makest grass grow for the cattle
    and green things for those who toil for man,
  bringing bread out of the earth
  and wine to gladden men's hearts,
  oil to make their faces shine
  and bread to sustain their strength.
    The trees of the Lord are green and leafy,
    the cedars of Lebanon which he planted;
  the birds build their nests in them,
  the stork makes her home in their tops.
  High hills are the haunt of the mountain-goat,
  and boulders a refuge for the rock-badger.

Thou hast made the moon to measure the year
  and taught the sun where to set.
When thou makest darkness and it is night,
all the beasts of the forest come forth;
  the young lions roar for prey,
  seeking their food from God.
  When thou makest the sun rise, they slink away
    and go to rest in their lairs;
  but man comes out to his work
    and to his labours until evening.
  Countless are the things thou hast made, O Lord.
  Thou hast made all by thy wisdom;
  and the earth is full of thy creatures,
  beasts great and small.
Here is the great immeasurable sea,
  in which move creatures beyond number.
  Here ships sail to and fro,
here is Leviathan whom thou hast made thy plaything.

All of them look expectantly to thee
  to give them their food at the proper time;
  what thou givest them they gather up;
  when thou openest thy hand, they eat their fill.
  Then thou hidest thy face, and they are restless and
    troubled;
  when thou takest away their breath, they fail
  [and they return to the dust from which they came];
but when thou breathest into them, they recover;
  thou givest new life to the earth.

May the glory of the Lord stand for ever
  and may he rejoice in his works!
When he looks at the earth, it quakes;
  when he touches the hills, they pour forth smoke.

I will sing to the Lord as long as I live,
all my life I will sing psalms to my God.
May my meditation please the Lord,
  as I show my joy in him!
Away with all sinners from the earth
and may the wicked be no more!

Bless the Lord, my soul.

  O praise the Lord.

The Song of Songs

BRIDE

I will sing the song of all songs to Solomon
that he may smother me with kisses.

Your love is more fragrant than wine,
fragrant is the scent of your perfume,
and your name like perfume poured out;
for this the maidens love you.
Take me with you, and we will run together;
bring me into your chamber, O king.

COMPANIONS

Let us rejoice and be glad for you;
let us praise your love more than wine,
and your caresses more than any song.

BRIDE

I am dark but lovely, daughters of Jerusalem,
like the tents of Kedar
or the tent-curtains of Shalmah.
Do not look down on me; a little dark I may be
because I am scorched by the sun.
My mother's sons were displeased with me,
they sent me to watch over the vineyards;
so I did not watch over my own vineyard.
Tell me, my true love,
where you mind your flocks,
where you rest them at midday,
that I may not be left picking lice
as I sit among your companions' herds.

BRIDEGROOM

If you yourself do not know,
O fairest of women,
go, follow the tracks of the sheep
and mind your kids by the shepherds' huts.

I would compare you, my dearest,
to Pharaoh's chariot-horses,
Your cheeks are lovely between plaited tresses,
your neck with its jewelled chains.

COMPANIONS

We will make you braided plaits of gold
set with beads of silver.

BRIDE

While the king reclines on his couch,
my spikenard gives forth its scent.
My beloved is for me a bunch of myrrh
as he lies on my breast,
my beloved is for me a cluster of henna-blossom
from the vineyards of En-gedi.

BRIDEGROOM

How beautiful you are, my dearest,
O how beautiful,
your eyes are like doves!

BRIDE

How beautiful you are, O my love,
and how pleasant!

BRIDEGROOM

Our couch is shaded with branches;
the beams of our house are of cedar,
our ceilings are all of fir.

BRIDE

I am an asphodel in Sharon,
a lily growing in the valley.

BRIDEGROOM

No, a lily among thorns
is my dearest among girls.

BRIDE

Like an apricot-tree among the trees of the wood,
so is my beloved among boys.
To sit in its shadow was my delight,
and its fruit was sweet to my taste.
He took me into the wine-garden
and gave me loving glances.
He refreshed me with raisins, he revived me with
apricots;
for I was faint with love.
His left arm was under my head, his right arm was
round me.

BRIDEGROOM

I charge you, daughters of Jerusalem,
by the spirits and the goddesses of the field:
Do not rouse her, do not disturb my love
until she is ready.

BRIDE

Hark! My beloved! Here he comes,
bounding over the mountains, leaping over the hills.
My beloved is like a gazelle
or a young wild goat:
there he stands outside our wall,
peeping in at the windows, glancing through the lattice.

My beloved answered, he said to me:
Rise up, my darling;
my fairest, come away.

For now the winter is past,
the rains are over and gone;
the flowers appear in the country-side;
the time is coming when the birds will sing,
and the turtle-dove's cooing will be heard in our land;
when the green figs will ripen on the fig-trees
and the vines give forth their fragrance.
Rise up, my darling;
my fairest, come away.

BRIDEGROOM

My dove, that hides in holes in the cliffs
or in crannies on the high ledges,
let me see your face, let me hear your voice;
for your voice is pleasant, your face is lovely.

COMPANIONS

Catch for us the jackals, the little jackals,
that spoil our vineyards, when the vines are in flower.

BRIDE

My beloved is mine and I am his;
he delights in the lilies.
While the day is cool and the shadows are dispersing,
turn, my beloved, and show yourself
a gazelle or a young wild goat
on the hills where cinnamon grows.

Night after night on my bed
I have sought my true love;
I have sought him but not found him,
I have called him but he has not answered.
I said, 'I will rise and go to the rounds of the city,
through the streets and the squares,
seeking my true love.'
I sought him but I did not find him,
I called him but he did not answer.
The watchmen, going the rounds of the city, met me,
and I asked, 'Have you seen my true love?'
Scarcely had I left them behind me
when I met my true love.
I seized him and would not let him go
until I had brought him to my mother's house,
to the room of her who conceived me.

BRIDEGROOM

I charge you, daughters of Jerusalem,
by the spirits and the goddesses of the field:
Do not rouse her, do not disturb my love
until she is ready.

COMPANIONS

What is this coming up from the wilderness
like a column of smoke
from burning myrrh or frankincense,
from all the powdered spices that merchants bring?
Look; it is Solomon carried in his litter;
sixty of Israel's chosen warriors
are his escort,
all of them skilled swordsmen,

all trained to handle arms,
each with his sword ready at his side
to ward off the demon of the night.

The palanquin which King Solomon had made for
himself
was of wood from Lebanon.
Its poles he had made of silver,
its head-rest of gold;
its seat was of purple stuff,
and its lining was of leather.

Come out, daughters of Jerusalem;
you daughters of Zion, come out and welcome King
Solomon,
wearing the crown with which his mother has
crowned him,
on his wedding day, on his day of joy.

BRIDEGROOM

How beautiful you are, my dearest, how beautiful!
Your eyes behind your veil are like doves,
your hair like a flock of goats streaming down Mount
Gilead.
Your teeth are like a flock of ewes just shorn
which have come up fresh from the dipping;
each ewe has twins and none has cast a lamb.
Your lips are like a scarlet thread,
and your words are delightful;
your parted lips behind your veil
are like a pomegranate cut open.
Your neck is like David's tower,
which is built with winding courses;
a thousand bucklers hang upon it,
and all are warriors' shields.
Your two breasts are like two fawns,
twin fawns of a gazelle.
While the day is cool and the shadows are dispersing,
I will go to the mountains of myrrh
and to the hills of frankincense.
You are beautiful, my dearest,
beautiful without a flaw.

Come from Lebanon, my bride;
come with me from Lebanon.
Hurry down from the top of Amana,
from Senir's top and Hermon's,
from the lions' lairs, and the hills the leopards haunt.

You have stolen my heart, my sister,
you have stolen it, my bride,
with one of your eyes, with one jewel of your necklace.
How beautiful are your breasts, my sister, my bride!
Your love is more fragrant than wine,
and your perfumes sweeter than any spices.
Your lips drop sweetness like the honeycomb, my bride,
syrup and milk are under your tongue,
and your dress has the scent of Lebanon.
Your two cheeks are an orchard of pomegranates,
an orchard full of rare fruits:
spikenard and saffron, sweet-cane and cinnamon

with every incense-bearing tree,
 myrrh and aloes
with all the choicest spices.
My sister, my bride, is a garden close-locked,
a garden close-locked, a fountain sealed.

BRIDE

The fountain in my garden is a spring of running water
 pouring down from Lebanon.
Awake, north wind, and come, south wind;
blow upon my garden that its perfumes may pour forth,
 that my beloved may come to his garden
 and enjoy its rare fruits.

BRIDEGROOM

I have come to my garden, my sister and bride,
 and have plucked my myrrh and my spices;
 I have eaten my honey and my syrup,
 I have drunk my wine and my milk.
Eat, friends, and drink,
 until you are drunk with love.

BRIDE

I sleep but my heart is awake.
 Listen! My beloved is knocking:

'Open to me, my sister, my dearest,
 my dove, my perfect one;
 for my head is drenched with dew,
 my locks with the moisture of the night.'

'I have stripped off my dress; must I put it on again?
I have washed my feet; must I soil them again?'

When my beloved slipped his hand through the
 latch-hole,
 my bowels stirred within me.
When I arose to open for my beloved,
 my hands dripped with myrrh;
the liquid myrrh from my fingers
 ran over the knobs of the bolt.
 With my own hands I opened to my love,
 but my love had turned away and gone by;
 my heart sank when he turned his back.
 I sought him but I did not find him,
 I called him but he did not answer.
The watchmen, going the rounds of the city, met me;
 they struck me and wounded me;
the watchmen on the walls took away my cloak.
 I charge you, daughters of Jerusalem,
if you find my beloved, will you not tell him
 that I am faint with love?

COMPANIONS

What is your beloved more than any other,
 O fairest of women?
What is your beloved more than any other,
 that you give us this charge?

BRIDE

My beloved is fair and ruddy,
 a paragon among ten thousand.
His head is gold, finest gold;
 his locks are like palm-fronds.
His eyes are like doves beside brooks of water,
 splashed by the milky water
 as they sit where it is drawn.
His cheeks are like beds of spices or chests full of
 perfumes;
his lips are lilies, and drop liquid myrrh;
his hands are golden rods set in topaz;
his belly a plaque of ivory overlaid with lapis lazuli.
His legs are pillars of marble in sockets of finest gold;
 his aspect is like Lebanon, noble as cedars.
His whispers are sweetness itself, wholly desirable.
Such is my beloved, such is my darling,
 daughters of Jerusalem.

COMPANIONS

Where has your beloved gone,
 O fairest of women?
Which way did your beloved go,
 that we may help you to seek him?

BRIDE

My beloved has gone down to his garden,
 to the beds where balsam grows,
to delight in the garden and to pick the lilies.
I am my beloved's, and my beloved is mine,
 he who delights in the lilies.

BRIDEGROOM

You are beautiful, my dearest, as Tirzah,
 lovely as Jerusalem.
 Turn your eyes away from me;
 they dazzle me.
Your hair is like a flock of goats streaming down Mount
 Gilead;
your teeth are like a flock of ewes come up fresh from
 the dipping,
each ewe has twins and none has cast a lamb.
 Your parted lips behind your veil
 are like a pomegranate cut open.
 There may be sixty princesses,
eighty concubines, and young women past counting,
but there is one alone, my dove, my perfect one,
 her mother's only child,
 devoted to the mother who bore her;
 young girls see her and call her happy,
 princesses and concubines praise her.
Who is this that looks out like the dawn,
beautiful as the moon, bright as the sun,
 majestic as the starry heavens?

I went down to a garden of nut-trees
 to look at the rushes by the stream,
to see if the vine had budded

or the pomegranates were in flower.
I did not know myself;
she made me feel more than a prince
reigning over the myriads of his people.

COMPANIONS

Come back, come back, Shulammite maiden,
come back, that we may gaze upon you.

BRIDEGROOM

How you love to gaze on the Shulammite maiden,
as she moves between the lines of dancers!

How beautiful are your sandalled feet, O prince's
daughter!
The curves of your thighs are like jewels,
the work of a skilled craftsman.
Your navel is a rounded goblet
that never shall want for spiced wine.
Your belly is a heap of wheat
fenced in by lilies.
Your two breasts are like two fawns,
twin fawns of a gazelle.
Your neck is like a tower of ivory.
Your eyes are the pools in Heshbon,
beside the gate of the crowded city.
Your nose is like towering Lebanon
that looks towards Damascus.
You carry your head like Carmel;
the flowing hair on your head is lustrous black,
your tresses are braided with ribbons.
How beautiful, how entrancing you are,
my loved one, daughter of delights!
You are stately as a palm-tree,
and your breasts are the clusters of dates.
I said, 'I will climb up into the palm
to grasp its fronds.'
May I find your breasts like clusters of grapes on the vine,
the scent of your breath like apricots,
and your whispers like spiced wine
flowing smoothly to welcome my caresses,
gliding down through lips and teeth.

BRIDE

I am my beloved's, his longing is all for me.
Come, my beloved, let us go out into the fields
to lie among the henna-bushes;
let us go early to the vineyards
and see if the vine has budded or its blossom opened,
if the pomegranates are in flower.
There will I give you my love,
when the mandrakes give their perfume,
and all rare fruits are ready at our door,
fruits new and old
which I have in store for you, my love.

If only you were my own true brother
that sucked my mother's breasts!
Then, if I found you outside, I would kiss you,
and no man would despise me.

I would lead you to the room of the mother who bore me,
bring you to her house for you to embrace me;
I would give you mulled wine to drink
and the fresh juice of pomegranates,
your left arm under my head and your right arm round me.

BRIDEGROOM

I charge you, daughters of Jerusalem:
Do not rouse her, do not disturb my love
until she is ready.

COMPANIONS

Who is this coming up from the wilderness
leaning on her beloved?

BRIDEGROOM

Under the apricot-trees I roused you,
there where your mother was in labour with you,
there where she who bore you was in labour.
Wear me as a seal upon your heart,
as a seal upon your arm;
for love is strong as death,
passion cruel as the grave;
it blazes up like blazing fire,
fiercer than any flame.
Many waters cannot quench love,
no flood can sweep it away;
if a man were to offer for love
the whole wealth of his house,
it would be utterly scorned.

COMPANIONS

We have a little sister
who has no breasts;
what shall we do for our sister
when she is asked in marriage?
If she is a wall,
we will build on it a silver parapet,
but if she is a door,
we will close it up with planks of cedar.

BRIDE

I am a wall and my breasts are like towers;
so in his eyes I am as one who brings contentment.
Solomon has a vineyard at Baal-hamon;
he has let out his vineyard to guardians,
and each is to bring for its fruit
a thousand pieces of silver.
But my vineyard is mine to give;
the thousand pieces are yours, O Solomon,
and the guardians of the fruit shall have two hundred.

BRIDEGROOM

My bride, you who sit in my garden,
what is it that my friends are listening to?
Let me also hear your voice.

BRIDE

Come into the open, my beloved,
and show yourself like a gazelle or a young wild goat
on the spice-bearing mountains.

The Book of Job

1–2
Prologue

There lived in the land of Uz a man of blameless and upright life named Job, who feared God and set his face against wrongdoing. He had seven sons and three daughters; and he owned seven thousand sheep and three thousand camels, five hundred yoke of oxen and five hundred asses, with a large number of slaves. Thus Job was the greatest man in all the East.

Now his sons used to foregather and give, each in turn, a feast in his own house; and they used to send and invite their three sisters to eat and drink with them. Then, when a round of feasts was finished, Job sent for his children and sanctified them, rising early in the morning and sacrificing a whole-offering for each of them; for he thought that they might somehow have sinned against God and committed blasphemy in their hearts. This he always did.

The day came when the members of the court of heaven took their places in the presence of the Lord, and Satan was there among them. The Lord asked him where he had been. 'Ranging over the earth', he said, 'from end to end.' Then the Lord asked Satan, 'Have you considered my servant Job? You will find no one like him on earth, a man of blameless and upright life, who fears God and sets his face against wrong-doing.' Satan answered the Lord, 'Has not Job good reason to be God-fearing? Have you not hedged him round on every side with your protection, him and his family and all his possessions? Whatever he does you have blessed, and his herds have increased beyond measure. But stretch out your hand and touch all that he has, and then he will curse you to your face.' Then the Lord said to Satan, 'So be it. All that he has is in your hands; only Job himself you must not touch.' And Satan left the Lord's presence.

When the day came that Job's sons and daughters were eating and drinking in the eldest brother's house, a messenger came running to Job and said, 'The oxen were ploughing and the asses were grazing near them, when the Sabaeans swooped down and carried them off, after putting the herdsmen to the sword; and I am the only one to escape and tell the tale.' While he was still speaking, another messenger arrived and said, 'God's fire flashed from heaven. It struck the sheep and the shepherds and burnt them up; and I am the only one to escape and tell the tale.' While he was still speaking, another arrived and said, 'The Chaldaeans, three bands of them, have made a raid on the camels and carried them off, after putting the drivers to the sword; and I am the only one to escape and tell the tale.' While this man was speaking, yet another arrived and said, 'Your sons and daughters were eating and drinking in the eldest brother's house, when suddenly a whirlwind swept across from the desert and struck the four corners of the house, and it fell on the young people and killed them; and I am the only one

to escape and tell the tale.' At this Job stood up and rent his cloak; then he shaved his head and fell prostrate on the ground, saying:

> *Naked I came from the womb,*
> *naked I shall return whence I came.*
> *The Lord gives and the Lord takes away;*
> *blessed be the name of the Lord.*

Throughout all this Job did not sin; he did not charge God with unreason.

Once again the day came when the members of the court of heaven took their places in the presence of the Lord, and Satan was there among them. The Lord asked him where he had been. 'Ranging over the earth,' he said, 'from end to end.' Then the Lord asked Satan, 'Have you considered my servant Job? You will find no one like him on earth, a man of blameless and upright life, who fears God and sets his face against wrongdoing. You incited me to ruin him without a cause, but his integrity is still unshaken.' Satan answered the Lord, 'Skin for skin! There is nothing the man will grudge to save himself. But stretch out your hand and touch his bone and his flesh, and see if he will not curse you to your face.'

Then the Lord said to Satan, 'So be it. He is in your hands; but spare his life.' And Satan left the Lord's presence, and he smote Job with running sores from head to foot, so that he took a piece of a broken pot to scratch himself as he sat among the ashes. Then his wife said to him, 'Are you still unshaken in your integrity? Curse God and die!' But he answered, 'You talk as any wicked fool of a woman might talk. If we accept good from God, shall we not accept evil?' Throughout all this, Job did not utter one sinful word.

When Job's three friends, Eliphaz of Teman, Bildad of Shuah, and Zophar of Naamah, heard of all these calamities which had overtaken him, they left their homes and arranged to come and condole with him and comfort him. But when they first saw him from a distance, they did not recognize him; and they wept aloud, rent their cloaks and tossed dust into the air over their heads. For seven days and seven nights they sat beside him on the ground, and none of them said a word to him; for they saw that his suffering was very great.

3:1–26
Job's complaint to God

After this Job broke silence and cursed the day of his birth:

> Perish the day when I was born
> and the night which said, 'A man is conceived'!
> May that day turn to darkness; may God above not look
>   for it,
> nor light of dawn shine on it.

May blackness sully it, and murk and gloom,
cloud smother that day, swift darkness eclipse its sun.
Blind darkness swallow up that night;
count it not among the days of the year,
reckon it not in the cycle of the months.
That night, may it be barren for ever,
no cry of joy be heard in it.
Cursed be it by those whose magic binds even the
    monster of the deep,
who are ready to tame Leviathan himself with spells.
May no star shine out in its twilight;
may it wait for a dawn that never comes,
nor ever see the eyelids of the morning,
because it did not shut the doors of the womb that
    bore me
and keep trouble away from my sight.
Why was I not still-born,
why did I not die when I came out of the womb?
Why was I ever laid on my mother's knees
or put to suck at her breasts?
Why was I not hidden like an untimely birth,
like an infant that has not lived to see the light?
For then I should be lying in the quiet grave,
asleep in death, at rest,
with kings and their ministers
who built themselves palaces,
with princes rich in gold
who filled their houses with silver.
There the wicked man chafes no more,
there the tired labourer rests;
the captive too finds peace there
and hears no taskmaster's voice;
high and low are there,
even the slave, free from his master.

Why should the sufferer be born to see the light?
Why is life given to men who find it so bitter?
They wait for death but it does not come,
they seek it more eagerly than hidden treasure.
They are glad when they reach the tomb,
and when they come to the grave they exult.
Why should a man be born to wander blindly,
hedged in by God on every side?
My sighing is all my food,
and groans pour from me in a torrent.
Every terror that haunted me has caught up with me,
and all that I feared has come upon me.
There is no peace of mind nor quiet for me;
I chafe in torment and have no rest. . . .

19

Then Job answered:

How long will you exhaust me
and pulverize me with words?
Time and time again you have insulted me
and shamelessly done me wrong.
If in fact I had erred,

the error would still be mine.
But if indeed you lord it over me
and try to justify the reproaches levelled at me,
I tell you, God himself has put me in the
    wrong,
he has drawn the net round me.
If I cry 'Murder!' no one answers;
if I appeal for help, I get no justice.
He has walled in my path so that I cannot break
    away,
and he has hedged in the road before me.
He has stripped me of all honour
and has taken the crown from my head.
On every side he beats me down and I am gone;
he has pulled up my tent-rope like a tree.
His anger is hot against me
and he counts me his enemy.
His raiders gather in force
and encamp about my tent.
My brothers hold aloof from me,
my friends are utterly estranged from me;
my kinsmen and intimates fall away,
my retainers have forgotten me;
my slave-girls treat me as a stranger,
I have become an alien in their eyes.
I summon my slave, but he does not answer,
though I entreat him as a favour.
My breath is noisome to my wife,
and I stink in the nostrils of my own family.
Mere children despise me
and, when I rise, turn their backs on me;
my intimate companions loathe me,
and those whom I love have turned against me.
My bones stick out through my skin,
and I gnaw my under-lip with my teeth.

Pity me, pity me, you that are my friends;
for the hand of God has touched me.
Why do you pursue me as God pursues me?
Have you not had your teeth in me long enough?
O that my words might be inscribed,
O that they might be engraved in an inscription,
cut with an iron tool and filled with lead
to be a witness in hard rock!
But in my heart I know that my vindicator lives
and that he will rise last to speak in court;
and I shall discern my witness standing at my side
and see my defending counsel, even God himself,
whom I shall see with my own eyes,
I myself and no other.

My heart failed me when you said,
'What a train of disaster he has brought on
    himself!
The root of the trouble lies in him.'
Beware of the sword that points at you,
the sword that sweeps away all iniquity;
then you will know that there is a judge. . . .

38–42:6
God's answer and Job's submission

Then the Lord answered Job out of the tempest:

Who is this whose ignorant words
cloud my design in darkness?
Brace yourself and stand up like a man;
I will ask questions, and you shall answer.
Where were you when I laid the earth's foundations?
Tell me, if you know and understand.
Who settled its dimensions? Surely you should know.
Who stretched his measuring-line over it?
On what do its supporting pillars rest?
Who set its corner-stone in place,
when the morning stars sang together
and all the sons of God shouted aloud?
Who watched over the birth of the sea,
when it burst in flood from the womb?—
when I wrapped it in a blanket of cloud
and cradled it in fog,
when I established its bounds,
fixing its doors and bars in place,
and said, 'Thus far shall you come and no farther,
and here your surging waves shall halt.'
In all your life have you ever called up the dawn
or shown the morning its place?
Have you taught it to grasp the fringes of the earth
and shake the Dog-star from its place;
to bring up the horizon in relief as clay under a seal,
until all things stand out like the folds of a cloak,
when the light of the Dog-star is dimmed
and the stars of the Navigator's Line go out one by one?
Have you descended to the springs of the sea
or walked in the unfathomable deep?
Have the gates of death been revealed to you?
Have you ever seen the door-keepers of the place of
  darkness?
Have you comprehended the vast expanse of the world?
Come, tell me all this, if you know.
Which is the way to the home of light
and where does darkness dwell?
And can you then take each to its appointed bound
and escort it on its homeward path?
Doubtless you know all this; for you were born already,
so long is the span of your life!

Have you visited the storehouse of the snow
or seen the arsenal where hail is stored,
which I have kept ready for the day of calamity,
for war and for the hour of battle?
By what paths is the heat spread abroad
or the east wind carried far and wide over the earth?
Who has cut channels for the downpour
and cleared a passage for the thunderstorm,
for rain to fall on land where no man lives
and on the deserted wilderness,
clothing lands waste and derelict with green
and making grass grow on thirsty ground?
Has the rain a father?

Who sired the drops of dew?
Whose womb gave birth to the ice,
and who was the mother of the frost from heaven,
which lays a stony cover over the waters
and freezes the expanse of ocean?
Can you bind the cluster of the Pleiades
or loose Orion's belt?
Can you bring out the signs of the zodiac in their
  season
or guide Aldebaran and its train?
Did you proclaim the rules that govern the heavens,
or determine the laws of nature on earth?
Can you command the dense clouds
to cover you with their weight of waters?
If you bid lightning speed on its way,
will it say to you, 'I am ready'?
Who put wisdom in depths of darkness
and veiled understanding in secrecy?
Who is wise enough to marshal the rain-clouds
and empty the cisterns of heaven,
when the dusty soil sets hard as iron,
and the clods of earth cling together?
Do you hunt her prey for the lioness
and satisfy the hunger of young lions,
as they crouch in the lair
or lie in wait in the covert?
Who provides the raven with its quarry
when its fledglings croak for lack of food?
Do you know when the mountain-goats are born
or attend the wild doe when she is in labour?
Do you count the months that they carry their young
or know the time of their delivery,
when they crouch down to open their wombs
and bring their offspring to the birth,
when the fawns grow and thrive in the open forest,
and go forth and do not return?
Who has let the wild ass of Syria range at will
and given the wild ass of Arabia its freedom?—
whose home I have made in the wilderness
and its lair in the saltings;
it disdains the noise of the city
and is deaf to the driver's shouting;
it roams the hills as its pasture
and searches for anything green.
Does the wild ox consent to serve you,
does it spend the night in your stall?
Can you harness its strength with ropes,
or will it harrow the furrows after you?
Can you depend on it, strong as it is,
or leave your labour to it?
Do you trust it to come back
and bring home your grain to the threshing-floor?

The wings of the ostrich are stunted;
her pinions and plumage are so scanty
that she abandons her eggs to the ground,
letting them be kept warm by the sand.
She forgets that a foot may crush them,
or a wild beast trample on them;
she treats her chicks heartlessly as if they were not hers,

not caring if her labour is wasted
(for God has denied her wisdom
and left her without sense),
while like a cock she struts over the uplands,
scorning both horse and rider.

Did you give the horse his strength?
Did you clothe his neck with a mane?
Do you make him quiver like a locust's wings,
when his shrill neighing strikes terror?
He shows his mettle as he paws and prances;
he charges the armoured line with all his might.
He scorns alarms and knows no dismay;
he does not flinch before the sword.
The quiver rattles at his side,
the spear and sabre flash.
Trembling with eagerness, he devours the ground
and cannot be held in when he hears the horn;
at the blast of the horn he cries 'Aha!'
and from afar he scents the battle.
Does your skill teach the hawk to use its pinions
and spread its wings towards the south?
Do you instruct the vulture to fly high
and build its nest aloft?
It dwells among the rocks and there it lodges;
its station is a crevice in the rock;
from there it searches for food,
keenly scanning the distance,
that its brood may be gorged with blood;
and where the slain are, there the vulture is.
Can you pull out the whale with a gaff
or can you slip a noose round its tongue?
Can you pass a cord through its nose
or put a hook through its jaw?
Will it plead with you for mercy
or beg its life with soft words?
Will it enter into an agreement with you
to become your slave for life?
Will you toy with it as with a bird
or keep it on a string like a song-bird for your maidens?
Do trading-partners haggle over it
or merchants share it out?

Then the Lord said to Job:

Is it for a man who disputes with the Almighty to be
stubborn?
Should he that argues with God answer back?

And Job answered the Lord:

What reply can I give thee, I who carry no weight?
I put my finger to my lips.
I have spoken once and now will not answer again;
twice have I spoken, and I will do so no more.

Then the Lord answered Job out of the tempest:

Brace yourself and stand up like a man;
I will ask questions, and you shall answer.

Dare you deny that I am just
or put me in the wrong that you may be right?
Have you an arm like God's arm,
can you thunder with a voice like his?
Deck yourself out, if you can, in pride and dignity,
array yourself in pomp and splendour;
unleash the fury of your wrath,
look upon the proud man and humble him;
look upon every proud man and bring him low,
throw down the wicked where they stand;
hide them in the dust together,
and shroud them in an unknown grave.
Then I in my turn will acknowledge
that your own right hand can save you.

Consider the chief of the beasts, the crocodile,
who devours cattle as if they were grass:
what strength is in his loins!
what power in the muscles of his belly!
His tail is rigid as a cedar,
the sinews of his flanks are closely knit,
his bones are tubes of bronze,
and his limbs like bars of iron.
He is the chief of God's works,
made to be a tyrant over his peers;
for he takes the cattle of the hills for his prey
and in his jaws he crunches all wild beasts.
There under the thorny lotus he lies,
hidden in the reeds and the marsh;
the lotus conceals him in its shadow,
the poplars of the stream surround him.
If the river is in spate, he is not scared,
he sprawls at his ease though the stream is in flood.
Can a man blind his eyes and take him
or pierce his nose with the teeth of a trap?
Can you fill his skin with harpoons
or his head with fish-hooks?
If ever you lift your hand against him,
think of the struggle that awaits you, and let be.

No, such a man is in desperate case,
hurled headlong at the very sight of him.
How fierce he is when he is roused!
Who is there to stand up to him?
Who has ever attacked him unscathed?
Not a man under the wide heaven.
I will not pass over in silence his limbs,
his prowess and the grace of his proportions.
Who has ever undone his outer garment
or penetrated his doublet of hide?
Who has ever opened the portals of his face?
for there is terror in his arching teeth.
His back is row upon row of shields,
enclosed in a wall of flints;
one presses so close on the other
that air cannot pass between them,
each so firmly clamped to its neighbour
that they hold and cannot spring apart.
His sneezing sends out sprays of light,
and his eyes gleam like the shimmer of dawn.

Firebrands shoot from his mouth,
and sparks come streaming out;
his nostrils pour forth smoke
like a cauldron on a fire blown to full heat.
His breath sets burning coals ablaze,
and flames flash from his mouth.
Strength is lodged in his neck,
and untiring energy dances ahead of him.
Close knit is his underbelly,
no pressure will make it yield.
His heart is firm as a rock,
firm as the nether millstone.
When he raises himself, strong men take fright,
bewildered at the lashings of his tail.
Sword or spear, dagger or javelin,
if they touch him, they have no effect.
Iron he counts as straw,
and bronze as rotting wood.
No arrow can pierce him,
and for him sling-stones are turned into chaff;
to him a club is a mere reed,
and he laughs at the swish of the sabre.
Armoured beneath with jagged sherds,
he sprawls on the mud like a threshing-sledge.
He makes the deep water boil like a cauldron,
he whips up the lake like ointment in a mixing-bowl.
He leaves a shining trail behind him,
and the great river is like white hair in his wake.
He has no equal on earth;
for he is made quite without fear.
He looks down on all creatures, even the highest;
he is king over all proud beasts.

Then Job answered the Lord:

I know that thou canst do all things
and that no purpose is beyond thee.
But I have spoken of great things which I have not
    understood,

things too wonderful for me to know.
I knew of thee then only by report,
but now I see thee with my own eyes.
Therefore I melt away;
I repent in dust and ashes.

42:7–17
Epilogue

When the Lord had finished speaking to Job, he said to Eliphaz the Temanite, 'I am angry with you and your two friends, because you have not spoken as you ought about me, as my servant Job has done. So now take seven bulls and seven rams, go to my servant Job and offer a whole-offering for yourselves, and he will intercede for you; I will surely show him favour by not being harsh with you because you have not spoken as you ought about me, as he has done.' Then Eliphaz the Temanite and Bildad the Shuhite and Zophar the Naamathite went and carried out the Lord's command, and the Lord showed favour to Job when he had interceded for his friends. So the Lord restored Job's fortunes and doubled all his possessions.

Then all Job's brothers and sisters and his former acquaintances came and feasted with him in his home, and they consoled and comforted him for all the misfortunes which the Lord had brought on him; and each of them gave him a sheep and a gold ring. Furthermore, the Lord blessed the end of Job's life more than the beginning; and he had fourteen thousand head of small cattle and six thousand camels, a thousand yoke of oxen and as many she-asses. He had seven sons and three daughters; and he named his eldest daughter Jemimah, the second Keziah and the third Kerenhappuch. There were no women in all the world so beautiful as Job's daughters; and their father gave them an inheritance with their brothers.

Thereafter Job lived another hundred and forty years, he saw his sons and his grandsons to four generations, and died at a very great age.

The Gospel According to Matthew

• • •

1:18–4
The coming of Christ

This is the story of the birth of the Messiah. Mary his mother was betrothed to Joseph; before their marriage she found that she was with child by the Holy Spirit. Being a man of principle, and at the same time wanting to save her from exposure, Joseph desired to have the marriage contract set aside quietly. He had resolved on this, when an angel of the Lord appeared to him in a dream. 'Joseph son of David,' said the angel, 'do not be afraid to take Mary home with you as your wife. It is by the Holy Spirit that she has conceived this child. She will bear a son; and you shall give him the name Jesus (Saviour), for he will save his people from their sins.' All this happened in order to fulfil what the Lord declared through the prophet: 'The virgin will conceive and bear a son, and he shall be called Emmanuel,' a name which means 'God is with us'. Rising from sleep Joseph did as the angel had directed him; he took Mary home to be his wife, but had no intercourse with her until her son was born. And he named the child Jesus.

Jesus was born at Bethlehem in Judaea during the reign of Herod. After his birth astrologers from the east arrived in Jerusalem, asking, 'Where is the child who is born to be king of the Jews? We observed the rising of his star, and we have come to pay him homage.' King Herod was greatly perturbed when he heard this; and so was the whole of Jerusalem. He called a meeting of the chief priests and lawyers of the Jewish people, and put before them the question: 'Where is it that the Messiah is to be born?' 'At Bethlehem in Judaea', they replied; and they referred him to the prophecy which reads: 'Bethlehem in the land of Judah, you are far from least in the eyes of the rulers of Judah; for out of you shall come a leader to be the shepherd of my people Israel.'

Herod next called the astrologers to meet him in private, and ascertained from them the time when the star had appeared. He then sent them on to Bethlehem, and said, 'Go and make a careful inquiry for the child. When you have found him, report to me, so that I may go myself and pay him homage.'

They set out at the king's bidding; and the star which they had seen at its rising went ahead of them until it stopped above the place where the child lay. At the sight of the star they were overjoyed. Entering the house, they saw the child with Mary his mother, and bowed to the ground in homage to him; then they opened their treasures and offered him gifts: gold, frankincense, and myrrh. And being warned in a dream not to go back to Herod, they returned home another way.

After they had gone, an angel of the Lord appeared to Joseph in a dream, and said to him, 'Rise up, take the child and his mother and escape with them to Egypt, and stay there until I tell you; for Herod is going to search for the child to do away with him.' So Joseph rose from sleep, and taking mother and child by night he went away with them to Egypt, and there he stayed till Herod's death. This was to fulfil what the Lord had declared through the prophet: 'I called my son out of Egypt.'

When Herod saw how the astrologers had tricked him he fell into a passion, and gave orders for the massacre of all children in Bethlehem and its neighbourhood, of the age of two years or less, corresponding with the time he had ascertained from the astrologers. So the words spoken through Jeremiah the prophet were fulfilled: 'A voice was heard in Rama, wailing and loud laments; it was Rachel weeping for her children, and refusing all consolation, because they were no more.'

The time came that Herod died; and an angel of the Lord appeared in a dream to Joseph in Egypt and said to him, 'Rise up, take the child and his mother, and go with them to the land of Israel, for the men who threatened the child's life are dead.' So he rose, took mother and child with him, and came to the land of Israel. Hearing, however, that Archelaus had succeeded his father Herod as king of Judaea, he was afraid to go there. And being warned by a dream, he withdrew to a region of Galilee; there he settled in a town called Nazareth. This was to fulfil the words spoken through the prophets: 'He shall be called a Nazarene.'

About that time John the Baptist appeared as a preacher in the Judaean wilderness; his theme was: 'Repent; for the kingdom of Heaven is upon you!' It is of him that the prophet Isaiah spoke when he said, 'A voice crying aloud in the wilderness, "Prepare a way for the Lord; clear a straight path for him."'

John's clothing was a rough coat of camel's hair, with a leather belt round his waist, and his food was locusts and wild honey. They flocked to him from Jerusalem, from all Judaea, and the whole Jordan valley, and were baptized by him in the River Jordan, confessing their sins.

When he saw many of the Pharisees and Sadducees coming for baptism he said to them: 'You vipers' brood! Who warned you to escape from the coming retribution? Then prove your repentance by the fruit it bears; and do not presume to say to yourselves, "We have Abraham for our father." I tell you that God can make children for Abraham out of these stones here. Already the axe is laid to the roots of the trees; and every tree that fails to produce good fruit is cut down and thrown on the fire. I baptize you with water, for repentance; but the one who comes after me is mightier than I. I am not fit to take off his shoes. He will baptize you with the Holy Spirit and with fire. His shovel is ready in his hand and he will winnow his threshing-floor; the wheat he will gather into his granary, but he will burn the chaff on a fire that can never go out.'

Then Jesus arrived at the Jordan from Galilee, and came to John to be baptized by him. John tried to dissuade him. 'Do you come to me?' he said; 'I need rather to be baptized by you.' Jesus replied, 'Let it be so for the present; we do well to conform in this way with all that God requires.' John then allowed him to come. After baptism Jesus came up out of the water at once, and at that moment heaven opened; he saw the Spirit of God descending like a dove to alight upon him; and a voice from heaven was heard saying, 'This is my Son, my Beloved, on whom my favour rests.'

Jesus was then led away by the Spirit into the wilderness, to be tempted by the devil.

For forty days and nights he fasted, and at the end of them he was famished. The tempter approached him and said, 'If you are the Son of God, tell these stones to become bread.' Jesus answered, 'Scripture says, "Man cannot live on bread alone; he lives on every word that God utters."'

The devil then took him to the Holy City and set him on the parapet of the temple. 'If you are the Son of God,' he said, 'throw yourself down; for Scripture says, "He will put his angels in charge of you, and they will support you in their arms, for fear you should strike your foot against a stone."' Jesus answered him, 'Scripture says again, "You are not to put the Lord your God to the test."'

Once again, the devil took him to a very high mountain, and showed him all the kingdoms of the world in their glory. 'All these,' he said, 'I will give you, if you will only fall down and do me homage.' But Jesus said, 'Begone, Satan! Scripture says, "You shall do homage to the Lord your God and worship him alone."'

Then the devil left him; and angels appeared and waited on him.

When he heard that John had been arrested, Jesus withdrew to Galilee; and leaving Nazareth he went and settled at Capernaum on the Sea of Galilee, in the district of Zebulun and Naphtali. This was to fulfil the passage in the prophet Isaiah which tells of the 'land of Zebulun, the land of Naphtali, the Way of the Sea, the land beyond Jordan, heathen Galilee', and says:

> 'The people that lived in darkness saw a great light;
> light dawned on the dwellers in the land of death's dark shadow.'

From that day Jesus began to proclaim the message: 'Repent; for the kingdom of Heaven is upon you.'

Jesus was walking by the Sea of Galilee when he saw two brothers, Simon called Peter and his brother Andrew, casting a net into the lake; for they were fishermen. Jesus said to them, 'Come with me, and I will make you fishers of men.' And at once they left their nets and followed him.

He went on, and saw another pair of brothers, James son of Zebedee and his brother John; they were in the boat with their father Zebedee, overhauling their nets. He called them, and at once they left the boat and their father, and followed him.

He went round the whole of Galilee, teaching in the synagogues, preaching the gospel of the Kingdom, and curing whatever illness or infirmity there was among the people. His fame reached the whole of Syria; and sufferers from every kind of illness, racked with pain, possessed by devils, epileptic, or paralysed, were all brought to him, and he cured them. Great crowds also followed him, from Galilee and the Ten Towns, from Jerusalem and Judaea, and from Transjordan.

5–7:29
The Sermon on the Mount

When he saw the crowds he went up the hill. There he took his seat, and when his disciples had gathered round him he began to address them. And this is the teaching he gave:

> 'How blest are those who know their need of God;
>   the kingdom of Heaven is theirs.
> How blest are the sorrowful;
>   they shall find consolation.
> How blest are those of a gentle spirit;
>   they shall have the earth for their possession.
> How blest are those who hunger and thirst to see right prevail;
>   they shall be satisfied.
> How blest are those who show mercy;
>   mercy shall be shown to them.
> How blest are those whose hearts are pure;
>   they shall see God.
> How blest are the peacemakers;
>   God shall call them his sons.
> How blest are those who have suffered persecution for the
>   cause of right;
>   the kingdom of Heaven is theirs.

'How blest you are, when you suffer insults and persecution and every kind of calumny for my sake. Accept it with gladness and exultation, for you have a rich reward in heaven; in the same way they persecuted the prophets before you.

'You are salt to the world. And if salt becomes tasteless, how is its saltness to be restored? It is now good for nothing but to be thrown away and trodden underfoot.

'You are light for all the world. A town that stands on a hill cannot be hidden. When a lamp is lit, it is not put under the meal-tub, but on the lamp-stand, where it gives light to everyone in the house. And you, like the lamp, must shed light among your fellows, so that, when they see the good you do, they may give praise to your Father in heaven.

'Do not suppose that I have come to abolish the Law and the prophets; I did not come to abolish, but to complete. I tell you this: so long as heaven and earth endure, not a letter, not a stroke, will disappear from the Law until all that must happen has happened. If any man therefore sets aside even the least of the Law's demands, and teaches others to do the same, he will have the lowest place in the kingdom of Heaven, whereas anyone who keeps the Law, and teaches others so, will stand high in the kingdom of Heaven. I tell you, unless you show yourselves far better men than the Pharisees and the doctors of the law, you can never enter the kingdom of Heaven.

'You have learned that our forefathers were told, "Do not commit murder; anyone who commits murder must be brought to judgement." But what I tell you is this: Anyone who nurses anger against his brother must be brought to judgement. If he abuses his brother he must answer for it in court; if he sneers at him he will have to answer for it in the fires of hell.

'If, when you are bringing your gift to the altar, you suddenly remember that your brother has a grievance against you, leave your gift where it is before the altar. First go and make your peace with your brother, and only then come back and offer your gift.

'If someone sues you, come to terms with him promptly while you are both on your way to court; otherwise he may hand you over to the judge, and the judge to the constable, and you will be put in jail. I tell you, once you are there you will not be let out till you have paid the last farthing.

'You have learned that they were told, "Do not commit adultery." But what I tell you is this: If a man looks on a woman with a lustful eye, he has already committed adultery with her in his heart.

'If your right eye is your undoing, tear it out and fling it away; it is better for you to lose one part of your body than for the whole of it to be thrown into hell. And if your right hand is your undoing, cut it off and fling it away; it is better for you to lose one part of your body than for the whole of it to go to hell.

'They were told, "A man who divorces his wife must give her a note of dismissal." But what I tell you is this: If a man divorces his wife for any cause other than unchastity he involves her in adultery; and anyone who marries a divorced woman commits adultery.

'Again, you have learned that our forefathers were told, "Do not break your oath," and, "Oaths sworn to the Lord must be kept." But what I tell you is this: You are not to swear at all—not by heaven, for it is God's throne, nor by earth, of it is his footstool, nor by Jerusalem, for it is the city of the great King, nor by your own head, because you cannot turn one hair of it white or black. Plain "Yes" or "No" is all you need to say; anything beyond that comes from the devil.

'You have learned that they were told, "Eye for eye, tooth for tooth." But what I tell you is this: Do not set yourself against the man who wrongs you. If someone slaps you on the right cheek, turn and offer him your left. If a man wants to sue you for your shirt, let him have your coat as well. If a man in authority makes you go one mile, go with him two. Give when you are asked to give; and do not turn your back on a man who wants to borrow.

'You have learned that they were told, "Love your neighbour, hate your enemy." But what I tell you is this: Love your enemies, and pray for your persecutors; only so can you be children of your heavenly Father, who makes his sun rise on good and bad alike, and sends the rain on the honest and the dishonest. If you love only those who love you, what reward can you expect? Surely the tax-gatherers do as much as that. And if you greet only your brothers, what is there extraordinary about that? Even the heathen do as much. There must be no limit to your goodness, as your heavenly Father's goodness knows no bounds.

'Be careful not to make a show of your religion before men; if you do, no reward awaits you in your Father's house in heaven.

'Thus, when you do some act of charity, do not announce it with a flourish of trumpets, as the hypocrites do in synagogue and in the streets to win admiration from men. I tell you this: they have their reward already. No; when you do some act of charity, do not let your left hand know what your right is doing; your good deed must be secret, and your Father who sees what is done in secret will reward you.

'Again, when you pray, do not be like the hypocrites; they love to say their prayers standing up in synagogue and at the street-corners, for everyone to see them. I tell you this: they have their reward already. But when you pray, go into a room by yourself, shut the door, and pray to your Father who is there in the secret place; and your Father who sees what is secret will reward you.

'In your prayers do not go babbling on like the heathen, who imagine that the more they say the more likely they are to be heard. Do not imitate them. Your Father knows what your needs are before you ask him.

'This is how you should pray:

"Our Father in heaven,
thy name be hallowed;
thy kingdom come,
thy will be done,
on earth as in heaven.
Give us today our daily bread.
Forgive us the wrong we have done,
as we have forgiven those who have wronged us.
And do not bring us to the test,
but save us from the evil one."

For if you forgive others the wrongs they have done, your heavenly Father will also forgive you; but if you do not forgive others, then the wrongs you have done will not be forgiven by your Father.

'So too when you fast, do not look gloomy like the hypocrites: they make their faces unsightly so that other people may see that they are fasting. I tell you this: they have their reward already. But when you fast, anoint your head and wash your face, so that men may not see that you are fasting, but only your Father who is in the secret place; and your Father who sees what is secret will give you your reward.

'Do not store up for yourselves treasures on earth, where it grows rusty and moth-eaten, and thieves break in to steal it. Store up treasure in heaven, where there is no moth and no rust to spoil it, no thieves to break in and steal. For where your treasure is, there will your heart be also.

'The lamp of the body is the eye. If your eyes are sound, you will have light for your whole body; if the eyes are bad, your whole body will be in darkness. If then the only light you have is darkness, the darkness is doubly dark.

'No servant can be the slave of two masters; for either he will hate the first and love the second, or he will be devoted to the first and think nothing of the second. You cannot serve God and Money.

'Therefore I bid you put away anxious thoughts about food and drink to keep you alive, and clothes to cover your body. Surely life is more than food, the body more than clothes. Look at the birds of the air; they do not sow and reap and store in barns, yet your heavenly Father feeds them. You are worth more than the birds! Is there a man of you who by anxious thought can add a foot to his height? And why be anxious about clothes? Consider how the lilies grow in the fields; they do not work, they do not spin; and yet, I tell you, even Solomon in all his splendour was not attired like one of these. But if that is how God clothes the grass in the fields, which is there today, and tomorrow is thrown on the stove, will he not all the more clothe you? How little faith you have! No, do not ask anxiously, "What are we to eat? What are we to drink? What shall we wear?" All these things for the heathen to run after, not for you, because your heavenly Father knows that you need them all. Set your mind on God's kingdom and his justice before everything else, and all the rest will come to you as well. So do not be anxious about tomorrow; tomorrow will look after itself. Each day has troubles enough of its own.

'Pass no judgement, and you will not be judged. For as you judge others, so you will yourselves be judged, and whatever measure you deal out to others will be dealt back to you. Why do you look at the speck of sawdust in your brother's eye, with never a thought of the great plank in your own? Or how can you say to your brother, ''Let me take the speck out of your eye,'' when all the time there is that plank in your own? You hypocrite! First take the plank out of your own eye, and then you will see clearly to take the speck out of your brother's.

'Do not give dogs what is holy; do not throw your pearls to the pigs; they will only trample on them, and turn and tear you to pieces.

'Ask, and you will receive; seek, and you will find; knock, and the door will be opened. For everyone who asks receives, he who seeks finds, and to him who knocks, the door will be opened.

'Is there a man among you who will offer his son a stone when he asks for bread, or a snake when he asks for fish? If you, then, bad as you are, know how to give your children what is good for them, how much more will your heavenly Father give good things to those who ask him!

'Always treat others as you would like them to treat you: that is the Law and the prophets.

'Enter by the narrow gate. The gate is wide that leads to perdition, there is plenty of room on the road, and many go that way; but the gate that leads to life is small and the road is narrow, and those who find it are few.

'Beware of false prophets, men who come to you dressed up as sheep while underneath they are savage wolves. You will recognize them by the fruits they bear. Can grapes be picked from briars, or figs from thistles? In the same way, a good tree always yields good fruit, and a poor tree bad fruit. A good tree cannot bear bad fruit, or a poor tree good fruit. And when a tree does not yield good fruit it is cut down and burnt. That is why I say you will recognize them by their fruits.

'Not everyone who calls me "Lord, Lord" will enter the kingdom of Heaven, but only those who do the will of my heavenly Father. When that day comes, many will say to me, "Lord, Lord, did we not prophesy in your name, cast out devils in your name, and in your name perform many miracles?" Then I will tell them to their face, "I never knew you; out of my sight, you and your wicked ways!"

'What then of the man who hears these words of mine and acts upon them? He is like a man who had the sense to build his house on rock. The rain came down, the floods rose, the wind blew, and beat upon that house; but it did not fall, because its foundations were on rock. But what of the man who hears these words of mine and does not act upon them? He is like a man who was foolish enough to build his house on sand. The rain came down, the floods rose, the wind blew, and beat upon that house; down it fell with a great crash.'

When Jesus had finished this discourse the people were astounded at his teaching; unlike their own teachers he taught with a note of authority.

First Corinthians

13

I may speak in tongues of men or of angels, but if I am without love, I am a sounding gong or a clanging cymbal. I may have the gift of prophecy, and know every hidden truth; I may have faith strong enough to move mountains; but if I have no love, I am nothing. I may dole out all I possess, or even give my body to be burnt, but if I have no love, I am none the better.

Love is patient; love is kind and envies no one. Love is never boastful, nor conceited, nor rude; never selfish, not quick to take offence. Love keeps no score of wrongs; does not gloat over other men's sins, but delights in the truth. There is nothing love cannot face; there is no limit to its faith, its hope, and its endurance.

Love will never come to an end. Are there prophets? their work will be over. Are there tongues of ecstasy? they will cease. Is there knowledge? it will vanish away; for our knowledge and our prophecy alike are partial, and the partial vanishes when wholeness comes. When I was a child, my speech, my outlook, and my thoughts were all childish. When I grew up, I had finished with childish things. Now we see only puzzling reflections in a mirror, but then we shall see face to face. My knowledge now is partial; then it will be whole, like God's knowledge of me. In a word, there are three things that last for ever: faith, hope, and love; but the greatest of them all is love.

Chapter

7

Late Roman Civilization

ST. AUGUSTINE

from *Confessions*

Book VIII

10

There are many abroad who talk of their own fantasies and lead men's minds astray. They assert that because they have observed that there are two wills at odds with each other when we try to reach a decision, we must therefore have two minds of different natures, one good, the other evil. *Let them vanish at God's presence as the smoke vanishes.* As long as they hold these evil beliefs they are evil themselves, but even they will be good if they see the truth and accept it, so that your apostle may say to them *Once you were all darkness; now, in the Lord you are all daylight.* These people want to be light, not in the Lord, but in themselves, because they think that the nature of the soul is the same as God. In this way their darkness becomes denser still, because in their abominable arrogance they have separated themselves still further from you, who are *the true Light which enlightens every soul born into the world.* I say to them, 'Take care what you say, and blush for shame. Enter God's presence, and find their enlightenment; *here is no room for downcast looks.'*

When I was trying to reach a decision about serving the Lord my God, as I had long intended to do, it was I who willed to take this course and again it was I who willed not to take it. It was I and I alone. But I neither willed to do it nor refused to do it with my full will. So I was at odds with myself. I was throwing myself into confusion. All this happened to me although I did not want it, but it did not prove that there was some second mind in me besides my own. It only meant that my mind was being punished. *My action did not come from me, but from the sinful principle that dwells in me.* It was part of the punishment of a sin freely committed by Adam, my first father.

If there were as many different natures in us as there are conflicting wills, we should have a great many more natures than merely two. Suppose that someone is trying to decide whether to go to the theatre or to the Manichees' meeting-house. The Manichees will say, 'Clearly he has two natures, the good one bringing him here to us and the bad one leading him away. Otherwise, how can you explain this dilemma of two opposing wills?' I say that the will to attend their meetings is just as bad as the will to go off to the theatre, but in their opinion it can only be a good will that leads a man to come to them. Suppose then that one of us is wavering between two conflicting wills and cannot make up his mind whether to go to the theatre or to our church. Will not the Manichees be embarrassed to know what to say? Either they must admit—which they will not do—that it is a good will which brings a man to our church, just as in their opinion it is a good will which brings their own communicants and adherents to their church; or they must presume that there are two evil natures and two evil minds in conflict in one man. If they think this, they will disprove their own theory that there is one good and one evil will in man. The only alternative is for them to be converted to the truth and to cease to deny that when a man tries to make a decision, he has one soul which is torn between conflicting wills.

So let us hear no more of their assertion, when they observe two wills in conflict in one man, that there are two opposing minds in him, one good and the other bad, and that they are in conflict because they spring from two opposing substances and two opposing principles. For you, O God of truth, prove that they are utterly wrong. You demolish their arguments and confound them completely. It may be that both the wills are bad. For instance, a man may be trying to decide whether to commit murder by poison or by stabbing; whether he should swindle another man out of one part of his property or another, that is, if he cannot obtain both; whether he should spend his money extravagantly on pleasure or hoard it like a miser; or whether he should go to the games in the circus or to the theatre, when there is a performance at both places on the same day. In this case there may be a third possibility, that he should go and rob another person's house, if he has the chance. There may even be a fourth choice open to him, because he may wonder whether to go and commit adultery, if the occasion arises at the same time. These possibilities may all occur at the same moment and all may seem equally desirable. The man cannot do all these things at once, and his mind is torn between four wills which cannot be reconciled—perhaps more than four, because there are a great many things that he might wish to do. But the Manichees do not claim that there are as many different substances in us as this.

It is just the same when the wills are good. If I question the Manichees whether it is good to find pleasure in reading Paul's Epistles or in the tranquil enjoyment of a Psalm or in a discussion of the Gospel, they will reply in each case that it is good. Supposing, then, that a man finds all these things equally attractive and the chance to do all of them occurs at the same time, is it not true that as long as he cannot make up his mind which of them he most wants to do his heart is torn between several different desires? All these different desires are good, yet they are in conflict with each other until he chooses a single course to which the will may apply itself as a single whole, so that it is no longer split into several different wills.

The same is true when the higher part of our nature aspires after eternal bliss while our lower self is held back by the love of temporal pleasure. It is the same soul that wills both, but it wills neither of them with the full force of the will. So it is wrenched in two and suffers great trials, because while truth teaches it to prefer one course, habit prevents it from relinquishing the other.

11

This was the nature of my sickness. I was in torment, reproaching myself more bitterly than ever as I twisted and turned in my chain. I hoped that my chain might be broken once and for all, because it was only a small thing that held me now. All the same it held me. And you, O Lord, never ceased to watch over my secret heart. In your stern mercy you lashed me with the twin scourge of fear and shame in case I should give way once more and the worn and slender remnant of my chain should not be broken but gain new strength and bind me all the faster. In my heart I kept saying 'Let it be now, let it be now!', and merely by saying this I was on the point of making the resolution. I was on the point of making it, but I did not succeed. Yet I did not fall back into my old state. I stood on the brink of resolution, waiting to take fresh breath. I tried again and came a little nearer to my goal, and then a little nearer still, so that I could almost reach out and grasp it. But I did not reach it. I could not reach out to it or grasp it, because I held back from the step by which I should die to death and become alive to life. My lower instincts, which had taken firm hold of me, were stronger than the higher, which were untried. And the closer I came to the moment which was to mark the great change in me, the more I shrank from its horror. But it did not drive me back or turn me from my purpose: it merely left me hanging in suspense.

I was held back by mere trifles, the most paltry inanities, all my old attachments. They plucked at my garment of flesh and whispered, 'Are you going to dismiss us? From this moment we shall never be with you again, for ever and ever. From this moment you will never again be allowed to do this thing or that, for evermore.' What was it, my God, that they meant when they whispered 'this thing or that?' Things so sordid and so shameful that I beg you in your mercy to keep the soul of your servant free from them! These voices, as I heard them, seemed less than half as loud as they had been before. They no longer barred my way, blatantly contradictory, but their mutterings seemed to reach me from behind, as though they were stealthily plucking at my back, trying to make me turn my head when I wanted to go forward. Yet, in my state of indecision, they kept me from tearing myself away, from shaking myself free of them and leaping across the barrier to the other side, where you were calling me. Habit was too strong for me when it asked 'Do you think you can live without these things?'

But by now the voice of habit was very faint. I had turned my eyes elsewhere, and while I stood trembling at the barrier, on the other side I could see the chaste beauty of Continence in all her serene, unsullied joy, as she modestly beckoned me to cross over and to hesitate no more. She stretched out loving hands to welcome and embrace me, holding up a host of good examples to my sight. With her were countless boys and girls, great numbers of the young and people of all ages, staid widows and women still virgins in old age. And in their midst was Continence herself, not barren but a fruitful mother of children, of joys born of you, O Lord, her Spouse. She smiled at me to give me courage, as though she were saying, 'Can you not do what these men and these women do? Do you think they find the strength to do it in themselves and not in the Lord their God? It was the Lord their God who gave me to them. Why do you try to stand in your own strength and fail? Cast yourself upon God and have no fear. He will not shrink away and let you fall. Cast yourself upon him without fear, for he will welcome you and cure you of your ills.' I was overcome with shame, because I was still listening to the futile mutterings of my lower self and I was still hanging in suspense. And again Continence seemed to say, 'Close your eyes to the unclean whispers of your body, so that it may be mortified. It tells you of things that delight you, but not such things as the law of the Lord your God has to tell.'

In this way I wrangled with myself, in my own heart, about my own self. And all the while Alypius stayed at my side, silently awaiting the outcome of this agitation that was new in me.

12

I probed the hidden depths of my soul and wrung its pitiful secrets from it, and when I mustered them all before the eyes of my heart, a great storm broke within me, bringing with it a great deluge of tears. I stood up and left Alypius so that I might weep and cry to my heart's content, for it occurred to me that tears were best shed in solitude. I moved away far enough to avoid being embarrassed even by his presence. He must have realized what my feelings were, for I suppose I had said something and he had known from the sound of my voice that I was ready to burst into tears. So I stood up and left him where we had been sitting, utterly bewildered. Somehow I flung myself down beneath a fig tree and gave way to the tears which now streamed from my eyes, the sacrifice that is acceptable to you. I had much to say to you, my God, not in these very words but in this strain: *Lord, will you never be content? Must we always taste your vengeance? Forget the long record of our sins.* For I felt that I was still the captive of my sins, and in my misery I kept crying 'How long shall I go on saying "tomorrow, tomorrow"? Why not now? Why not make an end of my ugly sins at this moment?'

I was asking myself these questions, weeping all the while with the most bitter sorrow in my heart, when all at once I heard the sing-song voice of a child in a nearby house. Whether it was the voice of a boy or a girl I cannot say, but again and again it repeated the refrain 'Take it and read, take it and read.' At this I looked up, thinking hard whether there was any kind of game in which children used to chant words

like these, but I could not remember ever hearing them before. I stemmed my flood of tears and stood up, telling myself that this could only be a divine command to open my book of Scripture and read the first passage on which my eyes should fall. For I had heard the story of Antony, and I remembered how he had happened to go into a church while the Gospel was being read and had taken it as a counsel addressed to himself when he heard the words *Go home and sell all that belongs to you. Give it to the poor, and so the treasure you have shall be in heaven; then come back and follow me.* By this divine pronouncement he had at once been converted to you.

So I hurried back to the place where Alypius was sitting, for when I stood up to move away I had put down the book containing Paul's Epistles. I seized it and opened it, and in silence I read the first passage on which my eyes fell: *Not in revelling and drunkenness, not in lust and wantonness, not in quarrels and rivalries. Rather, arm yourselves with the Lord Jesus Christ; spend no more thought on nature and nature's appetites.* I had no wish to read more and no need to do so. For in an instant, as I came to the end of the sentence, it was as though the light of confidence flooded into my heart and all the darkness of doubt was dispelled.

I marked the place with my finger or by some other sign and closed the book. My looks now were quite calm as I told Alypius what had happened to me. He too told me what he had been feeling, which of course I did not know. He asked to see what I had read. I showed it to him and he read on beyond the text which I had read. I did not know what followed, but it was this: *Find room among you for a man of over-delicate conscience.* Alypius applied this to himself and told me so. This admonition was enough to give him strength, and without suffering the distress of hesitation he made his resolution and took this good purpose to himself. And it very well suited his moral character, which had long been far, far better than my own.

Then we went in and told my mother, who was overjoyed. And when we went on to describe how it had all happened, she was jubilant with triumph and glorified you, *who are powerful enough, and more than powerful enough, to carry out your purpose beyond all our hopes and dreams.* For she saw that you had granted her far more than she used to ask in her tearful prayers and plaintive lamentations. You converted me to yourself, so that I no longer desired a wife or placed any hope in this world but stood firmly upon the rule of faith, where you had shown me to her in a dream so many years before. And you *turned her sadness into rejoicing,* into joy far fuller than her dearest wish, far sweeter and more chaste than any she had hoped to find in children begotten of my flesh.

from *The City of God*

Book XIV

Chapter 28
The Character of the Two Cities

We see then that the two cities were created by two kinds of love: the earthly city was created by self-love reaching the point of contempt for God, the Heavenly City by the love of God carried as far as contempt of self. In fact, the earthly city glories in itself, the Heavenly City glories in the Lord. The former looks for glory from men, the latter finds its highest glory in God, the witness of a good conscience. The earthly lifts up its head in its own glory, the Heavenly City says to its God: 'My glory; you lift up my head.' In the former, the lust for domination lords it over its princes as over the nations it subjugates; in the other both those put in authority and those subject to them serve one another in love, the rulers by their counsel, the subjects by obedience. The one city loves its own strength shown in its powerful leaders; the other says to its God, 'I will love you, my Lord, my strength.'

Consequently, in the earthly city its wise men who live by men's standards have pursued the goods of the body or of their own mind, or of both. Or those of them who were able to know God 'did not honour him as God, nor did they give thanks to him, but they dwindled into futility in their thoughts, and their senseless heart was darkened: in asserting their wisdom'—that is, exalting themselves in their wisdom, under the domination of pride—'they became foolish, and changed the glory of the imperishable God into an image representing a perishable man, or birds or beasts or reptiles'—for in the adoration of idols of this kind they were either leaders or followers of the general public—'and they worshipped and served created things instead of the Creator, who is blessed for ever.' In the Heavenly City, on the other hand, man's only wisdom is the devotion which rightly worships the true God, and looks for its reward in the fellowship of the saints, not only holy men but also holy angels, 'so that God may be all in all'.

Book XV

Chapter 4
Conflict and Peace in the Earthly City

The earthly city will not be everlasting; for when it is condemned to the final punishment it will no longer be a city. It has its good in this world, and rejoices to participate in it with such gladness as can be derived from things of such a kind. And since this is not the kind of good that causes no frustrations to those enamoured of it, the earthly city is generally divided against itself by litigation, by wars, by battles, by the pursuit of victories that bring death with them or at best are doomed to death. For if any section of that city has risen up in war against another part, it seeks to be victorious over other nations, though it is itself the slave of base passions; and if, when victorious, it is exalted in its arrogance, that victory brings death in its train. Whereas if it considers the human condition and the changes and chances common to mankind, and is more tormented by possible misfortunes than puffed up by its present success, then its victory is only doomed to death. For it will not be able to lord it permanently over those whom it has been able to subdue victoriously.

However, it would be incorrect to say that the goods which this city desires are not goods, since even that city is better, in its own human way, by their possession. For example, that city desires an earthly peace, for the sake of the lowest goods; and it is that peace which it longs to attain by making war. For if it wins the war and no one survives to resist, then there will be peace, which the warring sections did not enjoy when they contended in their unhappy poverty for the things which they could not both possess at the same time. This peace is the aim of wars, with all their hardships; it is this peace that glorious victory (so called) achieves.

Now when the victory goes to those who were fighting for the juster cause, can anyone doubt that the victory is a matter for rejoicing and the resulting peace is something to be desired? These things are goods and undoubtedly they are gifts of God. But if the higher goods are neglected, which belong to the City on high, where victory will be serene in the enjoyment of eternal and perfect peace—if these goods are neglected and those other goods are so desired as to be considered the only goods, or are loved more than the goods which are believed to be higher, the inevitable consequence is fresh misery, and an increase of the wretchedness already there.

Book XIX

Chapter 7
Human Society Divided by Differences of Language.
The Misery of War, Even When Just

After the city or town comes the world, which the philosophers reckon as the third level of human society. They begin with the household, proceed to the city, and then arrive at the world. Now the world, being like a confluence of waters, is obviously more full of danger than the other communities by reason of its greater size. To begin with, on this level the diversity of languages separates man from man. For if two men meet, and are forced by some compelling reason not to pass on but to stay in company, then if neither knows the other's language, it is easier for dumb animals, even of different kinds, to associate together than these men, although both are human beings. For when men cannot communicate their thoughts to each other, simply because of difference of language, all the similarity of their common nature is of no avail to unite them in fellowship. So true is this that the man would be more cheerful with his dog for company than with a foreigner. I shall be told that the Imperial City has been at pains to impose on conquered peoples not only her yoke but her language also, as a bond of peace and fellowship, so that there should be no lack of interpreters but even a profusion of them. True; but think of the cost of this achievement! Consider the scale of those wars, with all that slaughter of human beings, all the human blood that was shed!

Those wars are now past history; and yet the misery of these evils is not yet ended. For although there has been, and still is, no lack of enemies among foreign nations, against whom wars have always been waged, and are still being waged, yet the very extent of the Empire has given rise to wars of a worse kind, namely, social and civil wars, by which mankind is more lamentably disquieted either when fighting is going on in the hope of bringing hostilities eventually to a peaceful end, or when there are fears that hostilities will break out again. If I were to try to describe, with an eloquence worthy of the subject, the many and multifarious disasters, the dour and dire necessities, I could not possibly be adequate to the theme, and there would be no end to this protracted discussion. But the wise man, they say, will wage just wars. Surely, if he remembers that he is a human being, he will rather lament the fact that he is faced with the necessity of waging just wars; for if they were not just, he would not have to engage in them, and consequently there would be no wars for a wise man. For it is the injustice of the opposing side that lays on the wise man the duty of waging wars; and this injustice is assuredly to be deplored by a human being, since it is the injustice of human beings, even though no necessity for war should arise from it. And so everyone who reflects with sorrow on such grievous evils, in all their horror and cruelty, must acknowledge the misery of them. And yet a man who experiences such evils, or even thinks about them,

without heartfelt grief, is assuredly in a far more pitiable condition, if he thinks himself happy simply because he has lost all human feeling.

Chapter 8
The Friendship of Good Men Can Never Be Carefree,
Because of This Life's Dangers

If we are spared that kind of ignorance, akin to madness, which is a common affliction in the wretched condition of this life, an ignorance which leads men to believe an enemy to be a friend, or a friend an enemy, what consolation have we in this human society, so replete with mistaken notions and distressing anxieties, except the unfeigned faith and mutual affections of genuine, loyal friends? Yet the more friends we have and the more dispersed they are in different places, the further and more widely extend our fears that some evil may befall them from among all the mass of evils of this present world. For not only are we troubled and anxious because they may be afflicted by famine, war, disease, or captivity, fearing that in slavery they may suffer evils beyond our powers of imagination; there is the much more bitter fear, that their friendship be changed into treachery, malice and baseness. And when such things do happen (and the more numerous our friends, the more often they happen) and the news is brought to our ears, who, except one who has this experience, can be aware of the burning sorrow that ravages our hearts? Certainly we would rather hear that our friends were dead, although this also we could not hear without grief.

For if their life brought us the consoling delights of friendship, how could it be that their death should bring us no sadness? Anyone who forbids such sadness must forbid, if he can, all friendly conversation, must lay a ban on all friendly feeling or put a stop to it, must with a ruthless insensibility break the ties of all human relationships, or else decree that they must only be engaged upon so long as they inspire no delight in a man's soul. But if this is beyond all possibility, how can it be that a man's death should not be bitter if his life is sweet to us? For this is why the grief of a heart that has not lost human feeling is a thing like some wound or ulcer, and our friendly words of consolation are the healing application. And it does not follow that there is nothing to be healed simply because the nobler a man's spirit the quicker and easier the cure.

It is true, then, that the life of mortals is afflicted, sometimes more gently, sometimes more harshly, by the death of those most dear to us, and especially the death of those whose functions are necessary for human society; and yet we should prefer to hear, or even to witness, the death of those we love, than to become aware that they have fallen from faith or from moral conflict—that is, that they have died in their very soul. The earth is full of this vast mass of evils; that is why we find this in Scripture: 'Is man's life on earth anything but temptation?' And why the Lord himself says, 'Alas for the world, because of these obstacles'; and again, 'Because iniquity will increase beyond measure, the love of many will grow cold.' The result of this situation is that when good men die who are our friends we rejoice for them; and though their death brings us sadness, we find our surer consolation in this, that they have been spared those evils by which in this life even good men are crushed or corrupted, or at least are in danger of both these disasters.

Chapter 17
The Origin of Peace Between the Heavenly Society and the Earthly City, and of Discord Between Them

But a household of human beings whose life is not based on faith is in pursuit of an earthly peace based on the things belonging to this temporal life, and on its advantages, whereas a household of human beings whose life is based on faith looks forward to the blessings which are promised as eternal in the future, making use of earthly and temporal things like a pilgrim in a foreign land, who does not let himself be taken in by them or distracted from his course towards God, but rather treats them as supports which help him more easily to bear the burdens of 'the corruptible body which weighs heavy on the soul'; they must on no account be allowed to increase the load. Thus both kinds of men and both kinds of households alike make use of the things essential for this mortal life; but each has its own very different end in making use of them. So also the earthly city, whose life is not based on faith, aims at an earthly peace, and it limits the harmonious agreement of citizens concerning the giving and obeying of orders to the establishment of a kind of compromise between human wills about the things relevant to mortal life. In contrast, the Heavenly City—or rather that part of it which is on pilgrimage in this condition of mortality, and which lives on the basis of faith—must needs make use of this peace also, until this mortal state, for which this kind of peace is essential, passes away. And therefore, it leads what we may call a life of captivity in this earthly city as in a foreign land, although it has already received the promise of redemption, and the gift of the Spirit as a kind of pledge of it; and yet it does not hesitate to obey the laws of the earthly city by which those things which are designed for the support of this mortal life are regulated; and the purpose of this obedience is that, since this mortal condition is shared by both cities, a harmony may be preserved between them in things that are relevant to this condition.

But this earthly city has had some philosophers belonging to it whose theories are rejected by the teaching inspired by God. Either led astray by their own speculation or deluded by demons, these thinkers reached the belief that there are many gods who must be won over to serve human ends, and

also that they have, as it were, different departments with different responsibilities attached. Thus the body is the department of one god, the mind that of another; and within the body itself, one god is in charge of the head, another of the neck and so on with each of the separate members. Similarly, within the mind, one is responsible for natural ability, another for learning, another for anger, another for lust; and in the accessories of life there are separate gods over the departments of flocks, grain, wine, oil, forests, coinage, navigation, war and victory, marriage, birth, fertility, and so on. The Heavenly City, in contrast, knows only one God as the object of worship, and decrees, with faithful devotion, that he only is to be served with that service which the Greeks call *latreia*, which is due to God alone. And the result of this difference has been that the Heavenly City could not have laws of religion common with the earthly city, and in defence of her religious laws she was bound to dissent from those who thought differently and to prove a burdensome nuisance to them. Thus she had to endure their anger and hatred, and the assaults of persecution; until at length that City shattered the morale of her adversaries by the terror inspired by her numbers, and by the help she continually received from God.

While this Heavenly City, therefore, is on pilgrimage in this world, she calls out citizens from all nations and so collects a society of aliens, speaking all languages. She takes on account of any difference in customs, laws, and institutions, by which earthly peace is achieved and preserved—not that she annuls or abolishes any of those, rather, she maintains them and follows them (for whatever divergences there are among the diverse nations, those institutions have one single aim—earthly peace), provided that no hindrance is presented thereby to the religion which teaches that the one supreme and true God is to be worshipped. Thus even the Heavenly City in her pilgrimage here on earth makes use of the earthly peace and defends and seeks the compromise between human wills in respect of the provisions relevant to the mortal nature of man, so far as may be permitted without detriment to true religion and piety. In fact, that City relates the earthly peace to the heavenly peace, which is so truly peaceful that it should be regarded as the only peace deserving the name, at least in respect of the rational creation; for this peace is the perfectly ordered and completely harmonious fellowship in the enjoyment of God, and of each other in God. When we arrive at that state of peace, there will be no longer a life that ends in death, but a life that is life in sure and sober truth; there will be no animal body to 'weigh down the soul' in its process of corruption; there will be a spiritual body with no cravings, a body subdued in every part to the will. This peace the Heavenly City possesses in faith while on its pilgrimage, and it lives a life of righteousness, based on this faith, having the attainment of that peace in view in every good action it performs in relation to God, and in relation to a neighbour, since the life of a city is inevitably a social life.

Chapter
8

The Successors of Rome:
Byzantium, Islam, and the Early Medieval West

from *The Koran*

21
The Prophets

In the Name of God, the Compassionate, the Merciful

The Day of Reckoning for mankind is drawing near, yet they blithely persist in unbelief. They listen with ridicule to each fresh warning that their Lord gives them: their hearts are set on pleasure.

In private the wrongdoers say to each other: 'Is this man not a mortal like yourselves? Would you follow witchcraft with your eyes open?'

Say: 'My Lord has knowledge of whatever is said in heaven and earth. He hears all and knows all.'

Some say: 'It is but a medley of dreams.' Others: 'He has invented it himself.' And yet others: 'He is a poet: let him show us some sign, as did the apostles in days gone by.'

Yet though We showed them signs, the nations whom We destroyed before them did not believe either. Will *they* believe?

The apostles We sent before you were but men whom We inspired. Ask the People of the Book if you do not know this. The bodies We gave them could not dispense with food, nor were they immortal. Then We fulfilled Our promise: We delivered them and those We willed, and utterly destroyed the transgressors.

And now We have revealed a Book for your admonishment. Will you not give heed?

We have destroyed many a sinful nation and replaced them by other men. And when they felt Our might they took to their heels and fled. They were told: 'Do not run away. Return to your comforts and to your dwellings. You shall be questioned all.'

'Woe to us, we have done wrong!' was their reply. And this they kept repeating until We mowed them down and put out their light.

It was not in sport that We created the heavens and the earth and all that lies between them. Had it been Our will to find a pastime, We could have found one near at hand.

We will hurl Truth at Falsehood, until Truth shall triumph and Falsehood be no more. Woe shall befall you, for all the falsehoods you have uttered.

His are all who dwell in the heavens and on earth. Those who stand in His presence do not disdain to worship Him, nor are they ever wearied. They praise Him day and night, unflaggingly.

Have they chosen earthly deities? And can these deities restore the dead to life? Were there other gods in heaven or earth besides God, both heaven and earth would be ruined. Exalted be God, Lord of the Throne, above their falsehoods!

None shall question Him about His works, but they shall be questioned. Have they chosen other gods besides Him?

Say: 'Show us your proofs. Here are the Scriptures of today and those of long ago.' But most of them do not know the Truth, and this is why they give no heed.

We inspired all the apostles whom We sent before you, saying: 'There is no god but Me. Therefore serve Me.'

They say: 'The Merciful has begotten children.' God forbid! They are but His honoured servants. They do not speak till He has spoken: they act by His command. He knows what is before them and behind them. They intercede for none save those whom He accepts, and tremble for awe of Him. Whoever of them declares: 'I am a god besides Him,' shall be requited with Hell. Thus shall We reward the wrongdoers.

Are the disbelievers unaware that the heavens and the earth were but one solid mass which We tore asunder, and that We made every living thing of water? Will they not have faith?

We set firm mountains upon the earth lest it should move away with them, and hewed out highways in the rock so that they might be rightly guided.

We spread the heaven like a canopy and provided it with strong support: yet of its signs they are heedless.

It was He who created the night and the day, and the sun and the moon: each moves swiftly in an orbit of its own.

No man before you have We made immortal. If you yourself are doomed to die, will they live for ever?

Every soul shall taste death. We will prove you all with good and evil. To Us you shall return.

When the unbelievers see you, they scoff at you, saying: 'Is this the man who fulminates against your gods?' And they deny all mention of the Merciful.

Impatience is the very stuff man is made of. You shall before long see My signs: you need not ask Me to hasten them.

They say: 'When will this promise be fulfilled, if what you say be true?'

If only the unbelievers knew the day when they shall strive in vain to shield their faces and their backs from the fire of Hell; the day when none shall help them! It will overtake them unawares and stupefy them. They shall have no power to ward it off, nor shall they be reprieved.

Other apostles have been mocked before you; but those who scoffed at them were smitten by the very scourge they mocked.

Say: 'Who will protect you, by night and by day, from the Lord of Mercy?' Yet are they unmindful of their Lord's remembrance.

Have they other gods to defend them? Their idols shall be powerless over their own salvation, nor shall they be protected from Our scourge.

We have bestowed good things upon these men and upon their fathers, and made their lives too long. Can they not see how We invade their land and curtail its borders? Is it they who will triumph?

Say: 'I warn you only by that with which I am inspired.' But the deaf can hear nothing when they are warned.

Yet if the lightest whiff from the vengeance of your Lord touched them, they would say: 'Woe to us: we have done wrong!'

We shall set up just scales on the Day of Resurrection, so that no man shall in the least be wronged. Actions as small as a grain of mustard seed shall be weighed out. Our reckoning shall suffice.

We showed Moses and Aaron the distinction between right and wrong, and gave them a light and an admonition for righteous men: those who truly fear their Lord and dread the terrors of Judgement-day.

And in this We have revealed a blessed counsel. Will you then reject it?

We bestowed guidance on Abraham, for We knew him well. He said to his father and to his people: 'What are these images to which you are so devoted?'

They replied: 'They are the gods our fathers worshipped.'

He said: 'Then you and your fathers are in the grossest error.'

'Is it the truth that you are preaching,' they asked, 'or is this but a jest?'

'Indeed,' he answered, 'your Lord is the Lord of the heavens and the earth. It was He that made them: to this I bear witness. By the Lord, I will overthrow your idols as soon as you have turned your backs.'

He broke them all in pieces, except their supreme god, so that they might return to Him.

'Who has done this to our deities?' asked some. 'He must surely be a wicked man.'

Others replied: 'We have heard a youth called Abraham speak of them.'

They said: 'Then bring him here in sight of all the people, that they may act as witnesses.'

'Abraham,' they said, 'was it you who did this to our deities?'

'No,' he replied. 'It was their chief who smote them. Ask *them*, if they can speak.'

Thereupon they turned their thoughts upon themselves and said to each other: 'Surely you are the ones who have done wrong.'

Confounded as they were, they said to Abraham: 'You know they cannot speak.'

He answered: 'Would you then worship that, instead of God, which can neither help nor harm you? Shame on you and on your idols! Have you no sense?'

They cried: 'Burn him and avenge your gods, if you must punish him!'

'Fire,' We said, 'be cool to Abraham and keep him safe.'

They sought to lay a snare for him, but they themselves were ruined. We delivered him and Lot, and brought them to the land which We had blessed for all mankind.

We gave him Isaac, and then Jacob for a grandson; and We made each a righteous man. We ordained them leaders to guide mankind at Our behest, and enjoined on them charity, prayer and almsgiving. They served none but Ourself.

To Lot We gave wisdom and knowledge and delivered him from the Wicked City; for its inhabitants were men of iniquity and evil. We admitted him to Our mercy: he was a righteous man.

Before him Noah invoked Us, and We heard his prayer. We saved him and all his kinsfolk from the great calamity, and delivered him from those who had denied Our revelations. Evil men they were; We drowned them all.

And tell of David and Solomon: how they passed judgement regarding the cornfield in which strayed lambs had grazed by night. We gave Solomon insight into the case and bore witness to both their judgements.

We bestowed on them wisdom and knowledge, and caused the birds and mountains to join with David in Our praise. All this We have done.

We taught him the armourer's craft, so that you might have protection in your wars. Will you then give thanks?

To Solomon We subjected the raging wind: it sped at his bidding to the land which We had blessed. We have knowledge of all things.

We assigned him devils who dived for him into the sea and who performed other tasks besides. Over them We kept a watchful eye.

And tell of Job: how he called on his Lord, saying: 'I am sorely afflicted: but of all those that show mercy You are the most merciful.'

We heard his prayer and relieved his affliction. We restored to him his family and as many more with them: a blessing from Ourself and an admonition to worshippers.

And you shall also tell of Ishmael, Idīs, and Dhūl-Kifl, who all endured with patience. To Our mercy We admitted them, for they were upright men.

And of Dhūl-Nūn: how he went away in anger, thinking We had no power over him. But in the darkness he cried: 'There is no god but You. Glory be to You! I have done wrong.'

We answered his prayer and delivered him from distress. Thus shall We save the true believers.

And of Zacharias, who invoked his Lord, saying: 'Lord, let me not remain childless, though of all heirs You are the best.'

We answered his prayer and gave him John, curing his wife of sterility. They vied with each other in good works and called on Us with piety, fear, and submission.

And of the woman who kept her chastity. We breathed into her of Our spirit, and made her and her son a sign to all men.

Your religion is but one religion, and I am Your only Lord. Therefore serve Me. Men have divided themselves into factions, but to Us they shall all return. He that does good works in the fullness of his faith, his endeavours shall not be lost: We record them all.

It is ordained that no nation We have destroyed shall ever rise again. But when Gog and Magog are let loose and rush headlong down every hill; when the true promise nears its fulfilment; the unbelievers shall stare in amazement, crying: 'Woe to us! Of this we have been heedless. We have done wrong.'

You and your idols shall be the fuel of Hell; therein you shall all go down. Were they true gods, your idols would not go there: but there they shall abide for ever. They shall groan with anguish and be bereft of hearing.

But those to whom We have long since shown Our favour shall be far removed from Hell. They shall not hear its roar, but shall delight for ever in what their souls desire.

The Supreme Terror shall not grieve them, and the angels will receive them, saying: 'This is the day you have been promised.'

On that day We shall roll up the heaven like a scroll of parchment. As We first created man, so will We bring him back to life. This is a promise We shall assuredly fulfil.

We wrote in the Psalms after the Torah was revealed: 'The righteous among My servants shall inherit the earth.' That is an admonition to those who serve Us.

We have sent you forth but as a blessing to mankind. Say: 'It is revealed to me that your God is one God. Will you submit to Him?'

If they give no heed say: 'I have warned you all alike, though I cannot tell whether the scourge you are threatened with is imminent or far off. He knows your spoken words and hidden thoughts. This may be a test for you and a short reprieve.'

Say: 'Lord, judge with fairness. Our Lord is the Merciful, whose help We seek against your blasphemies.'

24:35–46
Light

• • •

God is the light of the heavens and the earth. His light may be compared to a niche that enshrines a lamp, the lamp within a crystal of star-like brilliance. It is lit from a blessed olive tree neither eastern nor western. Its very oil would almost shine forth, though no fire touched it. Light upon light; God guides to His light whom He will.

God speaks in metaphors to men. God has knowledge of all things.

His light is found in temples which God has sanctioned to be built for the remembrance of His name. In them, morning and evening, His praise is sung by men whom neither trade nor profit can divert from remembering Him, from offering prayers, or from giving alms; who dread the day when men's hearts and eyes shall writhe with anguish; who hope that God will requite them for their noblest deeds and lavish His grace upon them. God gives without measure to whom He will.

As for the unbelievers, their works are like a mirage in a desert. The thirsty traveller thinks it is water, but when he comes near he finds that it is nothing. He finds God there, who pays him back in full. Swift is God's reckoning.

Or like darkness on a bottomless ocean spread with clashing billows and overcast with clouds: darkness upon darkness. If he stretches out his hand he can scarcely see it. Indeed the man from whom God withholds His light shall find no light at all.

Do you not see how God is praised by those in heaven and those on earth? The very birds praise Him as they wing their flight. He notes the prayers and praises of all His creatures, and has knowledge of all their actions.

It is God who has sovereignty over the heavens and the earth. To Him shall all things return.

Do you not see how God drives the clouds, then gathers and piles them up in masses which pour down torrents of rain? From heaven's mountains He sends down the hail, pelting with it whom He will and turning it away from whom He pleases. The flash of His lightning almost snatches off men's eyes.

He makes the night succeed the day: surely in this there is a lesson for clear-sighted men.

God created every beast from water. Some creep upon their bellies, others walk on two legs, and others yet on four. God creates what He pleases. He has power over all things.

We have sent down revelations demonstrating the Truth. God guides whom He will to a straight path. . . .

BOETHIUS

from *The Consolation of Philosophy*

Book III

Chapter IX

• • •

'Even a blind man could see it,' I said, 'and you revealed it just now when you were trying to show the causes of false happiness. For unless I'm mistaken, true and perfect happiness is that which makes a man self-sufficient, strong, worthy of respect, glorious and joyful. And to show you that I have more than a superficial understanding, without a shadow of doubt I can see that happiness to be true happiness which, since they are all the same thing, can truly bestow any one of them.'

'You are blessed in this belief, my child, provided you add one thing.'

'What is that?'

'Do you think there is anything among these mortal and degenerate things which could confer such a state?'

'No, I don't, and you have proved it as well as anyone could wish.'

'Clearly, therefore, these things offer man only shadows of the true good, or imperfect blessings, and cannot confer true and perfect good.'

'Yes.'

'Since then you have realized the nature of true happiness and seen its false imitations, what remains now is that you should see where to find this true happiness.'

'Which is the very thing I have long and eagerly been waiting for.'

'But since in the *Timaeus* my servant Plato was pleased to ask for divine help even over small matters, what do you think we ought to do now in order to be worthy of discovering the source of that supreme good?'

'We ought to pray to the Father of all things. To omit to do so would not be laying a proper foundation.'

'Right,' she said, and immediately began the following hymn.

'O Thou who dost by everlasting reason rule,
Creator of the planets and the sky, who time
From timelessness didst bring, unchanging Mover,
No cause drove Thee to mould unstable matter, but
The form benign of highest good within Thee set.
All things Thou bringest forth from Thy high archetype:
Thou, height of beauty, in Thy mind the beauteous world
Dost bear, and in that ideal likeness shaping it,
Dost order perfect parts a perfect whole to frame.
The elements by harmony Thou dost constrain,
That hot to cold and wet to dry are equal made,
That fire grow not too light, or earth too fraught with weight.
The bridge of threefold nature madest Thou soul, which spreads
Through nature's limbs harmonious and all things moves.
The soul once cut, in circles two its motion joins,
Goes round and to itself returns encircling mind,
And turns in pattern similar the firmament.
From causes like Thou bringst forth souls and lesser lives,
Which from above in chariots swift Thou dost disperse
Through sky and earth, and by Thy law benign they turn
And back to Thee they come through fire that brings them home.

Grant, Father, that our minds Thy august seat may scan,
Grant us the sight of true good's source, and grant us light
That we may fix on Thee our mind's unblinded eye.
Disperse the clouds of earthly matter's cloying weight;
Shine out in all Thy glory; for Thou art rest and peace
To those who worship Thee; to see Thee is our end,
Who art our source and maker, lord and path and goal.'

Chapter X

'Since, then, you have seen the form both of imperfect and of perfect good, I think we now have to show where this perfect happiness is to be found.

'The first question to ask is, I think, whether any good of the kind I defined a moment ago can exist in the natural world. This will prevent our being led astray from the truth of the matter before us by false and ill-founded reasoning. But the existence of this good and its function as a kind of fountain-head of all good things cannot be denied; for everything that is said to be imperfect is held to be so by the absence of perfection. So that if a certain imperfection is visible in any class of things, it follows that there is also a proportion of perfection in it. For if you do away with perfection, it is impossible to imagine how that which is held to be imperfect could exist. The natural world did not take its origin from that which was impaired and incomplete, but issues from that which is unimpaired and perfect and then degenerates into this fallen and worn out condition. But we showed just now that there is a certain imperfect happiness in perishable good, so that there can be no doubt that a true and perfect happiness exists.'

'Which is a very sound and true conclusion,' I said.

'As to where it is to be found, then, you should think as follows. It is the universal understanding of the human mind that God, the author of all things, is good. Since nothing can be conceived better than God, everyone agrees that that which has no superior is good. Reason shows that God is so good that we are convinced that His goodness is perfect. Otherwise He couldn't be the author of creation. There would have to be something else possessing perfect goodness over and above God, which would seem to be superior to Him and of greater antiquity. For all perfect things are obviously superior to those that are imperfect. Therefore, to avoid an unending argument, it must be admitted that the supreme God is to the highest degree filled with supreme and perfect goodness. But we have agreed that perfect good is true happiness; so that it follows that true happiness is to be found in the supreme God.'

'I accept that. There is nothing in any way open to contradiction.'

'But,' she said, 'I must ask you to make sure that your approval of our statement that the supreme God is to the highest degree filled with supreme good is unqualified and final.'

'How do you mean?' I asked.

'By avoiding the assumption that this Father of creation has received this supreme good with which He is said to be filled from outside Himself, or that He possesses it by nature but in such a way as would lead you to suppose that the substance of God the possessor was a separate thing from the substance of the happiness He possesses. If you thought that He received it from outside Himself, you would be able to count the giver superior to the receiver. But we are in agreement that it is right to consider God the most excellent of things.

'On the other hand, if goodness is a natural property of God, but something logically distinct from Him, whenever we speak of God as the author of creation, an able mind might be able to imagine the existence of a power responsible for bringing together the two that were separate.

'Finally, if one thing is distinct from another, it cannot be the thing from which it is perceived to be distinct. So that which by its own nature is something distinct from supreme good, cannot be supreme good; but this is something we may not hold about Him to whom we agree there is nothing superior. It is impossible for anything to be by nature better than that from which it is derived. I would therefore conclude with perfect logic that that which is the origin of all things is in its own substance supreme good.'

'Perfectly right.'

'But we have agreed that supreme good is the same as happiness.'

'Yes.'

'So that we have to agree that God is the essence of happiness.'

'Your premises are incontestable and I see that this inference follows upon them.'

'Then consider whether this, too, can be firmly accepted: that it is impossible for two supreme goods to exist separate from one another. For it is clear that if the two goods are separate, the one cannot be the other, so that neither could be perfect when each is lacking to the other. But that which is not perfect is obviously not supreme. It is therefore impossible for there to be two separate supreme goods. However, we deduced that both happiness and God are supreme goodness, so that it follows that supreme happiness is identical with supreme divinity.'

'There could scarcely be a conclusion more true to reality, or more sure in its reasoning, or more worthy of God.'

'I will add something to it. Just as in geometry some additional inference may be drawn from a theorem that has been proved, called in technical language, in Greek a *porisma* and in Latin a corollary, I too will give you a kind of corollary. Since it is through the possession of happiness that people become happy, and since happiness is in fact divinity, it is clear that it is through the possession of divinity that they become happy. But by the same logic as men become just through the possession of justice, or wise through the possession of wisdom, so those who possess divinity necessarily become divine. Each happy individual is therefore divine. While only God is so by nature, as many as you like may become so by participation.'

'What you say is beautiful and valuable, whether you give it the Greek or the Latin name.'

'But the most beautiful thing is what logic leads us to add to all this.'

'What is that?'

'Are all the many things we see included under the word happiness like parts combining to form a single body, yet separate in their variety, or is there any one of them which can fully supply the essence of happiness and under which the others may be classed?'

'Could you clarify the question by being more specific?'

'Well, we consider happiness something good, don't we?'

'Yes, the supreme good.'

'You could say the same of all of them. Absolute sufficiency is judged to be the same as happiness, and so too are power, reverence, glory and pleasure. Well, the question is this, all these things—sufficiency, power and the others—are they good as if happiness were a body of which they were members, or is goodness a kind of heading to which they belong?'

'I understand the question which you are proposing we should ask, but I should like to hear what your answer would be.'

'This is how I would resolve it. If all these were related to happiness like limbs to a body, they would differ from one another, because it is the nature of parts that the body is one, but the parts that make it up are diverse. But all these things have been proved to be identical. So that they are not like limbs. Moreover it would appear that happiness was a body made up of a single limb, which is impossible.'

'There is no doubt of that; but I am eager for what is to come.'

'It is clear that the other properties are classed under good. It is just because sufficiency is judged a good that people want it, and it is just because it too is believed to be a good that power is sought after. And exactly the same conclusion may be reached about reverence, glory and pleasure.

'The chief point and reason, therefore, for seeking all things is goodness. For it is quite impossible for that which contains no good in itself whether real or apparent, to be an object of desire. On the other hand, things which are not good by nature are sought after if they nevertheless seem as if they were truly good.

'The result is, therefore, that there is justice in the belief that goodness is the chief point upon which the pursuit of everything hinges and by which it is motivated. What seems most to be desired is the thing that motivates the pursuit of something, as, for example, if a man wants to go riding for the sake of health; it is not so much the motion of horse-riding he desires as the resultant good health. Since, therefore, all things are desired for the sake of the good in them, no one desires them as much as the good itself. But we are agreed that the reason for desiring things is happiness. So that it is patently obvious that the good itself and happiness are identical.'

'I can see no reason for anyone to disagree.'

'But we have shown that God and happiness are one and the same thing.'

'Yes.'

'We may safely conclude, then, that God is to be found in goodness itself and nowhere else.

'Come hither now all you who captive are,
Whom false desire enchains in wicked bonds,
Desire that makes her home in earthly minds;
Here will you find release from grievous toil,
Here find a haven blessed with peaceful calm,
An ever open refuge from distress.
Not all the gold that Tagus' sands bestow,
That Hermus from his glittering banks casts up,
Or Indus, on whose torrid shores are strewn
Green emeralds intermixed with dazzling pearls,
May sharpen and make bright the intellect,
But wealth in its own darkness clouds the thoughts.
For all that thus excites and charms the mind
Dim earth has fostered in her caverns deep;
While that bright light which rules and animates
The sky, will shun such dark and ruined souls:
Whoever once shall see this shining light
Will say the sun's own rays are not so bright.'

BEDE

from *A History of the English Church and People*

Chapter 24
A Brother of the Monastery Is Found to Possess God's Gift of Poetry (A.D. 680)

In this monastery of Streanaeshalch lived a brother singularly gifted by God's grace. So skilful was he in composing religious and devotional songs that, when any passage of Scripture was explained to him by interpreters, he could quickly turn it into delightful and moving poetry in his own English tongue. These verses of his have stirred the hearts of many folk to despise the world and aspire to heavenly things. Others after him tried to compose religious poems in English, but none could compare with him; for he did not acquire the art of poetry from men or through any human teacher but received it as a free gift from God. For this reason he could never compose any frivolous or profane verses; but only such as had a religious theme fell fittingly from his devout lips. He had followed a secular occupation until well advanced in years without ever learning anything about poetry. Indeed it sometimes happened at a feast that all the guests in turn would be invited to sing and entertain the company; then, when he saw the harp coming his way, he would get up from table and go home.

On one such occasion he had left the house in which the entertainment was being held and went out to the stable, where it was his duty that night to look after the beasts. There when the time came he settled down to sleep. Suddenly in a dream he saw a man standing beside him who called him by name. 'Caedmon,' he said, 'sing me a song.' 'I don't know how to sing,' he replied. 'It is because I cannot sing that I left the feast and came here.' The man who addressed him then said: 'But you shall sing to me.' 'What should I sing about?' he replied. 'Sing about the Creation of all things,' the other answered. And Caedmon immediately began to sing verses in praise of God the Creator that he had never heard before, and their theme ran thus:

Praise we the Fashioner now of Heaven's fabric,
The majesty of his might and his mind's wisdom,
Work of the world-warden, worker of all wonders,
How he the Lord of Glory everlasting,
Wrought first for the race of men Heaven as a rooftree,
Then made he Middle Earth to be their mansion.

This is the general sense, but not the actual words that Caedmon sang in his dream; for verses, however masterly, cannot be translated literally from one language into another without losing much of their beauty and dignity. When Caedmon awoke, he remembered everything that he had sung in his dream, and soon added more verses in the same style to a song truly worthy of God.

Early in the morning he went to his superior the reeve, and told him about this gift that he had received. The reeve took him before the abbess, who ordered him to give an account of his dream and repeat the verses in the presence of many learned men, so that a decision might be reached by common consent as to their quality and origin. All of them agreed that Caedmon's gift had been given him by our Lord. And they explained to him a passage of scriptural history or doctrine and asked him to render it into verse if he could. He promised to do this, and returned next morning with excellent verses as they had ordered him. The abbess was delighted that God had given such grace to the man, and advised him to abandon secular life and adopt the monastic state. And when she had admitted him into the Community as a brother, she ordered him to be instructed in the events of sacred history. So Caedmon stored up in his memory all that he learned, and like one of the clean animals chewing the cud, turned it into such melodious verse that his delightful renderings turned his instructors into auditors. He sang of the creation of the world, the origin of the human race, and the whole story of Genesis. He sang of Israel's exodus from Egypt, the entry into the Promised Land, and many other events of scriptural history. He sang of the Lord's

Incarnation, Passion, Resurrection, and Ascension into heaven, the coming of the Holy Spirit, and the teaching of the Apostles. He also made many poems on the terrors of the Last Judgement, the horrible pains of Hell, and the joys of the Kingdom of Heaven. In addition to these, he composed several others on the blessings and judgements of God, by which he sought to turn his hearers from delight in wickedness and to inspire them to love and do good. For Caedmon was a deeply religious man, who humbly submitted to regular discipline and hotly rebuked all who tried to follow another course. And so he crowned his life with a happy end.

For, when the time of his death drew near, he felt the onset of physical weakness for fourteen days, but not seriously enough to prevent his walking or talking the whole time. Close by there was a house to which all who were sick or likely to die were taken. Towards nightfall on the day when he was to depart this life, Caedmon asked his attendant to prepare a resting-place for him in this house. The attendant was surprised at this request from a man who did not appear likely to die yet; nevertheless, he did as he was asked. So Caedmon went to the house, and conversed and jested cheerfully with those who were already there; and when it was past midnight, he asked: 'Is the Eucharist in the house?' 'Why do you want the Eucharist?' they enquired; 'you are not likely to die yet, when you are talking so cheerfully to us and seem to be in perfect health.' 'Nevertheless,' he said, 'bring me the Eucharist.' And taking It in his hands, Caedmon asked whether they were all charitably disposed towards him, and whether they had any complaint or ill-feeling against him. They replied that they were all most kindly disposed towards him, and free from all bitterness. Then in turn they asked him to clear his heart of bitterness towards them. At once he answered: 'Dear sons, my heart is at peace with all the servants of God.' Then, when he had fortified himself with the heavenly Viaticum, he prepared to enter the other life, and asked how long it would be before the brothers were roused to sing God's praises in the Night Office. 'Not long,' they replied. 'Good, then let us wait until then,' he answered; and signing himself with the holy Cross, he laid his head on the pillow and passed away quietly in his sleep. So, having served God with a simple and pure mind, and with tranquil devotion, he left the world and departed to his presence by a tranquil death. His tongue, which had sung so many inspiring verses in praise of his Maker, uttered its last words in his praise as he signed himself with the Cross and commended his soul into his hands. For, as I have already said, Caedmon seems to have had a premonition of his death.

EINHARD

from *The Life of Charlemagne*

Book III (The Emperor's Private Life)

• • •

§19.   Charlemagne was determined to give his children, his daughters just as much as his sons, a proper training in the liberal arts which had formed the subject of his own studies. As soon as they were old enough he had his sons taught to ride in the Frankish fashion, to use arms and to hunt. He made his daughters learn to spin and weave wool, use the distaff and spindle, and acquire every womanly accomplishment, rather than fritter away their time in sheer idleness. . . .

When the death of Hadrian, the Pope of Rome and his close friend, was announced to him, he wept as if he had lost a brother or a dearly loved son. He was firm and steady in his human relationships, developing friendship easily, keeping it up with care and doing everything he possibly could for anyone whom he had admitted to this degree of intimacy.

He paid such attention to the upbringing of his sons and daughters that he never sat down to table without them when he was at home, and never set out on a journey without taking them with him. His sons rode at his side and his daughters followed along behind. Hand-picked guards watched over them as they closed the line of march. These girls were extraordinarily beautiful and greatly loved by their father. It is a remarkable fact that, as a result of this, he kept them with him in his household until the very day of his death, instead of giving them in marriage to his own men or to foreigners, maintaining that he could not live without them. The consequence was that he had a number of unfortunate experiences, he who had been so lucky in all else that he undertook. However, he shut his eyes to all that happened, as if no suspicion of any immoral conduct had ever reached him, or as if the rumour was without foundation.

§20.   I did not mention with the others a son called Pepin who was born to Charlemagne by a concubine. He was handsome enough, but a hunchback. At a moment when his father was wintering in Bavaria, soon after the beginning of his campaign against the Huns, this Pepin pretended to be ill and conspired with certain of the Frankish leaders who had won him over to their cause by pretending to offer him the kingship. The plot was discovered and the conspirators were duly punished. Pepin was tonsured and permitted to take up, in the monastery of Prüm, the life of a religious for which he had already expressed a vocation.

Earlier on there had been another dangerous conspiracy against Charlemagne in Germany. All the plotters were exiled, some having their eyes put out first, but the others were not maltreated physically. Only three of them were killed. These resisted arrest, drew their swords and started to defend themselves. They slaughtered a few men in the process and had to be destroyed themselves, as there was no other way of dealing with them.

The cruelty of Queen Fastrada is thought to have been the cause of both these conspiracies, since it was under her influence that Charlemagne seemed to have taken actions which were fundamentally opposed to his normal kindliness and good nature. Throughout the remainder of his life he so won the love and favour of all his fellow human beings, both at home and abroad, that no one ever levelled against him the slightest charge of cruelty or injustice.

§21.   He loved foreigners and took great pains to make them welcome. So many visited him as a result that they were rightly held to be a burden not only to the palace, but to the entire realm. In his magnanimity he took no notice at all of this criticism, for he considered that his reputation for hospitality and the advantage of the good name which he acquired more than compensated for the great nuisance of their being there.

§22.   The Emperor was strong and well built. He was tall in stature, but not excessively so, for his height was just seven times the length of his own feet. The top of his head was round, and his eyes were piercing and unusually large. His nose was slightly longer than normal, he had a fine head of white hair and his expression was gay and good-humoured. As a result, whether he was seated or standing, he always appeared masterful and dignified. His neck was short and rather thick, and his stomach a trifle too heavy, but the proportions of the rest of his body prevented one from noticing these blemishes. His step was firm and he was manly in all his movements. He spoke distinctly, but his voice was thin for a man of his physique. His health was good, except that he suffered from frequent attacks of fever during the last four years of his life, and towards the end he was lame in one foot. Even then he continued to do exactly as he wished, instead of following the advice of his doctors, whom he came positively to dislike after they advised him to stop eating the roast meat to which he was accustomed and to live on stewed dishes.

He spent much of his time on horseback and out hunting, which came naturally to him, for it would be difficult to find another race on earth who could equal the Franks in this activity. He took delight in steam-baths at the thermal springs, and loved to exercise himself in the water whenever he could. He was an extremely strong swimmer and in this sport no one could surpass him. It was for this reason that he built his palace at Aachen and remained continuously in residence there during the last years of his life and indeed until the moment of his death. He would invite not only his sons to bathe with him, but his nobles and friends as well, and occasionally even a crowd of his attendants and body-guards, so that sometimes a hundred men or more would be in the water together.

§23. He wore the national dress of the Franks. Next to his skin he had a linen shirt and linen drawers; and then long hose and a tunic edged with silk. He wore shoes on his feet and bands of cloth wound round his legs. In winter he protected his chest and shoulders with a jerkin made of otter skins or ermine. He wrapped himself in a blue cloak and always had a sword strapped to his side, with a hilt and belt of gold or silver. Sometimes he would use a jewelled sword, but this was only on great feast days or when ambassadors came from foreign peoples. He hated the clothes of other countries, no matter how becoming they might be, and he would never consent to wear them. The only exception to this was one day in Rome when Pope Hadrian entreated him to put on a long tunic and a Greek mantle, and to wear shoes made in the Roman fashion; and then a second time, when Leo, Hadrian's successor, persuaded him to do the same thing. On feast days he walked in procession in a suit of cloth of gold, with jewelled shoes, his cloak fastened with a golden brooch and with a crown of gold and precious stones on his head. On ordinary days his dress differed hardly at all from that of the common people.

§24. He was moderate in his eating and drinking, and especially so in drinking; for he hated to see drunkenness in any man, and even more so in himself and his friends. All the same, he could not go long without food, and he often used to complain that fasting made him feel ill. He rarely gave banquets and these only on high feast days, but then he would invite a great number of guests. His main meal of the day was served in four courses, in addition to the roast meat which his hunters used to bring in on spits and which he enjoyed more than any other food. During his meal he would listen to a public reading or some other entertainment. Stories would be recited for him, or the doings of the ancients told again. He took great pleasure in the books of Saint Augustine and especially in those which are called *The City of God*. . . .

§25. He spoke easily and fluently, and could express with great clarity whatever he had to say. He was not content with his own mother tongue, but took the trouble to learn foreign languages. He learnt Latin so well that he spoke it as fluently as his own tongue; but he understood Greek better than he could speak it. He was eloquent to the point of sometimes seeming almost garrulous.

He paid the greatest attention to the liberal arts; and he had great respect for men who taught them, bestowing high honours upon them. When he was learning the rules of grammar he received tuition from Peter the Deacon of Pisa, who by then was an old man, but for all other subjects he was taught by Alcuin, surnamed Albinus, another Deacon, a man of the Saxon race who came from Britain and was the most learned man anywhere to be found. Under him the Emperor spent much time and effort in studying rhetoric, dialectic and especially astrology. He applied himself to mathematics and traced the course of the stars with great attention and care. He also tried to learn to write. With this object in view he used to keep writing-tablets and notebooks under the pillows on his bed, so that he could try his hand at forming letters during his leisure moments; but, although he tried very hard, he had begun too late in life and he made little progress. . . .

§29. Now that he was Emperor, he discovered that there were many defects in the legal system of his own people, for the Franks have two separate codes of law which differ from each other in many points. He gave much thought to how he could best fill the gaps, reconcile the discrepancies, correct the errors and rewrite the laws which were ill-expressed. None of this was ever finished; he added a few sections, but even these remained incomplete. What he did do was to have collected together and committed to writing the laws of all the nations under his jurisdiction which still remained unrecorded.

At the same time he directed that the age-old narrative poems, barbarous enough, it is true, in which were celebrated the warlike deeds of the kings of ancient times, should be written out and so preserved. He also began a grammar of his native tongue. . . .

from *Beowulf*

· · ·

        Gliding through the shadows came
the walker in the night; the warriors slept
whose task was to hold the horned building,
all except one. It was well-known to men
that the demon could not drag them to the shades
without God's willing it; yet the one man kept
unblinking watch. He awaited, heart swelling

with anger against his foe, the ordeal of battle.
Down off the moorlands' misting fells came
Grendel stalking; God's brand was on him.
The spoiler meant to snatch away
from the high hall some of human race.
He came on under the clouds, clearly saw at last
the gold-hall of men, the mead-drinking place
nailed with gold plates. That was not the first visit

he had paid to the hall of Hrothgar the Dane:
he never before and never after
harder luck nor hall-guards found.

Walking to the hall came this warlike creature
condemned to agony. The door gave way,
toughened with iron, at the touch of those hands.
Rage-inflamed, wreckage-bent, he ripped open
the jaws of the hall. Hastening on,
the foe then stepped onto the unstained floor,
angrily advanced: out of his eyes stood
an unlovely light like that of fire.
He saw then in the hall a host of young soldiers,
a company of kinsmen caught away in sleep,
a whole warrior-band. In his heart he laughed then,
horrible monster, his hopes swelling
to a gluttonous meal. He meant to wrench
the life from each body that lay in the place
before night was done. It was not to be;
he was no longer to feast on the flesh of mankind
after that night.
                    Narrowly the powerful
kinsman of Hygelac kept watch how the ravager
set to work with his sudden catches;
nor did the monster mean to hang back.
As a first step he set his hands on
a sleeping soldier, savagely tore at him,
gnashed at his bone-joints, bolted huge gobbets,
sucked at his veins, and had soon eaten
all of the dead man, even down to his
hands and feet.
                    Forward he stepped,
stretched out his hands to seize the warrior
calmly at rest there, reached out for him with his
unfriendly fingers: but the faster man
forestalling, sat up, sent back his arm.
The upholder of evils at once knew
he had not met, on middle earth's
extremest acres, with any man
of harder hand-grip: his heart panicked.
He was quit of the place no more quickly for that.

Eager to be away, he ailed for his darkness
and the company of devils; the dealings he had there
were like nothing he had come across in his lifetime.
Then Hygelac's brave kinsman called to mind
that evening's utterance, upright he stood,
fastened his hold till fingers were bursting.
The monster strained away: the man stepped closer.
The monster's desire was for darkness between them,
direction regardless, to get out and run
for his fen-bordered lair; he felt his grip's strength
crushed by his enemy. It was an ill journey
the rough marauder had made to Heorot.

The crash in the banqueting-hall came to the Danes,
the men of the guard that remained in the building,
with the taste of death. The deepening rage
of the claimants to Heorot caused it to resound.
It was indeed wonderful that the wine-supper-hall

withstood the wrestling pair, that the world's palace
fell not to the ground. But it was girt firmly,
both inside and out, by iron braces
of skilled manufacture. Many a figured
gold-worked wine-bench, as we heard it,
started from the floor at the struggles of that pair.
The men of the Danes had not imagined that
any of mankind by what method soever
might undo that intricate, antlered hall,
sunder it by strength—unless it were swallowed up in
the embraces of fire.
                    Fear entered into
the listening North Danes, as that noise rose up again
strange and strident. It shrilled terror
to the ears that heard it through the hall's side-wall,
the grisly plaint of God's enemy,
his song of ill-success, the sobs of the damned one
bewailing his pain. He was pinioned there
by the man of all mankind living
in this world's estate the strongest of his hands.

Not for anything would the earls' guardian
let his deadly guest go living:
he did not count his continued existence
of the least use to anyone. The earls ran
to defend the person of their famous prince;
they drew their ancestral swords to bring
what aid they could to their captain, Beowulf.
They were ignorant of this, when they entered the fight,
boldly-intentioned battle-friends,
to hew at Grendel, hunt his life
on every side—that no sword on earth,
not the truest steel, could touch their assailant;
for by a spell he had dispossessed all
blades of their bite on him.
                    A bitter parting
from life was that day destined for him;
the eldritch spirit was sent off on his
far faring into the fiends' domain.

It was then that this monster, who, moved by spite
against human kind, had caused so much harm
—so feuding with God—found at last
that flesh and bone were to fail him in the end;
for Hygelac's great-hearted kinsman
had him by the hand; and hateful to each
was the breath of the other.
                    A breach in the giant
flesh-frame showed then, shoulder-muscles
sprang apart, there was a snapping of tendons,
bone-locks burst. To Beowulf the glory
of this fight was granted; Grendel's lot
to flee the slopes fen-ward with flagging heart,
to a den where he knew there could be no relief,
no refuge for a life at its very last stage,
whose surrender-day had dawned. The Danish hopes
in this fatal fight had found their answer.

He had cleansed Heorot. He who had come from afar,
deep-minded, strong-hearted, had saved the hall

from persecution. He was pleased with his night's work,
the deed he had done. Before the Danish people
the Great captain had made good his boast,
had taken away all their unhappiness,
the evil menace under which they had lived,
enduring it by dire constraint,
no slight affliction. As a signal to all
the hero hung up the hand, the arm
and torn-off shoulder, the entire limb,
Grendel's whole grip, below the gable of the roof.

There was, as I heard it, at hall next morning
a great gathering in the gift-hall yard
to see the wonder. Along the wide highroads
the chiefs of the clans came from near and far
to see the foe's footprints. It may fairly be said
that his parting from life aroused no pity in any
who tracked the spoor-blood of his blind flight
for the monster's mere-pool; with mood flagging
and strength crushed, he had staggered onwards;
each step evidenced his ebbing life's blood.

The tarn was troubled; a terrible wave-thrash
brimmed it, bubbling; black-mingled,
the warm wound-blood welled upwards.
He had dived to his doom, he had died miserably;
here in his fen-lair he had laid aside
his heathen soul. Hell welcomed it.

Chapter

9

The High Middle Ages:
The Christian Centuries

from *The Song of Roland*

CLXXIV

Count Roland feels   the very grip of death
Which from his head   is reaching for his heart.
He hurries then   to go beneath a pine;
In the green grass   he lies down on his face,
Placing beneath him   the sword and Oliphant;
He turns his head   to look toward pagan Spain.
He does these things   in order to be sure
King Charles will say,   and with him all the Franks,
The noble count   conquered until he died.
He makes confession,   for all his sins laments,
Offers his glove   to God in penitence.

CLXXV

Now Roland feels   his time has all run out.
He looks toward Spain   from high on a steep hill,
And with one hand   beating his breast, he says:
"God, I have sinned   against Thy holy name.
Forgive the sins,   the great ones and the less,
That I committed   from my first hour of life
To this last day   when I have been struck down."
And now toward God   he raises his right glove;
A flight of angels   comes from the skies above.

CLXXVI

And now Count Roland,   lying beneath a pine,
Has turned his face   to look toward pagan Spain;
And he begins   remembering these things:
The many lands   his valor won the king,
Sweet France, his home,   the men of his own line,
And Charlemagne   who raised him in his house—
The memories   make him shed tears and sigh.
But not forgetting   how close he is to death,
He prays that God   forgive him all his sins:
"O my true Father,   O Thou who never lied,
Thou who delivered   Lazarus from the grave,
Who rescued Daniel   out of the lions' den,
Keep now my soul   from every peril safe,
Forgive the sins   that I have done in life."
Roland, in homage,   offers his glove to God.
Saint Gabriel comes   and takes it from his hand.
His head sinks down   to rest upon his arm;
Hands clasped in prayer,   the count has met his end.
God sends from heaven   the angel Cherubin,
Holy Saint Michael   who saves us from the sea,
And with these two   the Angel Gabriel flies.
Count Roland's soul   they bring to Paradise.

CLXXVII

Roland is dead;   his soul rests now with God.
The Emperor Charles   rides into Roncevaux;
On every road,   on every mountain path,
On every ell,   on every foot of land,
They find a body   of Frank or Saracen.
King Charles cries out,   "Fair nephew, where are you?
Where's the archbishop?   Where is Count Oliver?
Where is Count Gerin,   and Gerier his friend?
Oton—where is he,   and noble Bérengier,
Ivoire and Ivon,   those two I held so dear?
Tell me what happened   to Gascon Engelier,
Where are Duke Samson,   the valiant Anseïs,
And Old Gérard,   the Count of Roussillon?
Where are the peers,   the twelve who stayed behind?"
What good is asking   when no one can reply?
"God!" says the king,   "Now have I cause to grieve,
For where was I   when fighting here began!"
He pulls his beard   in anguish and in pain;
The lords of France   are weeping bitter tears,
And twenty thousand   faint in their grief and fall.
Duke Naimon feels   great sorrow for them all.

CLXXVIII

There is not one   among those noble lords
Who can refrain   from shedding tears of grief:
It is their sons,   their brothers that they mourn,
Their nephews, friends;   they weep for their liege lords.
Many among them   fall fainting to the ground.
Only Duke Naimon   can see what must be done;
He is the first   to tell the emperor:
"Look up ahead,   two leagues from where we stand,
See how the dust   is rising from the road—
There are the pagans,   and surely not a few.
Ride after them!   Let us avenge our grief!"
"O God," says Charles,   "they are already far—
Grant me this grace,   let me do what is right,
For they have stolen   the flower of sweet France!"
The king commands   Oton and Geboïn,
Thibault of Reims,   and also Count Milon:
"Guard well this field,   the valleys and the heights,
Let all the dead   remain just as they are,
But keep them safe   from lions and wild beasts;
Let no one touch them,   no servant and no squire—
I say to you,   let no man touch these dead
Until God brings us   back to this field again."
They answer him   with reverence and love:
"Right Emperor,   dear lord, as you command."
These four will keep   a thousand knights at hand.

CLXXIX

The Emperor Charles   has all his trumpets sound.
The mighty lord   rides onward with his host;
They find the tracks   made by the Saracens,
And all together   follow them in pursuit.
When the king sees   that evening will come soon,

In a green meadow   he gets down from his horse,
Kneels on the ground   and prays almighty God
To make the sun   stop moving through the sky,
Delay the night,   and let the day remain.
And then an angel,   who often spoke with him,
Came in great haste   to give him this command:
"Charles, speed you on!   The light won't fail you now.
God knows that you have lost   the flower of France.
You'll have your vengeance   on the vile Saracen!"
Already Charles   has mounted once again.

CLXXX

For Charlemagne   God worked a miracle:
The sun stops moving,   and stands still in the sky.
The pagans flee,   the Franks pursue them hard,
At Val-Tenebre   they overtake their foes;
Toward Saragossa   they chase them, sword in hand,
With mighty blows   cutting the pagans down,
Driving them off   the wide paths and the roads,
Until they find   the Ebro in their way.
Deep is the water,   and frightening and swift,
There are no boats,   no galleys, not a barge.
The Saracens   invoke their Tervagant;
They all jump in,   but nothing keeps them safe:
The men in armor   weigh more than all the rest,
Some of them sink   straight down into the depths,
Others are carried   by the swift-running stream,
Those least in danger   still drink, and far too much;
All of them drown   in anguish and in fear.
The French cry, "Roland,   if only you were here!"

CLXXXI

When Charlemagne   sees all the pagans dead,
Some slain in battle,   and many of them drowned,
Leaving great spoils   for all the Frankish knights,
The noble king,   dismounting from his horse,
Kneels on the ground,   and gives his thanks to God.
When he gets up,   he sees the sun has set.
The emperor says,   "We'll have to make camp here.
It's too late now   to ride to Roncevaux—
All of our horses   are weary and worn out.
Take off their saddles   and let their bridles go;
Free in these meadows,   they'll cool off as they should."
The Franks reply,   "My lord, your words are good."

CLXXXII

The Emperor Charles   has had his camp set up.
The French dismount   there in the wilderness,
The horses' saddles   are taken off their backs,
The golden bridles   are lifted from their heads,
They roam the meadows   where there is good fresh
        grass—
There are no other   provisions to be had.
Men who are weary   lie on the ground and sleep;
For on this night   there is no watch to keep.

CLXXXIII

Now in a meadow   the emperor lies down;
His mighty spear   he keeps close by his head,
For on this night   he wishes to stay armed.
He wears his hauberk   of saffron-burnished steel,
His helm is laced,   bright gems gleam in its gold;
Still at his side,   Joyeuse, the peerless sword,
Which changes color   thirty times every day.
We all have heard   what happened to the lance
With which Our Lord   was wounded on the Cross:
Charles has the spearhead—   almighty God be thanked—
He had it mounted   into the golden hilt,
And for that honor,   that sign of heaven's love,
The name Joyeuse   was given to the sword.
Let the French barons   remember this each time
They cry "Montjoie!"   in battle: let them know
That war cry means   they'll conquer any foe.

CLXXXIV

The night is clear,   the moon gleams in the sky.
King Charles lies down,   but for Count Roland grieves,
For Oliver   whose loss weighs on his heart,
For the twelve peers,   for all the men of France:
At Roncevaux   their bloodstained bodies lie.
He can't help weeping,   and bitterly laments,
Praying that God   have mercy on their souls.
The king is weary,   exhausted by his grief,
He falls asleep—   he can't do any more.
In all the meadows   the Franks are sleeping too.
There's not one horse   left standing on its feet;
Those who want grass   eat just what they can reach.
A man does well   to learn what pain can teach.

CLXXXV

Charles goes to sleep   worn out by grief and toil.
Then God in heaven   sends Saint Gabriel down,
Commanding him   to guard the emperor.
The angel stays   close by his head all night,
And in two visions   lets him see what will come:
Another foe   is marching on the king,

The dream shows clearly   the fighting will be grim.
The emperor sees   above him in the sky
Lightning and thunder,   and gusts of wind and hail,
Great are the tempests,   fearful and vast the storms,
The heavens gather   flickering fire and flames
Which all at once   fall down upon his men;
Ash-wood and apple,   their spear-shafts are ablaze,
Their shields are burning   down to the boss of gold,
The shafts snap off   from their keen-bladed spears,
Their chain-mail crumples,   and their strong helms of
   steel.
With great dismay   Charles sees his knights attacked
By vicious beasts—   by leopards and by bears,
Serpents and vipers,   dragons and devils too,
And there are griffons,   thirty thousand and more,
All of them leaping,   charging against the Franks,
The Franks who cry,   "Charlemagne, help us now!"
And overwhelmed   by pity and by grief,
He starts out toward them,   but something interferes:
A mighty lion   springs at him from a wood,
Fearful to look at,   raging and proud and bold;
He leaps, attacking   the person of the king.
Grappling each other   they wrestle violently:
But who will rise   a victor, who will fall?
The emperor sleeps   and does not wake at all.

CLXXXVI

Later that night   he had another dream:
He was in Aix;   on a dais he stood,
Holding a bear   bound tight with double chains.
Thirty more bears   came out of the Ardennes,
Each of them speaking   exactly like a man.
They said to Charles,   "Sire, give him back to us!
It isn't right   for you to keep him here;
We cannot choose   but bring our kinsman help."
Out of the palace   there came a hunting dog
Who then attacked   the largest of the bears;
On the green grass   apart from all the rest,
While the king watched,   they fought a dreadful fight—
He could not see   which one of them would lose.
All this God's angel   revealed to Charlemagne.
The king slept on   until it was bright day.

ANNA COMNENA

from *The Alexiad*

Book Eleven
The First Crusade
(1097–1104)

Bohemond and all the counts met at a place from which they intended to sail across to Kibotos, and with Godfrey they awaited the arrival of Saint-Gilles who was coming with the emperor. Thus with their forces united they would set out along the road to Nicaea. However, their numbers were so immense that further delay became impossible—the food-supplies were deficient. So they divided their army in two: one group drove on through Bithynia and Nicomedia towards Nicaea; the other crossed the strait to Kibotos and assembled in the same area later. Having approached Nicaea in this manner they allotted towers and intervening battlements to certain sections. The idea was to make the assault on the walls according to these dispositions; rivalry between the various contingents would be provoked and the siege pressed with greater vigour. The area allotted to Saint-Gilles was left vacant until he arrived. At this moment the emperor reached Pelekanum, with his eye on Nicaea (as I have already pointed out). The barbarians inside the city meanwhile sent repeated messages to the sultan asking for help, but he was still wasting time and as the siege had already gone on for many days, from sunrise right up to sunset, their condition was obviously becoming extremely serious. They gave up the fight, deciding that it was better to make terms with the emperor than to be taken by the Kelts. Under the circumstances they summoned Boutoumites, who had often promised in a never-ending stream of letters that this or that favour would be granted by Alexius, if only they surrendered to him. He now explained in more detail the emperor's friendly intentions and produced written guarantees. He was gladly received by the Turks, who had despaired of holding out against the overwhelming strength of their enemies; it was wiser, they thought, to cede Nicaea voluntarily to Alexius and share in his gifts, with honourable treatment, than to become the victims of war to no purpose. Boutoumites had not been in the place more than two days before Saint-Gilles arrived, determined to make an attempt on the walls without delay; he had siege engines ready for the task. Meanwhile a rumour spread that the sultan was on his way. At this news the Turks, inspired with courage again, at once expelled Boutoumites. As for the sultan, he sent a detachment of his forces to observe the Frankish offensive, with orders to fight if they met any Kelts. They were seen by Saint-Gilles's men from a distance and a battle took place—but it went ill for the Turks, for the other counts and Bohemond himself, learning of the engagement, set aside up to 200 men from each company, thus making up a considerable army, and sent them immediately to help. They overtook the barbarians and pursued them till

nightfall. Nevertheless, the sultan was far from downcast at this setback; at sunrise the next morning he was in full armour and with all his men occupied the plain outside the walls of Nicaea. The Kelts heard about it and they too armed themselves for battle. They descended on their enemies like lions. The struggle that then ensued was ferocious and terrible. All through the day it was indecisive, but when the sun went down the Turks fled. Night had ended the contest. On either side many fell and most of them were killed; the majority of the fighters were wounded. So the Kelts won a glorious victory. The heads of many Turks they stuck on the ends of spears and came back carrying these like standards, so that the barbarians, recognizing afar off what had happened and being frightened by this defeat at their first encounter, might not be so eager for battle in future. So much for the ideas and actions of the Latins. The sultan, realizing how numerous they were and after this onslaught made aware of their self-confidence and daring, gave a hint to the Turks in Nicaea: 'From now on do just what you consider best.' He already knew that they preferred to deliver up the city to Alexius than to become prisoners of the Kelts. Meanwhile Saint-Gilles, setting about the task allotted to him, was constructing a wooden tower, circular in shape; inside and out he covered it with leather hides and filled the centre with intertwined wickerwork. When it was thoroughly strengthened, he approached the so-called Gonatas Tower. His machine was manned by soldiers whose job was to batter the walls and also by expert sappers, equipped with iron tools to undermine them from below; the former would engage the defenders on the ramparts above, while the latter worked with impunity below. In place of the stones they prised out, logs of wood were put in and when their excavations reached the point where they were nearly through the wall and a gleam of light could be seen from the far side, they set light to these logs and burnt them. After they were reduced to ashes, Gonatas inclined even more, and merited its name even more than before. The rest of the walls were surrounded with a girdle of battering-rams and 'tortoises'; in the twinkling of an eye, so to speak, the outer ditch was filled with dust, level with the flat parts on either side of it. Then they proceeded with the siege as best they could.

The emperor, who had thoroughly investigated Nicaea, and on many occasions, judged that it could not possibly be captured by the Latins, however overwhelming their numbers. In his turn he constructed helepoleis of several types, but mostly to an unorthodox design of his own which surprised everyone. These he sent to the counts. He had, as we have already remarked, crossed with the available troops and was staying at Pelekanum near Mesampeloi, where in the old days a sanctuary was built in honour of George, the great martyr. Alexius would have liked to accompany the expedition against the godless Turks, but abandoned the project after carefully weighing the arguments for and against: he noted that the Roman army was hopelessly outnumbered by the enormous host of the Franks; he knew from long experience, too, how untrustworthy the Latins were. Nor was that all: the instability of these men and their treacherous nature might well sweep them again and again, like the tides of Euripus, from one extreme to the other; through love of money they were ready to sell their own wives and children for next to nothing. Such were the reasons which prevented him then from joining the enterprise. However, even if his presence was unwise, he realized the necessity of giving as much aid to the Kelts as if he were actually with them. The great strength of its walls, he was sure, made Nicaea impregnable; the Latins would never take it. But when it was reported that the sultan was bringing strong forces and all necessary food supplies across the lake, with no difficulty at all, and these were finding their way into the city, he determined to gain control of the lake. Light boats, capable of sailing on its waters, were built, hoisted on wagons and launched on the Kios side. Fully-armed soldiers were put on board, under the command of Manuel Boutoumites. Alexius gave them more standards than usual—so that they might seem far more numerous than they really were—and also trumpets and drums. He then turned his attention to the mainland. He sent for Taticius and Tzitas. With a force of brave peltasts, 2,000 in all, they were despatched to Nicaea; their orders were to load their very generous supply of arrows on mules as soon as they disembarked and seize the fort of St George; at a good distance from the walls of Nicaea they were to dismount from their horses, go on foot straight for the Gonatas Tower and there take up position; they were then to form ranks with the Latins and acting under their orders assault the walls. Obedient to the emperor's instructions Taticius reported to the Kelts that he had arrived with his army, whereupon everyone put on armour and attacked with loud shouts and war-cries. Taticius' men fired their arrows in great volleys while the Kelts made breaches in the walls and kept up a constant bombardment of stones from their catapults. On the side of the lake the enemy were panic-stricken by the imperial standards and the trumpets of Boutoumites, who chose this moment to inform the Turks of the emperor's promises. The barbarians were reduced to such straits that they dared not even peep over the battlements of Nicaea. At the same time they gave up all hope of the sultan's coming. They decided it was better to hand over the city and start negotiations with Boutoumites to that end. After the usual courtesies Boutoumites showed them the chrysobull entrusted to him by Alexius, in which they were not only guaranteed an amnesty, but also a liberal gift of money and honours for the sister and wife of the sultan. These offers were extended to all the barbarians in Nicaea without exception. With confidence in the emperor's promises the inhabitants allowed Boutoumites to enter the city. At once he sent a message to Taticius: 'The quarry is now in our hands. Preparations must be made for an assault on the walls.

The Kelts must be given that task too, but leave nothing to them except the wall-fighting round the ramparts. Invest the city at all points, as necessary, and make the attempt at sunrise.' This was in fact a trick to make the Kelts believe that the city had been captured by Boutoumites in fighting; the drama of betrayal carefully planned by Alexius was to be concealed, for it was his wish that the negotiations conducted by Boutoumites should not be divulged to the Kelts. On the next day the call to battle was sounded on both sides of the city: on one, from the mainland, the Kelts furiously pressed the siege; on the other Boutoumites, having climbed to the battlements and set up there the imperial sceptres and standards, acclaimed the emperor to the accompaniment of trumpets and horns. It was in this way that the whole Roman force entered Nicaea. Nevertheless, knowing the great strength of the Kelts, as well as their fickle nature and passionate, impulsive whims, Boutoumites guessed that they might well seize the fort if they once got inside. The Turkish satraps in Nicaea, moreover, were capable, if they wished, of throwing into chains and massacring his own force—in comparison with the Romans they were numerous. Therefore he took possession of the keys of the city gate at once. There was at this time only one gate allowing people to enter or leave, the others having been closed through fear of the Kelts just beyond the walls. With the keys of this particular gate in his hands, he determined to reduce the number of satraps by a ruse. It was essential to have them at his mercy, if he was himself to avoid a catastrophe. He sent for them and advised a visit to the emperor, if they wanted to receive from him large sums of money, to be rewarded with high distinctions and to find their names on the lists of annual pensioners. The Turks were persuaded and during the night the gate was opened; they were let out, a few at a time and at frequent intervals, to make their way across the nearby lake to Rodomer and the half-caste Monastras, who were stationed by St George's fort. Boutoumites' orders were that the satraps should be forwarded to the emperor immediately they disembarked; not even for a brief moment were they to be detained, lest uniting with the Turks sent on behind them they might plot some mischief against the Romans. This was in fact a simple prediction, an intuitive remark which could only be attributed to the man's long experience, for as long as the new arrivals were quickly sent on to Alexius the Romans were secure and no danger whatever hung over them; but when Rodomer and Monastras relaxed their vigilance they found themselves in peril from the barbarians whom they kept back. The Turks, as their numbers grew, planned to take one of two courses: either in the night they would attack and kill the Romans, or they would bring them as prisoners to the sultan. The latter was unanimously decided to be the better idea. They did attack in the night and took them away as their captives. The place they made for was the hill-top of Azala, . . . stades from the walls of Nicaea. Having arrived there they naturally dismounted to rest their horses. Now Monastras was a half-caste and understood the Turkish dialect; Rodomer, too, having been captured by the Turks long ago and having lived with them for a considerable time, was himself not unacquainted with their language. They tried hard to move their captors with persuasive arguments. 'Why are you mixing a lethal potion for us, as it were, without deriving the slightest benefit for yourselves? When the others without exception are enjoying great rewards from the emperor and having their names enrolled for annual pensions, you will be cutting yourselves off from all these privileges. Well now, don't be such fools, especially when you can live in safety without interference and return home exulting in riches. You may perhaps acquire new territory. Don't throw yourselves into certain danger. Maybe you'll meet Romans lying in ambush over there,' pointing to mountain streams and marshy parts; 'if you do, you'll be massacred and lose your lives for nothing. There are thousands of men lying in wait for you, not only Kelts and barbarians, but a multitude of Romans as well. Now if you take our advice, you will turn your horses' heads and come to the emperor with us. We swear, as God is our witness, that you will enjoy countless gifts at his hands, and then, when it pleases you, you will leave as free men, without hindrance.' These arguments convinced the Turks. Pledges were exchanged and both parties set out on their way to Alexius. On their arrival at Pelekanum, all were received with a cheerful smile (although inwardly he was very angry with Rodomer and Monastras). For the present they were sent off to rest, but on the next day all those Turks who were eager to serve him received numerous benefits; those who desired to go home were permitted to follow their own inclination— and they too departed with not a few gifts. It was only later that Alexius severely reprimanded Rodomer and Monastras for their folly, but seeing that they were too ashamed to look him in the face, he altered his attitude and with words of forgiveness strove to conciliate them. . . .

The work took up three whole days and nights. When it was completed, he used it as a protective covering while another strong-point of concrete was erected inside it, a base of operations for even fiercer attacks on the city defences. Two towers, moreover, were set up on either side of the harbour mouth and an iron chain was stretched across the intervening space. Thus help from the sea was excluded. At the same time he seized many of the forts along the coast: Argyrocastron, Marchapin, Gabala and certain others as far as the borders of Tripolis, places which formerly paid tribute to the Saracens, but afterwards were reunited with the Roman Empire by Alexius at the cost of much sweat and toil. Alexius reckoned that Laodicea should be invested from the land side as well. He had long experience of Bohemond's cunning and his stratagems (Alexius had a genius for appreciating a man's character quickly) and the count's traitorous, rebellious nature was well understood. Monastras was therefore sent overland with a powerful contingent to besiege Laodicea from land while Cantacuzenus shut it in by sea. But before Monastras arrived, his colleague had occupied both harbour and town; only the citadel (nowadays commonly referred to as the *koula*) was still in the hands of 500 Keltic infantry and a hundred of their knights. Bohemond heard of this and he was also told by the count responsible for the defence of the citadel that provisions were scarce. He concentrated all his own forces, therefore, with those of Tancred and Saint-Gilles and all kinds of edible supplies were loaded on mules. When he reached the city it was not long before they were transported to the *koula*. Bohemond also had an interview with Cantacuzenus. 'What's the idea of building these earthworks?' he asked. 'You

know,' replied Cantacuzenus, 'that you and your fellow counts swore to serve the emperor and agreed under oath to hand over to him whatever cities were captured by you. Later on you yourself lied about the oaths, set aside even the treaties of peace; you took this city and handed it over to us, then changed your mind and kept it, so that when I came here to accept the cities taken by you my visit was useless.' 'Have you come here hoping to take it from us with money or by force?' asked Bohemond. 'Our allies have received the money,' answered the Roman, 'for their gallantry in battle.' Bohemond was filled with wrath. 'Be sure of this: without money you wouldn't be able to capture even a watch-post.' Whereupon he provoked his troops to gallop right up to the gates of the city. As the Franks got near the walls they were driven back a little by Cantacuzenus' men guarding the ramparts, who fired arrows at them thick as snowflakes. Bohemond promptly rallied them and all (including himself) made their way into the citadel. The count defending Laodicea and his Kelts being suspect, Bohemond dismissed them and appointed a new commander. At the same time he destroyed the vineyards near the walls, so that his Latin cavalry should have freedom of movement. Then, having made these arrangements, he left the city and went off to Antioch. As for Cantacuzenus, he carried on the siege by every means available; hundreds of devices were tried, sudden assaults were made and helepoleis brought up to confound the Latins in the citadel. Monastras was also busy. Coming overland with the cavalry he occupied Longinias, Tarsus, Adana, Mamistra and indeed the whole of Cilicia.

Bohemond shuddered at the emperor's threats. Without means of defence (for he had neither an army on land nor a fleet at sea, and danger hung over him on both sides) he invented a plan, not very dignified, but amazingly crafty. First he left the city of Antioch in the hands of his nephew Tancred, the son of the Marquis Odo; then he spread rumours everywhere about himself: 'Bohemond,' it was said, 'is dead.' While still alive he convinced the world that he had passed away. Faster than the beating of a bird's wings the story was propagated in all quarters: 'Bohemond,' it proclaimed, 'is a corpse.' When he perceived that the story had gone far enough, a wooden coffin was made and a bireme prepared. The coffin was placed on board and he, a still breathing 'corpse', sailed away from Soudi, the port of Antioch, for Rome. He was being transported by sea as a corpse. To outward appearance (the coffin and the behaviour of his companions) he was a corpse. At each stop the barbarians tore out their hair and paraded their mourning. But inside Bohemond, stretched out at full length, was a corpse only thus far; in other respects he was alive, breathing air in and out through hidden holes. That is how it was at the coastal places, but when the boat was out at sea, they shared their food with him and gave him attention; then once more there were the same dirges, the same tomfoolery. However, in order that the corpse might appear to be in a state of rare putrefaction, they strangled or cut the throat of a cock and put that in the coffin with him. By the fourth or fifth day at the most, the horrible stench was obvious to anyone who could smell. Those who had been deceived by the outward show thought the offensive odour emanated from Bohemond's body, but Bohemond himself derived more pleasure than anyone from his imaginary misfortune. For my part I wonder how on earth he endured such a siege on his nose and still continued to live while being carried along with his dead companion. But that has taught me how hard it is to check all barbarians once they have set their hearts on something: there is nothing, however objectionable, which they will not bear when they have made up their minds once and for all to undergo self-inflicted suffering. This man Bohemond was not yet dead—he was dead only in pretence—yet he did not hesitate to live with dead bodies. In the world of our generation this ruse of Bohemond was unprecedented and unique, and its purpose was to bring about the downfall of the Roman Empire. Before it no barbarian or Greek devised such a plan against his enemies, nor, I fancy, will anyone in our lifetime ever see its like again. When he reached Corfu, as if he had reached some mountain peak, as if the island were a place of refuge and he was now free from danger, he rose from the 'presumed dead', left the coffin where his 'corpse' had lain, enjoyed the sunshine to the full, breathed in a cleaner air and walked around the city of Corfu. The inhabitants, seeing him dressed in outlandish, barbarian clothes, inquired about his family, his condition, his name; they asked where he came from and to whom he was going. Bohemond treated them all with lofty disdain and demanded to see the duke of the city. He was in fact a certain Alexius who came originally from the Armeniac theme. Coming face to face with him, Bohemond, arrogant in look and attitude, speaking with an arrogant tongue in a language wholly barbaric, ordered him to send this communication to the emperor: 'To you I, Bohemond, famous son of Robert, send this message. The past has taught you and your Empire how formidable are my bravery and my opposition. When I turn the scales of fortune, as God is my witness I will not leave unavenged the evils done to me in the past. Ever since I took Antioch on my march through Roman territory and with my spear enslaved the whole of Syria, I have had my fill of misery because of you and your army; my hopes, one after another, have been dashed; I have been thrust into a thousand misfortunes and a thousand barbarian wars. But now it is different. I want you to know that, although I was "dead", I have come back to life again; I have escaped your clutches. In the guise of a dead man I have avoided every eye, every hand, every plan. And now I live, I move, I breathe the air, and from this island of Corfu I send to Your Majesty offensive, hateful news. It will not make very pleasant reading for you. I have handed over the city of Antioch to my nephew Tancred, leaving him as a worthy adversary for your generals. I myself will go to my own country. As far as you and your friends are concerned, I am a corpse; but to myself and my friends it is manifest that I am a living man, plotting a diabolical end for you. In order to throw into tumult the Roman world which you rule, I who was alive became "dead"; now I who "died" am alive. If I reach the mainland of Italy and cast eyes on the Lombards and all the Latins and the Germans and our own Franks, men full of martial valour, then with many a murder I will make your cities and your provinces run with blood, until I set up my spear in Byzantium itself.' Such was the extreme bombast in which the barbarian exulted.

CHRÉTIEN DE TROYES
from *Arthurian Romances*

Lancelot

• • •

Late in the afternoon they arrive at a town, which, you must know, was very rich and beautiful. All three entered through the gate; the people are greatly amazed to see the knight borne upon the cart, and they take no pains to conceal their feelings, but small and great and old and young shout taunts at him in the streets, so that the knight hears many vile and scornful words at his expense. They all inquire: "To what punishment is this knight to be consigned? Is he to be flayed, or hanged, or drowned, or burned upon a fire of thorns? Tell us, thou dwarf, who art driving him, in what crime was he caught? Is he convicted of robbery? Is he a murderer, or a criminal?" And to all this the dwarf made no response, vouchsafing to them no reply. He conducts the knight to a lodging-place; and Gawain follows the dwarf closely to a tower, which stood on the same level over against the town. Beyond there stretched a meadow, and the tower was built close by, upon a lofty eminence of rock, whose face formed a sharp precipice. Following the horse and cart, Gawain entered the tower. In the hall they met a damsel elegantly attired, than whom there was none fairer in the land, and with her they saw coming two fair and charming maidens. As soon as they saw my lord Gawain, they received him joyously and saluted him, and then asked news about the other knight: "Dwarf, of what crime is this knight guilty, whom thou dost drive like a lame man?" He would not answer her question, but he made the knight get out of the cart, and then he withdrew, without their knowing whither he went. Then my lord Gawain dismounts, and valets come forward to relieve the two knights of their armour. The damsel ordered two green mantles to be brought, which they put on. When the hour for supper came, a sumptuous repast was set. The damsel sat at table beside my lord Gawain. They would not have changed their lodging-place to seek any other, for all that evening the damsel showed them great honour, and provided them with fair and pleasant company.

Vv. 463–538.—When they had sat up long enough, two long, high beds were prepared in the middle of the hall; and there was another bed alongside, fairer and more splendid than the rest; for, as the story testifies, it possessed all the excellence that one could think of in a bed. When the time came to retire, the damsel took both the guests to whom she had offered her hospitality; she shows them the two fine, long, wide beds, and says: "These two beds are set up here for the accommodation of your bodies; but in that one yonder no one ever lay who did not merit it: it was not set up to be used by you." The knight who came riding on the cart replies at once: "Tell me," he says, "for what cause this bed is inaccessible." Being thoroughly informed of this, she answers unhesitatingly: "It is not your place to ask or make such an inquiry. Any knight is disgraced in the land after being in a cart, and it is not fitting that he should concern himself with the matter upon which you have questioned me; and most of all it is not right that he should lie upon the bed, for he would soon pay dearly for his act. So rich a couch has not been prepared for you, and you would pay dearly for ever harbouring such a thought." He replies: "You will see about that presently." . . . "Am I to see it?" . . . "Yes." . . . "It will soon appear." . . . "By my head," the knight replies, "I know not who is to pay the penalty. But whoever may object or disapprove, I intend to lie upon this bed and repose there at my ease." Then he at once disrobed in the bed, which was long and raised half an ell above the other two, and was covered with a yellow cloth of silk and a coverlet with gilded stars. The furs were not of skinned vair but of sable; the covering he had on him would have been fitting for a king. The mattress was not made of straw or rushes or of old mats. At midnight there descended from the rafters suddenly a lance, as with the intention of pinning the knight through the flanks to the coverlet and the white sheets where he lay. To the lance there was attached a pennon all ablaze. The coverlet, the bedclothes, and the bed itself all caught fire at once. And the tip of the lance passed so close to the knight's side that it cut the skin a little, without seriously wounding him. Then the knight got up, put out the fire and, taking the lance, swung it in the middle of the hall, all this without leaving his bed; rather did he lie down again and slept as securely as at first.

Vv. 539–982.—In the morning, at daybreak, the damsel of the tower had Mass celebrated on their account, and had them rise and dress. When Mass had been celebrated for them, the knight who had ridden in the cart sat down pensively at a window, which looked out upon the meadow, and he gazed upon the fields below. The damsel came to another window close by, and there my lord Gawain conversed with her privately for a while about something, I know not what. I do not know what words were uttered, but while they were leaning on the window-sill they saw carried along the river through the fields a bier, upon which there lay a knight, and alongside three damsels walked, mourning bitterly. Behind the bier they saw a crowd approaching, with a tall knight in front, leading a fair lady by the horse's rein.

The knight at the window knew that it was the Queen. He continued to gaze at her attentively and with delight as long as she was visible. And when he could no longer see her, he was minded to throw himself out and break his body down below. And he would have let himself fall out had not my lord Gawain seen him, and drawn him back, saying: "I beg you, sire, be quiet now. For God's sake, never think again of committing such a mad deed. It is wrong for you to despise your life." "He is perfectly right," the damsel says; "for will not the news of his disgrace be known everywhere? Since he has been upon the cart, he has good reason to wish to die, for he would be better dead than alive. His life henceforth is sure to be one of shame, vexation, and unhappiness." Then the knights asked for their armour, and armed themselves, the damsel treating them courteously, with distinction and generosity; for when she had joked with the knight and ridiculed him enough, she presented him with a horse and lance as a token of her goodwill. The knights then courteously and politely took leave of the damsel, first saluting her, and then going off in the direction taken by the crowd they had seen. Thus they rode out from the town without addressing them. They proceeded quickly in the direction they had seen taken by the Queen, but they did not overtake the procession, which had advanced rapidly. After leaving the fields, the knights enter an enclosed place, and find a beaten road. They advanced through the woods until it might be six o'clock, and then at a crossroads they met a damsel, whom they both saluted, each asking and requesting her to tell them, if she knows, whither the Queen has been taken. Replying intelligently, she said to them: "If you would pledge me your word, I could set you on the right road and path, and I would tell you the name of the country and of the knight who is conducting her; but whoever would essay to enter that country must endure sore trials, for before he could reach there he must suffer much." Then my lord Gawain replies: "Damsel, so help me God, I promise to place all my strength at your disposal and service, whenever you please, if you will tell me now the truth." And he who had been on the cart did not say that he would pledge her all his strength; but he proclaims, like one whom love makes rich, powerful and bold for any enterprise, that at once and without hesitation he will promise her anything she desires, and he puts himself altogether at her disposal. "Then I will tell you the truth," says she. Then the damsel relates to them the following story: "In truth, my lords, Meleagant, a tall and powerful knight, son of the King of Gorre, has taken her off into the kingdom whence no foreigner returns, but where he must perforce remain in servitude and banishment." Then they ask her: "Damsel, where is this country? Where can we find the way thither?" She replies: "That you shall quickly learn; but you may be sure that you will meet with many obstacles and difficult passages, for it is not easy to enter there except with the permission of the king, whose name is Bademagu; however, it is possible to enter by two very perilous paths and by two very difficult passage-ways. One is called 'the water-bridge,' because the bridge is under water, and there is the same amount of water beneath it as above it, so that the bridge is exactly in the middle; and it is only a foot and a half in width and in thickness. This choice is certainly to be avoided, and yet it is the less dangerous of the two. In addition there are a number of other obstacles of which I will say nothing. The other bridge is still more impracticable and much more perilous, never having been crossed by man. It is just like a sharp sword, and therefore all the people call it 'the sword-bridge.' Now I have told you all the truth I know." But they ask of her once again: "Damsel, deign to show us these two passages." To which the damsel makes reply: "This road here is the most direct to the water-bridge, and that one yonder leads straight to the sword-bridge." Then the knight, who had been on the cart, says: "Sire, I am ready to share with you without prejudice: take one of these two routes, and leave the other one to me; take whichever you prefer." "In truth," my lord Gawain replies, "both of them are hard and dangerous: I am not skilled in making such a choice, and hardly know which of them to take; but it is not right for me to hesitate when you have left the choice to me: I will choose the water-bridge." The other answers: "Then I must go uncomplainingly to the sword-bridge, which I agree to do." Thereupon, they all three part, each one commending the others very courteously to God. And when she sees them departing, she says: "Each one of you owes me a favour of my choosing, whenever I may choose to ask it. Take care not to forget that." "We shall surely not forget it, sweet friend," both the knights call out. Then each one goes his own way, and he of the cart is occupied with deep reflections, like one who has no strength or defence against love which holds him in its sway. His thoughts are such that he totally forgets himself, and he knows not whether he is alive or dead, forgetting even his own name, not knowing whether he is armed or not, or whither he is going or whence he came. Only one creature he has in mind, and for her his thought is so occupied that he neither sees nor hears aught else. And his horse bears him along rapidly, following no crooked road, but the best and the most direct; and thus proceeding unguided, he brings him into an open plain. In this plain there was a ford, on the other side of which a knight stood armed, who guarded it, and in his company there was a damsel who had come on a palfrey. By this time the afternoon was well advanced, and yet the knight, unchanged and unwearied, pursued his thoughts. The horse, being very thirsty, sees clearly the ford, and as soon as he sees it, hastens toward it. Then he on the other side cries out: "Knight, I am guarding the ford, and forbid you to cross." He neither gives him heed, nor hears his words, being still deep in thought. In the meantime, his horse advanced rapidly toward the water. The knight calls out to him that he will do wisely to keep at a distance from the ford, for there is no passage that way; and he swears by the heart within his breast that he will smite him if he enters the water. But his threats are not heard, and he calls out to him a third time: "Knight, do not enter the ford against my will and prohibition; for, by my head, I shall strike you as soon as I see you in the ford." But he is so deep in thought that he does not hear him. And the horse, quickly leaving the bank, leaps into the ford and greedily begins to drink. And the knight says he shall pay for this, that his shield and the hauberk he wears upon his back shall afford him no protection. First, he puts his horse at a gallop, and from a gallop he urges him to a run, and he strikes the knight so hard that he knocks him down flat in the ford which he had forbidden him to cross. His lance flew

from his hand and the shield from his neck. When he feels the water, he shivers, and though stunned, he jumps to his feet, like one aroused from sleep, listening and looking about him with astonishment, to see who it can be who has struck him. Then face to face with the other knight, he said: "Vassal, tell me why you have struck me, when I was not aware of your presence, and when I had done you no harm." "Upon my word, you had wronged me," the other says; "did you not treat me disdainfully when I forbade you three times to cross the ford, shouting at you as loudly as I could? You surely heard me challenge you at least two or three times, and you entered in spite of me, though I told you I should strike you as soon as I saw you in the ford." Then the knight replies to him: "Whoever heard you or saw you, let him be damned, so far as I am concerned. I was probably deep in thought when you forbade me to cross the ford. But be assured that I would make you regret it, if I could just lay one of my hands on your bridle." And the other replies: "Why, what of that? If you dare, you may seize my bridle here and now. I do not esteem your proud threats so much as a handful of ashes." And he replies: "That suits me perfectly. However the affair may turn out, I should like to lay my hands on you." Then the other knight advances to the middle of the ford, where the other lays his left hand upon his bridle, and his right hand upon his leg, pulling, dragging and pressing him so roughly that he remonstrates, thinking that he would pull his leg out of his body. Then he begs him to let go, saying: "Knight, if it please thee to fight me on even terms, take thy shield and horse and lance, and joust with me." He answers: "That will I not do, upon my word; for I suppose thou wouldst run away as soon as thou hadst escaped my grip." Hearing this, he was much ashamed, and said: "Knight, mount thy horse, in confidence for I will pledge thee loyally my word that I shall not flinch or run away." Then once again he answers him: "First, thou wilt have to swear to that, and I insist upon receiving thy oath that thou wilt neither run away nor flinch, nor touch me, nor come near me until thou shalt see me on my horse; I shall be treating thee very generously, if, when thou art in my hands, I let thee go." He can do nothing but give his oath; and when the other hears him swear, he gathers up his shield and lance which were floating in the ford and by this time had drifted well down-stream; then he returns and takes his horse. After catching and mounting him, he seizes the shield by the shoulder-straps and lays his lance in rest. Then each spurs toward the other as fast as their horses can carry them. And he who had to defend the ford first attacks the other, striking him so hard that his lance is completely splintered. The other strikes him in return so that he throws him prostrate into the ford, and the water closes over him. Having accomplished that, he draws back and dismounts, thinking he could drive and chase away a hundred such. While he draws from the scabbard his sword of steel, the other jumps up and draws his excellent flashing blade. Then they clash again, advancing and covering themselves with the shields which gleam with gold. Ceaselessly and without repose they wield their swords; they have the courage to deal so many blows that the battle finally is so protracted that the Knight of the Cart is greatly ashamed in his heart, thinking that he is making a sorry start in the way he has undertaken, when he has spent so much time in defeating a single knight. If he had met yesterday a hundred such, he does not think or believe that they could have withstood him; so now he is much grieved and wroth to be in such an exhausted state that he is missing his strokes and losing time. Then he runs at him and presses him so hard that the other knight gives way and flees. However reluctant he may be, he leaves the ford and crossing free. But the other follows him in pursuit until he falls forward upon his hands; then he of the cart runs up to him, swearing by all he sees that he shall rue the day when he upset him in the ford and disturbed his revery. The damsel, whom the knight had with him, upon hearing the threats, is in great fear, and begs him for her sake to forbear from killing him; but he tells her that he must do so, and can show him no mercy for her sake, in view of the shameful wrong that he has done him. Then, with sword drawn, he approaches the knight who cries in sore dismay: "For God's sake and for my own, show me the mercy I ask of you." And he replies: "As God may save me, no one ever sinned so against me that I would not show him mercy once, for God's sake as is right, if he asked it of me in God's name. And so on thee I will have mercy; for I ought not to refuse thee when thou hast besought me. But first, thou shalt give me thy word to constitute thyself my prisoner whenever I may wish to summon thee." Though it was hard to do so, he promised him. At once the damsel said: "O knight, since thou hast granted the mercy he asked of thee, if ever thou hast broken any bonds, for my sake now be merciful and release this prisoner from his parole. Set him free at my request, upon condition that when the time comes, I shall do my utmost to repay thee in any way that thou shalt choose." Then he declares himself satisfied with the promise she has made, and sets the knight at liberty. Then she is ashamed and anxious, thinking that he will recognise her, which she did not wish. But he goes away at once, the knight and the damsel commending him to God, and taking leave of him. He grants them leave to go, while he himself pursues his way, until late in the afternoon he met a damsel coming, who was very fair and charming, well attired and richly dressed. The damsel greets him prudently and courteously, and he replies: "Damsel, God grant you health and happiness." Then the damsel said to him: "Sire, my house is prepared for you, if you will accept my hospitality; but you shall find shelter there only on condition that you will lie with me; upon these terms I propose and make the offer." Not a few there are who would have thanked her five hundred times for such a gift; but he is much displeased, and made a very different answer: "Damsel, I thank you for the offer of your house, and esteem it highly; but, if you please, I should be very sorry to lie with you." "By my eyes," the damsel says, "then I retract my offer." And he, since it is unavoidable, lets her have her way, though his heart grieves to give consent. He feels only reluctance now; but greater distress will be his when it is time to go to bed. The damsel, too, who leads him away, will pass through sorrow and heaviness. For it is possible that she will love him so that she will not wish to part with him. As soon as he had granted her wish and desire, she escorts him to a fortified place, than which there was none fairer in Thessaly; for it was entirely enclosed by a high wall and a deep moat, and there was no man within except him whom she brought with her.

Vv. 983–1042.—Here she had constructed for her residence a quantity of handsome rooms, and a large and roomy hall. Riding along a river bank, they approached their lodging-place, and a drawbridge was lowered to allow them to pass. Crossing the bridge, they entered in, and found the hall open with its roof of tiles. Through the open door they pass, and see a table laid with a broad white cloth, upon which the dishes were set, and the candles burning in their stands, and the gilded silver drinking-cups, and two pots of wine, one red and one white. Standing beside the table, at the end of a bench, they found two basins of warm water in which to wash their hands, with a richly embroidered towel, all white and clean, with which to dry their hands. No valets, servants, or squires were to be found or seen. The knight, removing his shield from about his neck, hangs it upon a hook, and, taking his lance, lays it above upon a rack. Then he dismounts from his horse, as does the damsel from hers. The knight, for his part, was pleased that she did not care to wait for him to help her to dismount. Having dismounted, she runs directly to a room and brings him a short mantle of scarlet cloth which she puts on him. The hall was by no means dark; for beside the light from the stars, there were many large twisted candles lighted there, so that the illumination was very bright. When she had thrown the mantle about his shoulders, she said to him: "Friend, here is the water and the towel; there is no one to present or offer it to you except me whom you see. Wash your hands, and then sit down, when you feel like doing so. The hour and the meal, as you can see, demand that you should do so." He washes, and then gladly and readily takes his seat, and she sits down beside him, and they eat and drink together, until the time comes to leave the table.

Vv. 1043–1206.—When they had risen from the table, the damsel said to the knight: "Sire, if you do not object, go outside and amuse yourself; but, if you please, do not stay after you think I must be in bed. Feel no concern or embarrassment; for then you may come to me at once, if you will keep the promise you have made." And he replies: "I will keep my word, and will return when I think the time has come." Then he went out, and stayed in the courtyard until he thought it was time to return and keep the promise he had made. Going back into the hall, he sees nothing of her who would be his mistress; for she was not there. Not finding or seeing her, he said: "Wherever she may be, I shall look for her until I find her." He makes no delay in his search, being bound by the promise he had made her. Entering one of the rooms, he hears a damsel cry aloud, and it was the very one with whom he was about to lie. At the same time, he sees the door of another room standing open, and stepping toward it, he sees right before his eyes a knight who had thrown her down, and was holding her naked and prostrate upon the bed. She, thinking that he had come of course to help her, cried aloud: "Help, help, thou knight, who art my guest. If thou dost not take this man away from me, I shall find no one to do so; if thou dost not succour me speedily, he will wrong me before thy eyes. Thou art the one to lie with me, in accordance with thy promise; and shall this man by force accomplish his wish before thy eyes? Gentle knight, exert thyself, and make haste to bear me aid." He sees that the other man held the damsel brutally uncovered to the waist, and he is ashamed and angered to see him assault her so; yet it is not jealousy he feels, nor will he be made a cuckold by him. At the door there stood as guards two knights completely armed and with swords drawn. Behind them there stood four men-at-arms, each armed with an axe—the sort with which you could split a cow down the back as easily as a root of juniper or broom. The knight hesitated at the door, and thought: "God, what can I do? I am engaged in no less an affair than the quest of Queen Guinevere. I ought not to have the heart of a hare, when for her sake I have engaged in such a quest. If cowardice puts its heart in me, and if I follow its dictates, I shall never attain what I seek. I am disgraced, if I stand here; indeed, I am ashamed even to have thought of holding back. My heart is very sad and oppressed: now I am so ashamed and distressed that I would gladly die for having hesitated here so long. I say it not in pride: but may God have mercy on me if I do not prefer to die honourably rather than live a life of shame! If my path were unobstructed, and if these men gave me leave to pass through without restraint, what honour would I gain? Truly, in that case the greatest coward alive would pass through; and all the while I hear this poor creature calling for help constantly, and reminding me of my promise, and reproaching me with bitter taunts." Then he steps to the door, thrusting in his head and shoulders; glancing up, he sees two swords descending. He draws back, and the knights could not check their strokes: they had wielded them with such force that the swords struck the floor, and both were broken in pieces. When he sees that the swords are broken, he pays less attention to the axes, fearing and dreading them much less. Rushing in among

them, he strikes first one guard in the side and then another. The two who are nearest him he jostles and thrusts aside, throwing them both down flat; the third missed his stroke at him, but the fourth, who attacked him, strikes him so that he cuts his mantle and shirt, and slices the white flesh on his shoulder so that the blood trickles down from the wound. But he, without delay, and without complaining of his wound, presses on more rapidly, until he strikes between the temples him who was assaulting his hostess. Before he departs, he will try to keep his pledge to her. He makes him stand up reluctantly. Meanwhile, he who had missed striking him comes at him as fast as he can, and, raising his arm again, expects to split his head to the teeth with the axe. But the other, alert to defend himself, thrusts the knight toward him in such a way that he receives the axe just where the shoulder joins the neck, so that they are cleaved apart. Then the knight seizes the axe, wresting it quickly from him who holds it; then he lets go the knight whom he still held, and looks to his own defence; for the knights from the door, and the three men with axes are all attacking him fiercely. So he leaped quickly between the bed and the wall, and called to them: "Come on now, all of you. If there were thirty-seven of you, you would have all the fight you wish, with me so favourably placed; I shall never be overcome by you." And the damsel watching him, exclaimed: "By my eyes, you need have no thought of that henceforth where I am." Then at once she dismisses the knights and the men-at-arms, who retire from there at once, without delay or objection. And the damsel continues: "Sire you have well defended me against the men of my household. Come now, and I'll lead you on." . . .

MARIE DE FRANCE
The Lay of the Dolorous Knight

Hearken now to the Lay that once I heard a minstrel chanting to his harp. In surety of its truth I will name the city where this story passed. The Lay of the Dolorous Knight, my harper called his song, but of those who hearkened, some named it rather, The Lay of the Four Sorrows.

In Nantes, of Brittany, there dwelt a dame who was dearly held of all, for reason of the much good that was found in her. This lady was passing fair of body, apt in book as any clerk, and meetly schooled in every grace that it becometh dame to have. So gracious of person was this damsel, that throughout the realm there was no knight could refrain from setting his heart upon her, though he saw her but one only time. Although the demoiselle might not return the love of so many, certainly she had no wish to slay them all. Better by far that a man pray and require in love all the dames of his country, than run mad in woods for the bright eyes of one. Therefore this dame gave courtesy and good will to each alike. Even when she might not hear a lover's words, so

sweetly she denied his wish that the more he held her dear and was the more her servant for that fond denial. So because of her great riches of body and of heart, this lady of whom I tell, was prayed and required in love by the lords of her country, both by night and by day.

Now in Brittany lived four young barons, but their names I cannot tell. It is enough that they were desirable in the eyes of maidens for reason of their beauty, and that men esteemed them because they were courteous of manner and open of hand. Moreover they were stout and hardy knights amongst the spears, and rich and worthy gentlemen of those very parts. Each of these four knights had set his heart upon the lady, and for love of her pained himself mightily, and did all that he was able, so that by any means he might gain her favour. Each prayed her privily for her love, and strove all that he could to make him worthy of the gift, above his fellows. For her part the lady was sore perplexed, and considered in her mind very earnestly, which of these four knights she should take as friend. But since they all were loyal and worthy gentlemen, she durst not choose amongst them; for she would not slay three lovers with her hand so that one might have content. Therefore to each and all, the dame made herself fair and sweet of semblance. Gifts she gave to all alike. Tender messages she sent to each. Every knight deemed himself esteemed and favoured above his fellows, and by soft words and fair service diligently strove to please. When the knights gathered together for the games, each of these lords contended earnestly for the prize, so that he might be first, and draw on him the favour of his dame. Each held her for his friend. Each bore upon him her gift—pennon, or sleeve, or ring. Each cried her name within the lists.

Now when Eastertide was come, a great tournament was proclaimed to be held beyond the walls of Nantes, that rich city. The four lovers were the appellants in this tourney, and from every realm knights rode to break a lance in honour of their dame. Frenchman and Norman and Fleming; the hardiest knights of Brabant, Boulogne and Anjou; each came to do his devoir in the field. Nor was the chivalry of Nantes backward in this quarrel, but till the vespers of the tournament was come, they stayed themselves within the lists, and struck stoutly for their lord. After the four lovers had laced their harness upon them, they issued forth from the city, followed by the knights who were of their company in this adventure. But upon the four fell the burden of the day, for they were known of all by the embroidered arms upon their surcoat, and the device fashioned on the shield. Now against the four lovers arrayed themselves four other knights, armed altogether in coats of mail, and helmets and gauntlets of steel. Of these stranger knights two were of Hainault, and the two others were Flemings. When the four lovers saw their adversaries prepare themselves for the combat, they had little desire to flee, but hastened to join them in battle. Each lowered his spear, and choosing his enemy, met him so eagerly that all men wondered, for horse and man fell to the earth. The four lovers recked little of their destriers, but freeing their feet from the stirrups bent over the fallen foe, and called on him to yield. When the friends of the vanquished knights saw their case, they hastened to their succour; so for their rescue there was a great press, and many a mighty stroke with the sword.

The damsel stood upon a tower to watch these feats of arms. By their blazoned coats and shields she knew her knights; she saw their marvellous deeds, yet might not say who did best, nor give to one the praise. But the tournament was no longer a seemly and ordered battle. The ranks of the two companies were confused together, so that every man fought against his fellow, and none might tell whether he struck his comrade or his foe. The four lovers did well and worshipfully, so that all men deemed them worthy of the prize. But when evening was come, and the sport drew to its close, their courage led them to folly. Having ventured too far from their companions, they were set upon by their adversaries, and assailed so fiercely that three were slain outright. As to the fourth he yet lived, but altogether mauled and shaken, for his thigh was broken, and a spear head remained in his side. The four bodies were fallen on the field, and lay with those who had perished in that day. But because of the great mischief these four lovers had done their

adversaries, their shields were cast despitefully without the lists; but in this their foemen did wrongfully, and all men held them in sore displeasure.

Great were the lamentation and the cry when the news of this mischance was noised about the city. Such a tumult of mourning was never before heard, for the whole city was moved. All men hastened forth to the place where the lists were set. Meetly to mourn the dead there rode nigh upon two thousand knights, with hauberks unlaced, and uncovered heads, plucking upon their beards. So the four lovers were placed each upon his shield, and being brought back in honour to Nantes, were carried to the house of that dame, whom so greatly they had loved. When the lady knew this distressful adventure, straightway she fell to the ground. Being returned from her swoon, she made her complaint, calling upon her lovers each by his name.

"Alas," she said, "what shall I do, for never shall I know happiness again. These four knights had set their hearts upon me, and despite their great treasure, esteemed my love as richer than all their wealth. Alas, for the fair and valiant knight! Alas, for the loyal and generous man! By gifts such as these they sought to gain my favour, but how might lady bereave three of life, so as to cherish one. Even now I cannot tell for whom I have most pity, or who was closest to my mind. But three are dead, and one is sore stricken; neither is there anything in the world which can bring me comfort. Only this is there to do—to give the slain men seemly burial, and, if it may be, to heal their comrade of his wounds."

So, because of her great love and nobleness, the lady caused these three distressful knights to be buried well and worshipfully in a rich abbey. In that place she offered their Mass penny, and gave rich offerings of silver and of lights besides. May God have mercy on them in that day. As for the wounded knight she commanded him to be carried to her own chamber. She sent for surgeons, and gave him into their hands. These searched his wounds so skilfully, and tended him with so great care, that presently his hurt commenced to heal. Very often was the lady in the chamber, and very tenderly she cherished the stricken man. Yet ever she felt pity for the three Knights of the Sorrows, and ever she went heavily by reason of their deaths.

Now on a summer's day, the lady and the knight sat together after meat. She called to mind the sorrow that was hers; so that, in a space, her head fell upon her breast, and she gave herself altogether to her grief. The knight looked earnestly upon his dame. Well he might see that she was far away, and clearly he perceived the cause.

"Lady," said he, "you are in sorrow. Open now your grief to me. If you tell me what is in your heart perchance I may find you comfort."

"Fair friend," replied she, "I think of what is gone, and remember your companions, who are dead. Never was lady of my peerage, however fair and good and gracious, ever loved by four such valiant gentlemen, nor ever lost them in one single day. Save you—who were so maimed and in such peril—all are gone. Therefore I call to mind those who loved me so dearly, and am the saddest lady beneath the sun. To remember these things, of you four I shall make a Lay, and will call it the Lay of the Four Sorrows."

When the knight heard these words he made answer very swiftly,

"Lady, name it not the Lay of the Four Sorrows, but, rather, the Lay of the Dolorous Knight. Would you hear the reason why it should bear this name? My three comrades have finished their course; they have nothing more to hope of their life. They are gone, and with them the pang of their great sorrow, and the knowledge of their enduring love for you. I alone have come, all amazed and fearful, from the net wherein they were taken, but I find my life more bitter than my comrades found the grave. I see you on your goings and comings about the house. I may speak with you both matins and vespers. But no other joy do I get—neither clasp nor kiss, nothing but a few empty, courteous words. Since all these evils are come upon me because of you, I choose death rather than life. For this reason your Lay should bear my name, and be called the Lay of the Dolorous Knight. He who would name it the Lay of the Four Sorrows would name it wrongly, and not according to the truth."

"By my faith," replied the lady, "this is a fair saying. So shall the song be known as the Lay of the Dolorous Knight."

Thus was the Lay conceived, made perfect, and brought to a fair birth. For this reason it came by its name; though to this day some call it the Lay of the Four Sorrows. Either name befits it well, for the story tells of both these matters, but it is the use and wont in this land to call it the Lay of the Dolorous Knight. Here it ends; no more is there to say. I heard no more, and nothing more I know. Perforce I bring my story to a close.

ST. FRANCIS OF ASSISI

The Canticle of Brother Sun

HERE BEGIN THE PRAISES OF THE CREATURES WHICH ST. FRANCIS MADE FOR THE PRAISE AND HONOR OF GOD WHEN HE WAS ILL AT SAN DAMIANO

Most High Almighty Good Lord,
Yours are the praises, the glory, the honor, and all
blessings!
To You alone, Most High, do they belong,
And no man is worthy to mention You.

Be praised, my Lord, with all Your creatures,
Especially Sir Brother Sun,
By whom You give us the light of day!
And he is beautiful and radiant with great splendor.
Of You, Most High, he is a symbol!

Be praised, my Lord, for Sister Moon and the Stars!
In the sky You formed them bright and lovely and fair.

Be praised, my Lord, for Brother Wind
And for the Air and cloudy and clear and all Weather,
By which You give sustenance to Your creatures!

Be praised, my Lord, for Sister Water,
Who is very useful and humble and lovely and chaste!

Be praised, my Lord, for Brother Fire,
By whom You give us light at night,
And he is beautiful and merry and mighty and strong!

Be praised, my Lord, for our Sister Mother Earth,
Who sustains and governs us,
And produces fruits with colorful flowers and leaves!

Be praised, my Lord, for those who forgive for love of You
And endure infirmities and tribulations.
Blessed are those who shall endure them in peace,
For by You, Most High, they will be crowned!

Be praised, my Lord, for our Sister Bodily Death,
From whom no living man can escape!
Woe to those who shall die in mortal sin!
Blessed are those whom she will find in Your most
holy will,
For the Second Death will not harm them.

Praise and bless my Lord and thank Him
And serve Him with great humility!

THE IS THE END OF THE BOOK ABOUT CERTAIN WONDERFUL DEEDS OF ST. FRANCIS AND HIS FIRST COMPANIONS. IN THE NAME OF OUR LORD JESUS CHRIST, FOR THE HONOR OF OUR MOST HOLY FATHER FRANCIS. GOD BE PRAISED!

ST. THOMAS AQUINAS
from *Summa Theologica*

Fifth Article

Whether Those Things That Are of Faith Can Be an Object of Science?

We proceed thus to the Fifth Article:—Objection 1. It would seem that those things that are of faith can be an object of science. For where science is lacking there is ignorance, since ignorance is the opposite of science. Now we are not in ignorance of those things we have to believe, since ignorance of such things savors of unbelief, according to 1 Tim. i. 13: *I did it ignorantly in unbelief.* Therefore things that are of faith can be an object of science.

Obj. 2. Further, science is acquired by reasons. Now sacred writers employ reasons to inculcate things that are of faith. Therefore such things can be an object of science.

Obj. 3. Further, things which are demonstrated are an object of science, since a *demonstration is a syllogism that produces science.* Now certain matters of faith have been demonstrated by the philosophers, such as the Existence and Unity of God, and so forth. Therefore things that are of faith can be an object of science.

Obj. 4. Further, opinion is further from science than faith is, since faith is said to stand between opinion and science. Now opinion and science can, in a way, be about the same object, as stated in *Poster.* i. Therefore faith and science can be about the same object also.

On the contrary, Gregory says (*Hom.* xxvi *in Ev.*) that *when a thing is manifest, it is the object, not of faith, but of perception.* Therefore things that are of faith are not the object of perception, whereas what is an object of science is the object of perception. Therefore there can be no faith about things which are an object of science.

I answer that, All science is derived from self-evident and therefore *seen* principles; wherefore all objects of science must needs be, in a fashion, seen.

Now as stated above (A. 4) it is impossible that one and the same thing should be believed and seen by the same person. Hence it is equally impossible for one and the same thing to be an object of science and of belief for the same person. It may happen, however, that a thing which is an object of vision or science for one, is believed by another: since we hope to see some day what we now believe about the Trinity, according to 1 Cor. xiii. 12: *We see now through a glass in a dark manner; but then face to face:* which vision the angels possess already; so that what we believe, they see. In like manner it may happen that what is an object of vision or scientific knowledge for one man, even in the state of a wayfarer, is, for another man, an object of faith, because he does not know it by demonstration.

Nevertheless that which is proposed to be believed equally by all, is equally unknown by all as an object of science: such are the things which are of faith simply. Consequently faith and science are not about the same things.

Reply Obj. 1. Unbelievers are in ignorance of things that are of faith, for neither do they see or know them in themselves, nor do they know them to be credible. The faithful, on the other hand, know them, not as by demonstration, but by the light of faith which makes them see that they ought to believe them, as stated above (A. 4, *ad* 2, 3).

Reply Obj. 2. The reasons employed by holy men to prove things that are of faith, are not demonstrations; they are either persuasive arguments showing that what is proposed to our faith is not impossible, or else they are proofs drawn from the principles of faith, i.e. from the authority of Holy Writ, as Dionysius declares (*Div. Nom.* ii). Whatever is based on these principles is as well proved in the eyes of the faithful, as a conclusion drawn from self-evident principles is in the eyes of all. Hence again, theology is a science, as we stated at the outset of this work (P. I, Q. 1, A. 2).

Reply Obj. 3. Things which can be proved by demonstration are reckoned among the articles of faith, not because they are believed simply by all, but because they are a necessary presupposition to matters of faith, so that those who do not know them by demonstration must know them first of all by faith.

Reply Obj. 4. As the Philosopher says (*loc. cit.*), *science and opinion about the same object can certainly be in different men,* as we have stated above about science and faith; yet it is possible for one and the same man to have science and faith about the same thing relatively, i.e. in relation to the object, but not in the same respect. For it is possible for the same person, about one and the same object, to know one thing and to think another: and, in like manner, one may know by demonstration the unity of the Godhead, and, by faith, the Trinity. On the other hand, in one and the same man, about the same object, and in the same respect, science is incompatible with either opinion or faith, yet for different reasons. Because science is incompatible with opinion about the same object simply, for the reason that science demands that its object should be deemed impossible to be otherwise, whereas it is essential to opinion, that its object should be deemed possible to be otherwise. Yet that which is the object of faith, on account of the certainty of faith, is also deemed impossible to be otherwise: and the reason why science and faith cannot be about the same object and in the same respect is because the object of science is something seen, whereas the object of faith is the unseen, as stated above.

DANTE ALIGHIERI
from *Inferno*
Canto I

The Dark Wood of Error

Midway in his allotted threescore years and ten, Dante comes to himself with a start and realizes that he has strayed from the True Way into the Dark Wood of Error (Worldliness). As soon as he has realized his loss, Dante lifts his eyes and sees the first light of the sunrise (the Sun is the Symbol of Divine Illumination) lighting the shoulders of a little hill (The Mount of Joy). It is the Easter Season, the time of resurrection, and the sun is in its equinoctial rebirth. This juxtaposition of joyous symbols fills Dante with hope and he sets out at once to climb directly up the Mount of Joy, but almost immediately his way is blocked by the Three Beasts of Worldliness: THE LEOPARD OF MALICE AND FRAUD, THE LION OF VIOLENCE AND AMBITION, and THE SHE-WOLF OF INCONTINENCE. These beasts, and especially the She-Wolf, drive him back despairing into the darkness of error. But just as all seems lost, a figure appears to him. It is the shade of VIRGIL, Dante's symbol of HUMAN REASON.

Virgil explains that he has been sent to lead Dante from error. There can, however, be no direct ascent past the beasts: the man who would escape them must go a longer and harder way. First he must descend through Hell (The Recognition of Sin), then he must ascend through Purgatory (The Renunciation of Sin), and only then may he reach the pinnacle of joy and come to the Light of God. Virgil offers to guide Dante, but only as far as Human Reason can go. Another guide (BEATRICE, symbol of DIVINE LOVE) must take over for the final ascent, for Human Reason is self-limited. Dante submits himself joyously to Virgil's guidance and they move off.

Midway in our life's journey, I went astray
  from the straight road and woke to find myself
  alone in a dark wood. How shall I say

what wood that was! I never saw so drear,
  so rank, so arduous a wilderness!
  Its very memory gives a shape to fear.

Death could scarce be more bitter than that place!
  But since it came to good, I will recount
  all that I found revealed there by God's grace.

How I came to it I cannot rightly say,
  so drugged and loose with sleep had I become
  when I first wandered there from the True Way.

But at the far end of that valley of evil
  whose maze had sapped my very heart with fear!
  I found myself before a little hill

and lifted up my eyes. Its shoulders glowed
  already with the sweet rays of that planet
  whose virtue leads men straight on every road,

and the shining strengthened me against the fright
  whose agony had wracked the lake of my heart
  through all the terrors of that piteous night.

Just as a swimmer, who with his last breath
  flounders ashore from perilous seas, might turn
  to memorize the wide water of his death—

so did I turn, my soul still fugitive
  from death's surviving image, to stare down
  that pass that none had ever left alive.

And there I lay to rest from my heart's race
  till calm and breath returned to me. Then rose
  and pushed up that dead slope at such a pace

each footfall rose above the last. And lo!
  almost at the beginning of the rise
  I faced a spotted Leopard, all tremor and flow

and gaudy pelt. And it would not pass, but stood
  so blocking my every turn that time and again
  I was on the verge of turning back to the wood.

This fell at the first widening of the dawn
  as the sun was climbing Aries with those stars
  that rode with him to light the new creation.

Thus the holy hour and the sweet season
  of commemoration did much to arm my fear
  of that bright murderous beast with their good omen.

Yet not so much but what I shook with dread
  at sight of a great Lion that broke upon me
  raging with hunger, its enormous head

held high as if to strike a mortal terror
  into the very air. And down his track,
  a She-Wolf drove upon me, a starved horror

ravening and wasted beyond all belief.
  She seemed a rack for avarice, gaunt and craving.
  Oh many the souls she has brought to endless grief!

She brought such heaviness upon my spirit
  at sight of her savagery and desperation,
  I died from every hope of that high summit.

And like a miser—eager in acquisition
  but desperate in self-reproach when Fortune's wheel
  turns to the hour of his loss—all tears and attrition

I wavered back; and still the beast pursued,
  forcing herself against me bit by bit
  till I slid back into the sunless wood.

And as I fell to my soul's ruin, a presence
  gathered before me on the discolored air,
  the figure of one who seemed hoarse from long
    silence.

At sight of him in that friendless waste I cried:
  "Have pity on me, whatever thing you are,
  whether shade or living man." And it replied:

"Not man, though man I once was, and my blood
  was Lombard, both my parents Mantuan.
  I was born, though late, *sub Julio,* and bred

in Rome under Augustus in the noon
  of the false and lying gods. I was a poet
  and sang of old Anchises' noble son

who came to Rome after the burning of Troy.
  But you—why do *you* return to these distresses
  instead of climbing that shining Mount of Joy

which is the seat and first cause of man's bliss?"
  "And are you then that Virgil and that fountain
  of purest speech?" My voice grew tremulous:

"Glory and light of poets! now may that zeal
  and love's apprenticeship that I poured out
  on your heroic verses serve me well!

For you are my true master and first author,
  the sole maker from whom I drew the breath
  of that sweet style whose measures have brought me
    honor.

See there, immortal sage, the beast I flee.
  For my soul's salvation, I beg you, guard me from her,
  for she has struck a mortal tremor through me."

And he replied, seeing my soul in tears:
  "He must go by another way who would escape
  this wilderness, for that mad beast that fleers

before you there, suffers no man to pass.
  She tracks down all, kills all, and knows no glut,
  but, feeding, she grows hungrier than she was.

She mates with any beast, and will mate with more
  before the Greyhound comes to hunt her down.
  He will not feed on lands nor loot, but honor

and love and wisdom will make straight his way.
  He will rise between Feltro and Feltro, and in him
  shall be the resurrection and new day

of that sad Italy for which Nisus died,
  and Turnus, and Euryalus, and the maid Camilla.
  He shall hunt her through every nation of sick pride

till she is driven back forever to Hell
  whence Envy first released her on the world.
  Therefore, for your own good, I think it well

you follow me and I will be your guide
  and lead you forth through an eternal place.
  There you shall see the ancient spirits tried

in endless pain, and hear their lamentation
  as each bemoans the second death of souls.
  Next you shall see upon a burning mountain

souls in fire and yet content in fire,
  knowing that whensoever it may be
  they yet will mount into the blessed choir.

To which, if it is still your wish to climb,
  a worthier spirit shall be sent to guide you.
  With her shall I leave you, for the King of Time,

who reigns on high, forbids me to come there
  since, living, I rebelled against his law.
  He rules the waters and the land and air

and there holds court, his city and his throne.
  Oh blessed are they he chooses!" And I to him:
  "Poet, by that God to you unknown,

lead me this way. Beyond this present ill
  and worse to dread, lead me to Peter's gate
  and be my guide through the sad halls of Hell."

And he then: "Follow." And he moved ahead
in silence, and I followed where he led.

Canto III

The Vestibule of Hell

THE OPPORTUNISTS

The Poets pass the Gate of Hell and are immediately assailed by cries of anguish. Dante sees the first of the souls in torment. They are THE OPPORTUNISTS, those souls who in life were neither for good nor evil but only for themselves. Mixed with them are those outcasts who took no sides in the Rebellion of the Angels. They are neither in Hell nor out of it. Eternally unclassified, they race round and round pursuing a wavering banner that runs forever before them through the dirty air; and as they run they are pursued by swarms of wasps and hornets, who sting them and produce a constant flow of blood and putrid matter which trickles down the bodies of the sinners and is feasted upon by loathsome worms and maggots who coat the ground.

The law of Dante's Hell is the law of symbolic retribution. As they sinned so are they punished. They took no sides, therefore they are given no place. As they pursued the ever-shifting illusion of their own advantage, changing their courses with every changing wind, so they pursue eternally an elusive, ever-shifting banner. As their sin was a darkness, so they move in darkness. As their own guilty conscience pursued them, so they are pursued by swarms of wasps and hornets. And as their actions were a moral filth, so they run eternally through the filth of worms and maggots which they themselves feed.

Dante recognizes several, among them POPE CELESTINE V, but without delaying to speak to any of these souls, the Poets move on to ACHERON, the first of the rivers of Hell. Here the newly-arrived souls of the damned gather and wait for monstrous CHARON to ferry them over to punishment. Charon recognizes Dante as a living man and angrily refuses him passage. Virgil forces Charon to serve them, but Dante swoons with terror, and does not reawaken until he is on the other side.

I AM THE WAY INTO THE CITY OF WOE.
I AM THE WAY TO A FORSAKEN PEOPLE.
I AM THE WAY INTO ETERNAL SORROW.

SACRED JUSTICE MOVED MY ARCHITECT.
I WAS RAISED HERE BY DIVINE OMNIPOTENCE,
PRIMORDIAL LOVE AND ULTIMATE INTELLECT.

ONLY THOSE ELEMENTS TIME CANNOT WEAR
WERE MADE BEFORE ME, AND BEYOND TIME I STAND.
ABANDON ALL HOPE YE WHO ENTER HERE.

These mysteries I read cut into stone
    above a gate. And turning I said: "Master,
    what is the meaning of this harsh inscription?"

And he then as initiate to novice:
    "Here must you put by all division of spirit
    and gather your soul against all cowardice.

This is the place I told you to expect.
    Here you shall pass among the fallen people,
    souls who have lost the good of intellect."

So saying, he put forth his hand to me,
    and with a gentle and encouraging smile
    he led me through the gate of mystery.

Here sighs and cries and wails coiled and recoiled
    on the starless air, spilling my soul to tears.
    A confusion of tongues and monstrous accents toiled

in pain and anger. Voices hoarse and shrill
    and sounds of blows, all intermingled, raised
    tumult and pandemonium that still

whirls on the air forever dirty with it
    as if a whirlwind sucked at sand. And I,
    holding my head in horror, cried: "Sweet Spirit,

what souls are these who run through this black haze?"
    And he to me: "These are the nearly soulless
    whose lives concluded neither blame nor praise.

They are mixed here with that despicable corps
    of angels who were neither for God nor Satan,
    but only for themselves. The High Creator

scourged them from Heaven for its perfect beauty,
    and Hell will not receive them since the wicked
    might feel some glory over them." And I:

"Master, what gnaws at them so hideously
    their lamentation stuns the very air?"
    "They have no hope of death," he answered me,

"and in their blind and unattaining state
    their miserable lives have sunk so low
    that they must envy every other fate.

No word of them survives their living season.
    Mercy and Justice deny them even a name.
    Let us not speak of them: look, and pass on."

I saw a banner there upon the mist.
    Circling and circling, it seemed to scorn all pause.
    So it ran on, and still behind it pressed

a never-ending rout of souls in pain.
    I had not thought death had undone so many
    as passed before me in that mournful train.

And some I knew among them; last of all
    I recognized the shadow of that soul
    who, in his cowardice, made the Great Denial.

At once I understood for certain: these
    were of that retrograde and faithless crew
    hateful to God and to His enemies.

These wretches never born and never dead
   ran naked in a swarm of wasps and hornets
   that goaded them the more the more they fled,

and made their faces stream with bloody gouts
   of pus and tears that dribbled to their feet
   to be swallowed there by loathsome worms and
     maggots.

Then looking onward I made out a throng
   assembled on the beach of a wide river,
   whereupon I turned to him: "Master, I long

to know what souls these are, and what strange usage
   makes them as eager to cross as they seem to be
   in this infected light." At which the Sage:

"All this shall be made known to you when we stand
   on the joyless beach of Acheron." And I
   cast down my eyes, sensing a reprimand

in what he said, and so walked at his side
   in silence and ashamed until we came
   through the dead cavern to that sunless tide.

There, steering toward us in an ancient ferry
   came an old man with a white bush of hair,
   bellowing: "Woe to you depraved souls! Bury

here and forever all hope of Paradise:
   I come to lead you to the other shore,
   into eternal dark, into fire and ice.

And you who are living yet, I say begone
   from these who are dead." But when he saw me stand
   against his violence he began again:

"By other windings and by other steerage
   shall you cross to that other shore. Not here! Not here!
   A lighter craft than mine must give you passage."

And my Guide to him: "Charon, bite back your spleen:
   this has been willed where what is willed must be,
   and is not yours to ask what it may mean."

The steersman of that marsh of ruined souls,
   who wore a wheel of flame around each eye,
   stifled the rage that shook his woolly jowls.

But those unmanned and naked spirits there
   turned pale with fear and their teeth began to chatter
   at sound of his crude bellow. In despair

they blasphemed God, their parents, their time on earth,
   the race of Adam, and the day and the hour
   and the place and the seed and the womb that gave
     them birth.

But all together they drew to that grim shore
   where all must come who lose the fear of God.
   Weeping and cursing they come for evermore,

and demon Charon with eyes like burning coals
   herds them in, and with a whistling oar
   flails on the stragglers to his wake of souls.

As leaves in autumn loosen and stream down
   until the branch stands bare above its tatters
   spread on the rustling ground, so one by one

the evil seed of Adam in its Fall
   cast themselves, at his signal, from the shore
   and streamed away like birds who hear their call.

So they are gone over that shadowy water,
   and always before they reach the other shore
   a new noise stirs on this, and new throngs gather.

"My son," the courteous Master said to me,
   "all who die in the shadow of God's wrath
   converge to this from every clime and country.

And all pass over eagerly, for here
   Divine Justice transforms and spurs them so
   their dread turns wish: they yearn for what they fear.

No soul in Grace comes ever to this crossing;
   therefore if Charon rages at your presence
   you will understand the reason for his cursing."

When he had spoken, all the twilight country
   shook so violently, the terror of it
   bathes me with sweat even in memory:

the tear-soaked ground gave out a sigh of wind
   that spewed itself in flame on a red sky,
   and all my shattered senses left me. Blind,

like one whom sleep comes over in a swoon,
I stumbled into darkness and went down.

Canto V

Circle Two

THE CARNAL

*The Poets leave Limbo and enter the SECOND CIRCLE. Here
begin the torments of Hell proper, and here, blocking the way, sits
MINOS, the dread and semi-bestial judge of the damned who
assigns to each soul its eternal torment. He orders the Poets back;
but Virgil silences him as he earlier silenced Charon, and the Poets
move on.*

*They find themselves on a dark ledge swept by a great
whirlwind, which spins within it the souls of the CARNAL, those
who betrayed reason to their appetites. Their sin was to abandon
themselves to the tempest of their passions: so they are swept
forever in the tempest of Hell, forever denied the light of reason
and of God. Virgil identifies many among them. SEMIRAMIS is
there, and DIDO, CLEOPATRA, HELEN, ACHILLES, PARIS,
and TRISTAN. Dante sees PAOLO and FRANCESCA swept
together, and in the name of love he calls to them to tell their sad
story. They pause from their eternal flight to come to him, and
Francesca tells their history while Paolo weeps at her side. Dante
is so stricken by compassion at their tragic tale that he swoons
once again.*

So we went down to the second ledge alone;
   a smaller circle of so much greater pain
   the voice of the damned rose in a bestial moan.

There Minos sits, grinning, grotesque, and hale.
   He examines each lost soul as it arrives
   and delivers his verdict with his coiling tail.

That is to say, when the ill-fated soul
   appears before him it confesses all,
   and that grim sorter of the dark and foul

decides which place in Hell shall be its end,
   then wraps his twitching tail about himself
   one coil for each degree it must descend.

The soul descends and others take its place:
   each crowds in its turn to judgment, each confesses,
   each hears its doom and falls away through space.

"O you who come into this camp of woe,"
   cried Minos when he saw me turn away
   without awaiting his judgment, "watch where you go

once you have entered here, and to whom you turn!
   Do not be misled by that wide and easy passage!"
   And my Guide to him: "That is not your concern;

it is his fate to enter every door.
   This has been willed where what is willed must be,
   and is not yours to question. Say no more."

Now the choir of anguish, like a wound,
   strikes through the tortured air. Now I have come
   to Hell's full lamentation, sound beyond sound.

I came to a place stripped bare of every light
   and roaring on the naked dark like seas
   wracked by a war of winds. Their hellish flight

of storm and counterstorm through time foregone,
   sweeps the souls of the damned before its charge.
   Whirling and battering it drives them on,

and when they pass the ruined gap of Hell
   through which we had come, their shrieks begin anew.
   There they blaspheme the power of God eternal.

And this, I learned, was the never ending flight
   of those who sinned in the flesh, the carnal and lusty
   who betrayed reason to their appetite.

As the wings of wintering starlings bear them on
   in their great wheeling flights, just so the blast
   wherries these evil souls through time foregone.

Here, there, up, down, they whirl and, whirling, strain
   with never a hope of hope to comfort them,
   not of release, but even of less pain.

As cranes go over sounding their harsh cry,
   leaving the long streak of their flight in air,
   so come these spirits, wailing as they fly.

And watching their shadows lashed by wind, I cried:
   "Master, what souls are these the very air
   lashes with its black whips from side to side?"

"The first of these whose history you would know,"
   he answered me, "was Empress of many tongues.
   Mad sensuality corrupted her so

that to hide the guilt of her debauchery
   she licensed all depravity alike,
   and lust and law were one in her decree.

She is Semiramis of whom the tale is told
   how she married Ninus and succeeded him
   to the throne of that wide land the Sultans hold.

The other is Dido; faithless to the ashes
   of Sichaeus, she killed herself for love.
   The next whom the eternal tempest lashes

is sense-drugged Cleopatra. See Helen there,
from whom such ill arose. And great Achilles,
who fought at last with love in the house of prayer.

And Paris. And Tristan." As they whirled above
he pointed out more than a thousand shades
of those torn from the mortal life by love.

I stood there while my Teacher one by one
named the great knights and ladies of dim time;
and I was swept by pity and confusion.

At last I spoke: "Poet, I should be glad
to speak a word with those two swept together
so lightly on the wind and still so sad."

And he to me: "Watch them. When next they pass,
call to them in the name of love that drives
and damns them here. In that name they will pause."

Thus, as soon as the wind in its wild course
brought them around, I called: "O wearied souls!
if none forbid it, pause and speak to us."

As mating doves that love calls to their nest
glide through the air with motionless raised wings,
borne by the sweet desire that fills each breast—

Just so those spirits turned on the torn sky
from the band where Dido whirls across the air;
such was the power of pity in my cry.

"O living creature, gracious, kind, and good,
going this pilgrimage through the sick night,
visiting us who stained the earth with blood,

were the King of Time our friend, we would pray His
    peace
on you who have pitied us. As long as the wind
will let us pause, ask of us what you please.

The town where I was born lies by the shore
where the Po descends into its ocean rest
with its attendant streams in one long murmur.

Love, which in gentlest hearts will soonest bloom
seized my lover with passion for that sweet body
from which I was torn unshriven to my doom.

Love, which permits no loved one not to love,
took me so strongly with delight in him
that we are one in Hell, as we were above.

Love led us to one death. In the depths of Hell
Caïna waits for him who took our lives."
This was the piteous tale they stopped to tell.

And when I had heard those world-offended lovers
I bowed my head. At last the Poet spoke:
"What painful thoughts are these your lowered brow
    covers?"

When at length I answered, I began: "Alas!
What sweetest thoughts, what green and young desire
led these two lovers to this sorry pass."

Then turning to those spirits once again,
I said: "Francesca, what you suffer here
melts me to tears of pity and of pain.

But tell me: in the time of your sweet sighs
by what appearances found love the way
to lure you to his perilous paradise?"

And she: "The double grief of a lost bliss
is to recall its happy hour in pain.
Your Guide and Teacher knows the truth of this.

But if there is indeed a soul in Hell
to ask of the beginning of our love
out of his pity, I will weep and tell:

On a day for dalliance we read the rhyme
of Lancelot, how love had mastered him.
We were alone with innocence and dim time.

Pause after pause that high old story drew
our eyes together while we blushed and paled;
but it was one soft passage overthrew

our caution and our hearts. For when we read
how her fond smile was kissed by such a lover,
he who is one with me alive and dead

breathed on my lips the tremor of his kiss.
That book, and he who wrote it, was a pander.
That day we read no further." As she said this,

the other spirit, who stood by her, wept
so piteously, I felt my senses reel
and faint away with anguish. I was swept

by such a swoon as death is, and I fell,
as a corpse might fall, to the dead floor of Hell.

Canto XIII

Circle Seven: Round Two

THE VIOLENT AGAINST THEMSELVES

*Nessus carries the Poets across the river of boiling blood and leaves
them in the Second Round of the Seventh Circle, THE WOOD OF
THE SUICIDES. Here are punished those who destroyed their
own lives and those who destroyed their substance.*

*The souls of the Suicides are encased in thorny trees whose
leaves are eaten by the odious HARPIES, the overseers of these
damned. When the Harpies feed upon them, damaging their leaves
and limbs, the wound bleeds. Only as long as the blood flows are
the souls of the trees able to speak. Thus, they who destroyed their
own bodies are denied a human form; and just as the supreme
expression of their lives was self-destruction, so they are permitted
to speak only through that which tears and destroys them. Only
through their own blood do they find voice. And to add one more
dimension to the symbolism, it is the Harpies—defilers of all they
touch—who give them their eternally recurring wounds.*

*The Poets pause before one tree and speak with the soul of
PIER DELLE VIGNE. In the same wood they see JACOMO DA
SANT' ANDREA, and LANO DA SIENA, two famous
SQUANDERERS and DESTROYERS OF GOODS pursued by a
pack of savage hounds. The hounds overtake SANT' ANDREA,
tear him to pieces and go off carrying his limbs in their teeth, a
self-evident symbolic retribution for the violence with which these
sinners destroyed their substance in the world. After this scene of
horror, Dante speaks to an UNKNOWN FLORENTINE SUICIDE
whose soul is inside the bush which was torn by the hound pack
when it leaped upon Sant' Andrea.*

Nessus had not yet reached the other shore
  when we moved on into a pathless wood
  that twisted upward from Hell's broken floor.

Its foliage was not verdant, but nearly black.
  The unhealthy branches, gnarled and warped and
    tangled,
  bore poison thorns instead of fruit. The track

of those wild beasts that shun the open spaces
  men till between Cecina and Corneto
  runs through no rougher nor more tangled places.

Here nest the odious Harpies of whom my Master
  wrote how they drove Aeneas and his companions
  from the Strophades with prophecies of disaster.

Their wings are wide, their feet clawed, their huge bellies
  covered with feathers, their necks and faces human.
  They croak eternally in the unnatural trees.

"Before going on, I would have you understand,"
  my Guide began, "we are in the second round
  and shall be till we reach the burning sand.

Therefore look carefully and you will see
  things in this wood, which, if I told them to you
  would shake the confidence you have placed in me."

I heard cries of lamentation rise and spill
  on every hand, but saw no souls in pain
  in all that waste; and, puzzled, I stood still.

I think perhaps he thought that I was thinking
  those cries rose from among the twisted roots
  through which the spirits of the damned were slinking

to hide from us. Therefore my Master said:
  "If you break off a twig, what you will learn
  will drive what you are thinking from your head."

Puzzled, I raised my hand a bit and slowly
  broke off a branchlet from an enormous thorn:
  and the great trunk of it cried: "Why do you break
    me?"

And after blood had darkened all the bowl
  of the wound, it cried again: "Why do you tear me?
  Is there no pity left in any soul?

Men we were, and now we are changed to sticks;
  well might your hand have been more merciful
  were we no more than souls of lice and ticks."

As a green branch with one end all aflame
  will hiss and sputter sap out of the other
  as the air escapes—so from that trunk there came

words and blood together, gout by gout.
  Startled, I dropped the branch that I was holding
  and stood transfixed by fear, half turned about

to my Master, who replied: "O wounded soul,
  could he have believed before what he has seen
  in my verses only, you would yet be whole,

for his hand would never have been raised against you.
  But knowing this truth could never be believed
  till it was seen, I urged him on to do

what grieves me now; and I beg to know your name,
  that to make you some amends in the sweet world
  when he returns, he may refresh your fame."

And the trunk: "So sweet those words to me that I
  cannot be still, and may it not annoy you
  if I seem somewhat lengthy in reply.

I am he who held both keys to Frederick's heart,
  locking, unlocking with so deft a touch
  that scarce another soul had any part

in his most secret thoughts. Through every strife
  I was so faithful to my glorious office
  that for it I gave up both sleep and life.

That harlot, Envy, who on Caesar's face
  keeps fixed forever her adulterous stare,
  the common plague and vice of court and palace,

inflamed all minds against me. These inflamed
  so inflamed him that all my happy honors
  were changed to mourning. Then, unjustly blamed,

my soul, in scorn, and thinking to be free
  of scorn in death, made me at last, though just,
  unjust to myself. By the new roots of this tree

I swear to you that never in word or spirit
  did I break faith to my lord and emperor
  who was so worthy of honor in his merit.

If either of you return to the world, speak for me,
  to vindicate in the memory of men
  one who lies prostrate from the blows of Envy."

The Poet stood. Then turned. "Since he is silent,"
  he said to me, "do not you waste this hour,
  if you wish to ask about his life or torment."

And I replied: "Question him for my part,
  on whatever you think I would do well to hear;
  I could not, such compassion chokes my heart."

The Poet began again: "That this man may
  with all his heart do for you what your words
  entreat him to, imprisoned spirit, I pray,

tell us how the soul is bound and bent
  into these knots, and whether any ever
  frees itself from such imprisonment."

At that the trunk blew powerfully, and then
  the wind became a voice that spoke these words:
  "Briefly is the answer given: when

out of the flesh from which it tore itself,
  the violent spirit comes to punishment,
  Minos assigns it to the seventh shelf.

It falls into the wood, and landing there,
  wherever fortune flings it, it strikes root,
  and there it sprouts, lusty as any tare,

shoots up a sapling, and becomes a tree.
  The Harpies, feeding on its leaves then, give it
  pain and pain's outlet simultaneously.

Like the rest, we shall go for our husks on Judgment Day,
  but not that we may wear them, for it is not just
  that a man be given what he throws away.

Here shall we drag them and in this mournful glade
  our bodies will dangle to the end of time,
  each on the thorns of its tormented shade."

We waited by the trunk, but it said no more;
  and waiting, we were startled by a noise
  that grew through all the wood. Just such a roar

and trembling as one feels when the boar and chase
  approach his stand, the beasts and branches crashing
  and clashing in the heat of the fierce race.

And there on the left, running so violently
  they broke off every twig in the dark wood,
  two torn and naked wraiths went plunging by me.

The leader cried, "Come now, O Death! Come now!"
  And the other, seeing that he was outrun
  cried out: "Your legs were not so ready, Lano,

in the jousts at the Toppo." And suddenly in his rush,
  perhaps because his breath was failing him,
  he hid himself inside a thorny bush

and cowered among its leaves. Then at his back,
  the wood leaped with black bitches, swift as
    greyhounds
  escaping from their leash, and all the pack

sprang on him; with their fangs they opened him
  and tore him savagely, and then withdrew,
  carrying his body with them, limb by limb.

Then, taking me by the hand across the wood,
  my Master led me toward the bush. Lamenting,
  all its fractures blew out words and blood:

"O Jacomo da Sant' Andrea!" it said,
  "what have you gained in making me your screen?
  What part had I in the foul life you led?"

And when my Master had drawn up to it
  he said: "Who were you, who through all our wounds
  blow out your blood with your lament, sad spirit?"

And he to us: "You who have come to see
  how the outrageous mangling of these hounds
  has torn my boughs and stripped my leaves from me,

O heap them round my ruin! I was born
  in the city that tore down Mars and raised the Baptist.
  On that account the God of War has sworn

her sorrow shall not end. And were it not
  that something of his image still survives
  on the bridge across the Arno, some have thought

those citizens who of their love and pain
afterwards rebuilt it from the ashes
left by Attila, would have worked in vain.

I am one who has no tale to tell:
I made myself a gibbet of my own lintel."

Chapter

10

The Late Middle Ages:
1300–1500

PETRARCH

from the *Canzoniere*

3

It was the day the sun's ray had turned pale
with pity for the suffering of his Maker
when I was caught, and I put up no fight,
my lady, for your lovely eyes had bound me.

It seemed no time to be on guard against
Love's blows; therefore, I went my way
secure and fearless—so, all my misfortunes
began in midst of universal woe.

Love found me all disarmed and found the way
was clear to reach my heart down through the eyes
which have become the halls and doors of tears.

It seems to me it did him little honour
to wound me with his arrow in my state
and to you, armed, not show his bow at all.

61

Oh blessèd be the day, the month, the year,
the season and the time, the hour, the instant,
the gracious countryside, the place where I
was struck by those two lovely eyes that bound me;

and blessèd be the first sweet agony
I felt when I found myself bound to Love,
the bow and all the arrows that have pierced me,
the wounds that reach the bottom of my heart.

And blessèd be all of the poetry
I scattered, calling out my lady's name,
and all the sighs, and tears, and the desire;

blessèd be all the paper upon which
I earn her fame, and every thought of mine,
only of her, and shared with no one else.

132

If it's not love, then what is it I feel?
But if it's love, by God, what is this thing?
If good, why then the bitter mortal sting?
If bad, then why is every torment sweet?

If I burn willingly, why weep and grieve?
And if against my will, what good lamenting?
O living death, O pleasurable harm,
how can you rule me if I not consent?

And if I do consent, it's wrong to grieve.
Caught in contrasting winds in a frail boat
on the high seas I am without a helm,

so light of wisdom, so laden of error,
that I myself do not know what I want,
and shiver in midsummer, burn in winter.

134

I find no peace, and I am not at war,
I fear and hope, and burn and I am ice;
I fly above the heavens, and lie on earth,
and I grasp nothing and embrace the world.

One keeps me jailed who neither locks nor opens,
nor keeps me for her own nor frees the noose;
Love does not kill, nor does he loose my chains;
he wants me lifeless but won't loosen me.

I see with no eyes, shout without a tongue;
I yearn to perish, and I beg for help;
I hate myself and love somebody else.

I thrive on pain and laugh with all my tears;
I dislike death as much as I do life:
because of you, lady, I am this way.

272

Life runs away and never rests a moment
and death runs after it with mighty stride,
and present things and things back from the past
and from the future, too, wage war on me:

anticipation, memory weigh down
my heart on either side so that, in truth,
if I did not take pity on myself,
I would, by now, be free of all such thoughts.

What little sweetness my sad heart once felt
comes back to me; but from the other side
I see turbulent winds blowing my sails;

I see a storm in port, and weary now
my helmsman, and my masts and lines destroyed,
and the fair stars I loved to look at, dead.

311

That nightingale so tenderly lamenting
perhaps his children or his cherished mate,
in sweetness fills the sky and countryside
with many notes of grief skilfully played,

and all night long he stays with me it seems,
reminding me of my harsh destiny;
I have no one to blame except myself
for thinking that Death could not take a goddess.

How easy to deceive one who is sure!
Those two lights, lovely, brighter than the sun,
whoever thought would turn the earth so dark?

And now I know what this fierce fate of mine
would have me learn as I live on in tears:
that nothing here can please and also last.

365

I go my way regretting those past times
I spent in loving something which was mortal
instead of soaring high, since I had wings
that might have taken me to higher levels.

You who see all my shameful, wicked errors,
King of all Heaven, invisible, immortal,
help this frail soul of mine for she has strayed,
and all her emptiness fill up with grace,

so that, having once lived in storms, at war,
I may now die in peace, in port; and if my stay
was vain, at least let my departure count.

Over that little life that still remains to me,
and at my death, deign that your hand be present:
You know You are the only hope I have.

GIOVANNI BOCCACCIO
from *The Decameron*
First Day

• • •

Whenever, fairest ladies, I pause to consider how compassionate you all are by nature, I invariably become aware that the present work will seem to you to possess an irksome and ponderous opening. For it carries at its head the painful memory of the deadly havoc wrought by the recent plague, which brought so much heartache and misery to those who witnessed, or had experience of it. But I do not want you to be deterred, for this reason, from reading any further, on the assumption that you are to be subjected, as you read, to an endless torrent of tears and sobbing. You will be affected no differently by this grim beginning than walkers confronted by a steep and rugged hill, beyond which there lies a beautiful and delectable plain. The degree of pleasure they derive from the latter will correspond directly to the difficulty of the climb and the descent. And just as the end of mirth is heaviness, so sorrows are dispersed by the advent of joy.

This brief unpleasantness (I call it brief, inasmuch as it is contained within few words) is quickly followed by the sweetness and the pleasure which I have already promised you, and which, unless you were told in advance, you would not perhaps be expecting to find after such a beginning as this. Believe me, if I could decently have taken you whither I desire by some other route, rather than along a path so difficult as this, I would gladly have done so. But since it is impossible without this memoir to show the origin of the events you will read about later, I really have no alternative but to address myself to its composition.

I say, then, that the sum of thirteen hundred and forty-eight years had elapsed since the fruitful Incarnation of the Son of God, when the noble city of Florence, which for its great beauty excels all others in Italy, was visited by the deadly pestilence. Some say that it descended upon the human race through the influence of the heavenly bodies, others that it was a punishment signifying God's righteous anger at our iniquitous way of life. But whatever its cause, it had originated some years earlier in the East, where it had claimed countless lives before it unhappily spread westward, growing in strength as it swept relentlessly on from one place to the next.

In the face of its onrush, all the wisdom and ingenuity of man were unavailing. Large quantities of refuse were cleared out of the city by officials specially appointed for the purpose, all sick persons were forbidden entry, and numerous instructions were issued for safeguarding the people's health, but all to no avail. Nor were the countless petitions humbly directed to God by the pious, whether by means of formal processions or in any other guise, any less ineffectual. For in the early spring of the year we have mentioned, the plague began, in a terrifying and extraordinary manner, to make its disastrous effects apparent. It did not take the form it had assumed in the East, where if anyone bled from the nose it was an obvious portent of certain death. On the contrary, its earliest symptom, in men and women alike, was the appearance of certain swellings in the groin or the armpit, some of which were egg-shaped whilst others were roughly the size of the common apple. Sometimes the swellings were large, sometimes not so large, and they were referred to by the populace as *gavòccioli*. From the two areas already mentioned, this deadly *gavòcciolo* would begin to spread, and within a short time it would appear at random all over the body. Later on, the symptoms of the disease changed, and many people began to find dark blotches and bruises on their arms, thighs, and other parts of the body, sometimes large and few in number, at other times tiny and closely spaced. These, to anyone unfortunate enough to contract them, were just as infallible a sign that he would die as the *gavòcciolo* had been earlier, and as indeed it still was.

Against these maladies, it seemed that all the advice of physicians and all the power of medicine were profitless and unavailing. Perhaps the nature of the illness was such that it allowed no remedy: or perhaps those people who were treating the illness (whose numbers had increased enormously because the ranks of the qualified were invaded by people, both men and women, who had never received any training in medicine), being ignorant of its causes, were not prescribing the appropriate cure. At all events, few of those who caught it ever recovered, and in most cases death occurred within three days from the appearance of the symptoms we have described, some people dying more rapidly than others, the majority without any fever or other complications.

But what made this pestilence even more severe was that whenever those suffering from it mixed with people who were still unaffected, it would rush upon these with the speed of a fire racing through dry or oily substances that happened to be placed within its reach. Nor was this the full extent of its evil, for not only did it infect healthy persons who conversed or had any dealings with the sick, making them ill or visiting an equally horrible death upon them, but it also seemed to transfer the sickness to anyone touching the clothes or other objects which had been handled or used by its victims.

It is a remarkable story that I have to relate. And were it not for the fact that I am one of many people who saw it with their own eyes, I would scarcely dare to believe it, let alone commit it to paper, even though I had heard it from a person whose word I could trust. The plague I have been describing was of so contagious a nature that very often it visibly did more than simply pass from one person to another. In other words, whenever an animal other than a human being touched anything belonging to a person who had been stricken or exterminated by the disease, it not only caught the sickness, but died from it almost at once. To all of this, as I have just said, my own eyes bore witness on more than one occasion. One day, for instance, the rags of a pauper who had died from the disease were thrown into the street, where they attracted the attention of two pigs. In their wonted fashion, the pigs first of all gave the rags a thorough mauling with their snouts after which they took them between their teeth and shook them against their cheeks. And within a short time they began to writhe as though they had been poisoned, then they both dropped dead to the ground, spreadeagled upon the rags that had brought about their undoing.

These things, and many others of a similar or even worse nature, caused various fears and fantasies to take root in the minds of those who were still alive and well. And almost without exception, they took a single and very inhuman precaution, namely to avoid or run away from the sick and their belongings, by which means they all thought that their own health would be preserved.

Some people were of the opinion that a sober and abstemious mode of living considerably reduced the risk of infection. They therefore formed themselves into groups and lived in isolation from everyone else. Having withdrawn to a comfortable abode where there were no sick persons, they locked themselves in and settled down to a peaceable existence, consuming modest quantities of delicate foods and precious wines and avoiding all excesses. They refrained from speaking to outsiders, refused to receive news of the dead or the sick, and entertained themselves with music and whatever other amusements they were able to devise.

Others took the opposite view, and maintained that an infallible way of warding off this appalling evil was to drink heavily, enjoy life to the full, go round singing and merrymaking, gratify all of one's cravings whenever the opportunity offered, and shrug the whole thing off as one enormous joke. Moreover, they practised what they preached to the best of their ability, for they would visit one tavern after another, drinking all day and night to immoderate excess; or alternatively (and this was their more frequent custom), they would do their drinking in various private houses, but only in the ones where the conversation was restricted to subjects that were pleasant or entertaining. Such places were easy to find, for people behaved as though their days were numbered, and treated their belongings and their own persons with equal abandon. Hence most houses had become common property, and any passing stranger could make himself at home as naturally as though he were the rightful owner. But for all their riotous manner of living, these people always took good care to avoid any contact with the sick.

In the face of so much affliction and misery, all respect for the laws of God and man had virtually broken down and been extinguished in our city. For like everybody else, those ministers and executors of the laws who were not either dead or ill were left with so few subordinates that they were unable to discharge any of their duties. Hence everyone was free to behave as he pleased.

There were many other people who steered a middle course between the two already mentioned, neither restricting their diet to the same degree as the first group, nor indulging so freely as the second in drinking and other forms of wantonness, but simply doing no more than satisfy their appetite. Instead of incarcerating themselves, these people moved about freely, holding in their hands a posy of flowers, or fragrant herbs, or one of a wide range of spices, which they applied at frequent intervals to their nostrils, thinking it an excellent idea to fortify the brain with smells of that particular sort; for the stench of dead bodies, sickness, and medicines seemed to fill and pollute the whole of the atmosphere.

Some people, pursuing what was possibly the safer alternative, callously maintained that there was no better or more efficacious remedy against a plague than to run away from it. Swayed by this argument, and sparing no thought for anyone but themselves, large numbers of men and women abandoned their city, their homes, their relatives, their estates and their belongings, and headed for the countryside, either in Florentine territory or, better still, abroad. It was as though they imagined that the wrath of God would not unleash this plague against men for their iniquities irrespective of where they happened to be, but would only be aroused against those who found themselves within the city walls; or possibly they assumed that the whole of the population would be exterminated and that the city's last hour had come.

Of the people who held these various opinions, not all of them died. Nor, however, did they all survive. On the contrary, many of each different persuasion fell ill here, there, and everywhere, and having themselves, when they were fit and well, set an example to those who were as yet unaffected, they languished away with virtually no one to nurse them. It was not merely a question of one citizen avoiding another, and of people almost invariably neglecting their neighbours and rarely or never visiting their relatives, addressing them only from a distance; this scourge had implanted so great a terror in the hearts of men and women that brothers abandoned brothers, uncles their nephews, sisters their brothers, and in many cases wives deserted their husbands. But even worse, and almost incredible, was the fact that fathers and mothers refused to nurse and assist their own children, as though they did not belong to them.

Hence the countless numbers of people who fell ill, both male and female, were entirely dependent upon either the charity of friends (who were few and far between) or the greed of servants, who remained in short supply despite the attraction of high wages out of all proportion to the services they performed. Furthermore, these latter were men and women of coarse intellect and the majority were unused to such duties, and they did little more than hand things to the invalid when asked to do so and watch over him when he was dying. And in performing this kind of service, they frequently lost their lives as well as their earnings.

As a result of this wholesale desertion of the sick by neighbours, relatives and friends, and in view of the scarcity of servants, there grew up a practice almost never previously heard of, whereby when a woman fell ill, no matter how gracious or beautiful or gently bred she might be, she raised no objection to being attended by a male servant, whether he was young or not. Nor did she have any scruples about showing him every part of her body as freely as she would have displayed it to a woman, provided that the nature of her infirmity required her to do so; and this explains why those women who recovered were possibly less chaste in the period that followed.

Moreover a great many people died who would perhaps have survived had they received some assistance. And hence, what with the lack of appropriate means for tending the sick, and the virulence of the plague, the number of deaths reported in the city whether by day or night was so enormous that it astonished all who heard tell of it, to say nothing of the people who actually witnessed the carnage. And it was perhaps inevitable that among the citizens who survived there arose certain customs that were quite contrary to established tradition.

It had once been customary, as it is again nowadays, for the women relatives and neighbours of a dead man to assemble in his house in order to mourn in the company of the women who had been closest to him; moreover his kinfolk would forgather in front of his house along with his neighbours and various other citizens, and there would be a contingent of priests, whose numbers varied according to the quality of the deceased; his body would be taken thence to the church in which he had wanted to be buried, being borne on the shoulders of his peers amidst the funeral pomp of candles and dirges. But as the ferocity of the plague began to mount, this practice all but disappeared entirely and was replaced by different customs. For not only did people die without having many women about them, but a great number departed this life without anyone at all to witness their going. Few indeed were those to whom the lamentations and bitter tears of their relatives were accorded; on the contrary, more often than not bereavement was the signal for laughter and witticisms and general jollification—the art of which the women, having for the most part suppressed their feminine concern for the salvation of the souls of the dead, had learned to perfection. Moreover it was rare for the bodies of the dead to be accompanied by more than ten or twelve neighbours to the church, nor were they borne on the shoulders of worthy and honest citizens, but by a kind of gravedigging fraternity, newly come into being and drawn from the lower orders of society. These people assumed the title of sexton, and demanded a fat fee for their services, which consisted in taking up the coffin and hauling it swiftly away, not to the church specified by the dead man in his will, but usually to the nearest at hand. They would be preceded by a group of four or six clerics, who between them carried one or two candles at most, and sometimes none at all. Nor did the priests go to the trouble of pronouncing solemn and lengthy funeral rites, but, with the aid of these so-called sextons, they hastily lowered the body into the nearest empty grave they could find.

As for the common people and a large proportion of the bourgeoisie, they presented a much more pathetic spectacle, for the majority of them were constrained, either by their poverty or the hope of survival, to remain in their houses. Being confined to their own parts of the city, they fell ill daily in their thousands, and since they had no one to assist them or attend to their needs, they inevitably perished almost without exception. Many dropped dead in the open streets, both by day and by night, whilst a great many others, though dying in their own houses, drew their neighbors' attention to the fact more by the smell of their rotting corpses than by any other means. And what with these, and the others who were dying all over the city, bodies were here, there and everywhere.

Whenever people died, their neighbours nearly always followed a single, set routine, prompted as much by their fear of being contaminated by the decaying corpse as by any charitable feelings they may have entertained towards the deceased. Either on their own, or with the assistance of bearers whenever these were to be had, they extracted the bodies of the dead from their houses and left them lying outside their front doors, where anyone going about the streets, especially in the early morning, could have observed countless numbers of them. Funeral biers would then be sent for, upon which the dead were taken away, though there were some who, for lack of biers, were carried off on plain boards. It was by no means rare for more than one of these biers to be seen with two or three bodies upon it at a time; on the contrary, many were seen to contain a husband and wife, two or three brothers and sisters, a father and son, or some other pair of close relatives. And times without number it happened that two priests would be on their way to bury someone, holding a cross before them, only to find that bearers carrying three or four additional biers would fall in behind them; so that whereas the priests had thought they had only one burial to attend to, they in fact had six or seven, and sometimes more. Even in these circumstances, however, there were no tears or candles or mourners to honour the dead; in fact, no more respect was accorded to dead people than would nowadays be shown towards dead goats. For it was quite apparent that the one thing which, in normal times, no wise man had ever learned to accept with patient resignation (even though it struck so seldom and unobtrusively), had now been brought home to the feeble-minded as well, but the scale of the calamity caused them to regard it with indifference.

Such was the multitude of corpses (of which further consignments were arriving every day and almost by the hour at each of the churches), that there was not sufficient consecrated ground for them to be buried in, especially if each was to have its own plot in accordance with long-established custom. So when all the graves were full, huge trenches were excavated in the churchyards, into which new arrivals were placed in their hundreds, stowed tier upon tier like ships' cargo, each layer of corpses being covered over with a thin layer of soil till the trench was filled to the top.

But rather than describe in elaborate detail the calamities were experienced in the city at that time, I must mention that, whilst an ill wind was blowing through Florence itself, the surrounding region was no less badly affected. In the fortified towns, conditions were similar to those in the city itself on a minor scale; but in the scattered hamlets and the countryside proper, the poor unfortunate peasants and their families had no physicians or servants whatever to assist them, and collapsed by the wayside, in their fields, and in their cottages at all hours of the day and night, dying more like animals than human beings. Like the townspeople, they too grew apathetic in their ways, disregarded their affairs, and neglected their possessions. Moreover they all behaved as though each day was to be their last, and far from making provision for the future by tilling their lands, tending their flocks, and adding to their previous labours, they tried in every way they could think of to squander the assets already in their possession. Thus it came about that oxen, asses, sheep, goats, pigs, chickens, and even dogs (for all their deep fidelity to man) were driven away and allowed to roam freely through the fields, where the crops lay abandoned and had not even been reaped, let alone gathered in. And after a whole day's feasting, many of these animals, as though possessing the power of reason, would return glutted in the evening to their own quarters, without any shepherd to guide them.

But let us leave the countryside and return to the city. What more remains to be said, except that the cruelty of heaven (and possibly, in some measure, also that of man) was so immense and so devastating that between March and July of the year in question, what with the fury of the pestilence and the fact that so many of the sick were inadequately cared for or abandoned in their hour of need because the healthy were too terrified to approach them, it is reliably thought that over a hundred thousand human lives were extinguished within the walls of the city of Florence? Yet before this lethal catastrophe fell upon the city, it is doubtful whether anyone would have guessed it contained so many inhabitants.

Ah, how great a number of splendid palaces, fine houses, and noble dwellings, once filled with retainers, with lords and with ladies, were bereft of all who had lived there, down to the tiniest child! How numerous were the famous families, the vast estates, the notable fortunes, that were seen to be left without a rightful successor! How many gallant gentlemen, fair ladies, and sprightly youths, who would have been judged hale and hearty by Galen, Hippocrates and Aesculapius (to say nothing of others), having breakfasted in the morning with their kinsfolk, acquaintances and friends, supped that same evening with their ancestors in the next world! . . .

GEOFFREY CHAUCER
from *The Canterbury Tales*
The Prologue

When in April the sweet showers fall
And pierce the drought of March to the root, and all
The veins are bathed in liquor of such power
As brings about the engendering of the flower,
When also Zephyrus with his sweet breath
Exhales an air in every grove and heath
Upon the tender shoots, and the young sun
His half-course in the sign of the *Ram* has run,
And the small fowl are making melody
That sleep away the night with open eye
(So nature pricks them and their heart engages)
Then people long to go on pilgrimages
And palmers long to seek the stranger strands
Of far-off saints, hallowed in sundry lands,
And specially, from every shire's end
Of England, down to Canterbury they wend
To seek the holy blissful martyr, quick
To give his help to them when they were sick.
 It happened in that season that one day
In Southwark, at *The Tabard*, as I lay
Ready to go on pilgrimage and start
For Canterbury, most devout at heart,
At night there came into that hostelry
Some nine and twenty in a company
Of sundry folk happening then to fall
In fellowship, and they were pilgrims all
That towards Canterbury meant to ride.
The rooms and stables of the inn were wide;

They made us easy, all was of the best.
And, briefly, when the sun had gone to rest,
I'd spoken to them all upon the trip
And was soon one with them in fellowship,
Pledged to rise early and to take the way
To Canterbury, as you heard me say.
 But none the less, while I have time and space,
Before my story takes a further pace,
It seems a reasonable thing to say
What their condition was, the full array
Of each of them, as it appeared to me,
According to profession and degree,
And what apparel they were riding in;
And at a Knight I therefore will begin.
There was a *Knight*, a most distinguished man,
Who from the day on which he first began
To ride abroad had followed chivalry,
Truth, honour, generousness and courtesy.
He had done nobly in his sovereign's war
And ridden into battle, no man more,
As well in Christian as in heathen places,
And ever honoured for his noble graces.
 When we took Alexandria, he was there.
He often sat at table in the chair
Of honour, above all nations, when in Prussia.
In Lithuania he had ridden, and Russia,
No Christian man so often, of his rank.
When, in Granada, Algeciras sank

Under assault, he had been there, and in
North Africa, raiding Benamarin;
In Anatolia he had been as well
And fought when Ayas and Attalia fell,
For all along the Mediterranean coast
He had embarked with many a noble host.
In fifteen mortal battles he had been
And jousted for our faith at Tramissene
Thrice in the lists, and always killed his man.
This same distinguished knight had led the van
Once with the Bey of Balat, doing work
For him against another heathen Turk;
He was of sovereign value in all eyes.
And though so much distinguished, he was wise
And in his bearing modest as a maid.
He never yet a boorish thing had said
In all his life to any, come what might;
He was a true, a perfect gentle-knight.

Speaking of his equipment, he possessed
Fine horses, but he was not gaily dressed.
He wore a fustian tunic stained and dark
With smudges where his armour had left mark;
Just home from service, he had joined our ranks
To do his pilgrimage and render thanks.

He had his son with him, a fine young *Squire*,
A lover and cadet, a lad of fire
With locks as curly as if they had been pressed.
He was some twenty years of age, I guessed.
In stature he was of a moderate length,
With wonderful agility and strength.
He'd seen some service with the cavalry
In Flanders and Artois and Picardy
And had done valiantly in little space
Of time, in hope to win his lady's grace.
He was embroidered like a meadow bright
And full of freshest flowers, red and white.
Singing he was, or fluting all the day;
He was as fresh as is the month of May.
Short was his gown, the sleeves were long and wide;
He knew the way to sit a horse and ride.
He could make songs and poems and recite,
Knew how to joust and dance, to draw and write.
He loved so hotly that till dawn grew pale
He slept as little as a nightingale.
Courteous he was, lowly and serviceable,
And carved to serve his father at the table.

There was a *Yeoman* with him at his side,
No other servant; so he chose to ride.
This Yeoman wore a coat and hood of green,
And peacock-feathered arrows, bright and keen
And neatly sheathed, hung at his belt the while
—For he could dress his gear in yeoman style,
His arrows never dropped their feathers low—
And in his hand he bore a mighty bow.
His head was like a nut, his face was brown.
He knew the whole of woodcraft up and down.
A saucy brace was on his arm to ward
It from the bow-string, and a shield and sword
Hung at one side, and at the other slipped
A jaunty dirk, spear-sharp and well-equipped.

A medal of St Christopher he wore
Of shining silver on his breast, and bore
A hunting-horn, well slung and burnished clean,
That dangled from a baldrick of bright green.
He was a proper forester, I guess.

There also was a *Nun*, a Prioress,
Her way of smiling very simple and coy.
Her greatest oath was only 'By St Loy!'
And she was known as Madam Eglantyne.
And well she sang a service, with a fine
Intoning through her nose, as was most seemly,
And she spoke daintily in French, extremely,
After the school of Stratford-atte-Bowe;
French in the Paris style she did not know.
At meat her manners were well taught withal;
No morsel from her lips did she let fall,
Nor dipped her fingers in the sauce too deep;
But she could carry a morsel up and keep
The smallest drop from falling on her breast.
For courtliness she had a special zest,
And she would wipe her upper lip so clean
That not a trace of grease was to be seen
Upon the cup when she had drunk; to eat,
She reached a hand sedately for the meat.
She certainly was very entertaining,
Pleasant and friendly in her ways, and straining
To counterfeit a courtly kind of grace,
A stately bearing fitting to her place,
And to seem dignified in all her dealings.
As for her sympathies and tender feelings,
She was so charitably solicitous
She used to weep if she but saw a mouse
Caught in a trap, if it were dead or bleeding.
And she had little dogs she would be feeding
With roasted flesh, or milk, or fine white bread.
And bitterly she wept if one were dead
Or someone took a stick and made it smart;
She was all sentiment and tender heart.
Her veil was gathered in a seemly way,
Her nose was elegant, her eyes glass-grey;
Her mouth was very small, but soft and red,
Her forehead, certainly, was fair of spread,
Almost a span across the brows, I own;
She was indeed by no means undergrown.
Her cloak, I noticed, had a graceful charm.
She wore a coral trinket on her arm,
A set of beads, the gaudies tricked in green,
Whence hung a golden brooch of brightest sheen
On which there first was graven a crowned A,
And lower, *Amor vincit omnia.*

Another *Nun*, the secretary at her cell,
Was riding with her, and *three Priests* as well.

A *Monk* there was, one of the finest sort
Who rode the country; hunting was his sport.
A manly man, to be an Abbot able;
Many a dainty horse he had in stable.
His bridle, when he rode, a man might hear
Jingling in a whistling wind as clear,
Aye, and as loud as does the chapel bell
Where my lord Monk was Prior of the cell.

The Rule of good St Benet or St Maur
As old and strict he tended to ignore;
He let go by the things of yesterday
And took the modern world's more spacious way.
He did not rate that text at a plucked hen
Which says that hunters are not holy men
And that a monk uncloistered is a mere
Fish out of water, flapping on the pier,
That is to say a monk out of his cloister.
That was a text he held not worth an oyster;
And I agreed and said his views were sound;
Was he to study till his head went round
Poring over books in cloisters? Must he toil
As Austin bade and till the very soil?
Was he to leave the world upon the shelf?
Let Austin have his labour to himself.

This Monk was therefore a good man to horse;
Greyhounds he had, as swift as birds, to course.
Hunting a hare or riding at a fence
Was all his fun, he spared for no expense.
I saw his sleeves were garnished at the hand
With fine grey fur, the finest in the land,
And on his hood, to fasten it at his chin
He had a wrought-gold cunningly fashioned pin;
Into a lover's knot it seemed to pass.
His head was bald and shone like looking-glass;
So did his face, as if it had been greased.
He was a fat and personable priest;
His prominent eyeballs never seemed to settle.
They glittered like the flames beneath a kettle;
Supple his boots, his horse in fine condition.
He was a prelate fit for exhibition,
He was not pale like a tormented soul.
He liked a fat swan best, and roasted whole.
His palfrey was as brown as is a berry.
There was a *Friar*, a wanton one and merry,
A Limiter, a very festive fellow.
In all Four Orders there was none so mellow,
So glib with gallant phrase and well-turned speech.
He'd fixed up many a marriage, giving each
Of his young women what he could afford her.
He was a noble pillar to his Order.
Highly beloved and intimate was he
With County folk within his boundary,
And city dames of honour and possessions;
For he was qualified to hear confessions,
Or so he said, with more than priestly scope;
He had a special licence from the Pope.
Sweetly he heard his penitents at shrift
With pleasant absolution, for a gift.
He was an easy man in penance-giving
Where he could hope to make a decent living;
It's a sure sign whenever gifts are given
To a poor Order that a man's well shriven,
And should he give enough he knew in verity
The penitent repented in sincerity.
For many a fellow is so hard of heart
He cannot weep, for all his inward smart.
Therefore instead of weeping and of prayer
One should give silver for a poor Friar's care.

He kept his tippet stuffed with pins for curls,
And pocket-knives, to give to pretty girls.
And certainly his voice was gay and sturdy,
For he sang well and played the hurdy-gurdy.
At sing-songs he was champion of the hour.
His neck was whiter than a lily-flower
But strong enough to butt a bruiser down.
He knew the taverns well in every town
And every innkeeper and barmaid too
Better than lepers, beggars and that crew,
For in so eminent a man as he
It was not fitting with the dignity
Of his position, dealing with a scum
Of wretched lepers; nothing good can come
Of commerce with such slum-and-gutter dwellers,
But only with the rich and victual-sellers.
But anywhere a profit might accrue
Courteous he was and lowly of service too.
Natural gifts like his were hard to match.
He was the finest beggar of his batch,
And, for his begging-district, paid a rent;
His brethren did no poaching where he went.
For though a widow mightn't have a shoe,
So pleasant was his holy how-d'ye-do
He got his farthing from her just the same
Before he left, and so his income came
To more than he laid out. And how he romped,
Just like a puppy! He was ever prompt
To arbitrate disputes on settling days
(For a small fee) in many helpful ways,
Not then appearing as your cloistered scholar
With threadbare habit hardly worth a dollar,
But much more like a Doctor or a Pope.
Of double-worsted was the semi-cope
Upon his shoulders, and the swelling fold
About him, like a bell about its mould
When it is casting, rounded out his dress.
He lisped a little out of wantonness
To make his English sweet upon his tongue.
When he had played his harp, or having sung,
His eyes would twinkle in his head as bright
As any star upon a frosty night.
This worthy's name was Hubert, it appeared.
There was a *Merchant* with a forking beard
And motley dress; high on his horse he sat,
Upon his head a Flemish beaver hat
And on his feet daintily buckled boots.
He told of his opinions and pursuits
In solemn tones, he harped on his increase
Of capital; there should be sea-police
(He thought) upon the Harwich-Holland ranges;
He was expert at dabbling in exchanges.
This estimable Merchant so had set
His wits to work, none knew he was in debt,
He was so stately in administration,
In loans and bargains and negotiation.
He was an excellent fellow all the same;
To tell the truth I do not know his name.
An *Oxford Cleric*, still a student though,
One who had taken logic long ago,

Was there; his horse was thinner than a rake,
And he was not too fat, I undertake,
But had a hollow look, a sober stare;
The thread upon his overcoat was bare.
He had found no preferment in the church
And he was too unworldly to make search
For secular employment. By his bed
He preferred having twenty books in red
And black, of Aristotle's philosophy,
Than costly clothes, fiddle or psaltery.
Though a philosopher, as I have told,
He had not found the stone for making gold.
Whatever money from his friends he took
He spent on learning or another book
And prayed for them most earnestly, returning
Thanks to them thus for paying for his learning.
His only care was study, and indeed
He never spoke a word more than was need,
Formal at that, respectful in the extreme,
Short, to the point, and lofty in his theme.
A tone of moral virtue filled his speech
And gladly would he learn, and gladly teach.

A *Serjeant at the Law* who paid his calls,
Wary and wise, for clients at St Paul's
There also was, of noted excellence.
Discreet he was, a man to reverence,
Or so he seemed, his sayings were so wise.
He often had been Justice of Assize
By letters patent, and in full commission.
His fame and learning and his high position
Had won him many a robe and many a fee.
There was no such conveyancer as he;
All was fee-simple to his strong digestion,
Not one conveyance could be called in question.
Though there was nowhere one so busy as he,
He was less busy than he seemed to be.
He knew of every judgement, case and crime
Ever recorded since King William's time.
He could dictate defences or draft deeds;
No one could pinch a comma from his screeds
And he knew every statute off by rote.
He wore a homely parti-coloured coat,
Girt with a silken belt of pin-stripe stuff;
Of his appearance I have said enough.

There was a *Franklin* with him, it appeared;
White as a daisy-petal was his beard.
A sanguine man, high-coloured and benign,
He loved a morning sop of cake in wine.
He lived for pleasure and had always done,
For he was Epicurus' very son,
In whose opinion sensual delight
Was the one true felicity in sight.
As noted as St Julian was for bounty
He made his household free to all the County.
His bread, his ale were finest of the fine
And no one had a better stock of wine.
His house was never short of bake-meat pies,
Of fish and flesh, and these in such supplies
It positively snowed with meat and drink
And all the dainties that a man could think.

According to the seasons of the year
Changes of dish were ordered to appear.
He kept fat partridges in coops, beyond,
Many a bream and pike were in his pond.
Woe to the cook unless the sauce was hot
And sharp, or if he wasn't on the spot!
And in his hall a table stood arrayed
And ready all day long, with places laid.
As Justice at the Sessions none stood higher;
He often had been Member for the Shire.
A dagger and a little purse of silk
Hung at his girdle, white as morning milk.
As Sheriff he checked audit, every entry.
He was a model among landed gentry.

A *Haberdasher*, a *Dyer*, a *Carpenter*,
A *Weaver* and a *Carpet-maker* were
Among our ranks, all in the livery
Of one impressive guild-fraternity.
They were so trim and fresh their gear would pass
For new. Their knives were not tricked out with brass
But wrought with purest silver, which avouches
A like display on girdles and on pouches.
Each seemed a worthy burgess, fit to grace
A guild-hall with a seat upon the dais.
Their wisdom would have justified a plan
To make each one of them an alderman;
They had the capital and revenue,
Besides their wives declared it was their due.
And if they did not think so, then they ought;
To be called '*Madam*' is a glorious thought,
And so is going to church and being seen
Having your mantle carried, like a queen.

They had a *Cook* with them who stood alone
For boiling chicken with a marrow-bone,
Sharp flavouring-powder and a spice for savour.
He could distinguish London ale by flavour,
And he could roast and seethe and broil and fry,
Make good thick soup and bake a tasty pie.
But what a pity—so it seemed to me,
That he should have an ulcer on his knee.
As for blancmange, he made it with the best.

There was a *Skipper* hailing from far west;
He came from Dartmouth, so I understood.
He rode a farmer's horse as best he could,
In a woollen gown that reached his knee.
A dagger on a lanyard falling free
Hung from his neck under his arm and down.
The summer heat had tanned his colour brown,
And certainly he was an excellent fellow.
Many a draught of vintage, red and yellow,
He'd drawn at Bordeaux, while the trader snored.
The nicer rules of conscience he ignored.
If, when he fought, the enemy vessel sank,
He sent his prisoners home; they walked the plank.
As for his skill in reckoning his tides,
Currents and many another risk besides,
Moons, harbours, pilots, he had such dispatch
That none from Hull to Carthage was his match.
Hardy he was, prudent in undertaking;
His beard in many a tempest had its shaking,

And he knew all the heavens as they were
From Gottland to the Cape of Finisterre,
And every creek in Brittany and Spain;
The barge he owned was called *The Maudelayne*.
 A *Doctor* too emerged as we proceeded;
No one alive could talk as well as he did
On points of medicine and of surgery,
For, being grounded in astronomy,
He watched his patient closely for the hours
When, by his horoscope, he knew the powers
Of favourable planets, then ascendent,
Worked on the images for his dependent.
The cause of every malady you'd got
He knew, and whether dry, cold, moist or hot;
He knew their seat, their humour and condition.
He was a perfect practising physician.
These causes being known for what they were,
He gave the man his medicine then and there.
All his apothecaries in a tribe
Were ready with the drugs he would prescribe
And each made money from the other's guile;
They had been friendly for a goodish while.
He was well-versed in Aesculapius too
And what Hippocrates and Rufus knew
And Dioscorides, now dead and gone,
Galen and Rhazes, Hali, Serapion,
Averroes, Avicenna, Constantine,
Scotch Bernard, John of Gaddesden, Gilbertine.
In his own diet he observed some measure;
There were no superfluities for pleasure,
Only digestives, nutritives and such.
He did not read the Bible very much.
In blood-red garments, slashed with bluish grey
And lined with taffeta, he rode his way;
Yet he was rather close as to expenses
And kept the gold he won in pestilences.
Gold stimulates the heart, or so we're told.
He therefore had a special love of gold.
 A worthy *woman* from beside *Bath* city
Was with us, somewhat deaf, which was a pity.
In making cloth she showed so great a bent
She bettered those of Ypres and of Ghent.
In all the parish not a dame dared stir
Towards the altar steps in front of her,
And if indeed they did, so wrath was she
As to be quite put out of charity.
Her kerchiefs were of finely woven ground;
I dared have sworn they weighed a good ten pound,
The ones she wore on Sunday, on her head.
Her hose were of the finest scarlet red
And gartered tight; her shoes were soft and new.
Bold was her face, handsome, and red in hue.
A worthy woman all her life, what's more
She'd had five husbands, all at the church door,
Apart from other company in youth;
No need just now to speak of that, forsooth.
And she had thrice been to Jerusalem,
Seen many strange rivers and passed over them;
She's been to Rome and also to Boulogne,
St James of Compostella and Cologne,

And she was skilled in wandering by the way.
She had gap-teeth, set widely, truth to say.
Easily on an ambling horse she sat
Well wimpled up, and on her head a hat
As broad as is a buckler or a shield;
She had a flowing mantle that concealed
Large hips, her heels spurred sharply under that.
In company she liked to laugh and chat
And knew the remedies for love's mischances,
An art in which she knew the oldest dances.
 A holy-minded man of good renown
There was, and poor, the *Parson* to a town,
Yet he was rich in holy thought and work.
He also was a learned man, a clerk,
Who truly knew Christ's gospel and would preach it
Devoutly to parishioners, and teach it.
Benign and wonderfully diligent,
And patient when adversity was sent
(For so he proved in much adversity)
He hated cursing to extort a fee,
Nay rather he preferred beyond a doubt
Giving to poor parishioners round about
Both from church offerings and his property;
He could in little find sufficiency.
Wide was his parish, with houses far asunder,
Yet he neglected not in rain or thunder,
In sickness or in grief, to pay a call
On the remotest, whether great or small,
Upon his feet, and in his hand a stave.
This noble example to his sheep he gave
That first he wrought, and afterwards he taught;
And it was from the Gospel he had caught
Those words, and he would add this figure too,
That if gold rust, what then will iron do?
For if a priest be foul in whom we trust
No wonder that a common man should rust;
And shame it is to see—let priests take stock—
A shitten shepherd and a snowy flock.
The true example that a priest should give
Is one of cleanness, how the sheep should live.
He did not set his benefice to hire
And leave his sheep encumbered in the mire
Or run to London to earn easy bread
By singing masses for the wealthy dead,
Or find some Brotherhood and get enrolled.
He stayed at home and watched over his fold
So that no wolf should make the sheep miscarry.
He was a shepherd and no mercenary.
Holy and virtuous he was, but then
Never contemptuous of sinful men,
Never disdainful, never too proud or fine,
But was discreet in teaching and benign.
His business was to show a fair behaviour
And draw men thus to Heaven and their Saviour,
Unless indeed a man were obstinate;
And such, whether of high or low estate,
He put to sharp rebuke, to say the least.
I think there never was a better priest.
He sought no pomp or glory in his dealings,
No scrupulosity had spiced his feelings.

Christ and His Twelve Apostles and their lore
He taught, but followed it himself before.
　There was a *Plowman* with him there, his brother;
Many a load of dung one time or other
He must have carted through the morning dew.
He was an honest worker, good and true,
Living in peace and perfect charity,
And, as the gospel bade him, so did he,
Loving God best with all his heart and mind
And then his neighbour as himself, repined
At no misfortune, slacked for no content,
For steadily about his work he went
To thrash his corn, to dig or to manure
Or make a ditch; and he would help the poor
For love of Christ and never take a penny
If he could help it, and, as prompt as any,
He paid his tithes in full when they were due
On what he owned, and on his earnings too.
He wore a tabard smock and rode a mare.
　There was a *Reeve*, also a *Miller*, there,
A College *Manciple* from the Inns of Court,
A papal *Pardoner* and, in close consort,
A Church-Court *Summoner*, riding at a trot,
And finally myself—that was the lot.
　The *Miller* was a chap of sixteen stone,
A great stout fellow big in brawn and bone.
He did well out of them, for he could go
And win the ram at any wrestling show.
Broad, knotty and short-shouldered, he would boast
He could heave any door off hinge and post,
Or take a run and break it with his head.
His beard, like any sow or fox, was red
And broad as well, as though it were a spade;
And, at its very tip, his nose displayed
A wart on which there stood a tuft of hair
Red as the bristles in an old sow's ear.
His nostrils were as black as they were wide.
He had a sword and buckler at his side,
His mighty mouth was like a furnace door.
A wrangler and buffoon, he had a store
Of tavern stories, filthy in the main.
His was a master-hand at stealing grain.
He felt it with his thumb and thus he knew
Its quality and took three times his due—
A thumb of gold, by God, to gauge an oat!
He wore a hood of blue and a white coat.
He liked to play his bagpipes up and down
And that was how he brought us out of town.
　The *Manciple* came from the Inner Temple;
All caterers might follow his example
In buying victuals; he was never rash
Whether he bought on credit or paid cash.
He used to watch the market most precisely
And got in first, and so he did quite nicely.
Now isn't it a marvel of God's grace
That an illiterate fellow can outpace
The wisdom of a heap of learned men?
His masters—he had more than thirty then—
All versed in the abstrusest legal knowledge,
Could have produced a dozen from their College

Fit to be stewards in land and rents and game
To any Peer in England you could name,
And show him how to live on what he had
Debt-free (unless of course the Peer were mad)
Or be as frugal as he might desire,
And make them fit to help about the Shire
In any legal case there was to try;
And yet this Manciple could wipe their eye.
　The *Reeve* was old and choleric and thin;
His beard was shaven closely to the skin,
His shorn hair came abruptly to a stop
Above his ears, and he was docked on top
Just like a priest in front; his legs were lean,
Like sticks they were, no calf was to be seen.
He kept his bins and garners very trim;
No auditor could gain a point on him.
And he could judge by watching drought and rain
The yield he might expect from seed and grain.
His master's sheep, his animals and hens,
Pigs, horses, dairies, stores and cattle-pens
Were wholly trusted to his government.
He had been under contract to present
The accounts, right from his master's earliest years.
No one had ever caught him in arrears.
No bailiff, serf or herdsman dared to kick,
He knew their dodges, knew their every trick;
Feared like the plague he was, by those beneath.
He had a lovely dwelling on a heath,
Shadowed in green by trees above the sward.
A better hand at bargains than his lord,
He had grown rich and had a store of treasure
Well tucked away, yet out it came to pleasure
His lord with subtle loans or gifts of goods,
To earn his thanks and even coats and hoods.
When young he'd learnt a useful trade and still
He was a carpenter of first-rate skill.
The stallion-cob he rode at a slow trot
Was dapple-grey and bore the name of Scot.
He wore an overcoat of bluish shade
And rather long; he had a rusty blade
Slung at his side. He came, as I heard tell,
From Norfolk, near a place called Baldeswell.
His coat was tucked under his belt and splayed.
He rode the hindmost of our cavalcade.
　There was a *Summoner* with us at that Inn,
His face on fire, like a cherubin,
For he had carbuncles. His eyes were narrow,
He was as hot and lecherous as a sparrow.
Black scabby brows he had, and a thin beard.
Children were afraid when he appeared.
No quicksilver, lead ointment, tartar creams,
No brimstone, no boracic, so it seems,
Could make a salve that had the power to bite,
Clean up or cure his whelks of knobby white
Or purge the pimples sitting on his cheeks.
Garlic he loved, and onions too, and leeks,
And drinking strong red wine till all was hazy.
Then he would shout and jabber as if crazy,
And wouldn't speak a word except in Latin
When he was drunk, such tags as he was pat in;

He had only a few, say two or three,
That he had mugged up out of some decree;
No wonder, for he heard them every day.
And, as you know, a man can teach a jay
To call out 'Walter' better than the Pope.
But had you tried to test his wits and grope
For more, you'd have found nothing in the bag.
Then '*Questio quid juris*' was his tag.
He was a noble varlet and a kind one,
You'd meet none better if you went to find one.
Why, he'd allow—just for a quart of wine—
Any good lad to keep a concubine
A twelvemonth and dispense him altogether!
And he had finches of his own to feather:
And if he found some rascal with a maid
He would instruct him not to be afraid
In such a case of the Archdeacon's curse
(Unless the rascal's soul were in his purse)
For in his purse the punishment should be.
'Purse is the good Archdeacon's Hell,' said he.
But well I know he lied in what he said;
A curse should put a guilty man in dread,
For curses kill, as shriving brings, salvation.
We should beware of excommunication.
Thus, as he pleased, the man could bring duress
On any young fellow in the diocese.
He knew their secrets, they did what he said.
He wore a garland set upon his head
Large as the holly-bush upon a stake
Outside an ale-house, and he had a cake,
A round one, which it was his joke to wield
As if it were intended for a shield.

  He and a gentle *Pardoner* rode together,
A bird from Charing Cross of the same feather,
Just back from visiting the Court of Rome.
He loudly sang '*Come hither, love, come home!*'
The Summoner sang deep seconds to this song,
No trumpet ever sounded half so strong.
This Pardoner had hair as yellow as wax,
Hanging down smoothly like a hank of flax.
In driblets fell his locks behind his head
Down to his shoulders which they overspread;
Thinly they fell, like rat-tails, one by one.
He wore no hood upon his head, for fun;
The hood inside his wallet had been stowed,
He aimed at riding in the latest mode;
But for a little cap his head was bare
And he had bulging eye-balls, like a hare.
He'd sewed a holy relic on his cap;
His wallet lay before him on his lap,
Brimful of pardons come from Rome, all hot.
He had the same small voice a goat has got.
His chin no beard had harboured, nor would harbour,
Smoother than ever chin was left by barber.
I judge he was a gelding, or a mare.

As to his trade, from Berwick down to Ware
There was no pardoner of equal grace,
For in his trunk he had a pillow-case
Which he asserted was Our Lady's veil.
He said he had a gobbet of the sail
Saint Peter had the time when he made bold
To walk the waves, till Jesu Christ took hold.
He had a cross of metal set with stones
And, in a glass, a rubble of pigs' bones.
And with these relics, any time he found
Some poor up-country parson to astound,
In one short day, in money down, he drew
More than the parson in a month or two,
And by his flatteries and prevarication
Made monkeys of the priest and congregation.
But still to do him justice first and last
In church he was a noble ecclesiast.
How well he read a lesson or told a story!
But best of all he sang an Offertory,
For well he knew that when that song was sung
He'd have to preach and tune his honey-tongue
And (well he could) win silver from the crowd.
That's why he sang so merrily and loud.

  Now I have told you shortly, in a clause,
The rank, the array, the number and the cause
Of our assembly in this company
In Southwark, at that high-class hostelry
Known as *The Tabard*, close beside *The Bell*.
And now the time has come for me to tell
How we behaved that evening; I'll begin
After we had alighted at the Inn,
Then I'll report our journey, stage by stage,
All the remainder of our pilgrimage.
But first I beg of you, in courtesy,
Not to condemn me as unmannerly
If I speak plainly and with no concealings
And give account of all their words and dealings,
Using their very phrases as they fell.
For certainly, as you all know so well,
He who repeats a tale after a man
Is bound to say, as nearly as he can,
Each single word, if he remembers it,
However rudely spoken or unfit,
Or else the tale he tells will be untrue,
The things pretended and the phrases new.
He may not flinch although it were his brother,
He may as well say one word as another.
And Christ Himself spoke broad in Holy Writ,
Yet there is no scurrility in it,
And Plato says, for those with power to read,
'The word should be as cousin to the deed.'
Further I beg you to forgive it me
If I neglect the order and degree
And what is due to rank in what I've planned.
I'm short of wit as you will understand. . . .

The Wife of Bath's Tale

When good King Arthur ruled in ancient days,
(A king that every Briton loves to praise.)
This was a land brim-full of fairy folk.
The Elf-Queen and her courtiers joined and broke
Their elfin dance on many a green mead,
Or so was the opinion once, I read,
Hundreds of years ago, in days of yore.
But no one now sees fairies any more,
For now the saintly charity and prayer
Of holy friars seem to have purged the air;
They search the countryside through field and stream
As thick as motes that speckle a sun-beam,
Blessing the halls, the chambers, kitchens, bowers,
Cities and boroughs, castles, courts and towers,
Thorpes, barns and stables, outhouses and dairies,
And that's the reason why there are no fairies.
Wherever there was wont to walk an elf
To-day there walks the holy friar himself
As evening falls or when the daylight springs,
Saying his mattins and his holy things,
Walking his limit round from town to town.
Women can now go safely up and down.
By every bush or under every tree;
There is no other incubus but he,
So there is really no one else to hurt you
And he will do no more than take your virtue.

Now it so happened, I began to say,
Long, long ago in good King Arthur's day,
There was a knight who was a lusty liver.
One day as he came riding from the river
He saw a maiden walking all forlorn
Ahead of him, alone as she was born.
And of that maiden, spite of all she said,
By very force he took her maidenhead.

This act of violence made such a stir,
So much petitioning of the king for her,
That he condemned the knight to lose his head
By course of law. He was as good as dead
(It seems that then the statutes took that view)
But that the queen, and other ladies too,
Implored the king to exercise his grace
So ceaselessly, he gave the queen the case
And granted her his life, and she could choose
Whether to show him mercy or refuse.

The queen returned him thanks with all her might,
And then she sent a summons to the knight
At her convenience, and expressed her will:
'You stand, for such is the position still,
In no way certain of your life,' said she,
'Yet you shall live if you can answer me:
What is the thing that women most desire?
Beware the axe and say as I require.

'If you can't answer on the moment, though,
I will concede you this: you are to go
A twelvemonth and a day to seek and learn
Sufficient answer, then you shall return.
I shall take gages from you to extort
Surrender of your body to the court.'

Sad was the knight and sorrowfully sighed,
But there! All other choices were denied,
And in the end he chose to go away
And to return after a year and day
Armed with such answer as there might be sent
To him by God. He took his leave and went.

He knocked at every house, searched every place,
Yes, anywhere that offered hope of grace.
What could it be that women wanted most?
But all the same he never touched a coast,
Country or town in which there seemed to be
Any two people willing to agree.

Some said that women wanted wealth and treasure,
'Honour,' said some, some 'Jollity and pleasure,'
Some 'Gorgeous clothes' and others 'Fun in bed,'
'To be oft widowed and remarried,' said
Others again, and some that what most mattered
Was that we should be cosseted and flattered.
That's very near the truth, it seems to me;
A man can win us best with flattery.
To dance attendance on us, make a fuss,
Ensnares us all, the best and worst of us.

Some say the things we most desire are these:
Freedom to do exactly as we please,
With no one to reprove our faults and lies,
Rather to have one call us good and wise.
Truly there's not a woman in ten score
Who has a fault, and someone rubs the sore,
But she will kick if what he says is true;
You try it out and you will find so too.
However vicious we may be within
We like to be thought wise and void of sin.
Others assert we women find it sweet
When we are thought dependable, discreet
And secret, firm of purpose and controlled,
Never betraying things that we are told.
But that's not worth the handle of a rake;
Women conceal a thing? For Heaven's sake!
Remember Midas? Will you hear the tale?

Among some other little things, now stale,
Ovid relates that under his long hair
The unhappy Midas grew a splendid pair
Of ass's ears; as subtly as he might,
He kept his foul deformity from sight;
Save for his wife, there was not one that knew.
He loved her best, and trusted in her too.

He begged her not to tell a living creature
That he possessed so horrible a feature.
And she—she swore, were all the world to win,
She would not do such villainy and sin
As saddle her husband with so foul a name;
Besides to speak would be to share the shame.
Nevertheless she thought she would have died
Keeping this secret bottled up inside;
It seemed to swell her heart and she, no doubt,
Thought it was on the point of bursting out.

Fearing to speak of it to woman or man,
Down to a reedy marsh she quickly ran
And reached the sedge. Her heart was all on fire
And, as a bittern bumbles in the mire,
She whispered to the water, near the ground,
'Betray me not, O water, with thy sound!
To thee alone I tell it: it appears
My husband has a pair of ass's ears!
Ah! My heart's well again, the secret's out!
I could no longer keep it, not a doubt.'
And so you see, although we may hold fast
A little while, it must come out at last,
We can't keep secrets; as for Midas, well,
Read Ovid for his story; he will tell.

This knight that I am telling you about
Perceived at last he never would find out
What it could be that women loved the best.
Faint was the soul within his sorrowful breast
As home he went, he dared no longer stay;
His year was up and now it was the day.

As he rode home in a dejected mood,
Suddenly, at the margin of a wood,
He saw a dance upon the leafy floor
Of four and twenty ladies, nay, and more.
Eagerly he approached, in hope to learn
Some words of wisdom ere he should return;
But lo! Before he came to where they were,
Dancers and dance all vanished into air!
There wasn't a living creature to be seen
Save one old woman crouched upon the green.
A fouler-looking creature I suppose
Could scarcely be imagined. She arose
And said, 'Sir knight, there's no way on from here.
Tell me what you are looking for, my dear,
For peradventure that were best for you;
We old, old women know a thing or two.'

'Dear Mother,' said the knight, 'alack the day!
I am as good as dead if I can't say
What thing it is that women most desire;
If you could tell me I would pay your hire.'
'Give me your hand,' she said, 'and swear to do
Whatever I shall next require of you
—If so to do should lie within your might—
And you shall know the answer before night.'
'Upon my honour,' he answered, 'I agree.'
'Then,' said the crone, 'I dare to guarantee
Your life is safe; I shall make good my claim.
Upon my life the queen will say the same.
Show me the very proudest of them all

In costly coverchief or jewelled caul
That dare say no to what I have to teach.
Let us go forward without further speech.'
And then she crooned her gospel in his ear
And told him to be glad and not to fear.

They came to court. This knight, in full array,
Stood forth and said, 'O Queen, I've kept my day
And kept my word and have my answer ready.'

There sat the noble matrons and the heady
Young girls, and widows too, that have the grace
Of wisdom, all assembled in that place,
And there the queen herself was throned to hear
And judge his answer. Then the knight drew near
And silence was commanded through the hall.

The queen then bade the knight to tell them all
What thing it was that women wanted most.
He stood not silent like a beast or post,
But gave his answer with the ringing word
Of a man's voice and the assembly heard:

'My liege and lady, in general,' said he,
'A woman wants the self-same sovereignty
Over her husband as over her lover,
And master him; he must not be above her.
That is your greatest wish, whether you kill
Or spare me; please yourself. I wait your will.'

In all the court not one that shook her head
Or contradicted what the knight had said;
Maid, wife and widow cried, 'He's saved his life!'

And on the word up started the old wife,
The one the knight saw sitting on the green,
And cried, 'Your mercy, sovereign lady queen!
Before the court disperses, do me right!
'Twas I who taught this answer to the knight,
For which he swore, and pledged his honour to it,
That the first thing I asked of him he'd do it,
So far as it should lie within his might.
Before this court I ask you then, sir knight,
To keep your word and take me for your wife;
For well you know that I have saved your life.
If this be false, deny it on your sword!'

'Alas!' he said, 'Old lady, by the Lord
I know indeed that such was my behest,
But for God's love think of a new request,
Take all my goods, but leave my body free.'
'A curse on us,' she said, 'if I agree!
I may be foul, I may be poor and old,
Yet will not choose to be, for all the gold
That's bedded in the earth or lies above,
Less than your wife, nay, than your very love!'

'My love?' said he. 'By Heaven, my damnation!
Alas that any of my race and station
Should ever make so foul a misalliance!'
Yet in the end his pleading and defiance
All went for nothing, he was forced to wed.
He takes his ancient wife and goes to bed.

Now peradventure some may well suspect
A lack of care in me since I neglect
To tell of the rejoicings and display
Made at the feast upon their wedding-day.

I have but a short answer to let fall;
I say there was no joy or feast at all,
Nothing but heaviness of heart and sorrow.
He married her in private on the morrow
And all day long stayed hidden like an owl,
It was such torture that his wife looked foul.
    Great was the anguish churning in his head
When he and she were piloted to bed;
He wallowed back and forth in desperate style.
His ancient wife lay smiling all the while;
At last she said 'Bless us! Is this, my dear,
How knights and wives get on together here?
Are these the laws of good King Arthur's house?
Are knights of his all so contemptuous?
I am your own beloved and your wife,
And I am she, indeed, that saved your life;
And certainly I never did you wrong.
Then why, this first of nights, so sad a song?
You're carrying on as if you were half-witted!
Say, for God's love, what sin have I committed?
I'll put things right if you will tell me how.'
    'Put right?' he cried. 'That never can be now!
Nothing can ever be put right again!
You're old, and so abominably plain,
So poor to start with, so low-bred to follow;
It's little wonder if I twist and wallow!
God, that my heart would burst within my breast!'
    'Is that,' said she, 'the cause of your unrest?'
    'Yes, certainly,' he said, 'and can you wonder?'
    'I could set right what you suppose a blunder,
That's if I cared to, in a day or two,
If I were shown more courtesy by you.
Just now,' she said, 'you spoke of gentle birth,
Such as descends from ancient wealth and worth.
If that's the claim you make for gentlemen
Such arrogance is hardly worth a hen.
Whoever loves to work for virtuous ends,
Public and private, and who most intends
To do what deeds of gentleness he can,
Take him to be the greatest gentleman.
Christ wills we take our gentleness from Him,
Not from a wealth of ancestry long dim,
Though they bequeath their whole establishment
By which we claim to be of high descent.
Our fathers cannot make us a bequest
Of all those virtues that became them best
And earned for them the name of gentleman,
But bade us follow them as best we can.
    'Thus the wise poet of the Florentines,
Dante by name, has written in these lines,
For such is the opinion Dante launches:
"Seldom arises by these slender branches
Prowess of men, for it is God, no less,
Wills us to claim of Him our gentleness."
For of our parents nothing can we claim
Save temporal things, and these may hurt and maim.
    'But everyone knows this as well as I;
For if gentility were implanted by
The natural course of lineage down the line,
Public or private, could it cease to shine

In doing the fair work of gentle deed?
No vice or villainy could then bear seed.
    'Take fire and carry it to the darkest house
Between this kingdom and the Caucasus,
And shut the doors on it and leave it there,
It will burn on, and it will burn as fair
As if ten thousand men were there to see,
For fire will keep its nature and degree,
I can assure you, sir, until it dies.
    'But gentleness, as you will recognize,
Is not annexed in nature to possessions,
Men fail in living up to their professions;
But fire never ceases to be fire.
God knows you'll often find, if you enquire,
Some lording full of villainy and shame.
If you would be esteemed for the mere name
Of having been by birth a gentleman
And stemming from some virtuous, noble clan,
And do not live yourself by gentle deed
Or take your fathers' noble code and creed,
You are no gentleman, though duke or earl.
Vice and bad manners are what make a churl.
    'Gentility is only the renown
For bounty that your fathers handed down,
Quite foreign to your person, not your own;
Gentility must come from God alone.
That we are gentle comes to us by grace
And by no means is it bequeathed with place.
    'Reflect how noble (says Valerius)
Was Tullius surnamed Hostilius,
Who rose from poverty to nobleness.
And read Boethius, Seneca no less,
Thus they express themselves and are agreed:
"Gentle is he that does a gentle deed."
And therefore, my dear husband, I conclude
That even if my ancestors were rude,
Yet God on high—and so I hope He will—
Can grant me grace to live in virtue still,
A gentlewoman only when beginning
To live in virtue and to shrink from sinning.
    'As for my poverty which you reprove,
Almighty God Himself in whom we move,
Believe and have our being, chose a life
Of poverty, and every man or wife
Nay, every child can see our Heavenly King
Would never stoop to choose a shameful thing.
No shame in poverty if the heart is gay,
As Seneca and all the learned say.
He who accepts his poverty unhurt
I'd say is rich although he lacked a shirt.
But truly poor are they who whine and fret
And covet what they cannot hope to get.
And he that, having nothing, covets not,
Is rich, though you may think he is a sot.
    'True poverty can find a song to sing.
Juvenal says a pleasant little thing:
"The poor can dance and sing in the relief
Of having nothing that will tempt a thief."
Though it be hateful, poverty is good,
A great incentive to a livelihood,

And a great help to our capacity
For wisdom, if accepted patiently.
Poverty is, though wanting in estate,
A kind of wealth that none calumniate.
Poverty often, when the heart is lowly,
Brings one to God and teaches what is holy,
Gives knowledge of oneself and even lends
A glass by which to see one's truest friends.
And since it's no offence, let me be plain;
Do not rebuke my poverty again.
   'Lastly you taxed me, sir, with being old.
Yet even if you never had been told
By ancient books, you gentlemen engage
Yourselves in honour to respect old age.
To call an old man "father" shows good breeding,
And this could be supported from my reading.
   'You say I'm old and fouler than a fen.
You need not fear to be a cuckold, then.
Filth and old age, I'm sure you will agree,
Are powerful wardens upon chastity.
Nevertheless, well knowing your delights,
I shall fulfil your worldly appetites.
   'You have two choices; which one will you try?
To have me old and ugly till I die,
But still a loyal, true and humble wife
That never will displease you all her life,
Or would you rather I were young and pretty
And chance your arm what happens in a city
Where friends will visit you because of me,
Yes, and in other places too, maybe.
Which would you have? The choice is all your own.'
   The knight thought long, and with a piteous groan
At last he said, with all the care in life,
'My lady and my love, my dearest wife,

I leave the matter to your wise decision.
You make the choice yourself, for the provision
Of what may be agreeable and rich
In honour to us both, I don't care which;
Whatever pleases you suffices me.'
   'And have I won the mastery?' said she,
'Since I'm to choose and rule as I think fit?'
'Certainly, wife,' he answered her, 'that's it.'
'Kiss me,' she cried. 'No quarrels! On my oath
And word of honour, you shall find me both,
That is, both fair and faithful as a wife;
May I go howling mad and take my life
Unless I prove to be as good and true
As ever wife was since the world was new!
And if to-morrow when the sun's above
I seem less fair than any lady-love,
Than any queen or empress east or west,
Do with my life and death as you think best.
Cast up the curtain, husband. Look at me!'
   And when indeed the knight had looked to see,
Lo, she was young and lovely, rich in charms.
In ecstasy he caught her in her arms,
His heart went bathing in a bath of blisses
And melted in a hundred thousand kisses,
And she responded in the fullest measure
With all that could delight or give him pleasure.
   So they lived ever after to the end
In perfect bliss; and may Christ Jesus send
Us husbands meek and young and fresh in bed,
And grace to overbid them when we wed.
And—Jesu hear my prayer!—cut short the lives
Of those who won't be governed by their wives;
And all old, angry niggards of their pence,
God send them soon a very pestilence!

from *Sir Gawain and the Green Knight*

VI

Erect stood the strong king, stately of mien,
Trifling time with talk before the topmost table.
Good Gawain was placed at Guinevere's side,
And Agravain of the Hard Hand sat on the other side,
Both the King's sister's sons, staunchest of knights.
Above, Bishop Baldwin began the board,
And Ywain, Urien's son, ate next to him.
These were disposed on the dais and with dignity
      served,
And many mighty men next, marshalled at side tables.
Then the first course came in with such cracking of
      trumpets,
(Whence bright bedecked blazons in banners hung)

Such din of drumming and a deal of fine piping,
Such wild warbles whelming in whirlpools of sound,
That hearts were uplifted high at the strains.
Then delicacies and dainties were delivered to the guests,
Fresh food in foison, such freight of full dishes
That space was scarce at the social tables
When the broth was brought in in bowls of silver
      To the cloth.
   Each feaster made free with the fare,
   Took lightly and nothing loth;
   Twelve plates were for every pair,
   Good beer and bright wine both.

VII

Of their meal I shall mention no more just now,
For it is evident to all that ample was served;
Near at hand the noise of a new fanfare
Gave the lords leave to lift food to their lips.
But barely had the blast of trump abated one minute
And the first course in the court been courteously
    served,
When there pressed in from the porch an appalling
    figure,
Who in height outstripped all earthly men.
From throat to thigh he was thickest and square;
His loins and limbs were so long and great

That he was half a giant on earth, I believe,
Yet mainly and most of all a man he seemed,
And the handsomest of horsemen, though huge, at that;
For though at back and at breast his body was broad,
His hips and haunches were elegant and small,
And perfectly proportioned were all parts of the man,
        As seen.
    Amazed at the hue of him,
    A foe with furious mien,
    Men gaped, for the giant grim
    Was coloured a gorgeous green.

VIII

And garments of green girt the fellow about—
A two-third length tunic, tight at the waist,
A comely cloak on top, accomplished with lining
Of the finest fur to be found, manifest to all,
Marvellous fur-trimmed material, with matching hood
Lying back from his locks and laid on his shoulders;
Fitly held-up hose, in hue the same green,
That was caught at the calf, with clinking spurs beneath
Of bright gold on bases of embroidered silk,
With shields for the shanks and shins when riding.
And verily his vesture was all vivid green,
So were the bars on his belt and the brilliants set
In ravishing array on his rich accoutrements.
It would be tedious to tell a tithe of the trifles
Embossed and embroidered, such as birds and flies,

In green gay and gaudy, with gold in the middle,
About himself and his saddle on silken work.
The breast-hangings of the horse, its haughty crupper,
The enamelled knobs and nails on its bridle,
And the stirrups that he stood on, were all stained with
    the same;
So were the saddle-bows and splendid tail-straps,
That ever glimmered and glinted with their green stones.
The steed that he spurred on was similar in hue
        To the sight,
    Green and huge of grain,
    Mettlesome in might
    And brusque with bit and rein—
    A steed to serve that knight!

IX

Yes, garbed all in green was the gallant rider.
His hair, like his horse in hue, hung light,
Clustering in curls like a cloak round his shoulders,
And a great bushy beard on his breast flowing down,
With the lovely locks hanging loose from his head,
Was shorn below the shoulder, sheared right round,

So that half his arms were under the encircling hair,
Covered as by a king's cape, that closes at the neck.
The mane of that mighty horse, much like the beard,
Well crisped and combed, was copiously plaited
With twists of twining gold, twinkling in the green,
First a green gossamer, a golden one next.

His flowing tail and forelock followed suit,
And both were bound with bands of bright green,
Ornamented to the end with exquisite stones,
While a thong running thwart threaded on high
Many bright golden bells, burnished and ringing.
Such a horse, such a horseman, in the whole wide world

Was never seen or observed by those assembled before,
    Not one.
Lightning-like he seemed
    And swift to strike and stun.
His dreadful blows, men deemed,
    Once dealt, meant death was done.

X

Yet hauberk and helmet had he none,
Nor plastron nor plate-armour proper to combat,
Nor shield for shoving, nor sharp spear for lunging;
But he held a holly cluster in one hand, holly
That is greenest when groves are gaunt and bare,
And an axe in his other hand, huge and monstrous,
An axe fell and fearsome, fit for a fable;
For fully forty inches frowned the head.
Its handle-base was hued in green, in hammered gold
    and steel.
The blade was burnished bright, with a broad edge,
Acutely honed for cutting, as keenest razors are.
The grim man gripped it by its great strong handle,
Which was wound with iron all the way to the end,
And graven in green with graceful designs.

A cord curved round it, was caught at the head,
Then hitched to the haft at intervals in loops,
With costly tassels attached thereto in plenty
On bosses of bright green embroidered richly.
In he rode, and up the hall, this man,
Pressing forward to the platform, no peril fearing.
He gave no one a greeting, but glared over all.
His opening utterance was, 'Who and where
Is the governor of this gathering? Gladly would I
Behold him with my eyes and have speech with him.'
    He frowned;
    He studied the standers-by
    And rolled his eye around,
    Essaying to espy
    The noble most renowned.

XI

The assembled folk stared, long scanning the man,
For all men marvelled what it might mean
That a chevalier and charger should achieve such a hue
As to grow green as grass, and greener yet, it seemed,
More gaudily glowing than green enamel on gold.
The people pondered him, in perplexity neared him,
With all the world's wonder as to what he would do.
For astonishing sights they had seen, but such a one never;
Therefore a phantom from Fairyland the folk there
    deemed him.

So even the doughty were daunted and dared not reply,
All standing stock-still, astounded by his voice.
Throughout the high hall was a hush like death;
Quiet suddenly descended, as if sleep had stolen them
    To rest;
    For some were still for fear,
    And others at honour's behest;
    But let him whom all revere
    Greet that gruesome guest.

XII

For Arthur sensed an exploit before the high dais,
And accorded him courteous greeting, no craven he,
Saying to him, 'Sir knight, you are certainly welcome.
I am king of this castle; I am called Arthur.
Please deign to dismount and dwell with us
Till you impart your purpose, at a proper time.'
'May He that sits in heaven help me,' said the knight,
'But my intention was not to tarry in this turreted hall.
But as your reputation, royal sir, stands in rare honour,
And your castle and cavaliers are accounted the best,
Your men the most mettlesome in mounted combat,
The most warlike, the worthiest the world has bred,
Most valiant to vie with in viril contests,
And as chivalry is shewn here, so I am assured,
My bent has brought me here now, I am bound to
      declare.

By this branch that I bear, you may be certain
That I proceed in peace, no peril seeking;
For had I fared forth in fighting gear,
My hauberk and helmet, both at home now,
My shield and sharp spear, all shining bright,
And other weapons to wield, I would have brought;
However, as I wish for no war here, I wear soft clothes.
But if you are as bold as brave men affirm,
You will gladly grant me the good sport I demand
      By right.'
      Then Arthur said to him
      In answer: 'Noble knight,
      If deadly duel's your whim,
      We'll fail you not in fight.'

XIII

'No, it is not combat I crave, for come to that,
There are only beardless boys at this banqueting board.
If I were hasped in armour on a high steed,
No man among you could catch me, your might being
      meagre.
Therefore in this court I crave a Christmas game,
For it is Yuletide and New Year, and young men abound
      here.
If any in this household is so hardy in spirit,
Of such mettlesome mind and so madly rash
As to strike a strong blow in return for another,
I shall offer to him this fine axe freely;
This axe, which is heavy enough, to handle as he please.

And I shall bide the first blow, as bare as I sit here.
If some intrepid man is tempted to try what I suggest,
Let him leap towards me and lay hold of this weapon,
Acquiring clear possession of it, no claim from me
      ensuing.
Then shall I stand up to his stroke, quite still on this
      floor—
So long as I shall have leave to launch a return blow
      Unchecked.
      Yet he shall have a year
      And a day's reprieve, I direct.
      Now hasten and let me hear
      Who answers, to what effect.'

XIV

If he had astonished them at the start, yet stiller now
Were the henchmen in hall of every rank.
The rider wrenched himself round in his saddle
And wrathfully rolled his red eyes about,
Bending on all his brows, bristling and green,
His beard swaying as he strained to see who would rise.
When none came to accord with him, he coughed aloud,
And hemmed heavily before uttering this:
'What, is this Arthur's house, the honour of which
Is bruited abroad so abundantly?
Has your pride disappeared? Your prowess gone?

Your victories, your valour, your vaunts, where are they?
The revel and renown of the Round Table
Is now overwhelmed by a word from one man's voice,
For all flinch for fear from a fight not begun!'
Upon this, he laughed so loudly that the lord grieved.
His fair face and features were suffused with blood
    For shame.
    He raged as roaring gale;
    His followers felt the shame.
    The King, not one to quail,
    To that cavalier then came.

XV

'By heaven,' then said Arthur, 'What you ask is foolish,
But as you firmly seek folly, find it you shall.
No good man here is aghast at your great words.
Hand me your axe now, for heaven's sake,
And I shall bestow the boon you bid us give.'
He leaped towards him lithely and laid hold of his hand,
And fiercely the other fellow footed the floor.
Now Arthur took his axe, holding the haft,
And swung it about sternly, as if to strike with it.
The bold man stood before him, big and tall,
Higher than any in the hall by a head and more.

He stroked his beard as he stood, stern of face,
Turning down his tunic in a tranquil manner,
Less unmanned and dismayed by the mighty strokes
Than if a banqueter at the bench had brought him a
    drink
    Of wine.
    Then Gawain at Guinevere's side
    Spoke to the King his design:
    'I beseech you fairly, confide
    This fight to me. May it be mine.'

XVI

'If you would grant, great lord,' said Gawain to the King,
'That I might stir from this seat and stand beside you,
Be allowed without lese-majesty to leave the table,
And if my liege lady would likewise allow it,
I should come there to counsel you before this court of nobles.
For it appears unmeet to me, as manners go,
When your hall hears uttered such a haughty request,
For your great self to go forward and gratify it,
When on the benches about you so many bold men sit,
The best-willed in the world, as I well believe,
And the finest in the field when the fight is joined.
I am the most wanting in wisdom, and the weakest, I know,

And loss of my life would be least, in truth.
My only asset is that my uncle is my king;
There is no blessing in my body but what your blood
    accords.
And since this affair is so foolish that it should not fall to you,
And I first asked it of you, make it over to me;
And if I speak dishonourably, may all the court judge
    Without blame.'
    Then wisely they whispered of it,
    And after, all said the same:
    That the crowned king should be quit,
    And Gawain given the game.

XVII

Then the King commanded the courtly knight to rise.
He directly uprose, made ready courteously,
Came to kneel to the King, and caught hold of the weapon.
Then Arthur happily handed it to him
And gave him God's blessing, and gladly urged him
To be strong in spirit and stout of sinew.
'Cousin, take care with your one cut,' then counselled
    the King,
'And if you strike home successfully, surely then
You will stand the return stroke he will strike afterwards!'
Gawain goes to the man, great axe in hand,
And boldly and unabashed abides the outcome.
Then the man garbed in green said to Gawain the noble,

'Let us affirm our pact freshly, before going farther.
I constrain you, knightly sir, to state your name;
Tell it me truly and trustworthily.'
'In good faith,' said the good knight, 'Gawain is my
    name,
And whatever happens after, I offer you this blow,
And in twelve months' time I shall take the return
With whatever weapon you wish, and without seconds
      To strive.'
   The other with pledge replied,
   'I'm the merriest man alive
   It's a blow from you I must bide,
   Sir Gawain, so may I thrive.'

XVIII

'By God,' said the Green Knight, 'Sir Gawain, I rejoice
That I shall meet from your mailed fist my demand here.
And you have gladly gone over, in good discourse,
The covenant I requested of the King in full,
Except that you shall assent, swearing in truth,
To seek me yourself, in such place as you think
To find me under the firmament, and fetch your
    payment
For what you deal me today before this dignified
    gathering.'
'How shall I hunt for you? How find your home?'
Said Gawain, 'By God that made me, I go in ignorance;
Nor, knight, do I know your name or your court.
But instruct me truly thereof, and tell me your name,
And my utmost effort shall urge me thither,

So I offer you my oath, on my honour as a knight.'
'That is enough this New Year, no more is needed,'
Said the gallant in green to Gawain the courteous,
'To tell you the truth, when I have taken the blow
After you have duly dealt it, I shall directly inform you
About my house and my home and my own name.
Then you may keep your covenant, and inquire how I do,
And if I waft you no words, then well may you prosper,
Stay long in your own land and look for no further
      Trial.
   Now grip your weapon grim;
   Let us see your fighting style.'
   'Gladly,' said Gawain to him,
   Stroking the steel the while.

XIX

On the ground the Green Knight graciously stood,
With head slightly slanting to expose the flesh.
His long and lovely locks he laid over his crown,
Neatly showing the naked neck, nape and all.
Gawain gripped his axe and gathered it on high,
Advanced the left foot before him on the ground,
And slashed swiftly down on the exposed part,
So that the sharp blade sheared through, shattering
    the bone,
Sank deep in the sleek flesh, split it in two,
And the scintillating steel struck the ground.
The fair head fell from the neck. On the floor it rolled,
So that people spurned and parried it as it passed
    their feet.
Then blood spurted from the body, bright against the
    green.

Yet the fellow did not fall, nor falter one whit,
But stoutly strode forward on legs still sturdy
To where the worthy knights stood, weirdly reached out,
Seized his splendid head and straightway lifted it.
Then he strode to his steed, snatched the bridle,
Stepped into the stirrup and swung aloft,
Holding his head by the hair in his hand.
He settled himself in the saddle as steadily
As if nothing had happened to him, though he had
        No head.
    He twisted his trunk about
    That gruesome body that bled;
    He caused much dread and doubt
    By the time his say was said.

XX

For he held the head in his hand upright,
Pointed the face at the fairest in fame on the dais;
And it lifted its eyelids and looked glaringly,
And menacingly said with its mouth as you may now
    hear:
'Be prepared to perform what you promised, Gawain;
Seek faithfully till you find me, my fine fellow,
According to your oath in this hall in these knights'
    hearing.
Go to the Green Chapel without gainsaying to get
—And gladly will it be given in the gleaming New Year—
Such a stroke as you have struck. Strictly you deserve it.
As the Knight of the Green Chapel I am known to many;

Therefore if you ask for me, I shall be found.
So come, or else be called coward accordingly!'
Then he savagely swerved, sawing at the reins,
Rushed out at the hall door, his head in his hand,
And the flint-struck fire flew up from the hooves.
What place he departed to no person there knew,
Nor could any account be given of the country he had
    come from.
        What then?
    At the Green Knight Gawain and King
    Grinned and laughed again;
    But plainly approved the thing
    As a marvel in the world of men.

CHRISTINE DE PIZAN
from *The Book of the City of Ladies*
Book I

1. Here Begins the Book of the City of Ladies, Whose First Chapter Tells Why and for What Purpose This Book Was Written.

One day as I was sitting alone in my study surrounded by books on all kinds of subjects, devoting myself to literary studies, my usual habit, my mind dwelt at length on the weighty opinions of various authors whom I had studied for a long time. I looked up from my book, having decided to leave such subtle questions in peace and to relax by reading some light poetry. With this in mind, I searched for some small book. By chance a strange volume came into my hands, not one of my own, but one which had been given to me along with some others. When I held it open and saw from its title page that it was by Mathéolus, I smiled, for though I had never seen it before, I had often heard that like other books it discussed respect for women. I thought I would browse through it to amuse myself. I had not been reading for very long when my good mother called me to refresh myself with some supper, for it was evening. Intending to look at it the next day, I put it down. The next morning, again seated in my study as was my habit, I remembered wanting to examine this book by Mathéolus. I started to read it and went on for a little while. Because the subject seemed to me not very pleasant for people who do not enjoy lies, and of no use in developing virtue or manners, given its lack of integrity in diction and theme, and after browsing here and there and reading the end, I put it down in order to turn my attention to more elevated and useful study. But just the sight of this book, even though it was of no authority, made me wonder how it happened that so many different men—and learned men among them—have been and are so inclined to express both in speaking and in their treatises and writings so many wicked insults about women and their behavior. Not only one or two and not even just this Mathéolus (for this book had a bad name anyway and was intended as a satire) but, more generally, judging from the treatises of all philosophers and poets and from all the orators—it would take too long to mention their names—it seems that they all speak from one and the same mouth. They all concur in one conclusion: that the behavior of women is inclined to and full of every vice. Thinking deeply about these matters, I began to examine my character and conduct as a natural woman and, similarly, I considered other women whose company I frequently kept, princesses, great ladies, women of the middle and lower classes, who had graciously told me of their most private and intimate thoughts, hoping that I could judge impartially and in good conscience whether the testimony of so many notable men could be true. To the best of my knowledge, no matter how long I confronted or dissected the problem, I could not see or realize how their claims could be true when compared to the natural behavior and character of women. Yet I still argued vehemently against women, saying that it would be impossible that so many famous men—such solemn scholars, possessed of such deep and great understanding, so clear-sighted in all things, as it seemed—could have spoken falsely on so many occasions that I could hardly find a book on morals where, even before I had read it in its entirety, I did not find several chapters or certain sections attacking women, no matter who the author was. This reason alone, in short, made me conclude that, although my intellect did not perceive my own great faults and, likewise, those of other women because of its simpleness and ignorance, it was however truly fitting that such was the case. And so I relied more on the judgment of others than on what I myself felt and knew. I was so transfixed in this line of thinking for such a long time that it seemed as if I were in a stupor. Like a gushing fountain, a series of authorities, whom I recalled one after another, came to mind, along with their opinions on this topic. And I finally decided that God formed a vile creature when He made woman, and I wondered how such a worthy artisan could have deigned to make such an abominable work which, from what they say, is the vessel as well as the refuge and abode of every evil and vice. As I was thinking this, a great unhappiness and sadness welled up in my heart, for I detested myself and the entire feminine sex, as though we were monstrosities in nature. And in my lament I spoke these words:

"Oh, God, how can this be? For unless I stray from my faith, I must never doubt that Your infinite wisdom and most perfect goodness ever created anything which was not good. Did You yourself not create woman in a very special way and since that time did You not give her all those inclinations which it pleased You for her to have? And how could it be that You could go wrong in anything? Yet look at all these accusations which have been judged, decided, and concluded against women. I do not know how to understand this repugnance. If it is so, fair Lord God, that in fact so many abominations abound in the female sex, for You Yourself say that the testimony of two or three witnesses lends credence, why shall I not doubt that this is true? Alas, God, why did You not let me be born in the world as a man, so that all my inclinations would be to serve You better, and so that I would not stray in anything and would be as perfect as a man is said to be? But since Your kindness has not been extended to me, then forgive my negligence in Your service, most fair Lord God, and may it not displease You, for the servant who receives fewer gifts from his lord is less obliged in his service."

I spoke these words to God in my lament and a great deal more for a very long time in sad reflection, and in my folly I considered myself most unfortunate because God had made me inhabit a female body in this world. . . .

27. Christine Asks Reason Whether God Has Ever Wished to Ennoble the Mind of Woman With the Loftiness of the Sciences; and Reason's Answer.

After hearing these things, I replied to the lady who spoke infallibly: "My lady, truly has God revealed great wonders in the strength of these women whom you describe. But please enlighten me again, whether it has ever pleased this God, who has bestowed so many favors on women, to honor the feminine sex with the privilege of the virtue of high understanding and great learning, and whether women ever have a clever enough mind for this. I wish very much to know this because men maintain that the mind of women can learn only a little."

She answered, "My daughter, since I told you before, you know quite well that the opposite of their opinion is true, and to show you this even more clearly, I will give you proof through examples. I tell you again—and don't doubt the contrary—if it were customary to send daughters to school like sons, and if they were then taught the natural sciences, they would learn as thoroughly and understand the subtleties of all the arts and sciences as well as sons. And by chance there happen to be such women, for, as I touched on before, just as women have more delicate bodies than men, weaker and less able to perform many tasks, so do they have minds that are freer and sharper whenever they apply themselves."

"My lady, what are you saying? With all due respect, could you dwell longer on this point, please. Certainly men would never admit this answer is true, unless it is explained more plainly, for they believe that one normally sees that men know more than women do."

She answered, "Do you know why women know less?"

"Not unless you tell me, my lady."

"Without the slightest doubt, it is because they are not involved in many different things, but stay at home, where it is enough for them to run the household, and there is nothing which so instructs a reasonable creature as the exercise and experience of many different things."

"My lady, since they have minds skilled in conceptualizing and learning, just like men, why don't women learn more?"

She replied, "Because, my daughter, the public does not require them to get involved in the affairs which men are commissioned to execute, just as I told you before. It is enough for women to perform the usual duties to which they are ordained. As for judging from experience, since one sees that women usually know less than men, that therefore their capacity for understanding is less, look at men who farm the flatlands or who live in the mountains. You will find that in many countries they seem completely savage because they are so simple-minded. All the same, there is no doubt that Nature provided them with the qualities of body and mind found in the wisest and most learned men. All of this stems from a failure to learn, though, just as I told you, among men and women, some possess better minds than others. Let me tell you about women who have possessed great learning and profound understanding and treat the question of the similarity of women's minds to men's."

30. Here She Speaks of Sappho, That Most Subtle Woman, Poet, and Philosopher.

"The wise Sappho, who was from the city of Mytilene, was no less learned than Proba. This Sappho had a beautiful body and face and was agreeable and pleasant in appearance, conduct, and speech. But the charm of her profound understanding surpassed all the other charms with which she was endowed, for she was expert and learned in several arts and sciences, and she was not only well-educated in the works and writings composed by others but also discovered many new things herself and wrote many books and poems. Concerning her, Boccaccio has offered these fair words couched in the sweetness of poetic language: 'Sappho, possessed of sharp wit and burning desire for constant study in the midst of bestial and ignorant men, frequented the heights of Mount Parnassus, that is, of perfect study. Thanks to her fortunate boldness and daring, she kept company with the Muses, that is, the arts and sciences, without being turned away. She entered the forest of laurel trees filled with may boughs, greenery, and different colored flowers, soft fragrances and various aromatic spices, where Grammar, Logic, noble Rhetoric, Geometry, and Arithmetic live and take their leisure. She went on her way until she came to the deep grotto of Apollo, god of learning, and found the brook and conduit of the fountain of Castalia, and took up the plectrum and quill of the harp and played sweet melodies, with the nymphs all the while leading the dance, that is, following the rules of harmony and musical accord.' From what Boccaccio says about her, it should be inferred that the profundity of both her understanding and of her learned books could only be known and understood by men of great perception and learning, according to the testimony of the ancients. Her writings and poems have survived to this day, most remarkably constructed and composed, and they serve as illumination and models of consummate poetic craft and composition to those who have come afterward. She invented different genres of lyric and poetry, short narratives, tearful laments and strange lamentations about love and other emotions, and these were so well made and so well ordered that they were named 'Sapphic' after her. Horace recounts, concerning her poems, that when Plato, the great philosopher who was Aristotle's teacher, died, a book of Sappho's poems was found under his pillow.

"In brief this lady was so outstanding in learning that in the city where she resided a statue of bronze in her image was dedicated in her name and erected in a prominent place so that she would be honored by all and be remembered forever. This lady was placed and counted among the greatest and most famous poets, and, according to Boccaccio, the honors of the diadems and crowns of kings and the miters of bishops are not any greater, nor are the crowns of laurel and victor's palm.

"I could tell you a great deal about women of great learning. Leontium was a Greek woman and also such a great philosopher that she dared, for impartial and serious reasons, to correct and attack the philosopher Theophrastus, who was quite famous in her time."

34. Here She Speaks of Minerva, Who Invented Many Sciences and the Technique of Making Armor from Iron and Steel.

"Minerva, just as you have written elsewhere, was a maiden of Greece and surnamed Pallas. This maiden was of such excellence of mind that the foolish people of that time, because they did not know who her parents were and saw her doing things which had never been done before, said she was a goddess descended from Heaven; for the less they knew about her ancestry, the more marvelous her great knowledge seemed to them, when compared to that of the women of her time. She had a subtle mind, of profound understanding, not only in one subject but also generally, in every subject. Through her ingenuity she invented a shorthand Greek script in which a long written narrative could be transcribed with far fewer letters, and which is still used by the Greeks today, a fine invention whose discovery demanded great subtlety. She invented numbers and a means of quickly counting and adding sums. Her mind was so enlightened with general knowledge that she devised various skills and designs which had never before been discovered. She developed the entire technique of gathering wool and making cloth and was the first who ever thought to shear sheep of their wool and then to pick, comb, and card it with iron spindles and finally to spin it with a distaff, and then she invented the tools needed to make the cloth and also the method by which the wool should finally be woven.

"Similarly she initiated the custom of extracting oil from different fruits of the earth, also from olives, and of squeezing and pressing juice from other fruits. At the same time she discovered how to make wagons and carts to transport things easily from one place to another.

"This lady, in a similar manner, did even more, and it seems all the more remarkable because it is far removed from a woman's nature to conceive of such things; for she invented the art and technique of making harnesses and armor from iron and steel, which knights and armed soldiers employ in battle and with which they cover their bodies, and which she first gave to the Athenians whom she taught how to deploy an army and battalions and how to fight in organized ranks.

"Similarly she was the first to invent flutes and fifes, trumpets and wind instruments. With her considerable force of mind, this lady remained a virgin her entire life. Because of her outstanding chastity, the poets claimed in their fictions that Vulcan, the god of fire, wrestled with her for a long time and that finally she won and overcame him, which is to say that she overcame the ardor and lusts of the flesh which so strongly assail the young. The Athenians held this maiden in such high reverence that they worshiped her as a goddess and called her the goddess of arms and chivalry because she was the first to devise their use, and they also called her the goddess of knowledge because of her learnedness.

"After her death they erected a temple in Athens dedicated to her, and there they placed a statue of her, portraying a maiden, as a representation of wisdom and chivalry. This statue had terrible and cruel eyes because chivalry has been instituted to carry out rigorous justice; they also signified that one seldom knows toward what end the meditation of the wise man tends. She wore a helmet on her head which signified that a knight must have strength, endurance, and constant courage in the deeds of arms, and further signified that the counsels of the wise are concealed, secret, and hidden. She was dressed in a coat of mail which stood for the power of the estate of chivalry and also taught that the wise man is always armed against the whims of Fortune, whether good or bad. She held some kind of spear or very long lance, which meant that the knight must be the rod of justice and also signified that the wise man casts his spears from great distances. A buckler or shield of crystal hung at her neck, which meant that the knight must always be alert and oversee everywhere the defense of his country and people and further signified that things are open and evident to the wise man. She had portrayed in the middle of this shield the head of a serpent called Gorgon, which teaches that the knight must always be wary and watchful over his enemies like the serpent, and furthermore, that the wise man is aware of all the malice which can hurt him. Next to this image they also placed a bird that flies by night, named the owl, as if to watch over her, which signified that the knight must be ready by night as well as by day for civil defense, when necessary, and also that the wise man should take care at all times to do what is profitable and fitting for him. For a long time this lady was held in such high regard and her great fame spread so far that in many places temples were founded to praise her. Even long afterward, when the Romans were at the height of their power, they included her image among their gods."

Book II

---

36. Against Those Men Who Claim It Is Not Good for Women to Be Educated.

Following these remarks, I, Christine, spoke, "My lady, I realize that women have accomplished many good things and that even if evil women have done evil, it seems to me, nevertheless, that the benefits accrued and still accruing because of good women—particularly the wise and literary ones and those educated in the natural sciences whom I mentioned above—outweigh the evil. Therefore, I am amazed by the opinion of some men who claim that they do not want their daughters, wives, or kinswomen to be educated because their mores would be ruined as a result."

She responded, "Here you can clearly see that not all opinions of men are based on reason and that these men are wrong. For it must not be presumed that mores necessarily grow worse from knowing the moral sciences, which teach the virtues, indeed, there is not the slightest doubt that moral education amends and ennobles them. How could anyone think or believe that whoever follows good teaching or doctrine is the worse for it? Such an opinion cannot be expressed or maintained. I do not mean that it would be good for a man or a woman to study the art of divination or those fields of learning which are forbidden—for the holy Church did not remove them from common use without good reason—but it should not be believed that women are the worse for knowing what is good.

"Quintus Hortensius, a great rhetorician and consummately skilled orator in Rome, did not share this opinion. He had a daughter, named Hortensia, whom he greatly loved for the subtlety of her wit. He had her learn letters and study the science of rhetoric, which she mastered so thoroughly that she resembled her father Hortensius not only in wit and lively memory but also in her excellent delivery and order of speech—in fact, he surpassed her in nothing. As for the subject discussed above, concerning the good which comes about through women, the benefits realized by this woman and her learning were, among others, exceptionally remarkable. That is, during the time when Rome was governed by three men, this Hortensia began to support the cause of women and to undertake what no man dared to undertake. There was a question whether certain taxes should be levied on women and on their jewelry during a needy period in Rome. This woman's eloquence was so compelling that she was listened to, no less readily than her father would have been, and she won her case.

"Similarly, to speak of more recent times, without searching for examples in ancient history, Giovanni Andrea, a solemn law professor in Bologna not quite sixty years ago, was not of the opinion that it was bad for women to be educated. He had a fair and good daughter, named Novella, who was educated in the law to such an advanced degree that when he was occupied by some task and not at leisure to present his lectures to his students, he would send Novella, his daughter, in his place to lecture to the students from his chair. And to prevent her beauty from distracting the concentration of her audience, she had a little curtain drawn in front of her. In this manner she could on occasion supplement and lighten her father's occupation. He loved her so much that, to commemorate her name, he wrote a book of remarkable lectures on the law which he entitled *Novella super Decretalium*, after his daughter's name.

"Thus, not all men (and especially the wisest) share the opinion that it is bad for women to be educated. But it is very true that many foolish men have claimed this because it displeased them that women knew more than they did. Your father, who was a great scientist and philosopher, did not believe that women were worth less by knowing science; rather, as you know, he took great pleasure from seeing your inclination to learning. The feminine opinion of your mother, however, who wished to keep you busy with spinning and silly girlishness, following the common custom of women, was the major obstacle to your being more involved in the sciences. But just as the proverb already mentioned above says, 'No one can take away what Nature has given,' your mother could not hinder in you the feeling for the sciences which you, through natural inclination, had nevertheless gathered together in little droplets. I am sure that, on account of these things, you do not think you are worth less but rather that you consider it a great treasure for yourself; and you doubtless have reason to.'

And I, Christine, replied to all of this, "Indeed, my lady, what you say is as true as the Lord's Prayer."

Everyman

Cast of Characters

MESSENGER	KNOWLEDGE
GOD	CONFESSION
DEATH	BEAUTY
EVERYMAN	STRENGTH
FELLOWSHIP	DISCRETION
KINDRED	FIVE-WITS
COUSIN	ANGEL
GOODS	DOCTOR
GOOD DEEDS	

Here Beginneth a Treatise How the High Father of Heaven Sendeth Death to Summon Every Creature to Come and Give Account of Their Lives in This World, and Is in Manner of a Moral Play

[*Enter* MESSENGER.]

MESSENGER.   I pray you all give your audience,
  And hear this matter with reverence,
  By figure a moral play.
  The Summoning of Everyman called it is,
  That of our lives and ending shows
  How transitory we be all day.
  The matter is wonder precious,
  But the intent of it is more gracious
  And sweet to bear away.
  The story saith: Man, in the beginning
  Look well, and take good heed to the ending,
  Be you never so gay.
  You think sin in the beginning full sweet,
  Which in the end causeth the soul to weep,
  When the body lieth in clay.
  Here shall you see how fellowship and jollity,
  Both strength, pleasure, and beauty,
  Will fade from thee as flower in May.
  For ye shall hear how our Heaven-King
  Calleth Everyman to a general reckoning.
  Give audience and hear what he doth say.

[*Exit* MESSENGER—*Enter* GOD.]

GOD. I perceive, here in my majesty,
   How that all creatures be to me unkind,
   Living without dread in worldly prosperity.
   Of ghostly sight the people be so blind,
   Drowned in sin, they know me not for their God.
   In worldly riches is all their mind:
   They fear not of my righteousness the sharp rod;
   My law that I showed when I for them died
   They forget clean, and shedding of my blood red.
   I hanged between two, it cannot be denied:
   To get them life I suffered to be dead.
   I healed their feet, with thorns hurt was my head.
   I could do no more than I did, truly—
   And now I see the people do clean forsake me.
   They use the seven deadly sins damnable,
   As pride, coveitise, wrath, and lechery
   Now in the world be made commendable.
   And thus they leave of angels the heavenly company.
   Every man liveth so after his own pleasure,
   And yet of their life they be nothing sure.
   I see the more that I them forbear,
   The worse they be from year to year:
   All that liveth appaireth fast.
   Therefore I will, in all the haste,
   Have a reckoning of every man's person.
   For, and I leave the people thus alone
   In their life and wicked tempests,
   Verily they will become much worse than beasts;
   For now one would by envy another up eat.
   Charity do they all clean forget.
   I hoped well that every man
   In my glory should make his mansion,
   And thereto I had them all elect.
   But now I see, like traitors deject,
   They thank me not for the pleasure that I to them meant,
   Nor yet for their being that I them have lent.
   I proffered the people great multitude of mercy,
   And few there be that asketh it heartily.
   They be so cumbered with worldly riches
   That needs on them I must do justice—
   On every man living without fear.
   Where art thou, Death, thou mighty messenger?

[*Enter* DEATH.]

DEATH. Almighty God, I am here at your will,
   Your commandment to fulfill.
GOD. Go thou to Everyman,
   And show him, in my name,
   A pilgrimage he must on him take,
   Which he in no wise may escape;
   And that he bring with him a sure reckoning
   Without delay or any tarrying.
DEATH. Lord, I will in the world go run over all,
   And cruelly out-search both great and small.

[*Exit* GOD.]

Everyman will I beset that liveth beastly
Out of God's laws, and dreadeth not folly.
He that loveth riches I will strike with my dart,
His sight to blind, and from heaven to depart—
Except that Almsdeeds be his good friend—
In hell for to dwell, world without end.
Lo, yonder I see Everyman walking:
Full little he thinketh on my coming;
His mind is on fleshly lusts and his treasure,
And great pain it shall cause him to endure
Before the Lord, Heaven-King.

[*Enter* EVERYMAN.]

   Everyman, stand still! Whither art thou going
   Thus gaily? Hast thou thy Maker forgeet?
EVERYMAN. Why askest thou?
   Why wouldest thou weet?
DEATH. Yea, sir, I will show you:
   In great haste I am sent to thee
   From God out of his majesty.
EVERYMAN. What! sent to me?
DEATH. Yea, certainly.
   Though thou have forgot him here,
   He thinketh on thee in the heavenly sphere,
   As, ere we depart, thou shalt know.
EVERYMAN. What desireth God of me?
DEATH. That shall I show thee:
   A reckoning he will needs have
   Without any longer respite.
EVERYMAN. To give a reckoning longer leisure I crave.
   This blind matter troubleth my wit.
DEATH. On thee thou must take a long journey:
   Therefore thy book of count with thee thou bring,
   For turn again thou cannot by no way.
   And look thou be sure of thy reckoning,
   For before God thou shalt answer and shew
   Thy many bad deeds and good but a few—
   How thou hast spent thy life and in what wise,
   Before the Chief Lord of Paradise.
   Have ado that we were in that way,
   For weet thou well thou shalt make none attornay.
EVERYMAN. Full unready I am such reckoning to give.
   I know thee not. What messenger art thou?
DEATH. I am Death that no man dreadeth,
   For every man I 'rest, and no man spareth;
   For it is God's commandment
   That all to me should be obedient.
EVERYMAN. O Death, thou comest when I had thee least
   in mind.
   In thy power it lieth me to save:
   Yet of my good will I give thee, if thou will be kind,
   Yea, a thousand pound shalt thou have—
   And defer this matter till another day.
DEATH. Everyman, it may not be, by no way.
   I set nought by gold, silver, nor riches,
   Nor by pope, emperor, king, duke, nor princes,
   For, and I would receive gifts great,

All the world I might get.
But my custom is clean contrary:
I give thee no respite. Come hence and not tarry!
EVERYMAN. Alas, shall I have no longer respite?
I may say Death giveth no warning.
To think on thee it maketh my heart sick,
For all unready is my book of reckoning.
But twelve year and I might have a biding,
My counting-book I would make so clear
That my reckoning I should not need to fear.
Wherefore, Death, I pray thee, for God's mercy,
Spare me till I be provided of remedy.
DEATH. Thee availeth not to cry, weep, and pray;
But haste thee lightly that thou were gone that journay,
And prove thy friends, if thou can.
For weet thou well the tide abideth no man,
And in the world each living creature
For Adam's sin must die of nature.
EVERYMAN. Death, if I should this pilgrimage take
And my reckoning surely make,
Show me, for saint charity,
Should I not come again shortly?
DEATH. No, Everyman. And thou be once there,
Thou mayst never more come here,
Trust me verily.
EVERYMAN. O gracious God in the high seat celestial,
Have mercy on me in this most need!
Shall I have company from this vale terrestrial
Of mine acquaintance that way me to lead?
DEATH. Yea, if any be so hardy
That would go with thee and bear thee company.
Hie thee that thou were gone to God's magnificence,
Thy reckoning to give before his presence.
What, weenest thou thy life is given thee,
And thy worldly goods also?
EVERYMAN. I had weened so, verily.
DEATH. Nay, nay, it was but lent thee.
For as soon as thou art go,
Another a while shall have it and then go therefro,
Even as thou hast done.
Everyman, thou art mad! Thou hast thy wits five,
And here on earth will not amend thy live!
For suddenly I do come.
EVERYMAN. O wretched caitiff! Whither shall I flee
That I might 'scape this endless sorrow?
Now, gentle Death, spare me till tomorrow,
That I may amend me
With good advisement.
DEATH. Nay, thereto I will not consent,
Nor no man will I respite,
But to the heart suddenly I shall smite,
Without any advisement.
And now out of thy sight I will me hie:
See thou make thee ready shortly,
For thou mayst say this is the day
That no man living may 'scape away.

[*Exit* DEATH.]

EVERYMAN. Alas, I may well weep with sighs deep:
Now have I no manner of company
To help me in my journey and me to keep.
And also my writing is full unready—
How shall I do now for to excuse me?
I would to God I had never be geet!
To my soul a full great profit it had be.
For now I fear pains huge and great.
The time passeth: Lord, help, that all wrought!
For though I mourn, it availeth nought.
The day passeth and is almost ago:
I wot not well what for to do.
To whom were I best my complaint to make?
What and I to Fellowship thereof spake,
And showed him of this sudden chance?
For in him is all mine affiance,
We have in the world so many a day
Be good friends in sport and play.
I see him yonder, certainly.
I trust that he will bear me company.
Therefore to him will I speak to ease my sorrow.

[*Enter* FELLOWSHIP.]

Well met, good Fellowship, and good morrow!
FELLOWSHIP. Everyman, good morrow, by this day!
Sir, why lookest thou so piteously?
If anything be amiss, I pray thee me say,
That I may help to remedy.
EVERYMAN. Yea, good Fellowship, yea:
I am in great jeopardy.
FELLOWSHIP. My true friend, show to me your mind.
I will not forsake thee to my life's end
In the way of good company.
EVERYMAN. That was well spoken, and lovingly!
FELLOWSHIP. Sir, I must needs know your heaviness.
I have pity to see you in any distress.
If any have you wronged, ye shall revenged be,
Though I on the ground be slain for thee,
Though that I know before that I should die.
EVERYMAN. Verily, Fellowship, gramercy.
FELLOWSHIP. Tush! by thy thanks I set not a stree.
Show me your grief and say no more.
EVERYMAN. If I my heart should to you break,
And then you to turn your mind fro me,
And would not me comfort when ye hear me speak,
Then should I ten times sorrier be.
FELLOWSHIP. Sir, I say as I will do, indeed.
EVERYMAN. Then be you a good friend at need.
I have found you true herebefore.
FELLOWSHIP. And so ye shall evermore.
For, in faith, and thou go to hell,
I will not forsake thee by the way.
EVERYMAN. Ye speak like a good friend. I believe you well.
I shall deserve it, and I may.
FELLOWSHIP. I speak of no deserving, by this day!
For he that will say and nothing do
Is not worthy with good company to go.
Therefore show me the grief of your mind,

As to your friend most loving and kind.

EVERYMAN.   I shall show you how it is:
Commanded I am to go a journay,
A long way, hard and dangerous,
And give a strait count, without delay,
Before the high judge Adonai.
Wherefore I pray you bear me company,
As ye have promised, in this journey.

FELLOWSHIP.   This is matter indeed! Promise is duty—
But, and I should take such a voyage on me,
I know it well, it should be to my pain.
Also it maketh me afeard, certain.
But let us take counsel here, as well as we can—
For your words would fear a strong man.

EVERYMAN.   Why, ye said if I had need,
Ye would me never forsake, quick ne dead,
Though it were to hell, truly.

FELLOWSHIP.   So I said, certainly,
But such pleasures be set aside, the sooth to say.
And also, if we took such a journey,
When should we again come?

EVERYMAN.   Nay, never again, till the day of doom.

FELLOWSHIP.   In faith, then will not I come there!
Who hath you these tidings brought?

EVERYMAN.   Indeed, Death was with me here.

FELLOWSHIP.   Now by God that all hath bought,
If Death were the messenger,
For no man that is living today
I will not go that loath journay—
Not for the father that begat me!

EVERYMAN.   Ye promised otherwise, pardie.

FELLOWSHIP.   I wot well I said so, truly.
And yet, if thou wilt eat and drink and make good
cheer,
Or haunt to women the lusty company,
I would not forsake you while the day is clear,
Trust me verily!

EVERYMAN.   Yea, thereto ye would be ready—
To go to mirth, solace, and play:
Your mind to folly will sooner apply
Than to bear me company in my long journey.

FELLOWSHIP.   Now in good faith, I will not that way.
But, and thou will murder or any man kill,
In that I will help thee with a good will.

EVERYMAN.   O that is simple advice, indeed!
Gentle fellow, help me in my necessity:
We have loved long, and now I need—
And now, gentle Fellowship, remember me!

FELLOWSHIP.   Whether ye have loved me or no,
By Saint John, I will not with thee go!

EVERYMAN.   Yet I pray thee take the labor and do so
much for me,
To bring me forward, for saint charity,
And comfort me till I come without the town.

FELLOWSHIP.   Nay, and thou would give me a new gown,
I will not a foot with thee go.
But, and thou had tarried, I would not have left thee so.
And as now, God speed thee in thy journey!
For from thee I will depart as fast as I may.

EVERYMAN.   Whither away, Fellowship? Will thou
forsake me?

FELLOWSHIP.   Yea, by my fay! To God I betake thee.

EVERYMAN.   Farewell, good Fellowship! For thee my
heart is sore.
Adieu forever—I shall see thee no more.

FELLOWSHIP.   In faith, Everyman, farewell now at the
ending:
For you I will remember that parting is mourning.

[*Exit* FELLOWSHIP.]

EVERYMAN.   Alack, shall we thus depart indeed—
Ah, Lady, help!—without any more comfort?
Lo, Fellowship forsaketh me in my most need!
For help in this world whither shall I resort?
Fellowship herebefore with me would merry make,
And now little sorrow for me doth he take.
It is said, "In prosperity men friends may find
Which in adversity be full unkind."
Now whither for succor shall I flee,
Sith that Fellowship hath forsaken me?
To my kinsmen I will, truly,
Praying them to help me in my necessity.
I believe that they will do so,
For kind will creep where it may not go.
I will go 'say—for yonder I see them—
Where be ye now my friends and kinsmen.

[*Enter* KINDRED *and* COUSIN.]

KINDRED.   Here be we now at your commandment:
Cousin, I pray you show us your intent
In any wise, and not spare.

COUSIN.   Yea, Everyman, and to us declare
If ye be disposed to go anywhither.
For, weet you well, we will live and die togither.

KINDRED.   In wealth and woe we will with you hold,
For over his kin a man may be bold.

EVERYMAN.   Gramercy, my friends and kinsmen kind.
Now shall I show you the grief of my mind.
I was commanded by a messenger
That is a high king's chief officer:
He bade me go a pilgrimage, to my pain—
And I know well I shall never come again.
Also I must give a reckoning strait,
For I have a great enemy that hath me in wait,
Which intendeth me to hinder.

KINDRED.   What account is that which ye must render?
That would I know.

EVERYMAN.   Of all my works I must show
How I have lived and my days spent;
Also of ill deeds that I have used
In my time sith life was me lent,
And of all virtues that I have refused.
Therefore I pray you go thither with me
To help me make mine account, for saint charity.

COUSIN.   What, to go thither? Is that the matter?
Nay, Everyman, I had liefer fast bread and water
All this five year and more!

EVERYMAN. Alas, that ever I was bore!
For now shall I never be merry
If that you forsake me.
KINDRED. Ah, sir, what? Ye be a merry man:
Take good heart to you and make no moan.
But one thing I warn you, by Saint Anne,
As for me, ye shall go alone.
EVERYMAN. My Cousin, will you not with me go?
COUSIN. No, by Our Lady! I have the cramp in my toe:
Trust not to me. For, so God me speed,
I will deceive you in your most need.
KINDRED. It availeth you not us to 'tice.
Ye shall have my maid with all my heart:
She loveth to go to feasts, there to be nice,
And to dance, and abroad to start.
I will give her leave to help you in that journey,
If that you and she may agree.
EVERYMAN. Now show me the very effect of your mind:
Will you go with me or abide behind?
KINDRED. Abide behind? Yea, that will I and I may!
Therefore farewell till another day.

[*Exit* KINDRED.]

EVERYMAN. How should I be merry or glad?
For fair promises men to me make,
But when I have most need they me forsake.
I am deceived. That maketh me sad.
COUSIN. Cousin Everyman, farewell now,
For verily I will not go with you;
Also of mine own an unready reckoning
I have to account—therefore I make tarrying.
Now God keep thee, for now I go.

[*Exit* COUSIN.]

EVERYMAN. Ah, Jesus, is all come hereto?
Lo, fair words maketh fools fain:
They promise and nothing will do, certain.
My kinsmen promised me faithfully
For to abide with me steadfastly,
And now fast away do they flee.
Even so Fellowship promised me.
What friend were best me of to provide?
I lose my time here longer to abide.
Yet in my mind a thing there is:
All my life I have loved riches;
If that my Good now help me might,
He would make my heart full light.
I will speak to him in this distress.
Where art thou, my Goods and riches?
GOODS. [*within*] Who calleth me? Everyman? What, hast thou haste?
I lie here in corners, trussed and piled so high,
And in chests I am locked so fast—
Also sacked in bags—thou mayst see with thine eye
I cannot stir, in packs low where I lie.
What would ye have? Lightly me say.
EVERYMAN. Come hither, Good, in all the haste thou may,
For of counsel I must desire thee.

[*Enter* GOODS.]

GOODS. Sir, and ye in the world have sorrow or adversity,
That can I help you to remedy shortly.
EVERYMAN. It is another disease that grieveth me:
In this world it is not, I tell thee so.
I am sent for another way to go,
To give a strait count general
Before the highest Jupiter of all.
And all my life I have had joy and pleasure in thee:
Therefore I pray thee go with me,
For, peradventure, thou mayst before God Almighty
My reckoning help to clean and purify.
For it is said ever among
That money maketh all right that is wrong.
GOODS. Nay, Everyman, I sing another song:
I follow no man in such voyages.
For, and I went with thee,
Thou shouldest fare much the worse for me;
For because on me thou did set thy mind,
Thy reckoning I have made blotted and blind,
That thine account thou cannot make truly—
And that hast thou for the love of me.
EVERYMAN. That would grieve me full sore
When I should come to that fearful answer.
Up, let us go thither together.
GOODS. Nay, not so, I am too brittle, I may not endure.
I will follow no man one foot, be ye sure.
EVERYMAN. Alas, I have thee loved and had great pleasure
All my life-days on good and treasure.
GOODS. That is to thy damnation, without leasing,
For my love is contrary to the love everlasting.
But if thou had me loved moderately during,
As to the poor to give part of me,
Then shouldest thou not in this dolor be,
Nor in this great sorrow and care.
EVERYMAN. Lo, now was I deceived ere I was ware,
And all I may wite misspending of time.
GOODS. What, weenest thou that I am thine?
EVERYMAN. I had weened so.
GOODS. Nay, Everyman, I say no.
As for a while I was lent thee;
A season thou hast had me in prosperity.
My condition is man's soul to kill;
If I save one, a thousand I do spill.
Weenest thou that I will follow thee?
Nay, from this world, not verily.
EVERYMAN. I had weened otherwise.
GOODS. Therefore to thy soul Good is a thief;
For when thou art dead, this is my guise—
Another to deceive in the same wise
As I have done thee, and all to his soul's repreef.
EVERYMAN. O false Good, cursed thou be,
Thou traitor to God, that hast deceived me
And caught me in thy snare!
GOODS. Marry, thou brought thyself in care,
Whereof I am glad:
I must needs laugh, I cannot be sad.
EVERYMAN. Ah, Good, thou hast had long my heartly love;

I gave thee that which should be the Lord's above.
But wilt thou not go with me, indeed?
I pray thee truth to say.
GOODS.   No, so God me speed!
Therefore farewell and have good day.

[*Exit* GOODS.]

EVERYMAN.   Oh, to whom shall I make my moan
For to go with me in that heavy journay?
First Fellowship said he would with me gone:
His words were very pleasant and gay,
But afterward he left me alone.
Then spake I to my kinsmen, all in despair,
And also they gave me words fair—
They lacked no fair speaking,
But all forsake me in the ending.
Then went I to my Goods that I loved best,
In hope to have comfort; but there had I least,
For my Goods sharply did me tell
That he bringeth many into hell.
Then of myself I was ashamed,
And so I am worthy to be blamed:
Thus may I well myself hate.
Of whom shall I now counsel take?
I think that I shall never speed
Till that I go to my Good Deed.
But alas, she is so weak
That she can neither go nor speak.
Yet will I venture on her now.
My Good Deeds, where be you?
GOOD DEEDS.   [*speaking from the ground*]   Here I lie,
cold in the ground:
Thy sins hath me sore bound
That I cannot stear.
EVERYMAN.   O Good Deeds, I stand in fear:
I must you pray of counsel,
For help now should come right well.
GOOD DEEDS.   Everyman, I have understanding
That ye be summoned, account to make,
Before Messiah of Jer'salem King.
And you do by me, that journey with you will I take.
EVERYMAN.   Therefore I come to you my moan to make:
I pray you that ye will go with me.
GOOD DEEDS.   I would full fain, but I cannot stand,
verily.
EVERYMAN.   Why, is there anything on you fall?
GOOD DEEDS.   Yea, sir, I may thank you of all:
If ye had perfectly cheered me,
Your book of count full ready had be.

[GOOD DEEDS *shows him the account book.*]

Look, the books of your works and deeds eke,
As how they lie under the feet,
To your soul's heaviness.
EVERYMAN.   Our Lord Jesus help me!
For one letter here I cannot see.
GOOD DEEDS.   There is a blind reckoning in time
of distress!
EVERYMAN.   Good Deeds, I pray you help me in this need,

Or else I am forever damned indeed.
Therefore help me to make reckoning
Before the Redeemer of all thing
That King is and was and ever shall.
GOOD DEEDS.   Everyman, I am sorry of your fall
And fain would help you and I were able.
EVERYMAN.   Good Deeds, your counsel I pray you
give me.
GOOD DEEDS.   That shall I do verily,
Though that on my feet I may not go;
I have a sister that shall with you also,
Called Knowledge, which shall with you abide
To help you to make that dreadful reckoning.

[*Enter* KNOWLEDGE.]

KNOWLEDGE.   Everyman, I will go with thee and be
thy guide,
In thy most need to go by thy side.
EVERYMAN.   In good condition I am now in everything,
And am whole content with this good thing,
Thanked be God my Creator.
GOOD DEEDS.   And when she hath brought you there
Where thou shalt heal thee of thy smart,
Then go you with your reckoning and your Good
Deeds together
For to make you joyful at heart
Before the blessed Trinity.
EVERYMAN.   My Good Deeds, gramercy!
I am well content, certainly,
With your words sweet.
KNOWLEDGE.   Now go we together lovingly
To Confession, that cleansing river.
EVERYMAN.   For joy I weep—I would we were there!
But I pray you give me cognition,
Where dwelleth that holy man Confession?
KNOWLEDGE.   In the House of Salvation:
We shall us comfort, by God's grace.

[KNOWLEDGE *leads* EVERYMAN *to* CONFESSION.]

Lo, this is Confession: kneel down and ask mercy,
For he is in good conceit with God Almighty.
EVERYMAN.   [*kneeling*]   O glorious fountain that all
uncleanness doth clarify,
Wash from me the spots of vice unclean,
That on me no sin may be seen.
I come with Knowledge for my redemption,
Redempt with heart and full contrition,
For I am commanded a pilgrimage to take
And great accounts before God to make.
Now I pray you, Shrift, mother of Salvation,
Help my Good Deeds for my piteous exclamation.
CONFESSION.   I know your sorrow well, Everyman:
Because with Knowledge ye come to me,
I will you comfort as well as I can,
And a precious jewel I will give thee,
Called Penance, voider of adversity.
Therewith shall your body chastised be—
With abstinence and perseverance in God's service.
Here shall you receive that scourge of me,

Which is penance strong that ye must endure,
To remember thy Saviour was scourged for thee
With sharp scourges, and suffered it patiently.
So must thou ere thou 'scape that painful pilgrimage.
Knowledge, keep him in this voyage,
And by that time Good Deeds will be with thee.
But in any wise be secure of mercy—
For your time draweth fast—and ye will saved be.
Ask God mercy and he will grant, truly.
When with the scourge of penance man doth him bind,
The oil of forgiveness then shall he find.

EVERYMAN.   Thanked be God for his gracious work,
For now I will my penance begin.
This hath rejoiced and lighted my heart,
Though the knots be painful and hard within.

KNOWLEDGE.   Everyman, look your penance that ye fulfill,
What pain that ever it to you be;
And Knowledge shall give you counsel at will
How your account ye shall make clearly.

EVERYMAN.   O eternal God, O heavenly figure,
O way of righteousness, O goodly vision,
Which descended down in a virgin pure
Because he would every man redeem,
Which Adam forfeited by his disobedience;
O blessed Godhead, elect and high Divine,
Forgive my grievous offense!
Here I cry thee mercy in this presence:
O ghostly Treasure, O Ransomer and Redeemer,
Of all the world Hope and Conduiter,
Mirror of joy, Foundator of mercy,
Which enlumineth heaven and earth thereby,
Hear my clamorous complaint, though it late be;
Receive my prayers, of thy benignity.
Though I be a sinner most abominable,
Yet let my name be written in Moses' table.
O Mary, pray to the Maker of all thing
Me for to help at my ending,
And save me from the power of my enemy,
For Death assaileth me strongly.
And Lady, that I may by mean of thy prayer
Of your Son's glory to be partner—
By the means of his passion I it crave.
I beseech you help my soul to save.
Knowledge, give me the scourge of penance:
My flesh therewith shall give acquittance.
I will now begin, if God give me grace.

KNOWLEDGE.   Everyman, God give you time and space!
Thus I bequeath you in the hands of our Saviour:
Now may you make your reckoning sure.

EVERYMAN.   In the name of the Holy Trinity
My body sore punished shall be:
Take this, body, for the sin of the flesh!
Also thou delightest to go gay and fresh,
And in the way of damnation thou did me bring,
Therefore suffer now strokes of punishing!
Now of penance I will wade the water clear,
To save me from purgatory, that sharp fire.

GOOD DEEDS.   I thank God, now can I walk and go,
And am delivered of my sickness and woe.
Therefore with Everyman I will go, and not spare:

His good works I will help him to declare.

KNOWLEDGE.   Now, Everyman, be merry and glad:
Your Good Deeds cometh now, ye may not be sad.
Now is your Good Deeds whole and sound,
Going upright upon the ground.

EVERYMAN.   My heart is light, and shall be evermore.
Now will I smite faster than I did before.

GOOD DEEDS.   Everyman, pilgrim, my special friend,
Blessed be thou without end!
For thee is preparate the eternal glory.
Ye have me made whole and sound
Therefore I will bide by thee in every stound.

EVERYMAN.   Welcome, my Good Deeds! Now I hear
thy voice,
I weep for very sweetness of love.

KNOWLEDGE.   Be no more sad, but ever rejoice:
God seeth thy living in his throne above.
Put on this garment to thy behove,
Which is wet with your tears—
Or else before God you may it miss
When ye to your journey's end come shall.

EVERYMAN.   Gentle Knowledge, what do ye it call?

KNOWLEDGE.   It is a garment of sorrow;
From pain it will you borrow:
Contrition it is
That getteth forgiveness;
It pleaseth God passing well.

GOOD DEEDS.   Everyman, will you wear it for your heal?

EVERYMAN.   Now blessed be Jesu, Mary's son,
For now have I on true contrition.
And let us go now without tarrying.
Good Deeds, have we clear our reckoning?

GOOD DEEDS.   Yea, indeed, I have it here.

EVERYMAN.   Then I trust we need not fear.
Now friends, let us not part in twain.

KNOWLEDGE.   Nay, Everyman, that will we not, certain.

GOOD DEEDS.   Yet must thou lead with thee
Three persons of great might.

EVERYMAN.   Who should they be?

GOOD DEEDS.   Discretion and Strength they hight,
And thy Beauty may not abide behind.

KNOWLEDGE.   Also ye must call to mind
Your Five-Wits as for your counselors.

GOOD DEEDS.   You must have them ready at all hours.

EVERYMAN.   How shall I get them hither?

KNOWLEDGE.   You must call them all togither,
And they will be here incontinent.

EVERYMAN.   My friends, come hither and be present,
Discretion, Strength, my Five-Wits, and Beauty!

[They enter.]

BEAUTY.   Here at your will we be all ready.
What will ye that we should do?

GOOD DEEDS.   That ye would with Everyman go
And help him in his pilgrimage.
Advise you: will ye with him or not in that voyage?

STRENGTH.   We will bring him all thither.
To his help and comfort, ye may believe me.

DISCRETION.   So will we go with him all togither.

EVERYMAN. Almighty God, loved might thou be!
  I give thee laud that I have hither brought
  Strength, Discretion, Beauty, and Five-Wits—lack I
  nought—
  And my Good Deeds, with Knowledge clear,
  All be in my company at my will here:
  I desire no more to my business.
STRENGTH. And I, Strength, will by you stand in
  distress,
  Though thou would in battle fight on the ground.
FIVE-WITS. And though it were through the world
  round,
  We will not depart for sweet ne sour.
BEAUTY. No more will I, until death's hour,
  Whatsoever thereof befall.
DISCRETION. Everyman, advise you first of all:
  Go with a good advisement and deliberation.
  We all give you virtuous monition
  That all shall be well.
EVERYMAN. My friends, hearken what I will tell;
  I pray God reward you in his heaven-sphere;
  Now hearken all that be here,
  For I will make my testament,
  Here before you all present:
  In alms half my good I will give with my hands twain,
  In the way of charity with good intent;
  And the other half, still shall remain,
  I 'queath to be returned there it ought to be.
  This I do in despite of the fiend of hell,
  To go quit out of his perel,
  Ever after and this day.
KNOWLEDGE. Everyman, hearken what I say:
  Go to Priesthood, I you advise,
  And receive of him, in any wise,
  The holy sacrament and ointment togither;
  Then shortly see ye turn again hither:
  We will all abide you here.
FIVE-WITS. Yea, Everyman, hie you that ye ready were.
  There is no emperor, king, duke, ne baron,
  That of God hath commission
  As hath the least priest in the world being:
  For of the blessed sacraments pure and bening
  He beareth the keys, and thereof hath the cure
  For man's redemption—it is ever sure—
  Which God for our souls' medicine
  Gave us out of his heart with great pine,
  Here in this transitory life for thee and me.
  The blessed sacraments seven there be:
  Baptism, confirmation, with priesthood good,
  And the sacrament of God's precious flesh and blood,
  Marriage, the holy extreme unction, and penance:
  These seven be good to have in remembrance,
  Gracious sacraments of high divinity.
EVERYMAN. Fain would I receive that holy body,
  And meekly to my ghostly father I will go.
FIVE-WITS. Everyman, that is the best that ye can do:
  God will you to salvation bring.
  For priesthood exceedeth all other thing:
  To us Holy Scripture they do teach,
  And converteth man from sin, heaven to reach;

God hath to them more power given
Than to any angel that is in heaven.
With five words he may consecrate
God's body in flesh and blood to make,
And handleth his Maker between his hands.
The priest bindeth and unbindeth all bands,
Both in earth and in heaven.
Thou ministers all the sacraments seven;
Though we kiss thy feet, thou were worthy;
Thou art surgeon that cureth sin deadly;
No remedy we find under God
But all only priesthood.
Everyman, God gave priests that dignity
And setteth them in his stead among us to be.
Thus be they above angels in degree.

[*Exit* EVERYMAN.]

KNOWLEDGE. If priests be good, it is so, surely.
  But when Jesu hanged on the cross with great smart,
  There he gave out of his blessed heart
  The same sacrament in great torment,
  He sold them not to us, that Lord omnipotent:
  Therefore Saint Peter the Apostle doth say
  That Jesu's curse hath all they
  Which God their Saviour do buy or sell,
  Or they for any money do take or tell.
  Sinful priests giveth the sinners example bad:
  Their children sitteth by other men's fires, I have
  heard;
  And some haunteth women's company
  With unclean life, as lusts of lechery.
  These be with sin made blind.
FIVE-WITS. I trust to God no such may we find.
  Therefore let us priesthood honor,
  And follow their doctrine for our souls' succor.
  We be their sheep and they shepherds be
  By whom we all be kept in surety.
  Peace, for yonder I see Everyman come,
  Which hath made true satisfaction.
GOOD DEEDS. Methink it is he indeed.

[*Re-enter* EVERYMAN.]

EVERYMAN. Now Jesu be your alder speed!
  I have received the sacrament for my redemption,
  And then mine extreme unction.
  Blessed be all they that counseled me to take it!
  And now, friends, let us go without longer respite.
  I thank God that ye have tarried so long.
  Now set each of you on this rood your hond
  And shortly follow me:
  I go before there I would be. God be our guide!
STRENGTH. Everyman, we will not from you go
  Till ye have done this voyage long.
DISCRETION. I, Discretion, will bide by you also.
KNOWLEDGE. And though this pilgrimage be never
  so strong,
  I will never part you fro.
STRENGTH. Everyman, I will be as sure by thee
  As ever I did by Judas Maccabee.

EVERYMAN.   Alas, I am so faint I may not stand—
My limbs under me doth fold!
Friends, let us not turn again to this land,
Not for all the world's gold.
For into this cave must I creep
And turn to earth, and there to sleep.
BEAUTY.   What, into this grave, alas?
EVERYMAN.   Yea, there shall ye consume, more and lass.
BEAUTY.   And what, should I smother here?
EVERYMAN.   Yea, by my faith, and nevermore appear.
In this world live no more we shall,
But in heaven before the highest Lord of all.
BEAUTY.   I cross out all this! Adieu, by Saint John—
I take my tape in my lap and am gone.
EVERYMAN.   What, Beauty, whither will ye?
BEAUTY.   Peace, I am deaf—I look not behind me,
Not and thou wouldest give me all the gold in thy
chest.

[*Exit* BEAUTY.]

EVERYMAN.   Alas, whereto may I trust?
Beauty goeth fast away fro me—
She promised with me to live and die!
STRENGTH.   Everyman, I will thee also forsake and deny.
Thy game liketh me not at all.
EVERYMAN.   Why then, ye will forsake me all?
Sweet Strength, tarry a little space.
STRENGTH.   Nay, sir, by the rood of grace,
I will hie me from thee fast,
Though thou weep till thy heart tobrast.
EVERYMAN.   Ye would ever bide by me, ye said.
STRENGTH.   Yea, I have you far enough conveyed!
Ye be old enough, I understand,
Your pilgrimage to take on hand:
I repent me that I hither came.
EVERYMAN.   Strength, you to displease I am to blame,
Yet promise is debt, this ye well wot.
STRENGTH.   In faith, I care not:
Thou art but a fool to complain;
You spend your speech and waste your brain.
Go, thrust thee into the ground.

[*Exit* STRENGTH.]

EVERYMAN.   I had weened surer I should you have
found.
He that trusteth in his Strength
She him deceiveth at the length.
Both Strength and Beauty forsaketh me—
Yet they promised me fair and lovingly.
DISCRETION.   Everyman, I will after Strength be gone:
As for me, I will leave you alone.
EVERYMAN.   Why Discretion, will ye forsake me?
DISCRETION.   Yea, in faith, I will go from thee.
For when Strength goeth before,
I follow after evermore.
EVERYMAN.   Yet I pray thee, for the love of the Trinity,
Look in my grave once piteously.
DISCRETION.   Nay, so nigh will I not come.
Farewell everyone!

[*Exit* DISCRETION.]

EVERYMAN.   O all thing faileth save God alone—
Beauty, Strength, and Discretion.
For when Death bloweth his blast
They all run fro me full fast.
FIVE-WITS.   Everyman, my leave now of thee I take.
I will follow the other, for here I thee forsake.
EVERYMAN.   Alas, then may I wail and weep,
For I took you for my best friend.
FIVE-WITS.   I will no longer thee keep.
Now farewell, and there an end!

[*Exit* FIVE-WITS.]

EVERYMAN.   O Jesu, help, all hath forsaken me!
GOOD DEEDS.   Nay, Everyman, I will bide with thee:
I will not forsake thee indeed;
Thou shalt find me a good friend at need.
EVERYMAN.   Gramercy, Good Deeds! Now may I true
friends see.
They have forsaken me every one—
I loved them better than my Good Deeds alone.
Knowledge, will ye forsake me also?
KNOWLEDGE.   Yea, Everyman, when ye to Death shall go,
But not yet, for no manner of danger.
EVERYMAN.   Gramercy, Knowledge, with all my heart!
KNOWLEDGE.   Nay, yet will I not from hence depart
Till I see where ye shall become.
EVERYMAN.   Methink, alas, that I must be gone
To make my reckoning and my debts pay,
For I see my time is nigh spent away.
Take example, all ye that this do hear or see,
How they that I best loved do forsake me,
Except my Good Deeds that bideth truly.
GOOD DEEDS.   All earthly things is but vanity.
Beauty, Strength, and Discretion do man forsake,
Foolish friends and kinsmen that fair spake—
All fleeth save Good Deeds, and that am I.
EVERYMAN.   Have mercy on me, God most mighty,
And stand by me, thou mother and maid, holy Mary!
GOOD DEEDS.   Fear not: I will speak for thee.
EVERYMAN.   Here I cry God mercy!
GOOD DEEDS.   Short our end, and 'minish our pain.
Let us go, and never come again.
EVERYMAN.   Into thy hands, Lord, my soul I commend:
Receive it, Lord, that it be not lost.
As thou me boughtest, so me defend,
And save me from the fiend's boast,
That I may appear with that blessed host
That shall be saved at the day of doom.
In manus tuas, of mights most,
Forever *commendo spiritum meum*.

[EVERYMAN *and* GOOD DEEDS *descend into the grave.*]
KNOWLEDGE.   Now hath he suffered that we all shall
endure,
The Good Deeds shall make all sure.
Now hath he made ending,
Methinketh that I hear angels sing
And make great joy and melody

Where Everyman's soul received shall be.
ANGEL. [*within*] Come, excellent elect spouse to Jesu!
  Here above thou shalt go
  Because of thy singular virtue.
  Now the soul is taken the body fro,
  Thy reckoning is crystal clear:
  Now shalt thou into the heavenly sphere—
  Unto the which all ye shall come
  That liveth well before the day of doom.

[*Enter* DOCTOR.]

DOCTOR. This memorial men may have in mind:
  Ye hearers, take it of worth, old and young,
  And forsake Pride, for he deceiveth you in the end.
  And remember Beauty, Five-Wits, Strength, and
  Discretion,

They all at the last do Everyman forsake,
Save his Good Deeds there doth he take—
But beware, for and they be small,
Before God he hath no help at all—
None excuse may be there for Everyman.
Alas, how shall he do than?
For after death amends may no man make,
For then mercy and pity doth him forsake.
If his reckoning be not clear when he doth come,
God will say, "*Ite, maledicti, in ignem eternum!*"
And he that hath his account whole and sound,
High in heaven he shall be crowned,
Unto which place God bring us all thither,
That we may live body and soul togither.
Thereto help, the Trinity!
Amen, say ye, for saint charity.

Chapter

11

The Early Renaissance:
Return to Classical Roots, 1400–1494

LEON BATTISTA ALBERTI

from *On Painting*

Book Two

Because this [process of] learning may perhaps appear a fatiguing thing to young people, I ought to prove here that painting is not unworthy of consuming all our time and study.

Painting contains a divine force which not only makes absent men present, as friendship is said to do, but moreover makes the dead seem almost alive. Even after many centuries they are recognized with great pleasure and with great admiration for the painter. Plutarch says that Cassander, one of the captains of Alexander, trembled through all his body because he saw a portrait of his King. Agesilaos, the Lacedaemonian, never permitted anyone to paint him or to represent him in sculpture; his own form so displeased him that he avoided being known by those who would come after him. Thus the face of a man who is already dead certainly lives a long life through painting. Some think that painting shaped the gods who were adored by the nations. It certainly was their greatest gift to mortals, for painting is most useful to that piety which joins us to the gods and keeps our souls full of religion. They say that Phidias made in Aulis a god Jove so beautiful that it considerably strengthened the religion then current.

The extent to which painting contributes to the most honourable delights of the soul and to the dignified beauty of things can be clearly seen not only from other things but especially from this: you can conceive of almost nothing so precious which is not made far richer and much more beautiful by association with painting. Ivory, gems and similar expensive things become more precious when worked by the hand of the painter. Gold worked by the art of painting outweighs an equal amount of unworked gold. If figures were made by the hand of Phidias or Praxiteles from lead itself—the lowest of metals—they would be valued more highly than silver. The painter, Zeuxis, began to give away his things because, as he said, they could not be bought. He did not think it possible to come to a just price which would be satisfactory to the painter, for in painting animals he set himself up almost as a god.

Therefore, painting contains within itself this virtue that any master painter who sees his works adored will feel himself considered another god. Who can doubt that painting is the master art or at least not a small ornament of things? The architect, if I am not mistaken, takes from the painter architraves, bases, capitals, columns, façades and other similar things. All the smiths, sculptors, shops and guilds are governed by the rules and art of the painter. It is scarcely possible to find any superior art which is not concerned with painting, so that whatever beauty is found can be said to be born of painting. *But also this, a dignified painting is held in high honour by many so that among all artists some smiths are named, only this is not the rule among smiths.* For this reason, I say among my friends that Narcissus who was changed into a flower, according to the poets, was the inventor of painting. Since painting is already the flower of every art, the story of Narcissus is most to the point. What else can you call painting but a similar embracing with art of what is presented on the surface of the water in the fountain?

Quintilian said that the ancient painters used to circumscribe shadows cast by the sun, and from this our art has grown. There are those who say that a certain Philocles, an Egyptian, and a Cleantes were among the first inventors of this art. The Egyptians affirm that painting was in use among them a good 6000 years before it was carried into Greece. They say that painting was brought to us from Greece after the victory of Marcellus over Sicily. But we are not interested in knowing who was the inventor of the art or the first painter, since we are not telling stories like Pliny. We are, however, building anew an art of painting about which nothing, as I see it, has been written in this age. They say that Euphranor of Isthmus wrote something about measure and about colours, that Antigonos and Xenocrates exchanged something in their letters about painting, and that Apelles wrote to Pelleus about painting. Diogenes Laertius recounts that Demetrius made commentaries on painting. Since all the other arts were recommended in letters by our great men, and since painting was not neglected by our Latin writers, I believe that our ancient Tuscan [ancestors] were already most expert masters in painting.

Trismegistus, an ancient writer, judged that painting and sculpture were born at the same time as religion, *for thus he answered Aesclepius: mankind portrays the gods in his own image from his memories of nature and his own origins.* Who can here deny that in all things public and private, profane and religious, painting has taken all the most honourable parts to itself so that nothing has ever been so esteemed by mortals?

The incredible prices of painted pictures have been recorded. Aristides the Theban sold a single picture for one hundred talents. They say that Rhodes was not burned by King Demetrius for fear that a painting of Protogenes' should perish. It could be said that the city of Rhodes was ransomed from the enemy by a single painting. Pliny collected many other such things in which you can see that good painters have always been greatly honoured by all. The most noble citizens, philosophers and quite a few kings not only enjoyed painted things but also painted with their own hands. Lucius Manilius, Roman citizen, and Fabius, a most noble man, were painters. Turpilius, a Roman knight, painted at Verona. Sitedius, praetor and proconsul, acquired renown as a painter. Pacuvius, tragic poet and nephew of the poet Ennius, painted Hercules in the Roman forum. Socrates, Plato, Metrodorus, Pyrrho were connoisseurs of painting. The emperors Nero, Valentinian, and Alexander Severus were most devoted to painting. It would be too long, however, to recount here how

many princes and kings were pleased by painting. Nor does it seem necessary to me to recount all the throng of ancient painters. Their number is seen in the fact that 360 statues, part on horseback and part in chariots, were completed in four hundred days for Demetrius Phalerius, son of Phanostratus. In a land in which there was such a great number of sculptors, can you believe that painters were lacking? I am certain that both these arts are related and nurtured by the same genius, painting with sculpture. But I always give higher rank to the genius of the painter because he works with more difficult things.

However, let us return to our work. Certainly the number of sculptors and painters was great in those times when princes and plebeians, learned and unlearned enjoyed painting, and when painted panels and portraits, considered the choicest booty from the provinces, were set up in the theatres. Finally L. Paulus Aemilius and not a few other Roman citizens taught their sons painting along with the fine arts and the art of living piously and well. This excellent custom was frequently observed among the Greeks who, because they wished their sons to be well educated, taught them painting along with geometry and music. It was also an honour among women to know how to paint. Martia, daughter of Varro, is praised by the writers because she knew how to paint. Painting had such reputation and honour among the Greeks that laws and edicts were passed forbidding slaves to learn painting. It was certainly well that they did this, for the art of painting has always been most worthy of liberal minds and noble souls.

As for me, I certainly consider a great appreciation of painting to be the best indication of a most perfect mind, even though it happens that this art is pleasing to the uneducated as well as to the educated. It occurs rarely in any other art that what delights the experienced also moves the inexperienced. In the same way you will find that many greatly desire to be well versed in painting. Nature herself seems to delight in painting, for in the cut faces of marble she often paints centaurs and faces of bearded and curly headed kings. It is said, moreover, that in a gem from Pyrrhus all nine Muses, each with her symbol, are to be found clearly painted by nature. Add to this that in no other art does it happen that both the experienced and the inexperienced of every age apply themselves so voluntarily to the learning and exercising of it. Allow me to speak of myself here. Whenever I turn to painting for my recreation, which I frequently do when I am tired of more pressing affairs, I apply myself to it with so much pleasure that I am surprised that three or four hours have passed. Thus this art gives pleasure and praise to whoever is skilled in it; riches and perpetual fame to one who is master of it. Since these things are so, since painting is the best and most ancient ornament of things, worthy of free men, pleasing to learned and unlearned, I greatly encourage our studious youth to exert themselves as much as possible in painting.

Therefore, I recommend that he who is devoted to painting should learn this art. The first great care of one who seeks to obtain eminence in painting is to acquire the fame and renown of the ancients. It is useful to remember that avarice is always the enemy of virtue. Rarely can anyone given to acquisition of wealth acquire renown. I have seen many in the first flower of learning suddenly sink to money-making. As a result they acquire neither riches nor praise. However, if they had increased their talent with study, they would have easily soared into great renown. Then they would have acquired much riches and pleasure. . . .

GIOVANNI PICO DELLA MIRANDOLA
from *On the Dignity of Man*

Most venerable fathers, I have read in the records of the Arabians that Abdul the Saracen, on being asked what thing on, so to speak, the world's stage, he viewed as most greatly worthy of wonder, answered that he viewed nothing more wonderful than man. And Mercury's, "a great wonder, Asclepius, is man!" agrees with that opinion. On thinking over the reason for these sayings, I was not satisfied by the many assertions made by many men concerning the outstandingness of human nature: that man is the messenger between creatures, familiar with the upper and king of the lower; by the sharpsightedness of the senses, by the hunting-power of reason, and by the light of intelligence, the interpreter of nature; the part in between the standstill of eternity and the flow of time, and, as the Persians say, the bond tying the world together, nay, the nuptial bond; and, according to David, "a little lower than the angels." These reasons are great but not the chief ones, that is, they are not reasons for a lawful claim to the highest wonder as to a prerogative. Why should we not wonder more at the angels themselves and at the very blessed heavenly choirs?

Finally, it seemed to me that I understood why man is the animal that is most happy, and is therefore worthy of all wonder; and lastly, what the state is that is allotted to man in the succession of things, and that is capable of arousing envy not only in the brutes but also in the stars and even in minds beyond the world. It is wonderful and beyond belief. For this is the reason why man is rightly said and thought to be a great marvel and the animal really worthy of wonder. Now hear what it is, fathers; and with kindly ears and for the sake of your humanity, give me your close attention:

Now the highest Father, God the master-builder, had, by the laws of his secret wisdom, fabricated this house, this world which we see, a very superb temple of divinity. He had adorned the super-celestial region with minds. He had animated the celestial globes with eternal souls; he had filled with a diverse throng of animals the cast-off and residual parts of the lower world. But, with the work finished, the Artisan desired that there be someone to reckon up the reason of such a big work, to love its beauty, and to wonder at its greatness. Accordingly, now that all things had been completed, as Moses and Timaeus testify, He lastly considered creating man. But there was nothing in the archetypes from which He could mold a new sprout, nor anything in His storehouses which He could bestow as a heritage upon a new son, nor was there an empty judiciary seat where this contemplator of the universe could sit. Everything was filled up; all things had been laid out in the highest, the lowest, and the middle orders. But it did not belong to the paternal power to have failed in the final parturition, as though exhausted by child-bearing; it did not belong to wisdom, in a case of necessity, to have been tossed back and forth through want of a plan; it did not belong to the loving-kindness which was going to praise divine liberality in others to be forced to condemn itself. Finally, the best of workmen decided that that to which nothing of its very own could be given should be, in composite fashion, whatsoever had belonged individually to each and every thing. Therefore He took up man, a work of indeterminate form; and, placing him at the midpoint of the world, He spoke to him as follows:

"We have given to thee, Adam, no fixed seat, no form of thy very own, no gift peculiarly thine, that thou mayest feel as thine own, have as thine own, possess as thine own the seat, the form, the gifts which thou thyself shalt desire. A limited nature in other creatures is confined within the laws written down by Us. In conformity with thy free judgment, in whose hand We have placed thee, thou art confined by no bounds; and thou wilt fix limits of nature for thyself. I have placed thee at the center of the world, that from there thou mayest more conveniently look around and see whatsoever is in the world. Neither heavenly nor earthly, neither mortal nor immortal have We made thee. Thou, like a judge appointed for being honorable, art the molder and maker of thyself; thou mayest sculpt thyself into whatever shape thou dost prefer. Thou canst grow downward into the lower natures which are brutes. Thou canst again grow upward from thy soul's reason into the higher natures which are divine."

O great liberality of God the Father! O great and wonderful happiness of man. It is given him to have that which he chooses and to be that which he wills. As soon as brutes are born, they bring with them, "from their dam's bag," as Lucilius says, what they are going to possess. Highest spirits have been, either from the beginning or soon after, that which they are going to be throughout everlasting eternity. At man's birth the Father placed in him every sort of seed and sprouts of every kind of life. The seeds that each man cultivates will grow and bear their fruit in him. If he cultivates vegetable seeds, he will become a plant. If the seeds of sensation, he will grow into brute. If rational, he will come out a heavenly animal. If intellectual, he will be an angel, and a son of God. And if he is not contented with the lot of any creature but takes himself up into the center of his own unity, then, made one spirit with God and settled in the solitary darkness of the Father, who is above all things, he will stand ahead of all things. Who does not wonder at this chameleon which we are? Or who at all feels more wonder at anything else whatsoever? It was not unfittingly that Asclepius the Athenian said that man was symbolized by Prometheus in the secret rites, by reason of our nature sloughing its skin and transforming itself; hence metamorphoses were popular among the Jews and the Pythagoreans. For the more secret Hebrew theology at one time reshapes holy Enoch into an angel of divinity, whom they call *malach hashechina,* and at other times reshapes other men into other divinities. According to the Pythagoreans, wicked men are deformed into brutes and, if you believe Empedocles, into plants too. And copying them, Maumeth [Mohammed] often had it on his lips that he who draws back from divine law becomes a brute. And his saying so was reasonable: for it is not the rind which makes the plant, but a dull and non-sentient nature; not the hide which makes a beast of burden, but a brutal and sensual soul; not the spherical body which makes the heavens, but right reason; and not a separateness from the body but a spiritual intelligence which makes an angel. For example, if you see a man given over to his belly and crawling upon the ground, it is a bush not a man that you see. If you see anyone blinded by the illusions of his empty and Calypso-like imagination, seized by the desire of scratching, and delivered over to the senses, it is a brute not a man that you see. If you come upon a philosopher winnowing out all things by right reason, he is a heavenly not an earthly animal. If you come upon a pure contemplator, ignorant of the body, banished to the innermost places of the mind, he is not an earthly, not a heavenly animal; he more superbly is a divinity clothed with human flesh.

Who is there that does not wonder at man? And it is not unreasonable that in the mosaic and Christian holy writ man is sometimes denoted by the name "all flesh" and at other times by that of "every creature"; and man fashions, fabricates, transforms himself into the shape of all flesh, into the character of every creature. Accordingly, where Evantes the Persian tells of the Chaldaean theology, he writes that man is not any inborn image of himself, but many images coming in from the outside: hence that saying of the Chaldaeans: *enosh hu shinuy vekamah tevaoth baal chayim,* that is, man is an animal of diverse, multiform, and destructible nature.

But why all this? In order for us to understand that, after having been born in this state so that we may be what we will to be, then, since we are held in honor, we ought to take particular care that no one may say against us that we do not know that we are made similar to brutes and mindless beasts of burden. But rather, as Asaph the prophet says: "Ye are all gods, and sons of the most high," unless by abusing the very indulgent liberality of the Father, we make the free choice, which he gave to us, harmful to ourselves instead of helpful toward salvation. Let a certain holy ambition invade the mind, so that we may not be content with mean things but may aspire to the highest things and strive with all our forces to attain them: for if we will to, we can. Let us spurn earthly things; let us struggle toward the heavenly. Let us put in last place whatever is of the world; and let us fly beyond the chambers of the world to the chamber nearest the most lofty divinity. There, as the sacred mysteries reveal, the seraphim, cherubim, and thrones occupy the first places. Ignorant of how to yield to them and unable to endure the second places, let us compete with the angels in dignity and glory. When we have willed it, we shall be not at all below them. . . .

Chapter

12

The High Renaissance and Early Mannerism: 1494–1564

NICCOLÒ MACHIAVELLI

from *The Prince*

VIII. Those who come to power by crime

As there are also two ways of becoming a prince which cannot altogether be attributed either to fortune or to prowess, I do not think I ought to leave them out, even though one of them can be dealt with at greater length under the heading of republics. The two I have in mind are when a man becomes prince by some criminal and nefarious method, and when a private citizen becomes prince of his native city with the approval of his fellow citizens. In dealing with the first method, I shall give two examples, one from the ancient world, one from the modern, without otherwise discussing the rights and wrongs of this subject, because I imagine that these examples are enough for anyone who has to follow them.

Agathocles, the Sicilian, not only from the status of a private citizen but from the lowest, most abject condition of life, rose to become king of Syracuse. At every stage of his career this man, the son of a potter, behaved like a criminal; nonetheless he accompanied his crimes with so much audacity and physical courage that when he joined the militia he rose through the ranks to become praetor of Syracuse. After he had been appointed to this position, he determined

to make himself prince and to possess by force and without obligation to others what had been voluntarily conceded to him. He reached an understanding about this ambition of his with Hamilcar the Carthaginian, who was campaigning with his armies in Sicily. Then one morning he assembled the people and Senate of Syracuse, as if he meant to raise matters which affected the republic; and at a prearranged signal he had all the senators, along with the richest citizens, killed by his soldiers; and when they were dead he seized and held the government of that city, without encountering any other internal opposition. Although he was twice routed and finally besieged by the Carthaginians, not only did he successfully defend the city, but, leaving some of his troops to defend it, he invaded Africa with the rest, and in a short time lifted the siege and reduced the Carthaginians to severe straits. They were compelled to make a pact with him, contenting themselves with the possession of Africa and leaving Sicily to Agathocles. So whoever studies that man's actions will discover little or nothing that can be attributed to fortune, inasmuch as he rose through the ranks of the militia, as I said, and his progress was attended by countless difficulties and dangers; that was how he won his principality, and he maintained his position with many audacious and dangerous enterprises. Yet it cannot be called prowess to kill fellow citizens, to betray friends, to be treacherous, pitiless, irreligious. These ways can win a prince power but not glory. One can draw attention to the prowess of Agathocles in confronting and surviving danger, and his courageous spirit in enduring and overcoming adversity, and it appears that he should not be judged inferior to any eminent commander; nonetheless, his brutal cruelty and inhumanity, his countless crimes, forbid his being honoured among eminent men. One cannot attribute to fortune or prowess what was accomplished by him without the help of either.

In our own time, during the pontificate of Alexander VI, there was Oliverotto of Fermo. Years before, he had been left fatherless as a small boy and was brought up by a maternal uncle called Giovanni Fogliani. In his early youth he was sent to serve as a soldier under Paulo Vitelli so that he could win high command after being trained by him. When Paulo died, Oliverotto soldiered under Vitelozzo, his brother; and in a very short time, as he was intelligent, and a man of courage and audacity, he became Vitelozzo's chief commander. But he thought it was servile to take orders from others, and so he determined that, with the help of some citizens of Fermo to whom the enslavement of their native city was more attractive than its liberty, and with the favour and help of the Vitelli, he would seize Fermo for himself. He wrote to Giovanni Fogliano saying that, having been many years away from home he wanted to come and see him and his city and to make some investigation into his own estate. He had worked for nothing else except honour, he went on, and in order that his fellow citizens might see that he had not spent his time in vain, he wanted to come honourably, with a mounted escort of a hundred companions and servants. He begged Giovanni to arrange a reception which would bring honour to Giovanni as well as to himself, as he was Giovanni's foster child. Giovanni failed in no duty of hospitality towards his nephew. He had him honourably welcomed by the citizens of Fermo and lodged him in his own mansion. There, after a few days had passed during which he waited in order to complete the secret arrangements for his future crime, Oliverotto prepared a formal banquet to which he invited Giovanni Fogliani and the leading citizens of Fermo. After they had finished eating and all the other entertainment usual at such banquets was done with, Oliverotto artfully started to touch on subjects of grave importance, talking of the greatness of Pope Alexander and of Cesare his son, and of their enterprises. When Giovanni and the others began to discuss these subjects in turn, he got to his feet all of a sudden, saying that these were things to be spoken of somewhere more private, and he withdrew to another room, followed by Giovanni and all the other citizens. And no sooner were they seated than soldiers appeared from hidden recesses, and killed Giovanni and all the others. After this slaughter, Oliverotto mounted his horse, rode through the town, and laid siege to the palace of the governing council; consequently they were frightened into obeying him and into setting up a government of which he made himself the prince. And having put to death all who, because they would resent his rule, might injure him, he strengthened his position by founding new civil and military institutions. In this way, in the space of the year that he held the principality, he not only established himself in the city of Fermo but also made himself formidable to all the neighbouring states. His overthrow would have proved as difficult as that of Agathocles, if he had not let himself be tricked by Cesare Borgia when, at Sinigaglia, as was recounted above, Cesare trapped the Orsini and the Vitelli. Oliverotto was also trapped there, and a year after he committed parricide he was strangled along with Vitellozzo, the teacher as regards both his virtues and his crimes.

One might well wonder how it was that Agathocles, and others like him, after countless treacheries and cruelties, could live securely in his own country and hold foreign enemies at bay, with never a conspiracy against him by his countrymen, inasmuch as many others, because of their cruel behaviour, have not been able to maintain their rule even in peaceful times, let alone in the uncertain times of war. I believe that here it is a question of cruelty used well or badly. We can say that cruelty is used well (if it is permissible to talk in this way of what is evil) when it is employed once for all, and one's safety depends on it, and then it is not persisted in but as far as possible turned to the good of one's subjects. Cruelty badly used is that which, although infrequent to start with, as time goes on, rather than disappearing, grows in intensity. Those who use the first method can, with divine and human assistance, find some means of consolidating their position, as did Agathocles; the others cannot possibly stay in power.

So it should be noted that when he seizes a state the new ruler must determine all the injuries that he will need to inflict. He must inflict them once for all, and not have to renew them every day, and in that way he will be able to set men's minds at rest and win them over to him when he confers benefits. Whoever acts otherwise, either through timidity or bad advice, is always forced to have the knife ready in his hand and he can never depend on his subjects because they, suffering fresh and continuous violence, can never feel secure with regard to him. Violence must be inflicted once for all; people will then forget what it tastes like and so be less resentful. Benefits must be conferred gradually; and in that way they will taste better. Above all, a prince must live with his subjects in such a way that no development, either favourable or adverse, makes him vary his conduct. For, when adversity brings the need for it, there is no time to inflict harm; and the favours he may confer are profitless, because they are seen as being forced, and so they earn no thanks.

• • •

'But to come to specific details, I judge that the first and true profession of the courtier must be that of arms; and this above everything else I wish him to pursue vigorously. Let him also stand out from the rest as enterprising, bold, and loyal to whomever he serves. And he will win a good reputation by demonstrating these qualities whenever and wherever possible, since failure to do so always incurs the gravest censure. Just as once a woman's reputation for purity has been sullied it can never be restored, so once the reputation of a gentleman-at-arms has been stained through cowardice or some other reproachful behaviour, even if only once, it always remains defiled in the eyes of the world and covered with ignominy. The more our courtier excels in this art, therefore, the more praise he will deserve, although I do not think he needs to have the professional knowledge of such things and the other qualities appropriate to a military commander. However, since the subject of what constitutes a great captain takes us into very deep waters, we shall be content, as we said, for the courtier to show complete loyalty and an undaunted spirit, and for these to be always in evidence. For men demonstrate their courage far more often in little things than in great. Very often in the face of appalling danger but where there are numerous witnesses one will find those who, though ready to drop dead with fear, driven on by shame or the presence of others, will press forward, with their eyes closed, and do their duty; and only God knows how. But in things of trifling importance, when they believe they can avoid danger without its being noticed, they are only too willing to play for safety. As for those who, even when they are sure they are not being observed or seen or recognized by anyone, are full of ardour and avoid doing anything, no matter how trivial, for which they would incur reproach, they possess the temper and quality we are looking for in our courtier. All the same, we do not wish the courtier to make a show of being so fierce that he is always blustering and bragging, declaring that he is married to his cuirass, and glowering with the haughty looks that we know only too well in Berto. To these may very fairly be said what a worthy lady once remarked jokingly, in polite company, to a certain man (I don't want just now to mention him by name) whom she had honoured by asking him to dance and who not only refused but would not listen to music or take part in the many other entertainments offered, protesting all the while that such frivolities were not his business. And when at length the lady asked what his business was, he answered with a scowl: "Fighting . . ."

' "Well then," the lady retorted, "I should think that since you aren't at war at the moment and you are not engaged in fighting, it would be a good thing if you were to have yourself well greased and stowed away in a cupboard with all your fighting equipment, so that you avoid getting rustier than you are already."

'And of course everyone burst out laughing at the way she showed her contempt for his stupid presumption.

'Therefore,' Count Lodovico went on, 'the man we are seeking should be fierce, rough and always to the fore, in the presence of the enemy; but anywhere else he should be kind, modest, reticent and anxious above all to avoid ostentation or the kind of outrageous self-glorification by which a man always arouses loathing and disgust among those who have to listen to him.' . . .

'I should like our courtier to be a more than average scholar, at least in those studies which we call the humanities; and he should have a knowledge of Greek as well as Latin, because of the many different things that are so beautifully written in that language. He should be very well acquainted with the poets, and no less with the orators and historians, and also skilled at writing both verse and prose, especially in our own language; for in addition to the satisfaction this will give him personally, it will enable him to provide constant entertainment for the ladies, who are usually very fond of such things. But if because of his other activities or through lack of study he fails to achieve a commendable standard in his writing, then he should take pains to suppress his work, to avoid ridicule, and he should show it only to a friend he can trust. And the exercise of writing will be profitable for him at least to the extent that it will teach him how to judge the work of others. For it is very unusual for someone who is not a practised writer, however erudite he may be, to understand completely the demanding work done by writers, or appreciate their stylistic accomplishments and triumphs and those subtle details characteristic of the writers of the ancient world. Moreover, these studies will make our courtier well informed and eloquent and (as Aristippus said to the tyrant) self-confident and assured no matter whom he is talking to. However, I should like our courtier to keep one precept firmly in mind: namely, that in what I have just discussed and in everything else he should always be diffident and reserved rather than forward, and he should be on his guard against assuming that he knows what he does not know. For we are instinctively all too greedy for praise, and there is no sound or song that comes sweeter to our ears; praise, like Sirens' voices, is the kind of music that causes shipwreck to the man who does not stop his ears to its deceptive harmony. Recognizing this danger, some of the philosophers of the ancient world wrote books giving advice on how a man can tell the difference between a true friend and a flatterer. Even so, we may well ask what use is this, seeing that there are so many who realize perfectly well that they are listening to flattery, and yet love the flatterer and detest the one who tells them the truth. Indeed, very often, deciding that the one who praises them is not being fulsome enough, they lend him a hand themselves and say such things that even the most outrageous flatterer feels ashamed. Let us leave these blind fools to their errors and decide that our courtier should possess such good judgement that he will not be told that black is white or presume anything of himself unless he is certain that it is true, and especially in regard to those flaws which, if you remember, when he was suggesting his game for the evening Cesare recalled we had often used to demonstrate the particular folly of this person or another. To make no mistake at all, the courtier should, on the contrary, when he knows the praises he receives are deserved, not assent to them too openly nor let them pass without some protest. Rather he should tend to disclaim them modestly, always giving the impression that arms are, as indeed they should be, his chief profession, and that all his other fine accomplishments serve merely as adornments; and this should especially be his attitude when he is in the company of soldiers, lest he behave like those who in the world of scholarship want to be taken for warriors and among warriors want to seem men of letters. In this way, as we have said, he will avoid affectation, and even his modest achievements will appear great.'

At this point, Pietro Bembo interrupted: 'I cannot see, my dear Count, why you wish this courtier, who is so literate and so well endowed with other worthy qualities, to regard everything as serving to adorn the profession of arms, and not arms and the rest as serving to adorn the profession of letters, which, taken by themselves, are as superior in dignity to arms as is the soul to the body, since letters are a function of the soul, just as arms are of the body.'

Then the Count answered: 'On the contrary, the profession of arms pertains both to the soul and to the body. But I should not want you to be the judge of this, Pietro, because by one of the parties concerned it would be assumed that you were prejudiced. And as this is a controversy that the wisest men have already thrashed out, there is no call to re-open it. As it is, I consider that it has been settled in favour of arms; and since I may form our courtier as I wish, I want him to be of the same opinion. If you think the contrary, wait until you hear of a contest in which the man who defends the cause of arms is allowed to use them, just as those who defend the cause of letters make use of letters in their defence; for if each one uses his own weapons, you will see that the men of letters will lose.'

'Ah,' said Pietro Bembo, 'you were only too ready earlier on to damn the French for their scant appreciation of letters, and you mentioned the glory that they bring to men and the way they make a man immortal. And now you seem to have changed your mind. Do you not remember that:

> *Giunto Alessandro alla famosa tomba*
> *del fero Achille, sospirando disse:*
> *O fortunato, che sì chiara tromba*
> *trovasti, e chi di te sì alto scrisse!**

*The first quatrain of a sonnet by Petrarch, literally: 'When Alexander reached the famous tomb of fierce Achilles, he sighed and said: O happy man, who found so illustrious a trumpet, and one to write of you so nobly!'

And if Alexander was envious of Achilles not because of what he had done himself but because of the way he was blessed by fortune in having his deeds celebrated by Homer, we must conclude that he put a higher value on the writings of Homer than on the arms of Achilles. What other judge do you want, or what other verdict on the relative worth of arms and letters than the one delivered by one of the greatest commanders that has ever lived?'

The Count replied: 'I blame the French for believing that letters are harmful to the profession of arms, and I maintain myself that it is more fitting for a warrior to be educated than for anyone else; and I would have these two accomplishments, the one helping the other, as is most fitting, joined together in our courtier. I do not think that this means I have changed my opinion. But, as I said, I do not wish to argue which of them is more praiseworthy. Let it be enough that men of letters hardly ever choose to praise other than great men and glorious deeds, which deserve praise both on their own account and because, in addition, they provide writers with a truly noble theme. And this subject-matter embellishes what is written and, no doubt, is the reason why such writings endure, for otherwise, if they dealt not with noble deeds but with vain and trivial subjects, they would surely be read and appreciated less. And if Alexander was envious of Achilles because he was praised by Homer, it still does not necessarily follow that he thought more of letters than of arms; and if he had thought that he was as inferior to Achilles as a soldier as he believed that all those who would write about him were inferior to Homer as writers, he would, I am sure, have far preferred brave exploits on his own part to brave talk from others. Therefore I believe that when he said what he did, Alexander was tacitly praising himself, and expressing a desire for what he thought he lacked, namely supreme ability as a writer, rather than for what he took for granted he already had, namely prowess as a warrior, in which he was far from acknowledging Achilles as his superior. So when he called Achilles fortunate he meant that if so far his own fame did not rival that of Achilles (which had been made bright and illustrious through so inspired a poem) this was not because his valour and merits were less notable or less deserving of the highest praise but because of the way fortune had granted Achilles a born genius to be his herald and to trumpet his deeds to the world. Moreover, perhaps Alexander wanted to encourage some gifted person to write about him, showing that his pleasure in this would be as great as his love and respect for the sacred monuments of literature. And now we have said enough about this subject.'

'Indeed, far too much,' remarked signor Lodovico, 'for I don't think that one could discover anywhere in the world a vessel big enough to hold all the things you want to put into our courtier.' . . .

. . . Thus just as it is very fitting that a man should display a certain robust and sturdy manliness, so it is well for a woman to have a certain soft and delicate tenderness, with an air of feminine sweetness in her every movement, which, in her going and staying and whatsoever she does, always makes her appear a woman, without any resemblance to a man. If this precept be added to the rules that these gentlemen have taught the courtier, then I think that she ought to be able to make use of many of them, and adorn herself with the finest accomplishments, as signor Gaspare says. For I consider that many virtues of the mind are as necessary to a woman as to a man; as it is to be of good family; to shun affectation: to be naturally graceful; to be well mannered, clever and prudent; to be neither proud, envious or evil-tongued, nor vain, contentious or clumsy; to know how to gain and keep the favour of her mistress and of everyone else; to perform well and gracefully the sports suitable for women. It also seems to me that good looks are more important to her than to the courtier, for much is lacking to a woman who lacks beauty. She must also be more circumspect and at greater pains to avoid giving an excuse for someone to speak ill of her; she should not only be beyond reproach but also beyond even suspicion, for a woman lacks a man's resources when it comes to defending herself. And now, seeing that Count Lodovico has explained in great detail what should be the principal occupation of a courtier, namely, to his mind, the profession of arms, it seems right for me to say what I consider ought to be that of the lady at Court. And when I have done this, then I shall believe that most of my task has been carried out.

'Leaving aside, therefore, those virtues of the mind which she must have in common with the courtier, such as prudence, magnanimity, continence and many others besides, and also the qualities that are common to all kinds of women, such as goodness and discretion, the ability to take good care, if she is married, of her husband's belongings and house and children, and the virtues belonging to a good mother, I say that the lady who is at Court should properly have, before all else, a certain pleasing affability whereby she will know how to entertain graciously every kind of man with charming and honest conversation, suited to the time and the place and the rank of the person with whom she is talking. And her serene and modest behaviour, and the candour that ought to inform all her actions, should be accompanied by a quick and vivacious spirit by which she shows her freedom from boorishness; but with such a virtuous manner that she makes herself thought no less chaste, prudent and benign than she is pleasing, witty and discreet. Thus she must observe a certain difficult mean, composed as it were of contrasting qualities, and take care not to stray beyond certain fixed limits. . . .

'Now since signor Gaspare also asks what are the many things a lady at Court should know about, how she ought to converse, and whether her virtues should be such as to contribute to her conversation, I declare that I want her to

understand what these gentlemen have said the courtier himself ought to know; and as for the activities we have said are unbecoming to her, I want her at least to have the understanding that people can have of things they do not practise themselves; and this so that she may know how to value and praise the gentlemen concerned in all fairness, according to their merits. And, to repeat in just a few words something of what has already been said, I want this lady to be knowledgeable about literature and painting, to know how to dance and play games, adding a discreet modesty and the ability to give a good impression of herself to the other principles that have been taught the courtier. And so when she is talking or laughing, playing or jesting, no matter what, she will always be most graceful, and she will converse in a suitable manner with whomever she happens to meet, making use of agreeable witticisms and jokes. And although continence, magnanimity, temperance, fortitude of spirit, prudence and the other virtues may not appear to be relevant in her social encounters with others, I want her to be adorned with these as well, not so much for the sake of good company, though they play a part in this too, as to make her truly virtuous, and so that her virtues, shining through everything she does, make her worthy of honour.'

'I am quite surprised,' said signor Gaspare with a laugh, 'that since you endow women with letters, continence, magnanimity and temperance, you do not want them to govern cities as well, and to make laws and lead armies, while the men stay at home to cook and spin.'

The Magnifico replied, also laughing: 'Perhaps that would not be so bad, either.'

Then he added: 'Do you not know that Plato, who was certainly no great friend of women, put them in charge of the city and gave all the military duties to the men? Don't you think that we might find many women just as capable of governing cities and armies as men? But I have not imposed these duties on them, since I am fashioning a Court lady and not a queen. I'm fully aware that you would like by implication to repeat the slander that signor Ottaviano made against women yesterday, namely, that they are most imperfect creatures, incapable of any virtuous act, worth very little and quite without dignity compared with men. But truly both you and he would be very much in error if you really thought this.' . . .

Allen Ginsberg, "A Supermarket in California" from *Howl and Other Poems*. Copyright © 1956, 1959 Allen Ginsberg. Reprinted by permission of City Lights Books.

Johann Wolfgang Goethe, *Faust*, Part One. Translated by Phillip Wayne. Copyright © 1949. Used by permission of Penguin USA Inc.

Great Hymns of the Aten, from *Wings of the Falcon: Life and Thought in Ancient Egypt*. Edited and translated by Joseph Kaster. Copyright © 1968. Reprinted by permission of Holt, Rhinehart, & Winston, Inc.

Horace, *Odes*. Translated by W. G. Shepherd. Copyright © 1983 by W. G. Shepherd. Used by permission of Penguin USA Inc.

Langston Hughes, "Theme for English B." from *A Montage of a Dream Deferred*. Reprinted by permission of Harold Ober Associated Incorporated. Copyright 1951 by Langston Hughes. Copyright renewed 1979 by George Houston Bass. "Harlem" from *The Panther and the Lash*. Copyright 1951 by Langston Hughes. Reprinted by permission of Alfred A Knopf, Inc. "Negro Speaks of Rivers" from *Selected Poems of Langston Hughes*. Copyright 1965 by Langston Hughes. Reprinted by permission of Alfred A. Knopf, Inc.

Zora Neale Hurston, "How it Feels to Be Colored Me" in *The Norton Anthology of Literature by Women*. Edited by Sandra M. Gilbert and Susan Gubar. Copyright © 1985 by W. W. Norton & Co. Inc. Reprinted by permission of the estate of Zora Neale Hurston.

David Hume, *A Treatise of Human Nature*, edited by L. A. Selby-Bigge. Copyright © 1978. Reprinted by permission of Oxford University Press.

Inanna: Queen of Heaven and Earth, translated by Diane Wolkstein and Samuel Noah Kramer. Copyright © 1983. Reprinted by permission of HarperCollins Publishers, Inc.

James Joyce, *Ulysses*. Copyright © 1934. Reprinted by permission of Modern Library, a division of Random House, Inc.

Juvenal, *Sixteen Satires*, translated by Peter Green. Copyright © 1967 by Peter Green. Used by permission of Penguin USA Inc.

Franz Kafka, *The Metamorphosis*, edited and translated by Stanley Corngold. Copyright © 1972. Reprinted by permission of Bantam Doubleday Dell Publishing Group, Inc.

Martin Luther King, Jr., "I Have a Dream" from a tape recording, printed by permission of Joan Daves. Copyright © 1963 by Martin Luther King, Jr.

Maxine Hong Kingston, "No Name Woman" from *The Woman Warrior*. Copyright © 1975, 1976. Reprinted by permission of Random House, Inc.

Koran, translated by N. J. Dawood. Copyright © 1956. Used by permission of Penguin USA Inc.

Milan Kundera, *The Unbearable Lightness of Being*, translated by Michael Henry Heim. Copyright © 1984. Reprinted by permission of HarperCollins Publishers, Inc.

Niccolò Macchiavelli, *The Prince*, translated by George Bull. Copyright © 1961. Used by permission of Penguin USA Inc.

Christopher Marlowe, *Dr. Faustus*, edited by Paul H. Kocher. Copyright © 1950. Reprinted by permission of Harlan Davidson, Inc.

Menander, *The Girl from Samos*, translated by Lionel Casson. Copyright © 1972. Reprinted by permission of New York University Press.

Molière, *The Misanthrope*, from *The Misanthrope and Tartuffe*, translated by Richard Wilbur. Copyright © 1954. Reprinted by permission of Harcourt Brace Jovanovich, Inc.

Michel de Montaigne, "On Cannibals" in *The Complete Essays of Montaigne*, translated by Donald M. Frame. Copyright © 1958 by the Board of Trustees of the Leland Stanford Junior University. Reprinted by permission of the publishers, Stanford University Press.

Sir Thomas More, *Utopia*, edited and translated by H. V. S. Ogden. Copyright © 1949. Reprinted by permission of Harlan Davidson, Inc.

Friedrich Nietzsche, *The Gay Science* and *Thus Spoke Zarathustra* from *The Portable Nietzsche*, edited and translated by Walter Kaufmann. Copyright © 1982. Used by permission of Penguin USA Inc.

Tim O'Brien, "How to Tell a True War Story" from *The Things They Carried*. Copyright © 1990. Reprinted by permission of Houghton Mifflin Inc.

Ovid, *The Metamorphosis of Ovid*, translated by Mary M. Innes. Copyright © 1955. Used by permission of Penguin USA Inc.

Petrarch, *Selections from the Canzioniere and Other Works*, translated by Mark Musa. Copyright © 1985. Reprinted by permission of Oxford University Press.

Christine de Pizan, *The Book of the City of Ladies*, translated by Earl Jeffrey Richards. Copyright © 1982. Reprinted by permission of Persea Books.

Plato, *The Republic and Phaedo* from *Great Dialogues of Plato*, translated by W. H. D. Rouse. Copyright © 1961. Reprinted by permission of New American Library.

François Rabelais, *The Histories of Gargantua and Pantagruel*, translated by J. M. Cohen. Copyright © 1955. Used by permission of Penguin USA Inc.

Jean Racine, *Phaedra*, translated by Richard Wilbur. Copyright © 1986. Reprinted by permission of Harcourt Brace Jovanovich, Inc.

Adrienne Rich, "The Burning of Paper Instead of Children" from *The Fact of a Doorframe, Poems Selected and New, 1950–1984*. Copyright © 1984. Reprinted by permission of W. W. Norton & Co. Inc.

Jean-Jacques Rousseau, *The Confessions of Jean-Jacques Rousseau*, translated by J. M. Cohen. Copyright © 1953. Used by permission of Penguin USA Inc.

St. Augustine, *Confessions*, translated by R. S. Pine-Coffin. Copyright © 1961. Used by permission of Penguin USA Inc.

St. Augustine, *The City of God*, translated by Henry Bettenson. Copyright © 1972. Used by permission of Penguin USA Inc.

Sappho, *Sappho and the Greek Lyric Poets*, translated by Willis Barnstone. Copyright © 1988 by Willis Barnstone. Reprinted by permission of Schocken Books, published by Pantheon Books, a division of Random House, Inc.

Jean-Paul Sartre, "The Humanism of Existentialism" from *Essays in Existentialism*, edited by Wade Baskin, copyright © 1965. Translated from "L'Esistentialisme Est